Contents

Introduction

Amsterdam is many things to many people. Some come to marvel at the picturesque backdrop provided by cobblestone streets, gabled houses and impossibly quaint canals; for others, the coffeeshops and Red Light District satisfy an entirely different set of needs. But the Dutch city's allure goes way beyond its photogenic appearance or its tolerance for hedonism; it's what the holiday snaps don't capture that makes this city truly unique. Long possessed of a liberal, open-minded outlook, Amsterdam is a laid-back city whose inhabitants are determined to enjoy all that life has to offer – there's a creative energy and spirit here that's both inspiring and infectious.

Whether you're into culture, food, design or partying until sunrise, Amsterdam delivers all the buzz of a big city in a small space. A compact, easy-to-navigate centre means you're never more than a short cycle ride from anything: internationally acclaimed museums; 24-hour nightclubs; peaceful parks; inventive restaurants and world-class shopping. Above all, Amsterdam is a city that rewards exploration. No matter how long your visit, take the time to go beyond the clichés and you'll find there's so much more to the 'Venice of the North' than canals and coffeeshops.

ABOUT THE GUIDE

This is one of a series of Time Out guidebooks to cities across the globe. Written by local experts, our guides are thoroughly researched and meticulously updated. They aim to be inspiring, irreverent, well-informed and trustworthy.

Time Out Amsterdam is divided into five sections: Discover, Explore, Experience, Understand and Plan.

Discover introduces the city and provides inspiration for your visit.

Explore is the main sightseeing section of the guide and includes detailed listings and reviews for sights, museums, restaurants ⑩, bars ⑩, coffeeshops ⑩ and shops ⑩, all organised by area with a corresponding street map. To help navigation, each area of Amsterdam has been assigned its own unique colour.

Experience covers the cultural life of the city in depth, including festivals, film, LGBTQ, music, nightlife, theatre and more.

Understand provides in-depth background information that places Amsterdam in its historical and cultural context.

Plan offers practical visitor information, including accommodation options and details of public transport.

Hearts

We use hearts ❤ to pick out venues, sights and experiences in the city that we particularly recommend. The very best of these are featured in the Top 20 (*see p10*) and receive extended coverage in the guide.

Maps

A detachable fold-out map can be found on the inside back cover. There's also an overview map (*see p8*) and individual streets maps for each area of the city. All the venues featured in the guide have been given a grid reference so that you can find them easily on the maps and on the ground.

Prices

All our **restaurant listings** are marked with a euro symbol category from budget to blow-out (**€-€€€€**), indicating the price you should expect to pay for an average main course: **€** = under €10; **€€** = €10-€20; **€€€** = €20-€30; **€€€€** = over €30.

A similar system is used in our **Accommodation** chapter based on a hotel's standard prices for one night in a double room: Budget = under €100; Moderate = €100-€200; Expensive = €200-€300; Luxury = over €300.

Discover

Langestraat

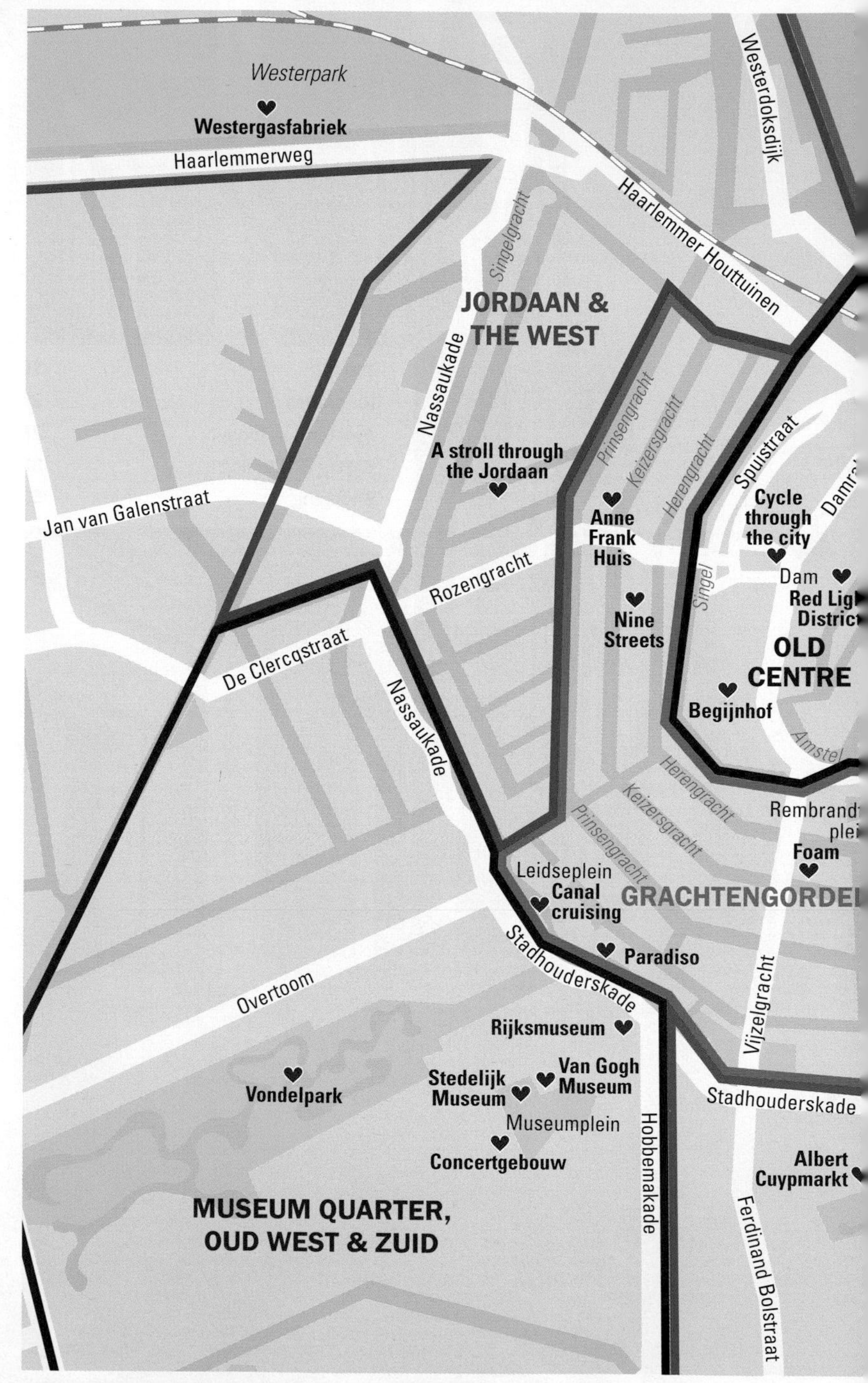
Westerpark
Westergasfabriek
Haarlemmerweg
Westerdoksdijk
Haarlemmer Houttuinen
Singelgracht
JORDAAN & THE WEST
Nassaukade
A stroll through the Jordaan
Prinsengracht
Keizersgracht
Herengracht
Spuistraat
Jan van Galenstraat
Anne Frank Huis
Cycle through the city
Rozengracht
Singel
Dam
Red Ligh
Distric
Nine Streets
OLD CENTRE
De Clercqstraat
Nassaukade
Begijnhof
Amstel
Herengracht
Keizersgracht
Prinsengracht
Rembrand
plei
Foam
Leidseplein
Canal cruising
GRACHTENGORDE
Stadhouderskade
Paradiso
Overtoom
Vijzelgracht
Rijksmuseum
Vondelpark
Stedelijk Museum
Van Gogh Museum
Museumplein
Stadhouderskade
Concertgebouw
Hobbemakade
Albert Cuypmarkt
Ferdinand Bolstraat
MUSEUM QUARTER, OUD WEST & ZUID

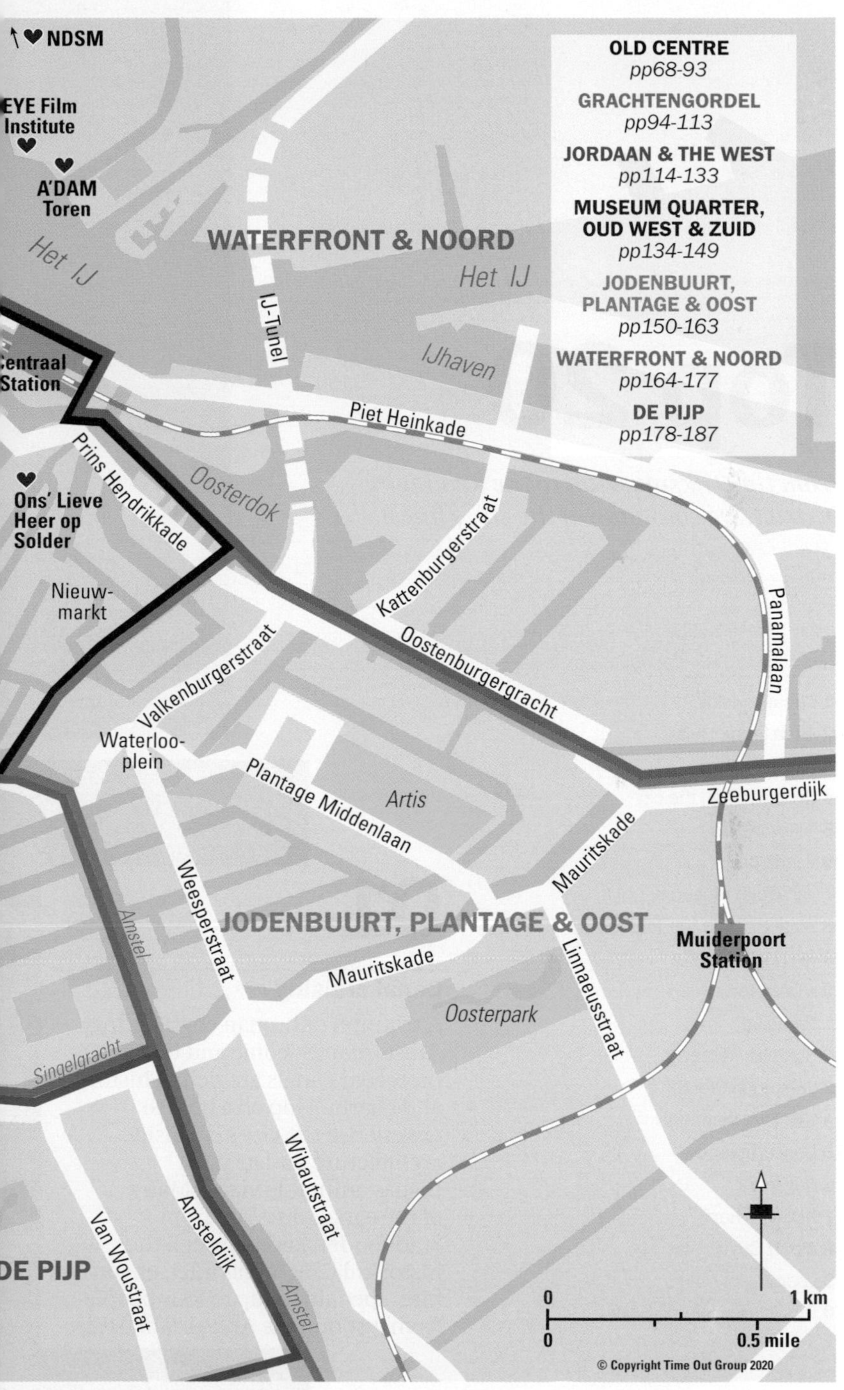
NDSM
EYE Film Institute
A'DAM Toren
Het IJ
WATERFRONT & NOORD
Het IJ
IJ-Tunel
IJhaven
Centraal Station
Piet Heinkade
Prins Hendrikkade
Oosterdok
Ons' Lieve Heer op Solder
Kattenburgerstraat
Nieuwmarkt
Panamalaan
Oostenburgergracht
Valkenburgerstraat
Waterlooplein
Plantage Middenlaan
Artis
Zeeburgerdijk
Mauritskade
Weesperstraat
Amstel
JODENBUURT, PLANTAGE & OOST
Linnaeusstraat
Muiderpoort Station
Mauritskade
Oosterpark
Singelgracht
Wibautstraat
Amsteldijk
Van Woustraat
DE PIJP
Amstel
0
1 km
0
0.5 mile
© Copyright Time Out Group 2020
OLD CENTRE pp68-93
GRACHTENGORDEL pp94-113
JORDAAN & THE WEST pp114-133
MUSEUM QUARTER, OUD WEST & ZUID pp134-149
JODENBUURT, PLANTAGE & OOST pp150-163
WATERFRONT & NOORD pp164-177
DE PIJP pp178-187

Top 20

From the Rijksmuseum to the Red Light District, we count down the city's finest

01 Canal cruising
02 Anne Frank Huis
03 Rijksmuseum
04 Cycle through the city
05 Nine Streets
06 Vondelpark
07 Van Gogh Museum
08 Stroll through the Jordaan
09 Red Light District
10 A'DAM Toren
11 Paradiso
12 Stedelijk Museum
13 Westergasfabriek
14 EYE Film Institute
15 Concertgebouw
16 Begijnhof
17 NDSM Wharf
18 Albert Cuypmarkt
19 Foam
20 Ons' Lieve Heer op Solder

01

Canal cruising *p99*

A triumph of human engineering, Amsterdam's iconic and UNESCO-protected canals are rich in history and charm. Hop on a boat to experience the city's canalside architecture and its most Instagrammable views. Many of the canal tours run from Stadhouderskade through the historical Grachtengordel, or you can hire a pedalo for up to four people from just outside Anne Frank Huis.

Anne Frank Huis *p102*

One of the 20th-century's most famous and bestselling authors died in a concentration camp at the age of 15. Her book, *The Diary of Anne Frank,* documents the two years her Jewish family spent hiding from the Nazis in a small Amsterdam backhouse. The family's preserved hiding place and the accompanying exhibitions resonate with a simple message – 'Never again' – which remains as relevant as ever.

03

Rijksmuseum *p140*

The nation's 'treasure house' makes one proud to be human – which is always refreshing. It's also reassuring to discover that Rembrandt's *The Night Watch* and Vermeer's *The Milkmaid* are not at all overrated. The Rijksmuseum's palatial interior – all gold leaf and intricate art nouveau woodwork and patterns – is worthy of a day's admiration in itself. As for the artworks, you'll need a week.

04

Cycle through the city *p65*

They don't call it the city on two wheels for nothing. Cycling is a quintessential part of Amsterdam culture and by far the cheapest and easiest way to get around. Pedal through the city's photogenic Grachtengordel and along the scenic paths of Vondelpark, or join a guided cycle tour to see the city and learn fun facts about its history along the way.

05

Nine Streets *p101*

The UNESCO-crowned Grachtengordel is essential viewing on any visit to Amsterdam, but make sure you don't miss the intersecting streets, where most of the city's living, eating and drinking take place. The Nine Streets are great for quirky shopping – from wonderful cheeses to designer couture to toothbrushes to 19th-century spectacles to 21st-century denim.

06

Vondelpark *p146*

In the 1970s, KLM airways lured American longhairs to visit Amsterdam with the slogan: 'Come sleep in Hippie Park'. Today, Vondelpark is a people's park where locals hang out in their thousands on sunny days. During the summer, you are likely to hear the echo of bass from whatever pop-up festival is being held in the park at the time.

07

Van Gogh Museum *p142*

Van Gogh's paintings may be familiar all over the world, thanks to reproductions on posters, T-shirts and homewares, but there's still nothing quite like admiring the real thing. The permanent exhibition features some 200 paintings and 500 drawings by Van Gogh, while temporary shows explore his contemporaries and his influence on other artists.

08

Stroll through the Jordaan *p120*

Laid-back Jordaan is a compelling neighbourhood and the perfect place for a spot of aimless wandering. Higgledy-piggledy streets offer a surprise round almost every corner: it may be a seemingly forgotten café, a hip art gallery or a window into a living room filled with plain weird stuff.

09

Red Light District *p74*

Yes, this is a red-light district where women get paid for sex. But Amsterdam's sleaze zone is also one of the city's oldest neighbourhoods and, as such, contains many ancient houses, squares and churches, along with nurseries, schools and locals casually going about their business.

10

A'DAM Toren *p174*

The former Royal Dutch Shell tower is now a landmark destination in Noord, complete with offices, cafés, restaurants, music rooms, a nightclub and rooftop terrace. If you fancy an unrivalled view of the city and an adrenaline hit, the A'DAM Lookout boasts a 360° panorama and the highest swing in Europe.

11

Paradiso *p227*

Paradiso was never technically a church, rather a congregational meeting hall. But with all the stained glass, it's churchy enough. Since the 1960s, it's been the city's undisputed 'music temple', attracting the world's biggest musical legends, who regularly forego a stadium gig to play here. And in its smaller upstairs hall, Paradiso books the legends of tomorrow, who lure in party-loving locals throughout the week.

12

Stedelijk Museum *p139*

With approximately 90,000 works of art and objects dating back to 1870, this is the largest museum of modern and contemporary art in the Netherlands, showcasing movements such as Bauhaus, abstract expressionism and conceptual art to great acclaim.

13

Westergasfabriek *p132*

The city's vast former gasworks on the western edge of the city have been transformed into an award-winning cultural park with clubs, music venues, restaurants, the Het Ketelhuis art-house cinema (*see p210*) and plenty of green space for concerts and festivals. It's a wonderful example of urban reuse.

14

EYE Film Institute *p173*

This stunning building is a treasure trove for film lovers. Carefully curated exhibitions focus on the cinematic greats, while the quirky programming includes cult classics, themed seasons and films shot in 70mm. There's an excellent gift shop and a bar serving craft ales and local tipples too.

15

Concertgebouw *p237*

Could this late 19th-century building topped with a shiny golden lyre have the best acoustics on the planet? Sink into one of the comfy seats and decide for yourself as you absorb the sound of world-class orchestras, conductors, ensembles and soloists.

17

16

Begijnhof *p90*

This hidden courtyard, near the consumer chaos of Kalverstraat, is the perfect place to regain a sense of peace. Begijnhof and its two churches are also handily adjacent to Spui (with its Friday book market and numerous bookshops and cafés) and the freely accessible Civic Guard's Gallery of the Amsterdam Museum (*see p87*).

17

NDSM Wharf *p176*

Once the largest shipyard in Amsterdam, NDSM has since been redeveloped into an 'Art City' with gritty post-industrial architecture and a creative, experimental atmosphere. Just 20 minutes by free ferry from Centraal Station, it is home to a host of restaurants, bars, studios, festivals and cultural venues, and even boasts a man-made urban beach during the summer months.

18

Albert Cuypmarkt *p184*

Amsterdam's most famous street market, the 'Cuyp' is an absolute must for anyone looking to bag a bargain or simply soak up the lively Dutch atmosphere. From Monday to Saturday, the wide street is lined with vibrant stalls selling everything from crazy wigs to delicious local delicacies, including raw herring and *stroopwaffles*.

19

Foam *p111*

The Photography Museum Amsterdam, located in a renovated canal house, displays a comprehensive array of camera-clicking talent, from global photography icons, such as William Klein and Diane Arbus, to up-and-coming artists on the domestic scene. There are courses, events and pop-ups, and an excellent café on site too.

20

Ons' Lieve Heer op Solder *p79*

Translating to 'Museum of Our Lord in the Attic', this 17th-century canal house holds what was once Amsterdam's best-kept secret: a church used by Catholics after the Alteration. The church has been beautifully preserved and is still used for services and even weddings today.

Itineraries

Don't spend your day in a coffeeshop daze; expand your mind and horizons with a tailored tour of the city

Van Gogh Museum

ESSENTIAL WEEKEND

Amsterdam in two days
Budget €200-€250 per person
Getting around Cycling, walking, tram

► *Budgets include transport, meals and admission prices, but not accommodation and shopping.*

DAY 1

Morning

Start the morning on two wheels like a true Amsterdammer. Rent a bike from, for example, **StarBikes** (*see p290*), just east of Centraal Station. Its rental supply is always high and its coffee is always hot. Naturally, you've pre-booked a ticket online for the **Van Gogh Museum** (*see p142*) or **Rijksmuseum** (*see p140*), so you can skip the queues. Cycle there via art and antique gallery streets Nieuwe Spiegelstraat and Spiegelgracht. If pushed for time, head straight for Floor 2 in the Rijksmuseum for the Gallery of Honour and its masterpieces. Alternatively, there are more than 700 pieces of art on display at the Van Gogh Museum.

Vondelpark

Afternoon

When you've had your fill of culture, pedal through the affluent **Museum Quarter** towards the city's green space – **Vondelpark** (*see p146*). Treat yourself to lunch with a view in the flying saucer-shaped **'t Blauwe Theehuis** (*see p146*) right in the middle of the park itself.

Head back north via the quirky retail offerings of the **Nine Streets** (*see p101*), a series of side streets connecting the three main canals of the UNESCO-listed Grachtengordel. From there it's just a short pedal past Westerkerk to the **Anne Frank Huis** (*see p102*) – again, you've really been on the ball and pre-booked a ticket online. If you need to return your bike, go via the 350-year-old distillery **Wynand Fockink** (*see p85*) for a shot or two of *jenever*, the original gin. Opt for a *kopstoot* ('head butt'), which pairs the shot with a beer.

Les Negresses Vertes, Paradiso

Evening

From StarBikes, stroll through the Old Centre past **Oude Kerk** (*see p80*) and the **Royal Palace** (*see p88*) to catch the sunset from the roof terrace of the **W Lounge** (*see p92*). You don't need a reservation for a drink, just head on up to the sixth floor for a view of the skyline you won't forget. Head down Spuistraat to fuel up at **Haesje Claes** (*see p89*) before catching that excellent gig likely to be happening at **Paradiso** (*see p227*) or the **Melkweg** (*see p230*).

DAY 2

Canal cruise

Morning

You've earned a big breakfast after all the exploring yesterday. Head to trendy neighbourhood **De Pijp** (*see p178*) for brunch at Australian-inspired café **Little Collins** (*see p185*). Walk off your meal with a stroll down **Albert Cuypmarkt** (*see p184*), Monday to Saturday, or **Sarphatipark** (*see p182*) if it's a Sunday, before jumping on Metro 52 at De Pijp towards Centraal. Catch a ferry across to Noord and the **A'DAM Toren** (*see p174*), taking in the breathtaking views from 'Over The Edge', Europe's highest swing.

EYE Film Institute

Artis

Afternoon

Grab some of the modern sharing plates at **Tolhuistuin** (*see p176*) and a spot on the terrace if the weather is nice. The bar-restaurant at the **EYE Film Institute** (*see p173*) is a great alternative, with stunning views over the IJ back towards Centraal.

Jump back on a ferry to Centraal. Walk down Damrak, across Dam Square, and down the main shopping drag of Kalverstraat, before exploring the ancient hidden courtyard, **Begijnhof** (*see p90*). Just make sure you leave enough time to get to the **Amsterdam Boat Centre** (*see p99*), a two-minute walk up Singel, for your Classic Canal Cruise, which you've already pre-booked online, of course. Once you're back on dry land, take a short walk through Spui to jump on tram 14 from Amsterdam Rokin to Pontanusstraat in Oost and walk across the bridge to enjoy some locally brewed beer in the shadow of a windmill on the packed terrace of **Brouwerij 't IJ** (*see p163*). Afterwards, walk back towards town through stunning park **Artis**, home to the city's 19th-century zoo (*see p158*).

Carmen, Nationale Opera

Concertgebouw

Evening

What better way to conclude your visit than with dinner and a show? Dine in style in a former orangerie at **Plantage** (*see p157*), before catching a performance at the **Nationale Opera & Ballet** (*see p238*), nearby. Or jump on the tram across town to enjoy a world-class concert at the **Concertgebouw** (*see p237*) or a show-stopping musical at the **DeLaMar Theater** (*see p242*).

Concertgebouw

BUDGET BREAK

For the euro-conscious visitor
Budget €40-€50 per person
Getting around Walking, plus one tram ride, return ferry

Morning

Nab a complimentary coffee at various branches of **Albert Heijn** to set you up to explore the bustling **Noordermarkt** (*see p124*) in the Jordaan. On Saturdays, the whole square is taken over by organic food, and if you happen to visit on a Monday, you may be able to bag a bargain at the weekly flea market. Afterwards, take time to explore the area's hidden *hofjes* (*see p118*) or one of Jordaan's smaller galleries where it's possible to browse art for free (*see p125*). Get your fill of the city's contemporary art scene before grabbing a cheap sandwich (or *broodje*) at **Comestibles Kinders** (*see p118*).

Noordermarkt

NDSM crane

Afternoon

Catch tram 5 to the lively Museumplein public space, bordered by the **Rijksmuseum** (*see p140*) and **Van Gogh Museum** (*see p142*). Wander through the Rijksmuseum's cavernous bicycle passage, which is a spectacle in itself with high ceilings and stunning architecture by Cruz y Ortiz. The museum has a free garden open to the public, which is the setting for an annual sculpture display. From Museumplein, saunter through the Old Centre as far as Centraal Station to catch a free ferry to shipyard turned urban cultural hub **NDSM** (*see p176*). If you've timed it right, you might get to browse the monthly flea market, or check out the goings-on at **Pllek** (*see p175*), where affordable food, live music and an urban beach draw in the punters.

Evening

You could either spend the whole evening at Pllek, or return to Centraal Station on the ferry to try dinner at **China Sichuan** on Warmoesstraat (*see p82*) or at rustic hideaway **Hannekes Boom** (*see p172*). If energy reserves are still high, then the full-on sights, sounds and smells of the **Red Light District** (*see p74*) make it perfect for a late-night wander.

In the know
Tuesday concert

If you happen to be visiting on a Tuesday, enjoy a free classical lunch concert in the foyer of Dutch Nationale Opera & Ballet, from September to May 12.30-1pm. This is occasionally followed by a behind-the-scenes tour (*see p238*).

FAMILY DAY OUT

Keeping the kids amused

Budget €250-€300 for a family of four
Getting around Canal boat, walking, trams, return ferry

Morning

Start your day at the **Hollandsche Manege** riding school in Amsterdam's Vondelpark (*see p147*), by catching tram 2 or 12 from Centraal Station. Enjoy a coffee while watching the horses, before taking a stroll through **Vondelpark** to Museumplein.

Take your pick from the many food stalls lining **Museumplein** (*see p138*) for a cheap and easy bite to eat. For something authentically Amsterdam, grab a serving or two of *bitterballen* for the family to share. If it's a sunny day, enjoy a family picnic on the grass or by the fountains near the **Rijksmuseum** (*see p140*), which offers guided family tours should you wish to venture inside; the Van Gogh museum also has a great family programme. If you're visiting November to February, the winter ice-skating rink is a wonderful way to keep kids occupied.

Rijksmuseum

Nemo Science Museum

Afternoon

After re-energising at lunch, explore the city's **Grachtengordel** (*see p94*). Walk for ten minutes to Stadhouderskade to board a 'Kidscruise' with the **Blue Boat Company** (*see p99*). Adults get a grown-up set of headphones while the kids are taken on an adventure by Johnny the mouse and Harold the cat. Afterwards, take tram 16 to the **NEMO Science Museum** (*see p169*) on Amsterdam's waterfront. Featuring a hands-on laboratory and a 'Maker Space', the museum is dedicated to blowing minds.

Evening

Walk along the waterfront back to Centraal Station, and take the brood for a bite to eat at **Sea Palace** (020 626 4777, seapalace.nl), where you can enjoy uninterrupted views of the IJ and Old Centre. Then, depending on the age of your offspring, either take them to a puppet show at the **Marionetten Theater** (*see p242*) or treat yourself to some much-deserved alone time with the help of a babysitting service, such as **Kriterion** (020 624 5848, www.oppascentralekriterion.nl). Register online and apply for a babysitter at the time and location you desire.

When to Visit

Amsterdam by season

Thanks to its cultural riches, Amsterdam can be enjoyed at any time of year. But each season brings its own character and atmosphere to the city, not to mention a calendar full of special events and festivals (*see pp198-205* Events).

Keukenhof

Spring

The sun is out, blue skies are abundant and Holland's iconic tulips are popping up to say hello. Many would say that spring is the best season of the year to visit Amsterdam: the winter frost is receding and the city's beauty is more vibrant than ever. And because you're avoiding the summer crowds, you can relax and enjoy it. The Dutch don't waste any time awakening from the cold spell – they spring into the season with a host of events and activities. If you're here in April or early May, a trip to **Keukenhof** (*see p192*) is an absolute must.

Summer

As spring merges into summer, both the calendar and the city become even more packed. Whether you want to party for 48 hours straight at a music festival, catch some rays from a canal boat or sit back and take it all in at Vondelpark, Amsterdam caters for every experience-seeker. However, if you're a first timer and don't want to spend half your holiday waiting in a lengthy museum queue, you may want to come back later in the year. Prices also tend to take a hike around this time – so if you're visiting between May and August, best book tickets in advance and eat at local haunts rather than tourist hotspots. But for a bona fide taste of Dutch life, complete with terrace parties, urban beaches and a Vitamin D-induced buzz, the city is at its finest in summer.

The Flying Dutch festival

Vondelpark

Ice skating in front of the Rijksmuseum

Autumn

The crowds of tourists fade away in the autumn to reveal empty cobbled streets covered in red, yellow and gold leaves. Ironically, it is now – as temperatures drops and the nights draw in – that Amsterdam's charm enters full bloom. With picturesque canals and cultural events galore, autumn is the perfect time for a city break before the chill sets in and street wandering becomes limited. You'll find fewer visitors at the main tourist sights, so this is a great time for art lovers to spend hours at the city's showcase museums; **Museum Night** (*see p205*) is a unique way to experience them. Towards the end of the season, festive energy takes hold of the city, with various Christmas events and an appearance from the man himself, St Nicholas.

Winter

Sure, it's cold (and most likely wet) outside but that doesn't dampen Amsterdam's warming display of seasonal cheer. From traditional Dickensian Christmas markets and ice skating to trendy festivals in converted industrial buildings, there's a winter attraction for just about everyone; the **Amsterdam Light Festival** (*see p205*) is the pick of the non-festive bunch. What's more, Amsterdam has a host of cosy venues designed for eating, drinking and making merry, which come into their own as the temperature drops. Be wary of the festive price hikes, however; travelling during December can leave your wallet worse for wear. For many in the Netherlands, 5 December is the most important day of the festive season. Although 24 and 25 December are celebrated, the city doesn't grind to a halt, and many businesses stay open over Christmas.

Amsterdam Today

'Some tourists think of Amsterdam as a city of sin, but in truth it is a city of freedom. And in freedom, most people find sin.' John Green, The Fault in Our Stars

---

The freedom to 'sin' may be one of Amsterdam's most infamous qualities, but this freedom is played out against a picturesque backdrop of gabled houses, cobbled streets and glittering canals. The historical merchant city turned thriving 21st-century metropolis has managed to maintain its laid-back local vibe, while at the same time emerging as a key player on the European cultural stage. What's more, Amsterdam has sustained its reputation as a hotbed for creative entrepreneurs in turbulent political times. This ingenious balancing act is perhaps what draws visitors to the city in increasing numbers. And, while the council tries to find space for both residents and tourists by expanding the cultural offering and building up and out, the 17th-century city continues to thrive at its core.

Dam Sqaure

The new 'Golden Age' loses its shine

The Netherlands remains one of the fastest growing tourist destinations on the planet, with Amsterdam and its surrounding area the jewel in its crown. According to the Netherlands Board of Tourism and Conventions (NBTC), 18 million people paid the country a visit in 2018, a number that's forecast to swell to well over 30 million by 2030. Of course, the more visitors to Amsterdam, the merrier the tourist industry and the more robust the city's finances – tourism earns the economy around €82bn and accounts for 761,000 jobs – but for the modest permanent population of 800,000, that's a lot of *bezoekers* ('visitors') with which to share Amsterdam's narrow, frequently photographed streets. Indeed, in early 2019 the Board adopted a remarkable policy – it would no longer actively promote the country as a tourist destination, because 'more is not always better'.

Many locals lament the 'Disneyfication' of inner-city neighbourhoods, which are being transformed from resident-based dwellings to tourist-heavy playgrounds

Such vast number have understandably caused problems. Many locals lament what's been dubbed the 'Disneyfication' of inner-city neighbourhoods, which they say are being transformed from resident-based dwellings to tourist-heavy playgrounds. The council, keen to appease all sides, has taken note, and is trying to preserve the city's authenticity; in 2016, the mayor's office put a moratorium on hotel construction in some parts of the city. But a lack of affordable hotel beds has played a huge role in the rise of homestay network Airbnb, with unscrupulous property owners effectively operating unlicensed hostels. The council has belatedly tried to fight back: hosts are banned from renting their properties for more than 30 days per year, and a cap of four visitors per property per night is now in place. But these moves haven't been entirely successful; stories still abound of party animals carousing all night in quiet residential areas,

The tourist board's Iamsterdam letters provide an Insta-friendly photo opportunity for visitors. There's a permanent set at Schiphol airport and another two sets at changing locations around town.

Sex and the City

Prostitution in Amsterdam

The recorded history of prostitution in the city dates back to the 13th century, when Amsterdam was a small fishing town. Two centuries later, it had grown into a bustling port attracting plenty of money, rich merchants and sailors, which in turn increased the amount of sex for sale. However, it wasn't only lascivious men who influenced the industry's growth, but also the fact that many local women, separated from their seafaring husbands for months on end, were left with little or no means to sustain themselves or their children. Prostitution was one of the few money-making options available.

In the Middle Ages, the city's prostitutes were permitted to work at one of the brothels located on what is now Damstraat. Keeping a whorehouse was the exclusive privilege of Amsterdam's sheriff, and women found working elsewhere in the city were marched to the said sheriff to the 'sound of drums and flutes'. In the 15th century, however, prostitutes began working the area around Zeedijk; and by the 17th century, some were walking through the Old Side with red lanterns to advertise their profession. Soon after, enterprising women started 'advertising' themselves in the windows of their own homes or from front-facing rooms rented from other homeowners – and it's from this practice that today's rather more garish window trade is descended.

Working as a prostitute has been legal in Amsterdam since 1911; the women have had their own union since 1984 (De Rode Draad, or 'the Red Thread'); and prostitution was defined as a legal and taxable profession in 1988. However, it wasn't until 2000 that the ban on brothels was lifted, thus formally permitting window and brothel sex work (a tactic intended to make taxation easier).

With the legalisation of brothels came bureaucratisation: now, all sex workers must be in possession of an EU passport, and a 200-page rule book governs the selling of sexual services – everything from fire escapes to the appropriate length of a prostitute's fingernails.

Although the legal changes mean that sex workers have access to social services and can legitimately band together to improve their working conditions, the stigma remains. It's still difficult for prostitutes to get bank accounts, mortgages and insurance, despite being liable for taxes and generating an estimated half a billion euros a year.

In 2007, Project 1012 was launched to clean up Amsterdam's infamous Red Light District (1012 is the area's postcode) by then-deputy mayor Lodewijk Asscher. New legislation gave the city the power to withdraw property rights from those suspected of criminal activities and to buy their properties under compulsory purchase orders. Since then, almost 130 windows have been shut, despite protests from local brothel owners. The city authorities originally intended to close 200 of the nearly 500 window brothels and 26 of the 76 coffeeshops in order to gentrify the Red Light District with luxury boutiques and upscale cafés. However, following a march on city hall and accusations that politicians were using the sex trade as an excuse to grab valuable property, the closure of sex windows was halted at the end of 2015. Nevertheless, the impact of Project 1012 is very evident in the area and the clean-up initiative continues. Critics believe reducing the number of windows has pushed the sex industry underground where it can't be regulated – thereby making conditions for sex workers far worse.

---

disrespecting neighbours and generally being disruptive and anti-social.

Airbnb is also partly blamed for a steep hike in property prices, which rose nine per cent in 2018 and are almost double what they were just a few years ago. Indeed, in some areas they're approaching London levels, fuelled by a surging economy and the ever-burgeoning expat community. All of this has been bad news for the artists, entrepreneurs and students who have traditionally innovated and invigorated

Amsterdam's cultural mix: they've been pushed to the margins quite literally, forced ever further east, west or across the water to Noord to find cheap-enough spaces to survive. Initiatives such as the Bureau Broedplaatsen ('Incubator Bureau'), which helps would-be squatters transform abandoned buildings – be they former dockyards in Noord, office buildings in Oost, churches or war bunkers in Zuid and Oud West – into live and work spaces for artists and entrepreneurs, have helped somewhat, but many complain that not nearly enough is being done to stop the very fabric of the city being irredeemably altered by over-gentrification.

As the city has grown, so too has its need for better and more infrastructure. Major public works, and the consequent upheaval, have been a constant on the city's streets for a number of years. Centraal Station and the surrounding concourse; most of Rokin; and huge swathes of Oostelijke Eilanden En Kadijken have all been extensively renovated, with more developments in the pipeline. And then there's the much delayed – and much derided – new Metro Noord/

NDSM Wharf is one of the areas of the city experiencing rapid development and new construction.

Zuidlijn, which finally opened in summer 2018 (seven years late and €1.64 billion over budget) to provide a link to the abandoned dockyards now converted into achingly trendy bars, clubs and art houses in Noord.

Despite the disruption, Amsterdam remains an easy city to get around, with the public transport network maintaining an air of calm, cleanliness and efficiency not seen in most European metropolises. And this, despite the swarms of tourists clogging up the centre during the summer months and weekends. The city's historic heart – all those cobbled streets and cute little canals – remain as lovely as ever, but the feeling among locals is that Amsterdam has become the victim of its own success and that a breaking point is looming. Soon, the city authorities will have to decide who the city is for and then direct policy accordingly, or risk losing the quaint charm – and the people – that make Amsterdam what it is.

Bicycles are the quickest way of getting round the city.

Maintaining stability in turbulent times

For centuries, displaced people and minority groups have found a safe haven in Amsterdam. The city's famed cocktail of political tolerance and intellectual freedom has made it a refuge for thinkers and dreamers since René Descartes decided to call it home. But in the context of the controversy surrounding foreign immigration to the EU – not to mention the rise of populism and nationalism across Western democracies – Amsterdam has experienced its fair share of political conflict.

The city's famed cocktail of political tolerance and intellectual freedom has made it a refuge for thinkers and dreamers

As in many major Western European cities, Amsterdam's famously liberal politics do not reflect the mood in the rest of the country, which has started leaning increasingly to the right. The rise of the intensely blond and vehemently anti-Islam populist politician Geert Wilders and his Freedom Party (PVV) has been well documented; sadly, it seems that more and more Dutch people, particularly in the south

Drugs and the Dutch

The rise and fall of the coffeeshop

The Netherland's apparently relaxed attitude to soft drugs has come to define the country (and particularly Amsterdam) in the minds of many visitors. And, despite a recent backlash against drug culture in the Netherlands, about a third of all visitors to Amsterdam step into one of the city's coffeeshops at some point. Strictly speaking, soft drugs are *not* legal in the Netherlands, but their sale and use is tolerated under strict conditions. In 1976, a vaguely worded law, or '*gedoogbeleid*', was passed to make a distinction between hard and soft drugs, meaning that the authorities would no longer prosecute members of the public for carrying or using a small quantity (five grams) of cannabis (marijuana or hash) and would also tolerate the sale of the same amount of the drug, as long as alcohol was not sold or consumed on the same premises. Thus, the 'front door' of the coffeeshop was effectively decriminalised, even though the 'back door' was still served by an illegal distribution system. Though flawed, this system has largely worked, allowing law enforcement, education and health policies to focus on tackling the use of hard drugs (cocaine, LSD, heroin, morphine or MDMA), which remains strictly forbidden and rigorously prosecuted. In recent years, however, the power of the anti-coffeeshop movement has grown, resulting in increasingly tight regulations 'to combat the nuisance and crime associated with coffeeshops and the sale of drugs' (www.government.nl).

Since 2013, coffeeshops in some other towns in the Netherlands have only been permitted to sell to a local clientele, who hold a so-called 'Weed Pass'. Although Amsterdam is exempt from this, it has had to comply with a 2017 decision that bans coffeeshops from operating within 250 metres of a school, resulting in the closure of the world's oldest coffeeshop, Mellow Yellow. And, more generally, the Europe-wide tendency towards right-wing populism means that coffeeshop regulation may become even more draconian in the coming years.

Coffeeshop rules

Each coffeeshop has a different ambience, but all are bound by strict regulations: licensed premises must display a white and green sticker; they can only sell five grams of cannabis to each customer per day; they are not permitted to sell alcohol, and they are banned from advertising (so if a coffeeshop has a website at all, it will be a 'fan site'). Under-18s are not permitted to enter a coffeeshop.

Smoking tobacco is not allowed in public spaces in the Netherlands (including, perversely, coffeeshops), so you can only smoke 'pure' weed, although many shops have sealed rooms for tobacco smoking, or may offer bongs, vapourisers or herbal mixes as alternatives. Others sell spacecakes and hash brownies; be very careful if you choose to indulge in these edible forms of the drug, however, as the effects can take a while to kick in and may be very intense. Magic mushrooms are no longer legal.

When you first walk in, ask to see a menu: it will list the available drugs and their prices. Seek the advice of the staff, who can explain the effects of each option and give you a look and a smell. Prices vary: expect to pay an average of €8 for a gram, but prices can go up to around €40, depending on quality. Coffeeshops in the centre tend to be more expensive than those in outlying districts.

Hash is typically named after its country of origin (Moroccan, Afghan, Lebanese), whereas weed usually bears invented names loosely referring to an element of the strain (White Widow, Super Skunk, Silver Haze). Beware homegrown Dutch weed, which is notoriously strong, containing more than 15 per cent of the intoxicating THC (tetrahydro-cannabinol), and should be avoided. (There have been moves to reclassify such strains as 'hard drugs', with accompanying stiff penalties.)

All shops provide free rolling papers and tips, and if you're in a hurry, pre-rolled joints are always available; these usually contain low-grade ingredients, although a few shops pride themselves on excellent pre-rolls.

of the country, sympathise with his views regarding the 'Islamisation of the Netherlands'. The PVV remains the second biggest party in parliament, while another far-right populist party, the Forum for Democracy stunned the political establishment by winning the biggest share of the votes in 2019's provincial elections. That ballot was held in a febrile atmosphere – just two days before, a Turkish-born male was arrested following a shooting in Utrecht that left three people dead. Since then, debate has continued to rage about what a future Dutch society might look like and how welcoming to outsiders it should be.

Even within Amsterdam, an almost defiantly left-wing town, such issues have come to the fore in recent years, particularly regarding social housing and the forces of gentrification that are reshaping neighbourhoods. In the 20th century, nondescript grey apartment blocks made of prefabricated concrete were constructed for immigrants and the poor in industrial zones away from the picturesque centre – out of sight, out of mind. Now, however, the city's sprawl is such that many of these estates find themselves slap bang in the

Dutch politics has seen the rise of the populist right in the last few years – even in traditionally left-wing Amsterdam.

middle of prime real estate – and the pressure to redevelop is building. Some would happily raze them to the ground, to be replaced by bijou hangouts and million-euro townhouses; others (correctly) point to the importance of neighbourly ties built up over generations, and the unfairness inherent in pushing entire communities further away from the city centre. It's a telling example of how Amsterdam's storied past and liberal reputation now seem in open conflict with the realities of hyper-connected 21st-century urban life.

Amsterdam's storied past and liberal reputation now seem in open conflict with the realities of hyper-connected 21st-century urban life

A new future, a new city?

The Dutch have always been pragmatic folk, with a keen sense as to which way the wind is blowing. To them, the future is a land of opportunity, one they have no desire to miss out on, and Amsterdam's desire to paint itself as a gleaming bastion of modernity is as much rooted in cold, hard economics as it is in loftier, more noble ideals. Much effort is being expended on facing 21st-century challenges, including climate change, social cohesion and ever-more transient notions of employment. Aware of the density and cost of living anywhere near the centre, the city plans to construct 52,500 new homes by 2025 in a variety of new hubs. NDSM is one, as are other parts of Noord, so too Oost and the waterfront, especially Cruquiuseiland and the series of islands stretching down to Ijburg. Mindful of an aging population, the city is also heavily investing in educating its own population and in attracting the top tech talent from elsewhere – it's all part of the drive to increase (and diversify) the city's knowledge base and to lead the digital revolution.

It remains a top destination for business, attracted mainly by a soft tax regime and generous incentives. It's quietly become the EU's new centre of financial trading infrastructure and has benefitted from the uncertainty

The Zuidas, Amsterdam's business district, has become a top destination for international companies.

Startup Village, in Amsterdam Science Park, opened as a community working space for new science-related businesses.

surrounding Brexit: the European Medicines Agency moved here from London in 2019, and corporate giants such as Sony are relocating their EU headquarters here too. Yet while shiny new towers and an influx of big-name HQs make for nice headlines and improve the balance sheet, there's been open grumbling about the prospect of yet more expats moving in. Where, citizens ask, is the concern over inner city schools, affordable housing and creaking public services?

Since the time of Rembrandt, Amsterdam's cultural offerings have been second to none, its creative arts fostering a deep-rooted attitude of curiosity and enterprise. But for young creatives today, Amsterdam has somewhat lost its shine. Cost is the main factor, but so is a creeping sense that the freedom described by John Green is slowly being curtailed. Amsterdam has lost its gritty edge, and the more polished façade it likes to present to the world has led to a certain homogeneity – in art, nightlife and society. The great challenge the city faces going forward is how to balance its rich cultural credentials with its aspirations to be a sleek metropolitan hub. Its ability to balance creativity with practicality is being tested like never before; how Amsterdam responds will determine how much of its famously unique atmosphere survives. The future will be interesting, to say the least.

Eating & Drinking

So much more than herring and potatoes

Wander around the centre of Amsterdam, and it can seem like every third building is a bar, café or restaurant with a bustling terrace spilling onto the pavement. Although the city doesn't have an especially distinguished culinary history, its food and drink scene is thriving. Tourist numbers continue to rise, thanks to the city's reinvigorated cultural offerings, and the hotel-restaurant-café business, or *horeca*, is clearly benefitting. Amsterdam's foodie movement reflects the trends currently in vogue in other major cities, with Instagram-friendly pop-ups, guest chefs and sustainable fare taking centre stage, but it also adds a uniquely Dutch spin to both international and local flavours.

As for Amsterdam's bars, they are far more sophisticated than the inebriated stag-and-hen-doers roaming the streets may have you believe. Whether you like your drinks brewed, distilled or caffeinated, the city has a liquid offering to suit most tastes. Drinking in Amsterdam is enough of a pleasure to make you forget the coffeeshops entirely.

CT Coffee & Coconuts *p185*

Netherlands on a plate

Admittedly light on culinary accolades when compared to its Western European counterparts, Amsterdam hasn't typically been a pinnacle of gastronomic glamour. But the country where cheese reigns supreme is fast becoming a key player in the food-enthusiast game. Well-travelled native chefs have returned home to apply their skills to fresh, local and often organic ingredients (source your own at **Noordermarkt**'s Saturday organic market; *see p124*).

The land is most suited to growing spuds, cabbage, kale and carrots, but the future-focused nation is making sustainable strides with greenhouses growing a startling array of ingredients, year-round. Organic eating is well and truly trendy, thanks largely to the revival of the city's post-industrial Noord area. Here, abandoned warehouses have been converted into sustainable restaurants such as **Pllek** (*see p175*) and **Café de Ceuvel** (*see p172*), which has its own rooftop farm. Both menus only feature locally sourced organic produce. Then there's **Vuurtoreneiland** ('Lighthouse Island' – *see p190*), on which the only building is an eco-friendly greenhouse restaurant.

❤ Best Dutch cuisine

Bistro Bij Ons *p105*
What better place to enjoy Dutch cuisine than overlooking a canal?

Hap Hmm *p145*
Home cooking at bargain prices.

Winkel 43 *p122*
The apple pie to end all apple pies.

❤ Best blowout restaurants

Moon *p175*
A high-end meal with a twist, literally. The restaurant revolves as you dine.

&moshik *p171*
Molecular, witty and expensive.

La Rive *p157*
The city's poshest of posh eateries is still going strong.

Pesca *p127*

In the know
Price categories

All our restaurant listings are marked with a euro symbol category, indicating the price you should expect to pay for a standard main course. The final bill will of course depend on the number of courses and drinks consumed.

€ = under €10

€€ = €10-€20

€€€ = €20-€30

€€€€ = over €30

Some Like it Hot

Where to find the best Indonesian food in town

Following Indonesian independence in 1949, 180,000 residents of the 'Spice Islands' emigrated to the Netherlands to become Dutch citizens. As a result, even Amsterdam's ubiquitous snackbars serve bastardised versions of Indonesian cuisine. Coming from an archipelago of more than a thousand islands, with historical influences ranging from Chinese and Arabian to Portuguese and Dutch, Indonesian food mingles many cuisines with an almost infinite range of dishes.

To add to the confusion are the many Chin-Indo-Suri eateries, which serve cheap dishes that have taken on the tones of the many immigrants from China (often via Indonesia) and Suriname, another former colony whose Caribbean style is usually represented by the pancake-like roti. The usual dishes on offer at these places are satay, *gado gado* (steamed veg and boiled egg served with rice and satay sauce), *nasi goreng* (onion-fried rice with meat, veg and egg) and *bami goreng* (the same but with noodles). While those are great for the monetarily challenged, all visitors should stretch their funds to visit an official purveyor of *rijsttafel* ('rice table') – a Dutch construct of a set meal that nobly tries to include as many dishes as possible.

While in days gone by, connoisseurs would have sent you to the Hague for the most authentic Indonesian restaurants, Amsterdam now offers ample choices of its own. There's **Tempo Doeloe** (*see p112*) and the crowd favourite **Sampurna** (Singel 498, Old Centre, 625 3264), which has been in business for over 25 years. And if you like it really hot, **Jun** (Frederik Hendrikstraat 98, Jordaan, 785 9185) will certainly sort you out. Then, of course, there are the stellar cheap takeaways, such as **Toko Joyce** (Nieuwmarkt 38, Old Centre, 020 427 9091, www.tokojoyce.nl) and **Sari Citra** (Ferdinand Bolstraat 52, De Pijp, 020 675 4102).

Top of the pile, however, is the relatively expensive **Blauw** in Oud West (Amstelveenseweg 158-160, 020 675 5000, www.restaurantblauw.nl). The restaurant serves authentic dishes, but with a twist. Its 'rice table' is a feast for the well-walleted.

Blauw

In medieval days it was fish, gruel and beer that formed the holy diet. During the Golden Age, the rich indulged in hogs and pheasants enlivened by spices, sugar and exotic fruits from the burgeoning Dutch Empire. The potato reigned supreme in the following centuries, until, after World War II, the rich, spicy food of Indonesia reawoke the Dutch palate. Indonesian *rijsttafel* ('rice table'), along with fondue – a 'national' dish shamelessly stolen from the Swiss because its shared pot appealed to the Dutch sense of democracy – are both foods of choice for any celebratory meals. Other waves of immigration helped create today's vortex of culinary diversity.

That said, there's still nothing quite like the hotchpotch of mashed potato, crispy bacon and crunchy greens, holding a well of gravy and loads of smoked sausage, to prove that traditional Dutch food can still hit the spot. The most feverish buzz remains around places that combine straight and honest cookery with eccentric ingredients and often out-of-the-way locations. Besides the watery ones, there's **De Kas** (*see p163*) in an old greenhouse and **As** (Beatrixpark, 020 644 0100, www.restaurantas.nl) in a remodelled modernist church.

Diners' demands for a more hands-on experience has driven the likes of **Foodhallen** (*see p144*), an industrial indoor food hall, and **Pesca** (*see p127*), the 'theatre of fish' that has guests selecting their meal from an on-site seafood market before it is cooked in front of them.

This 'nouveau rough' school of cookery, which combines rough interiors, an obsession for fresh and responsible ingredients, and reasonable prices, is also exemplified by rotisserie specialists **Rijsel** (*see p163*) in Oost, **Café Modern** (*see p172*) in Noord and **VOLT** (*see p185*) in De Pijp. The move towards unpretentious and straightforward cooking is also evident in the popularity of street food (*see p44* Street Eats).

&moshik *p171*

❤ Best global flavours

Blauw *p41*
Indonesian rice tables worth going out of your way for.

Café Bern *p82*
Swiss fondue in a Dutch brown café.

Nam Kee *p83*
Chinatown classic serving legendary oysters with black bean sauce.

Semhar *p122*
Spicy Ethiopian food with *enjeras* – perfect for sharing.

In the know
Essentials

Restaurants generally open in the evening from 5pm until 11pm (though some may close as early as 9pm or 10pm); many are closed on Monday and Tuesday. Most restaurants will accept at least one type of credit card, but it's best to have cash to be safe, especially since UK-issued Visa and Mastercard debit cards are often mistaken for credit cards. Service charges are included in café and restaurant bills. It's polite to round up to the nearest euro for small bills or the nearest five for larger sums, although tipping 10% is becoming more common.

Fento, Foodhallen

Where to eat

Several 'culinary boulevards' have recently staked their claim. One is located on a stretch of connected streets in the Jordaan that has become known as 'Little Italy' because of its highly regarded restaurants such as **Toscanini** (*see p122*); but there are also other options, such as Dutch 'eating café' **Vlaming** (Lindengracht 95, 020 622 2716, www.restaurantvlaming.com). Another culinary strip is Amstelveenseweg, bordering the south end of Vondelpark. It includes the Indonesian **Blauw** (*see p41* Some Like it Hot) and **Ron Gastrobar** (*see p149*).

If you enjoy a stroll that involves picking out where you're going to eat dinner, here are a few tips: go to De Pijp or Amsterdam East if you crave economical ethnic; cruise the eateries of Haarlemmerstraat, Utrechtsestraat, Nieuwmarkt, the 'Nine Streets' area and Reguliersdwarsstraat if you want something more upmarket; and only surrender to Leidseplein if you don't mind being overcharged for a cardboard steak or day-old sushi.

In the know
Appy meal

The internet is a good resource for local culinary knowledge. The website www.specialbite.nl is a good start, reliably offering the scoop on all the latest restaurant openings. For insider knowledge from prominent food bloggers, head to www.amsterdamfoodie.nl, www.yourlittleblackbook.me/en, or download the Amsterdam Food Guide app at thefoodguide.de.

Street Eats

From 'fat bites' to food trucks, this is the best fast food in town

Amsterdam's street food has gained some serious street cred in recent years. From the opening of **Foodhallen**, an indoor market lined with 20 high-end vendors (*see p144*), to the success of acclaimed chef Robert Kranenborg's Thrill Grill burger trucks-turned-restaurants, culinary entrepreneurs have found creative ways to satisfy the city's growing demand for superior street eats.

These are showcased at markets and food festivals, including the hugely popular **Rollende Keukens** (Rolling Kitchens; *see p201*) and **Taste Of Amsterdam** (tasteofamsterdam.com), a four-day event that takes over Amstelpark. Keep your eye out, too, for **The Kitchen of the Unwanted Animal** (dekeukenvanhetongewenstdier.nl), which serves meat that would otherwise end up as food waste. Delicacies include *bitterballen* (deep-fried meatballs) made from the geese that are killed in the name of keeping Schiphol Airport safe for jets.

Yet, although the burgeoning foodie scene has brought welcome innovation and quality to Amsterdam's street snacks, there are still some traditional Dutch treats that you shouldn't leave town without trying.

Broodjes

Traditional Dutch sandwiches filled with all manner of meats and cheese are available from bakers and butchers, but you can also try more creative variations that highlight the city's multiculturalism, such as spicy Surinamese *broodjes* from Chin-Indo-Suri snack bars (*see p41* Some Like it Hot), and rolled 'pizzas' from Turkish bakeries.

Frites

The best are the chunky Belgian ones (*Vlaamse frites*), double-fried to ensure a crispy exterior and creamy interior. Enjoy them along with your pick of toppings, such as *oorlog* ('war'): mayo, spicy peanut sauce and onions. **Vleminckx** (*see p90*) and **Manneken Pis** (Damrak 41, near Centraal Station) are two of the best places to eat them. But if you don't have the time (or patience) to wait in a long line, **Chipsy King** (www.chipsyking.nl) has two shops in the Old Centre, at Muntplein 5 and Damstraat 8.

Haring

In Amsterdam you must – yes, you really must – try raw herring. The fish is at its

Jambugo, Foodhallen

best between May and July when the plump Hollandse Nieuwe catch hits the stands and the sweet flesh can be eaten unadulterated by onions and pickles. There's a quality fish stall or shop round most corners; they also provide smoked eel and other fishy sandwich fillings.

Taste of Amsterdam

Vette hap

The local term for a greasy snack translates literally as 'fat bite'. At the ubiquitous **FEBO**, you can put your change into the glowing vending machine and, in return, get a hot hamburger, *bamibal* (a deep-fried noodle ball of vaguely Indonesian descent), or a *kaas soufflé* (a cheese treat). The most popular choice – and rightly so – are *kroketten*. The Dutch answer to Spanish *croquetas*, *kroketten* are a melange of meat and potato with deep-fried skins, best served on a bun with hot mustard and washed down with a pint.

Van Dobben (*see p112*), a 1945-vintage late-night venue just off Rembrandtplein, is the uncontested champion when it comes to *bitterballen*, though you can find a more refined shrimp version at nearby **Patisserie Holtkamp** (Vijzelgracht 15, 020 624 8757).

Taste of Amsterdam

Café or bar?

The café (or bar – the line between the two is suitably blurred) is central to Dutch social life, serving as a home from home at all hours of the day and night (most cafés open in the morning and don't shut until 1am; some stay open as late as 3am or 4am at weekends). Whatever the hour, you're as likely to find punters sipping a coffee (*see p48* The Brown Stuff) or a cola as the foaming head of a pils – or a shot of local *jenever*.

What to drink

Wine buffs may find themselves underwhelmed in Amsterdam's traditional *bruin cafés*, so called because they've been stained brown by decades of smoking and spilt coffee. But there are plenty of other options if you are aghast at the prospect of a beaker of unspecified red or white. Head to **Alex + Pinard** (*see p161*), **Bubbles & Wines** (*see p83*) or **La Oliva** (*see p119*), all examples of a well-respected breed of establishments specialising in pairing posh food with fine wine.

Cocktails, of course, remain ever popular, be they the ultra-posh secret concoctions made at **Vesper** (*see p131*) and **Hiding in Plain Sight**,

❤ Best beer

Arendsnest *p106*
Dutch beers of distinction with snacks to match.

Brouwerij 't IJ *p163*
A brewery under a windmill. Enough said.

Butcher's Tears *p149*
Small and sociable brewery and tasting room.

Gollem's Proeflokaal *p148*
A gathering place for the beers and people of the world.

Oedipus *p162*

or drinks with a view at the likes of **Twenty Third Bar** or **W Lounge**.

A barfly can score some major points by giving the Dutch their rightful credit for inventing gin. In around 1650 a doctor in Leiden came up with the process that allowed juniper berries to be infused into distilled spirits, and gin was born – or rather *jenever*, as the local version is called. A few decades later, the Dutch were exporting 10 million gallons of the stuff, as a supposedly innocuous cure for stomach and kidney ailments. They graded the gin by age – *jong*, *oud* and *zeer oud* (young, old and very old) – but also by adding various herbs, spices and flavours. Such liquid elixirs can still be found at *proeflokalen* (tasting houses) such as **Wynand Fockink** and **Distilleerderij 't Nieuwe Diep** (*see p160*).

Beer, though, is resoundingly the local drink of choice: in most places the pils is Heineken or Amstel, but every bar offers a range of Belgian brews and there are several specialist beer bars, such as **Brouwerij 't IJ** (*see p162* What's Brewing). For a real taste of all the Low Countries' native brews, **Arendsnest** has a huge range to choose from. Perhaps the most fundamental rule for Brits is not to whine

't Blauwe Theehuis *p146*

❤ Best cocktails

Door 74 *p113*
Speakeasy-style cocktail bar behind a hidden door.

Hiding in Plain Sight *p157*
Embrace liquid danger with a cocktail in cosy surrounds.

Twenty Third Bar *p186*
Top-class cocktails in a top-floor location.

W Lounge *p92*
Dip your feet into the infinity pool and delight your palate.

Twenty Third Bar

❤ Best traditional drinking dens

Café de Dokter *p92*
It doesn't come much more old school than this.

Café Nol *p123*
Regular brown bar by day, neon-lit karaoke paradise by night.

Café Welling *p143*
Brown café with a classical touch thanks to neighbour Concertgebouw.

Wynand Fockink *p85*
Taste the original gin, *jenever*, in surroundings that haven't changed in 300 years.

The Brown Stuff

There's another kind of coffeeshop fuelling Amsterdammers – think bean, not weed

The Dutch played a fundamental role in establishing the global coffee market. In 1690, a cheeky Dutchman plucked away the coffee monopoly from the Arabs by smuggling a coffee plant out of Mocha, Yemen. It ended up in Amsterdam's **Hortus Botanicus** (*see p158*), where descendants of the original *Arabica* plant still survive. Some clones went off to Dutch colonies in Sumatra, Java, Ceylon (now Sri Lanka) and Suriname, where they flourished.

Now, more than three centuries later, Amsterdam is regaining its status as a java hub. The city was home to the European headquarters of Starbucks until 2014 when it relocated to London, and big global coffee franchises are held in check by the ubiquitous local Coffee Company. But it's the independent coffee houses – run by caffeine obsessives – that add new-found energy and interest to the city's café scene.

Screaming Beans (Runstraat 6, Grachtengordel, 062 202 8077, screamingbeans.nl) was one of the first to roast its own beans, but new players in the high-end caffeine game have taken hold in recent years. Australian coffee fanatics **Lot Sixty One** supply quality beans to cafés and restaurants across the city, as well as having their own sit-in corner on the Kinkerstraat (*see p145*). Over in De Pijp, **CT Coffee & Coconuts** (*see p185*) and **Scandinavian Embassy** (*see p93*) set a high bar when it comes to caffeine, but the likes of **Little Collins** (*see p185*) and **Bakers & Roasters** (*see p183*) manage to meet it.

In the west, **Espressofabriek** provides a focal point for local baristas at its main location at the Westergasfabriek (Gosschalklaan 7, 486 2106, www.espressofabriek.nl). Coffeeheads come to talk shop and admire the state-of-the-art equipment.

In the east meanwhile, coffee lovers flock to **NewWerktheater** (*see p172*) for their ever-changing range of exotic roasts (and excellent brunch) and **Rum Baba Bakery & Roastery** (Pretoriusstraat 15h, www.rumbaba.nl), where the cakes and daily baked treats are every bit as good as the beans.

Bakers & Roasters

Hannekes Boom

about the 'two fingers' of head that comes with a glass of draft pils (lager). You are not being ripped off; it's the 'crown', and the reasoning behind it is sound: by letting a head form during tapping, the beer's hoppy aroma – and hence full flavour – is released, and the drinker's gas intake is minimised (leaving more room for more beer, of course).

Bar snacks

Another handy tip is to avoid getting completely legless by acquiring a sound knowledge of *borrelhapjes* (booze bites). These tasty bar snacks are formulated to line the stomach during drinking sessions. Inevitably, such menus begin with the strongest of stereotype reinforcers: *kaas* (cheese), which can be ingested either via *tostis* (grilled cheese sandwiches), or pure with dipping mustard. But the most universal and tastiest of *hapjes* are definitely *bitterballen*. These round *kroketten* are called 'bitter balls' because they were originally meant to be served with *bittertje* – a small glass of *jenever*.

❤ Best outdoor venues

't Blauwe Theehuis *p146*
Flying saucer-shaped venue in the heart of Vondelpark with expansive patio.

Distilleerderij 't Nieuwe Diep *p160*
This old mill in a park in deepest Oost serves home-brewed elixirs.

Hannekes Boom *p172*
This shack-style bar with a huge terrace is the place for a few lively sundowners.

Pllek *p175*
Amsterdam's revived Noord at its finest.

't Smalle *p123*
So gorgeously charming, the Japanese recreated it for a theme park.

Where to drink

A cool yet hard-drinking kind of crowd can be found at **Café Eijlders** (*see p106*) and other cafés along Marnixstraat, just off Leidseplein. A short hop in the other direction is Reguliersdwarsstraat, the centre of both the gay scene and an emerging more mixed trendy scene as exemplified by **Taboo Bar** (Reguliersdwarsstraat 45, www.taboobar.nl). And one of Amsterdam's best mixed gay bars, **PRIK** (*see p216*), which serves everyone's favourite bubbly – prosecco – on tap, is but a ten-minute walk away.

Away from the neon, the Jordaan is awash with *bruin* cafés. You can spot them on most street corners, but for a story you'll tell for years head to **Café Nol** (*see p123*), probably the best-known bar in the neighbourhood. Not far away stands the **Westergasfabriek** (*see p132*), which has several appealing drinking spots, including the WestergasTerras. A similar scene to the Jordaan is to be found in De Pijp, a great place to wander between trendy bars and more salt-of-the-earth watering holes. To soak up the city's most impressive revival, head across the IJ to **Pllek** (*see p175*) or **Café de Ceuvel** (*see p172*) for drinks with a view of the city.

Jenever *p47*

Pllek

Shopping

From mainstream malls to backstreet boutiques

Amsterdam's shopping scene has come a long way since the 'tulip mania' of the 17th-century Golden Age, when single bulbs were traded for cash, castles and mountains of cheese (though the latter is still a consumer crowd favourite). Today, the city streets are flanked by an array of stores that are as interesting and varied as the people that frequent them. From the tacky neon-lit tourist digs in the Red Light District to the high-end boutiques along PC Hoofstraat, the city's shops cater to just about any buyer or budget.

King Louie *p107*

The buoyancy of the retail sector could be explained by the simple fact that the Netherlands is a relatively wealthy country. Yet while the Dutch clearly spend, the population is perhaps less obsessed with shopping than residents of other countries. The influence of Calvinism, that most pared-down of lifestyle choices, is still etched deep into the national psyche, and most people are happy to pack a cheese sandwich for lunch rather than eat out at a stylish café. Contradictions abound, but there is clearly a lot to be enjoyed in the world of Amsterdam shopping.

Otherist

❤ Best gifts and souvenirs

Art Unlimited *p113*
The most comprehensive collection of international photographs and posters in the country.

Concrete Matter *p107*
The ultimate 'man cave' store with unusual gifts and vintage fashion.

the Otherist *p108*
Quirky gifts made for quirky minds.

Markets

Tulips are perhaps what Amsterdam is best known for exporting, and you can certainly pick up bargains at the floating flower market **Bloemenmarkt**. At the more traditional general markets, you'll find people truly enjoying shopping as they bounce between vendors while sniffing out special offers. With food as the great unifier, the market is among the few places at which the multi-ethnic diversity of the city is visible.

Bloemenmarkt

❤ Best markets

Albert Cuypmarkt *p184*
The nation's longest street market.

Bloemenmarkt *p113*
Floral overload.

Foodhallen *p144*
An indoor street food market perfect for a rainy day.

Noordermarkt *p124*
Monday morning flea market not to be missed.

Pekmarkt *p176*
The perfect excuse to pop over to the buzzing Noord district.

People from all walks of life are certainly brought together at the **Albert Cuypmarkt**, which claims to be one of Europe's longest street markets, and forms a line all the way through the heart of De Pijp. The daily market offers plenty of snacks, ranging from raw herring to Surinamese sherbets, along with all manner of household goods. It lies in close proximity to many pretty cafés, in which you can recharge over a cool drink.

Other neighbourhoods in the city tend to have their own markets: **Pekmarkt** in Noord and the **Dappermarkt** (*see p163*) in Oost are all worth a trip for an authentic shopping experience. In the Jordaan, Saturday's **Noordermarkt** is the place to buy organic farm produce amid well-heeled shoppers; the same crowd is back on Monday morning to pick through bric-a-brac and antiques at a much smaller (yet infinitely superior) variation on Waterlooplein's tourist trap **flea market** (*see p157*).

Fashion

The Dutch haven't traditionally had the best reputation for fashion but the city's creative types and young blood are transforming the stereotype with style. If you wander through the city's network of streets or people-watch from a canalside café, you'll notice that the Dutch favour a casual-chic look. Trainers are paired with just about any outfit and a 'less is more' approach makes for a simplistic and timeless style.

A fair few designers have also achieved success in Amsterdam, and the country can hold its head high in the catwalk stakes – after all, it's the home city of avant-garde darlings Viktor & Rolf and ever-charming Marlies Dekkers, who turns shoppers' heads with her feminine lingerie. Locally produced gentleman's style journal *Fantastic Man* is setting trends for fashion magazines across the planet.

Moooi

❤ Best fashion

Azzurro Due *p144*
Credit card at the ready.

Bij Ons Vintage *p93*
Because authentic 1960s wear will always be in style.

Jutka & Riska *p133*
Vintage fashion and up-and-coming designers.

Things I Like Things I Love *p187*
A wonderful collection of new and pre-loved fashion.

❤ Best design

Blom & Blom *p176*
Industrial home deco at its finest.

Droog *p85*
Design for home, garden and beyond.

Moooi *p124*
Marcel Wanders and friends ask for the big bucks.

Public House of Art *p113*
Its ethos: 'Art is for all – to disrupt not bankrupt'.

Droog *p85*

A couple of Dutch brands have brought street style home: Gsus and G-Star Raw. Affordable high-end wear from Scotch & Soda is also doing its part to put the international spotlight on Amsterdam.

The city's fashion map is divided along clear lines: head to PC Hooftstraat, as star footballers do, for top-end designer clothes; visit the Kalverstraat for high-street stalwarts such as H&M and HEMA. Even though Amsterdam has long lacked an abundance of good boutiques, a wander around the Jordaan, the Nine Streets and Damstraat areas will lead to the discovery of outlets selling quirkier and home-grown labels.

For something trendy, De Pijp certainly delivers, with eclectic boutique offerings at **Things I Like Things I Love** (*see p187*) and permanent hipster department store, **Hutspot** (*see p187*), which sells arty homewares alongside its clothing.

In the know
Essentials

In general, local shops are open from 1pm to 6pm on Mondays (if they open at all on this quiet day), 10am to 6pm from Tuesday to Friday (with many open until 9pm on Thursday), and 9am to 5pm on Saturday. Amsterdam has regular Sunday shopping, especially along Kalverstraat, PC Hooftstraat and the Nine Streets, with stores usually open between noon and 5pm. Smaller shops tend to have more erratic opening hours. Credit card and foreign bank card payment is not quite universally accepted, so as a rule of thumb, make sure you take enough cash with you when you go out shopping.

Where to Spend it

Amsterdam's shopping districts – the cheat sheet

Old Centre *p85, p93*

Stretching east from Dam Square, **Damstraat** is a rather eclectic mix of predictable tourist tackiness and trendy unassuming boutiques. Be warned, window-shopping here can sometimes be spoiled by laddish overflow from the Red Light District. South and north of Dam Square, pedestrianised **Kalverstraat** and its scruffier extension **Nieuwendijk** are where the locals go for their consumer kicks. Shops here are familiar high-street names and they get insanely busy at weekends. Make sure you follow the unwritten law of keeping to the left as you stroll up or down the street. Right behind Dam Square, the **Magna Plaza** mall is housed in a former post office and is a tourist favourite.

Grachtengordel *p106, p113*

The **Nine Streets** (*see p101*) connecting Prinsengracht, Keizersgracht and Herengracht in between Raadhuisstraat and Leidsegracht offer a very diverse mix of boutiques, antique shops and a good range of quirky speciality stores. To the south, between Koningsplein and Leidseplein, **Leidsestraat** is peppered with fine shoe shops and more high-street stores, but you'll have to dodge trams to shop there. More upmarket is the **Spiegelkwartier**, across from the Rijksmuseum. This area is packed with antique shops selling real treasures at suitably high prices. Dress for success and keep your nose in the air if you want to fit in with the big-spending locals here.

Jordaan & the West *p123, p128, p133*

Tiny backstreets laced with twisting canals, cosy boutiques, lush markets, bakeries, galleries, restful old-fashioned cafés and bars. The Jordaan captures the spirit of Amsterdam like nowhere else in the city. The 'hood is also handily cut in half by furnishings- and design-rich street **Rozengracht**. Forming the Jordaan's northern boundary, **Haarlemmerstraat** and **Haarlemmerdijk** have bloomed into a remarkable boutique shopping destination.

Museum Quarter *p144*

PC Hooftstraat, Amsterdam's elite shopping strip, is undeniably high-end and expensive. Its designer shops embrace both established and up-and-coming names. Come here for the world's biggest luxury brands and to see how the other half live.

De Pijp *p187*

This bustling district is notable mainly for the **Albert Cuypmarkt** and its ethnic food shops, but more fashion boutiques are filling the continually gentrifying gaps.

Leidsestraat

Interior design and homewares

Sneak a peek into just about any Amsterdam home and the city's interior design prowess will become apparent (*see p277* Design for Life). To feed your eyes with design of all kinds, from seriously high-end homeware to truly swanky jewellery, check out **Utrechtsestraat.** Overtoom, Rozengracht and Haarlemmerstraat/ Haarlemmerdijk are also the destinations of much-coveted furnishings.

Open books

The Dutch are freakishly bookish. They enjoy reading, collecting bookends, participating in book weeks – and even book months. So if you're a bookworm, you'll be in good company. Head straight to Spui, to be greeted by the **Friday book market**. Another singular browsing experience awaits if you cross the Rokin to reach Oudemanhuispoort, a covered passageway belonging to the University of Amsterdam where books and prints have been sold since the 18th century.

Incredible edibles

If you're hoping to pick up edible souvenirs, you'll be spoilt for choice in Amsterdam; head to **De Kaaskamer** (Runstraat 7, 020 623 3483, www.kaaskamer.nl) and you'll see a mountain of cheese – there are more than 200 varieties, including plenty of local specialities such as the popular *reypenaer*. For fishy dishes, you can pick up smoked eel, raw herring or tiny North Sea shrimps from any number of fish stalls dotted around town. Head to **Patisserie Holtkamp** (Vijzelgracht 15, 020 624 8757) for an array of cakes displayed in a beautiful interior; you will also be able to see how this gourmet shop cooks the humble *kroket*. If you fancy locally produced, organic food, visit **Marqt** (*see p148*) – if it happens to have lamb from the North Sea island of Texel, or white asparagus, make sure you try some.

❤ Best books and music

Flesch Records *p124*
All your vinyl and veg needs under one roof.

Book Market at the Spui *p93*
The already bookish Spui square has a weekly antiquarian book bonanza.

Book Market at the Spui

In the know
Shopping culture

Museum shops are some of the best places to find great presents, or books on art, design and architecture. In particular, try the EYE Film Institute (*see p173*) and the Van Gogh and Rijksmuseum's joint Museum Shop on the Museumplein (*see p138*).

Explore

A'DAM Lookout *p174*

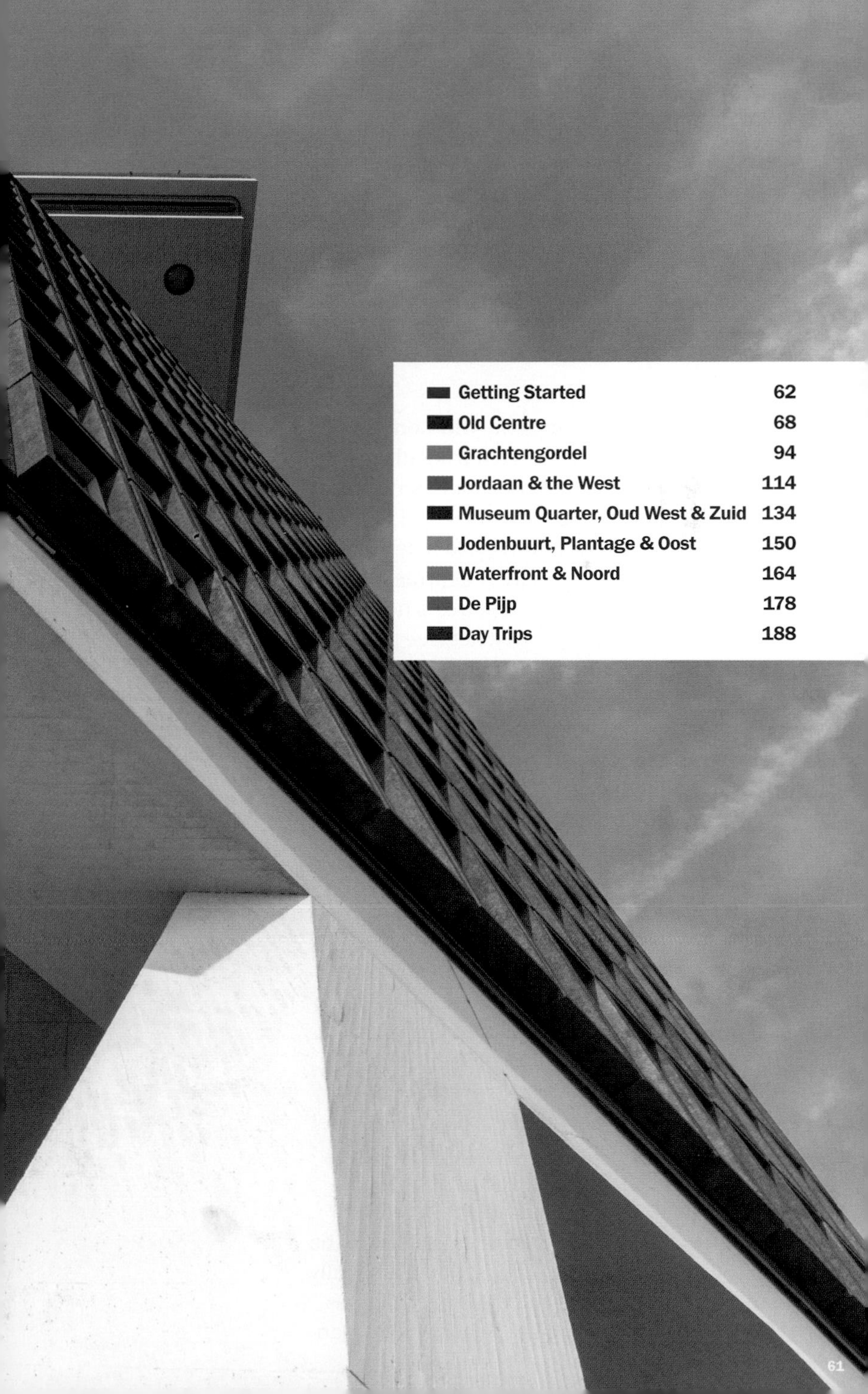

Getting Started

The heart of Amsterdam is the **Old Centre**, which is bounded by Prins Hendrikkade to the north, Oudeschans and Zwanenburgwal to the east, the Amstel to the south and Singel to the west. Within these borders, the Old Side, roughly covering the triangle formed by Centraal Station, the Nieuwmarkt and Dam Square, is notorious for hosting the Red Light District (see *p72*). However, the area is also home to historical sights, including Oude Kerk and De Waag.

The New Side, on the other hand, is the Old Side's gentler sister, featuring a history entwined with the intelligentsia, thanks to its many bookshops, brown cafés and the various buildings of the University of Amsterdam. The serene Begijnhof (*see p90*) is here too.

The **Grachtengordel** ('girdle of canals') that guards the Old Centre is pleasant, idyllic and uniquely Dutch. It is also home to Anne Frank Huis (*see p102*) and the Westerkerk, as well as more modern attractions such as Foam (*see p111*), Paradiso (*see p227*) and the boutiques and cafes of the Nine Streets (*see p101*). For ease of use, we have divided the Grachtengordel into two sections: Western Canal Belt denotes the stretch of canals to the west and north of Leidsestraat, taking in Leidseplein, whereas Southern Canal Belt covers the area that lies to the east, and Rembrandtplein. This split is historically justified by the fact that the western girdle was complete before work on the eastern half began.

❤ Best viewpoints

A'DAM Lookout *p174*
Dangle your feet over the 17th-century skyline from the tallest swing in Europe.

Westerkerk *p104*
Climb the stairs of one of Amsterdam's tallest churches for a bird's eye view of Jordaan's pretty streets.

SkyLounge at DoubleTree by Hilton *p283*
Treat yourself to sundowners overlooking both the Old Centre and Noord.

Zoku *p284*
Chill on a hammock on Zoku's rooftop garden terrace, a perfect suntrap above Oost.

Westerkerk *p104*

View from Westerkerk *p104*

The area around Waterlooplein, just east of the Old Centre, was settled by Jews four centuries ago, and so took its name, **Jodenbuurt**, from this rich culture. This is in evidence at Joods Historisch Museum. Oases of flora occupy the **Plantage** neighbourhood, east and south-east of Waterlooplein, among them the Hortus Botanicus and Artis. Further east (**Oost**) lies the Tropenmuseum (*see p161*).

Hortus Botanicus *p158*

Once the gateway to prosperity, Amsterdam's **Waterfront** has emerged as the setting for some of Europe's most inspired architecture. Traditional sights may be few, but the eastern stretch in particular has attracted thousands of new residents and has developed into a boulevard of contemporary arts and nightlife. Across the IJ from Centraal, the redeveloped **Noord** is now one of the city's hippest areas – with its landmark A'DAM Toren (*see p174*), eye-catchingly futuristic EYE Film Institute (*see p173*) and, further to the north, NSDM Wharf (*see p176*).

Over in the other direction, the Westelijke Eilanden link up nicely with Westerpark, Westergasfabriek (*see p132*) and the charming neighbourhood of the **Jordaan**, bordered by

❤ Cycle through the city

With over 800,000 in the city, there are almost more bikes than people in Amsterdam. What better way, then, to explore the 16th-century streets than on your own set of wheels? While the city is compact, there is an incredible amount of things to see, and pedalling will get you further than two feet. It's easy to see why the bike (or *fiets* – as the Dutch call it) has been embraced as the city's preferred mode of transport, and cyclists are exceptionally well catered for, with flat roads and well-marked bike lanes aplenty. Whether you just want to nip from Centraal Station to the Begijnhof or go further afield, the bike lanes make riding a breeze. If you're not confident in the busier areas, there's no shame in walking your wheels through the narrow streets of De Wallen and surrounds to avoid colliding with the crowds of wandering tourists. You can always jump back on when there's more room to move.

When cycling, remember that unless indicated otherwise by signs, traffic from the right has priority, and watch out for pedestrians stepping into your path. Bike lights are compulsory in the dark; police set up periodic checkpoints and will fine you on the spot if you don't have any. Avoid catching your tyre in the tram rails (always cross them at an angle) and never leave a bike unlocked – Amsterdam has one of the highest bicycle theft rates in the world. If someone on the street offers you a bike for sale (*fiets te koop*), don't be tempted: it's almost certainly stolen.

With its prime location in the Old Centre, Dam Square is a great place to pick up a bike for your visit, but there are also dozens of rental shops throughout the city (*see p290* Getting Around). Keep in mind, these shops can only stock a certain number of bikes, so if you're visiting during peak season or on a public holiday you'd do well to book in advance. Prices are €10-€20 per bike per day.

If you're unsteady and would rather cycle with a professional, there are plenty of guided bike tours on offer year-round. Companies including **Yellow Bike** (020 620 6940, www.yellowbike.nl) and **Mike's Bike Tours** (020 233 0216, www.mikesbiketoursamsterdam.com) have multiple starting points throughout the city.

For the more intrepid, free self-guided bike tours can be downloaded from www.Iamsterdam.com, and for a day trip out of the city, *see p190* Waterland.

Note that almost every bicycle in Amsterdam now uses the reverse pedal braking system rather than a pair of manual brakes attached to the handlebars. Those who are used to the latter will find it takes some time to adjust, so be sure to allow yourself time to practise before setting out on the streets.

Rijksmuseum

Brouwersgracht, Prinsengracht, Leidsegracht and Lijnbaansgracht. While lacking the grandiose architecture of the Grachtengordel, this area wants for nothing in terms of character, and is a great place for a stroll (*see p120*).

Amsterdam's **Museum Quarter** is centred round the Museumplein and its world-class Van Gogh Museum (*see p142*), Stedelijk Museum (*see p139*), Rijksmuseum (*see 140*) and Concertgebouw (*see p237*). Nearby is the city's central green space, Vondelpark (*see p146*), separating the affluent and leafy **Oud West** neighbourhood and business district, Zuid.

Against all the odds, **De Pijp** – location of Albert Cuypmarkt (*see p184*) – has remained a cultural melting pot, even though the area has been thoroughly gentrified over the last few years. It proves that the city is still full of charm – you may not even feel the desire to enter a museum.

❤ Best Dutch clichés

Amnesia *p106*
This coffeeshop's name says it all.

Bloemenmarkt *p113*
Tulips of every colour at the floating flower market.

Brouwerij 't IJ *p163*
Why not have a craft beer in the shadow of a windmill?

Erotic Museum *p78*
If you really can't leave it at a quick gawp in the Red Light District.

In the know
Travel apps

Get a digital head start with www.9292.nl, GVB's excellent door-to-door route-planner. If you're not so great at navigating paper maps, download free transport app Citymapper to your smartphone before arriving. It will lay out all of your transport options with a cost and time estimate for each to save you the faff. Wi-Fi is readily available at key landmarks and most cafés throughout the city if you don't want to spend a fortune on roaming charges.

Getting around

Most sights lie within half an hour's walk from one another, and the excellent network of trams (*see pull-out map*) provides back-up for those low on energy. You can join the slipstream of locals on a bike (although beware of trams and cycle thieves); or, better still, beg or borrow a boat to absorb the views on a cruise down the canals – surely the angle from which the city was meant to be seen. There's also a bewildering array of other modes of transport: metro, bus, ferry, and even horse and carriage (from Dam Square) or bike taxi (hail one near Dam Square, Damrak or Leidsplein).

Information and advice

The main tourist office, **Iamsterdam**, is outside Centraal Station. Look out for the cheerful 'Welcome Teams' dressed in red, waiting at Centraal and other busy central locations, to help tourists with directions, transport and tips for events. If you're a diligent traveller and want to start your research before arrival, head to www.Iamsterdam.com for all the key information you'll need.

Prices and discounts

There's good news for under-13s: they have free admission to many of the nation's museums. Even for older visitors, prices are still reasonable; despite the fact that most museums charge for admission, prices are rarely more than €20. However, if you're thinking of taking in a few museums in one go, then the **Museumkaart** (Museum Card or MK) is a steal at €64.90 for adults and €32.45 for under-19s (plus a €4.95 administration fee for first-timers). The card offers users free or discounted admission to more than 400 attractions in the Netherlands, and for non-residents is valid for one month from the date of purchase (residents get a full year). The museums with discounted or free entry for cardholders are denoted in this guide's listings by the letters 'MK'. You can purchase the card at museums participating in the scheme (check www.museumkaart.nl for more details).

The Amsterdam Tourist Board (outside Centraal) also sells a savings pass, the **Iamsterdam City Card**, which gives you free entry to major museums, free rides on public transport and a complimentary canal trip, along with a hefty 25 per cent discount at certain tourist attractions and restaurants. It costs €60 for 24 hours, €80 for 48 hours, €95 for 72 hours, €105 for 96 hours, and €115 for a full five days.

Tours

There is a wide range of tours readily available throughout all major areas in the city. Whether you're on two feet, two wheels (*see p65*) or navigating the canals, the compact nature of Amsterdam makes it a perfect place for self-guided exploration. But for first timers, guided tours are a great way to see the historical sights while hearing stories told by a local expert.

On foot

On a budget? No problem. Self-guided walking tours are available for free download at www.Iamsterdam.com. If you'd rather soak up the knowledge of a local expert, **Sandeman's New Amsterdam Free Walking Tour** (www.neweuropetours.eu/amsterdam) explains the city's wild history of prostitution and drug decriminalisation as you wander through historical landmarks. For foodies with a bit more dough to spend, **Eating Amsterdam Food Tours** (www.eatingeurope.com/amsterdam) are sure to satisfy.

On water

For an eel's-eye view of the UNESCO-listed Grachtengordel, pedal boats can be hired from major sights in the city for up to two hours of self-guided exploration. If you'd rather not navigate the crowded canals yourself, larger tourist boats, including **Amsterdam Canal Cruises**, pick up from the central Stadhouderskade, with many more operating from the Damrak directly in front of Centraal. If you fancy a bit of romance, companies like the **Blue Boat Company** offer candle-lit cruises by night.

► *For further information on exploring the canals, see p99 Canal cruising; for details of bike tours, see p65 Cycle through the city.*

Old Centre

The Old Centre was where the city was first established, and it is where today's visitors spend much of their time. It's a full-on sensory experience: Golden Age architecture lines picturesque canals; alleyways are crowded with tourists and tramlines. The cloying scent of waffles mingles with the unmistakable waft of marijuana, and women tout their wares from behind gaudily lit windows. This is Amsterdam's ground zero of vice, consumerism and entertainment but also its compelling historic core.

The Old Centre is bounded by the refurbished Centraal Station, Singel and Zwanenburgwal, and has bustling Dam Square at its heart. This is where the first dam was constructed in 1270 to prevent the flooding of a city that had been built – arguably against logic – on boggy marshlands surrounding the river Amstel. The medieval town initially developed around the Oude Kerk (Old Church); this is Amsterdam's oldest building, dating back to the 14th century. Just as old, however, is the history of prostitution in the area's notorious Red Light District. To the west is the rather more respectable Nieuwe Zijde (New Side), whose origins go back to the 15th century.

❤ Don't miss

1 Red Light District *p72, p74*
Amsterdam's oldest trade in its (not so) glamorous glory.

2 Begijnhof *p90*
Peaceful courtyard for a break from the buzz.

3 Ons' Lieve Heer op Solder *p79*
17th-century secrets in an attic church.

4 Oude Kerk *p80*
Solace for the soul in the heart of Sin City.

5 Amsterdam Museum *p87*
Explore Amsterdam's DNA.

Oude Kerk *p80*

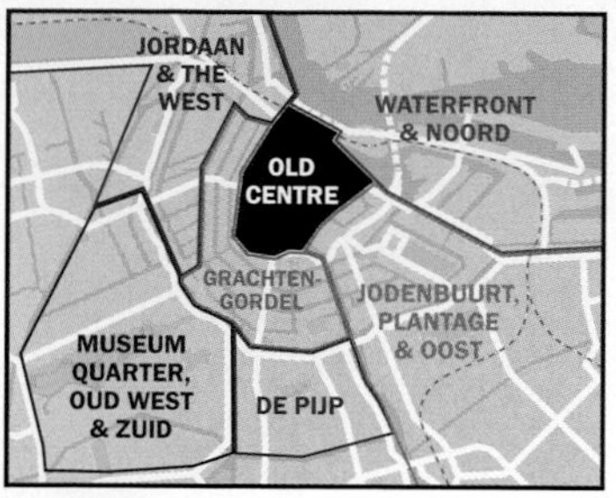

OLD CENTRE

Restaurants & cafés

1. 1e Klas *p81*
2. A Fusion *p81*
3. De Bakkerswinkel *p81*
4. Bird *p81*
5. Blauw aan de Wal *p82*
6. Bridges *p82*
7. Café Bern *p82*
8. China Sichuan *p82*
9. Gartine *p89*
10. Gebroeders Niemeijer *p89*
11. Haesje Claes *p89*
12. Hoi Tin *p83*
13. Juice by Nature *p83*
14. Kantjil & de Tijger *p89*
15. Latei *p83*
16. Nam Kee *p83*
17. Oriental City *p83*
18. d'Vijff Vlieghen *p90*
19. Vleminckx *p90*

Bars

1. 5&33 *p90*
2. Belgique *p90*
3. Bierfabriek *p83*
4. Brouwerij de Prael *p83*
5. Bubbles & Wines *p83*
6. Café de Dokter *p92*
7. Café Hoppe *p92*
8. Café de Jaren *p83*
9. Café 't Mandje *p83*
10. Kapitein Zeppos *p84*
11. Mata Hari *p84*
12. Proeflokkal de Ooievaar *p84*
13. TonTon Club Centrum *p84*
14. W Lounge *p92*
15. Wynand Fockink *p85*

Coffeeshops

1. Abraxas *p92*
2. Basjoe *p85*
3. Dampkring *p92*
4. Green House Centrum *p85*
5. Greenhouse Effect *p85*
6. Rusland *p85*
7. Tweede Kamer *p93*

Shops & services

1. A Boeken Stoffen & Fournituren *p85*
2. Albert Heijn *p93*
3. De Bierkoning *p93*
4. Bij Ons Vintage *p93*
5. Book Market at the Spui *p93*
6. Condomerie *p85*
7. Copa Football Store *p93*
8. Droog *p85*
9. HEMA *p93*
10. De Hoed van Tijn *p85*
11. Lambiek *p86*
12. Mark Raven *p93*
13. Nieuwmarkt Antique Market *p86*
14. Oudemanhuis Book Market *p86*
15. Toko Dun Yong *p86*
16. De Wijnerij *p86*

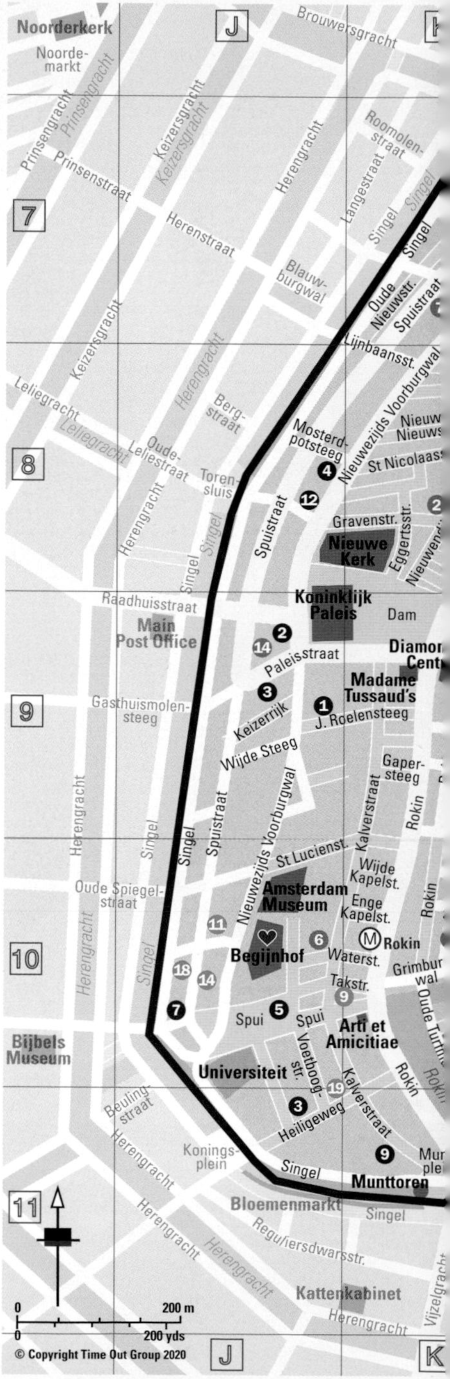

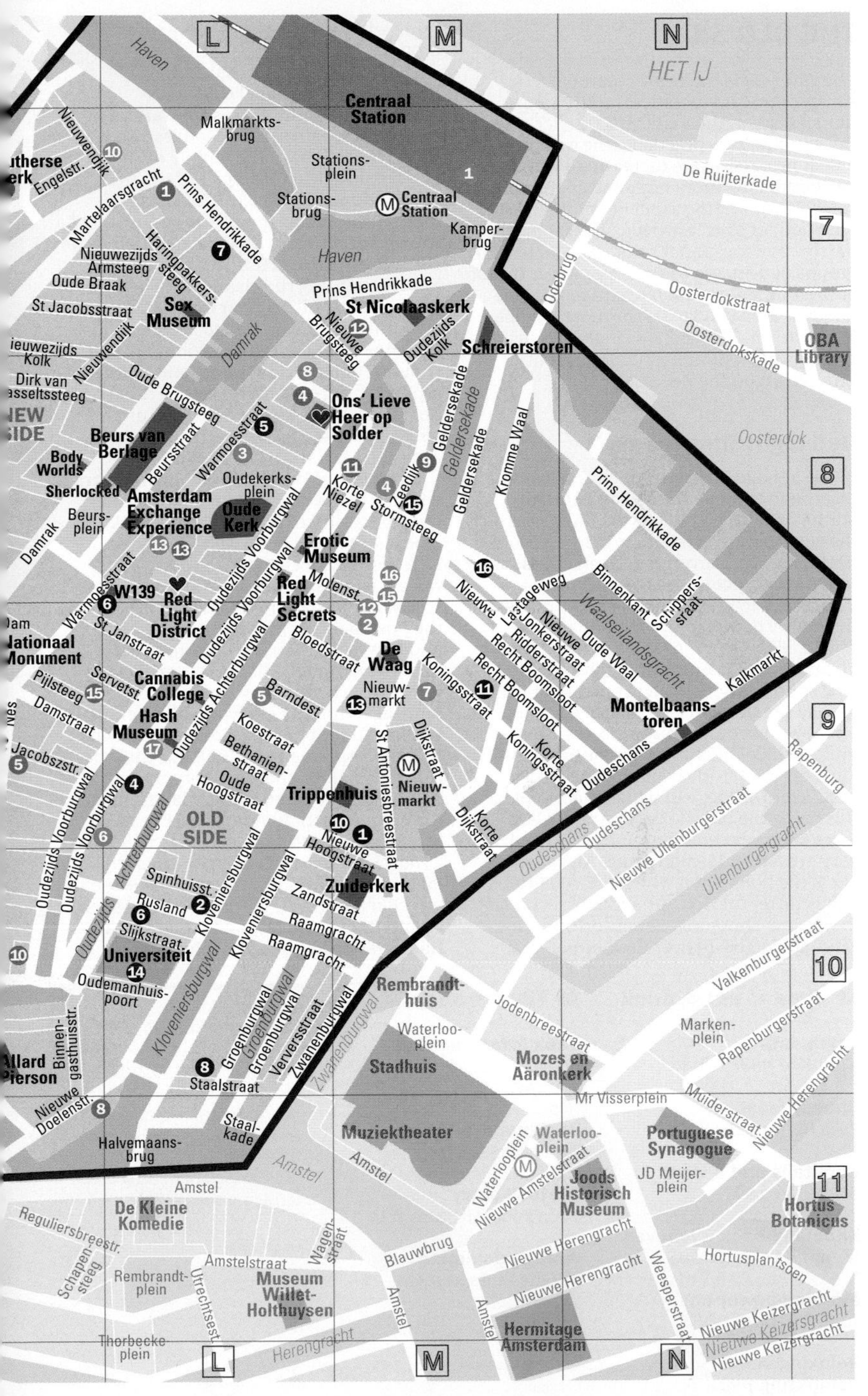
L
M
N
HET IJ
Centraal Station
Malkmarkts-brug
Stations-plein
Stations-brug
Centraal Station
Kamper-brug
Haven
De Ruijterkade
Prins Hendrikkade
St Nicolaaskerk
Schreierstoren
Oosterdokstraat
Oosterdokskade
OBA Library
Oosterdok
Sex Museum
Damrak
Ons' Lieve Heer op Solder
Beurs van Berlage
Body Worlds
Sherlocked
Amsterdam Exchange Experience
Oude Kerk
Erotic Museum
W139
Red Light District
Red Light Secrets
De Waag
Nationaal Monument
Cannabis College
Hash Museum
Montelbaanstoren
Trippenhuis
OLD SIDE
NEW SIDE
Zuiderkerk
Universiteit
Allard Pierson
Rembrandthuis
Waterlooplein
Stadhuis
Mozes en Aäronkerk
Muziektheater
Portuguese Synagogue
Joods Historisch Museum
Hortus Botanicus
De Kleine Komedie
Museum Willet-Holthuysen
Hermitage Amsterdam
Rembrandtplein
Thorbecke plein
Amstel
Halvemaansbrug
Staalstraat
Kalkmarkt
Oudeschans
Nieuwe Herengracht
Nieuwe Keizersgracht
7
8
9
10
11

THE OLD SIDE

The Old Side is the edgiest part of Amsterdam and includes the city's most unusual asset, the Red Light District, where the window girls practising the world's oldest profession are increasingly being surrounded by more high-end shops and cafés. However, the scent of marijuana still pours out of overcrowded coffeeshops in the narrow byways, and it's not unusual to hear groups of drunken tourists singing at the top of their lungs at 4am. It's hard to imagine that this area used to be the most religious part of town. The Old Side is also home to a very small, but nonetheless authentic, Chinatown on the Zeedijk.

Red Light District

The Red Light District, which is situated in a rough triangle formed by Centraal Station, Nieuwmarkt and the Dam, is at the very root of Amsterdam's international notoriety. While overheated imaginations might construct images of wild sexual abandon framed in red neon-lit windows, the reality depicted in the postcards on sale locally is a sort of small, cutesy version of Las Vegas. If truth be told, the cheesy joke shop has here been supplanted by the cheesy sex shop: instead of electric palm buzzers and comedy nose glasses, you get multi-orifice inflatables and huge dildos. Most of the historical significance of the Red Light District – of which there is plenty, this being the oldest part of Amsterdam – has been veneered by another old and very greasy trade: marketing. Although sex is the hook upon which the whole area hangs its reputation, it's actually secondary to window-shopping. People do buy – it's estimated to be an over €500m-per-year trade – but mostly they simply wander around, gawping at the live exhibits.

Oudezijds Voorburgwal and its neighbouring canal Oudezijds Achterburgwal, known as **De Wallen**, is where carnal sin screams loudest. So it's ironic that, right in the middle of Sin City, you'll stumble across a pair of old churches. The **Oude Kerk** (*see p80*), Amsterdam's oldest building, is literally in the centre of the sleazy action, with hookers in windows surrounding the mammoth church like bullies taunting the class geek. The attic church, **Ons' Lieve Heer op Solder** (*see p79*), meanwhile, is tucked away some distance from the red-lit action, but still shouldn't be overlooked on your journey around the area. A 17th-century canal house holds a well-preserved hidden church, which was used by the Catholics for worship after the Alteration (*see p249*).

Just west of De Wallen is **Warmoesstraat**, which – believe it or not – was once the most beautiful of lanes. It is Amsterdam's oldest street and has a rich history: the 17th-century poet Joost van den Vondel ran a hosiery business at Warmoesstraat 101; Mozart's dad tried to flog tickets at the posh bars for his young son's concerts; and Marx came here to write in peace (or so he claimed – he was more likely in town to borrow money from his cousin by marriage, the extremely wealthy Gerard Philips, founder of the globe-dominating Philips corporate machine). But with the influx of sailors, the law of supply and demand engineered a heavy fall from grace for Warmoesstraat. Adam and Eve in their salad days can still be seen etched in stone at no.25, but for the most part, this street has fallen to accommodating only the low-end traveller. However, hipper hangouts such as excellent breakfast and lunch spot **De Bakkerswinkel** (*see p81*), plus shops such

❤ Time to eat & drink

Asian eats
Nam Kee *p83*

Cheesy feast
Café Bern *p82*

Cocktails and a view
W Lounge *p92*

Knocking back a *jenever*
Wynand Fockink *p85*

Morning power-up
Juice by Nature *p83*

Relaxing smoke
Dampkring *p92*

❤ Time to shop

Book lovers' market
Book Market at the Spui *p93*

Designer everything
Droog *p85*

Football crazy
Copa Football Store *p93*

Vintage goldmine
Bij Ons Vintage *p93*

In the know
Getting around

Trams 2, 4, 11, 12, 13, 14, 17, 24 and 26 run to and from Centraal Station, the transport hub of the city on the border of the Old Centre. For details of nearby canal cruises, *see p99*.

Centraal Station

Gateway to the city

Constructed on three artificial islands on the edge of the IJ lake and opened to great fanfare in 1889, Centraal was designed by renowned Dutch architect Pierre Cuypers, who was also responsible for the Rijksmuseum (*see p140*). The station displays the same Gothic, Renaissance Revival style that was so in vogue at the time, with turrets, stone reliefs and a palatial facade lending it an air of regal grandeur to match its sister building on the other side of town. When it was unveiled, locals and visitors paid 25 cents to marvel at its magnificence. However, its position at the northern end of the Old Centre with its back to the waterfront also had the unintended consequence of blocking the city's view of the harbour and, thus, of its own maritime past. This psychological cleavage continued throughout the 20th century as the city focused on the development of its inland infrastructure.

In the 21st century, the construction of the metro's Noord/Zuidlijn saw nearly two decades of building work in and around Centraal Station, as developers tunnelled their way beneath the 19th-century building. In the process, the city's main transport hub gained a new bus station and food hall, plus revamped passenger and bike tunnels, which now run directly underneath the tracks to the ferry dock on the north side. Most importantly, perhaps, the station acquired a direct link to the fast-developing Noord neighbourhood, making it a gateway to the city's newly prized waterfront as well as to its established urban centre.

❤ A walk through the Red Light District

Begin at the entrance to Zeedijk, where the district's debauchery began in the 15th and 16th centuries. The **Prins Hendrik Hotel** at Prins Hendrikkade 53 (020 623 7969, www.hotel-prinshendrik.nl) is where jazz legend Chet Baker took his final curtain call in 1988 – onto a cement parking pole – from a window (second floor on the left). You'll see a brass plaque commemorating the crooning trumpeter has been put up to the left of the hotel's entrance. Continuing along Zeedijk, you'll find **Casablanca** (no.26), one of the few after-hours spots still functioning as a shadow of what it was. Before his death, Chet came to jam and hang out at this club alongside fellow crooner Gerry Mulligan in the 1950s. Further down at no.63 is **Café 't Mandje** (*see p83*), where the first openly gay establishment appeared in the 1930s, closed and then reopened. Back then, the subculture marked Zeedijk as a place where heroin could be scored with comparative ease and Amsterdam's reputation subsequently became littered with needles and foil. There was even a time when a German tour operator tried to run a 'criminal safari' along Zeedijk and street cleaners needed armed escorts, but as you'll notice nowadays the street is very safe – mostly thanks to the efforts of local residents and shopkeepers.

At the next intersection, either continue south on Zeedijk into the heart of Amsterdam's tiny Chinatown (*see p82*) or make a right on Korte Niezel and turn left before you cross the bridge to land in the district's main drag, **Oudezijds Achterburgwal**, which is essentially dominated by sleaze. A short walk away at no.37 is the **Bananenbar** (020 627 8954, www.bananenbar.nl), where improbably dexterous female genitalia can be seen performing night after night – and, as the central part of their belief-beggaring act, spitting out an average 15kg (33lb) of fruit every evening. A former owner of the Bananenbar once tried to stave off taxmen – and get round the fact that his drinking licence had lapsed – by picking Satan as a deity and registering the Bananenbar as a church. It was a scam that worked for years – until 1988, when the 'Church of Satan' claimed a membership of 40,000 overseen by a council of nine anonymous persons. The tax police were called in to bust the joint, but the bar was tipped off and the 'church' disbanded. Now under the same ownership as the **Erotic Museum** (*see p78*), the

Bananenbar has kept its name and returned to its roots as a purveyor of sleaze.

When you reach the next bridge, make a right on **Molensteeg** to cross the canal before continuing left down Oudezijds Achterburgwal on the opposite side. Stop in at no.60, the **Red Light Secrets Museum of Prostitution** (*see p81*), which although it's tourist-orientated, does allow you a glimpse behind the scenes, enabling visitors to empathise with the job of the sex worker (and take a nice snap of yourself in an S&M room). Further down at no.106 you'll find **Casa Rosso** nightclub (020 627 8954, www.casarosso.nl). This happens to be one of Amsterdam's most popular venues for live erotic entertainment, should you be wishing to tick that off your bucket list.

If you want to see Red Light ladies in all their window-working glory, take your

next right down **Stoofsteeg** – just make sure your camera is well away. Featuring an eclectic mix of window workers and cafés, the narrow passageway is an apt reflection of the controversial gentrification transforming the area (*see p31* Sex and the City). Make a right on **Oudezijds Voorburgwal** and ogle the array of sex shops and erotic boutiques on your way back to **Oude Kerk** (*see p80*), Amsterdam's oldest building and church, ironically situated in the centre of its Sin City. See if you can spot the small brass bosom laid by a mystery artist into the pavement by the front entrance. If you want to know more about the history and current state of the sex work industry, wander round to the other side of the building and finish up at the **Prostitution Information Centre** (Enge Kerk Steeg 3, 020 420 7328, www.pic-amsterdam.com).

as the **Condomerie** (*see p85*) and gallery **W139** (*see p81*), have ensured that the strip has retained some brighter and less corporate colours.

When Warmoesstraat was in its prime and still proper, it drew a sharp contrast to its evil and rowdy twin, **Zeedijk** on the east side of the district (*see p74* A Walk Through the Red Light District). Before Zeedijk was built, some time around 1300, Amsterdam was a fishing village with barely enough bog to stand on. By the 15th and 16th centuries, with the East India Company raking in the imperialist spoils, Zeedijk was the street where sailors came to catch up on their boozing, brawling and bonking – or 'doing the St Nicolaas', as it was fondly termed in those days (a tribute to their patron saint, an extremely busy chap who watches over children, thieves, prostitutes and the city of Amsterdam). Coincidentally, the city's major Catholic church, **Nicolaaskerk** (Prins Hendrikkade 73, 020 330 7812, www.nicolaas-parochie.nl), is also named after him. It was built in 1887.

Sailors who had lost all their money could trade in their pet monkey for a flea-infested bed at Zeedijk 1, which still retains its original name – **In't Aepjen**, meaning 'In the Monkeys' – and is today one of the oldest and most charming wooden houses in the city centre and still in business as a bar. Just off the street, down Oudezijds Kolk, is the **Schreierstoren**, aka the 'Weeping Tower'. Built in 1487, and successfully restored in 1966, it's the most interesting relic of Amsterdam's medieval city wall. It is said that wives would cry there (perhaps with relief) when their husbands set off on a voyage, then cry again if the ship returned with news that said spouse was lost at sea. If the latter happened, it was but a short walk to Zeedijk, where the bereaved lady would often continue life as a 'merry widow'. Prostitution was the female equivalent of joining the navy: the last economic option. During the 20th century, Zeedijk

In the know
Red Light etiquette

Contrary to what the hordes of obnoxious tourists frequenting the area may suggest, not everything goes in the Red Light District. It is completely forbidden to take a photo of a window prostitute, and this law is strictly enforced thanks to 24-hour surveillance in most areas. The majority of sex workers will agree on a price for their services beforehand, and only accept payment up front. They also take their healthcare very seriously and will insist clients use a condom.

was enlivened by the influx of different nationalities, in particular the Chinese, who established the city's very small **Chinatown** with a number of award-winning eateries (*see p82* Chinatown).

Southern Old Side

Just as Warmoesstraat stretches north from the Nationaal Monument towards Centraal Station, **Nes** leaves the same spot to the south, parallel and to the west of Oudezijds Achterburgwal. Dating from the Middle Ages, this street was once home to the city's tobacco trade and the Jewish philosopher Benedict Spinoza (1623-77), who saw body and mind as the two aspects of a single entity. Appropriate, then, that you can now witness the alignment of body and mind on the stages of the theatres that have long graced this street. You can also stop, recharge and realign your own essence at one of the many charming cafés that can be found hereabouts.

At the end of Nes, either cross over to the Spui in the New Side (*see p87*) or head east across a bridge towards **Oudemanhuis Book Market** (*see p86*). It's located where Van Gogh bought prints to decorate his room in a building owned by the University of Amsterdam, which has its roots in the 17th century. The institution was initially founded to train students in trade and philosophy. The **Agnietenkapel** (Oudezijds Voorburgwal 231) is one of Amsterdam's 17 medieval convents. Built in the 1470s and part of the University of Amsterdam since its foundation in 1632, the chapel has an austere Calvinistic beauty highlighted by its stained-glass windows, wooden beams and benches, not to mention a collection of portraits of humanist thinkers. The Grote Gehoorzaal (Large Auditorium), the country's oldest lecture hall, is where 17th-century scholars Vossius and Barlaeus first taught; the wooden ceiling is painted with soberly ornamental Renaissance motifs including angels and flowers. Now it's used mostly for readings and congresses, and the occasional exhibition.

The **Spinhuis**, a former convent tucked away at the southern end of Oudezijds Achterburgwal (on Spinhuissteeg), used to set 'wayward women' to work spinning wool. The male equivalent was over on the New Side at Heiligeweg 9 – now an entrance to the Kalvertoren shopping complex – where audiences came to watch the prisoners being branded and beaten with a bull's penis. In a rather curious foreshadowing of Amsterdam's contemporary S&M scene, the original entrance gate sports a statue that bears a striking resemblance to a scolding dominatrix.

Nieuwmarkt and around

The Nieuwmarkt is one of the city's oldest central squares, dominated by one of its oldest buildings, **De Waag**, whose origins may date from as long ago as 1425. Previously known as St Antoniespoort, when it was part of the defensive medieval city wall, it was redubbed De Waag in the 17th century when it became the weighing hall (built in 1614) where merchants calculated the weight and subsequent value of grains and other goods arriving in Amsterdam by ship. It's easy to see why it's located here. Look north down the Geldersekade and you'll see the IJ; this canal used to be an unimpeded thoroughfare that led directly to the harbour.

While the weighing hall downstairs was bustling with trade, upstairs the city's medical guild was employed with another kind of business altogether – the cutting up of human bodies. The topmost tower was an anatomical theatre, where the city's physicians would perform dissections on executed convicts to describe to an audience of doctors, noblemen and laymen how the body functioned.

Tour guides like to tell visitors that this is where Rembrandt painted his famous group portrait, *The Anatomy Lesson of Dr Nicolaes Tulp* (1632), but that isn't strictly accurate. The tower that houses the anatomical theatre wasn't built until 1639, a full seven years after Tulp's commemorated lesson. Though there was probably a more informal dissection chamber in the building before that, Rembrandt would have painted the picture in his studio on Sint Antoniesbreestraat (*see p156* Rembrandt van Rijn). Today, De Waag is home to the **Waag Society** (020 557 9898, www.waag.org), an institute for art, science and technology, which surfs the interface between technology and culture, and organises events in the former anatomical theatre.

The market around De Waag has been in operation since the city's Golden Age. It was a particularly popular trading spot for the city's Sephardic Jews, who had been migrating to this neighbourhood since the Spanish Inquisition. During World War II, the Nieuwmarkt was the site of far more grim business: rounding up Amsterdam's Jewish residents for deportation to the Nazi concentration camps. A popular fascist magazine, *De Waag*, was also published here.

Back in 1980, Nieuwmarkt was the site of riots when the city demolished housing to make way for the metro. In 1991, it was saved by a citizens' committee from being irrevocably revamped by designer Philippe Starck.

These days, there's an outdoor market where all kinds of activities take place; on Saturdays, a farmers' market offers freshly baked artisan breads, cheeses and locally grown veg, along with antiques and crafts. There are occasional carnivals here (on King's Night), and on New Year's Eve it becomes detonation-central for fireworks displays. But most of the day-to-day activity takes place around the square, in two dozen popular cafés and bars.

Running south from Nieuwmarkt, **Sint Antoniesbreestraat** is home to assorted shops, bars and cafés, along with modern yet tasteful council housing designed by local architect Theo Bosch. In contrast, there's the Italian Renaissance-style **Pintohuis** at no.69, which was grandly remodelled in the late 17th century by Isaac de Pinto. A Jewish refugee who had fled the inquisition in Portugal, de Pinto became one of the main investors in the lucrative Dutch East India Company.

Across the street, pop through the bizarre skull-adorned entrance between nos.130 and 132 to enter the restful square, formerly a graveyard, near the Zuiderkerk (South Church). Designed by master builder Hendrick De Keyser and built between 1603 and 1614, the **Zuiderkerk** was the first Protestant church to appear after the Reformation. Three of Rembrandt's children were buried here, and the church was painted by Monet during a visit to the Netherlands.

Sights & museums

Allard Pierson

Oude Turfmarkt 127-129 (020 525 2556, allardpierson.nl). Tram 4, 14, 24, or Metro Rokin. ***Open*** *10am-5pm Tue-Fri; 1-5pm Sat, Sun.* ***Admission*** *€10; €5 reductions; free under-4s, Iamsterdam, MK.* ***Map*** *p70 K10.*

Established in 1934, the Allard Pierson – The Collections of the University of Amsterdam is home to one of the world's richest university archaeological collections, and contains archaeological exhibits from Ancient Egypt, Greece, Rome and the Near East. The Allard Pierson is also the place to view the University of Amsterdam's Special Collections: documents, prints, maps, photos and endless rows of books. The invaluable pre-1850 collection is especially strong on the history of printing, Hebrew and Judaica studies, Protestantism, and medicine; the post-1850 collection focuses more on meritorious design, with exhibitions ranging from Shakespeare in the Netherlands to sacred books from Ethiopia.

Allard Pierson *p77*

Erotic Museum

Amsterdam Exchange Experience

Beursplein 5 (020 721 4333, www.aex.nl). Tram 4, 14, 24. ***Open*** *9am-5pm Mon-Fri (tours only, book ahead online).* ***Admission*** *€7.50.* ***Map*** *p70 L8.*

The Amsterdam Stock Exchange offers an 'experience' tour that gives visitors a taste of the manic world of trading and exchange. Group tours (for 25) can be arranged for any day, individuals must join the Wednesday morning tour, at 11am.

Beurs van Berlage

Damrak 243. Entrance at Beursplein 1 (020 530 4141, www.beursvanberlage.nl). Tram 4, 14, 24. ***Admission*** *varies.* ***Map*** *p70 L8.*

Designed in 1896 by Hendrik Berlage as the city's stock exchange, the palatial Beurs, while incorporating a broad range of traditional building styles, represents a break from the prevailing tastes of 19th-century architects and, as such, prepared the way for the Amsterdam School. Although critics thought it 'a big block with a cigar box on top', it's now considered the country's most important piece of 20th-century architecture and a powerful socialist statement: much of the artwork warns against capitalism, and each of the nine million bricks was intended to represent the individual, with the building as a whole standing for society. Having long driven out the money changers, the Beurs is now all things to all other people: a conference centre, a café-restaurant, and an exhibition space for shows that range from Dutch design to beer festivals.

► *For more on the Amsterdam School's vision and works, see p266.*

Cannabis College

Oudezijds Achterburgwal 124 (020 423 4420, www.cannabiscollege.com). Tram 4, 14, 24, or Metro Nieuwmarkt. ***Open*** *11am-7pm daily.* ***Admission*** *free.* ***Map*** *p70 L9.*

Founded by hemp activist Henk Poncin and a group called Green Prisoners Release, Cannabis College is a non-profit organisation, whose mission is to provide free, accurate and unbiased information concerning all aspects of the cannabis plant. The volunteer staff ask for a small donation if you want to wander around the indoor garden.

Erotic Museum

Oudezijds Achterburgwal 54 (020 627 8954, www.erotisch-museum.nl). Tram 4, 14, 24 or Metro Nieuwmarkt. ***Open*** *11am-1am Sun-Thur, 11am-2pm Fri, Sat.* ***Admission*** *€7. No cards.* ***Map*** *p70 L8.*

While the **Sexmuseum** (Damrak 18, www.sexmuseumamsterdam.nl) benefits from its Damrak site in terms of passing trade, the Erotic Museum is in the more appropriate location: slap bang in the middle of the Red Light District. That's not to say, though, that it's any more authentic or interesting. Its prize exhibits are a bicycle-powered dildo and a few of John Lennon's erotic drawings, while lovers of Bettie Page (and there are many) will enjoy the original photos of the S&M muse on display. It also puts on temporary exhibits in the Sexy Art Gallery on the third floor. In general, the museum's name is somewhat inaccurate: despite its best intentions and desperate desire to shock, it's as unsexy as can be. You're probably best off going to one of the many nearby sex shops for your kicks.

❤ Ons' Lieve Heer op Solder

Oudezijds Voorburgwal 38 (624 6604, www.opsolder.nl). Tram 2, 4, 11, 12, 13, 14, 17, 24 or Metro Nieuwmarkt. **Open** *10am-6pm Mon-Sat; 1-6pm Sun.* **Admission** *€12.50; €5 reductions; free under-5s, Iamsterdam, MK.* **Map** *p70 L8.*

'Our Lord in the Attic' is one of Amsterdam's most unusual spots and used to be one of its best-kept secrets. Visitors can explore the narrow corridors of the lower canal house, which have been wonderfully preserved since the 17th century, and imagine what life might have been like in the Dutch Golden Age. It's fascinating to walk through the historically furnished living rooms, kitchens and bedrooms, but the main attraction is clear when you arrive upstairs to find a church in the attic.

Built in 1663, this attic church was used by Catholics when they were banned from public worship after the Alteration (*see p249*). The authorities knew of the then-illicit activity but turned a blind eye rather than reprimanding those who attended the services. Their actions (or lack thereof) were an appropriate reflection of the religious tolerance in the Netherlands, which is a central theme at the museum today. The attic has been beautifully preserved and sympathetically renovated, and the altarpiece features a painting by the 18th-century artist Jacob de Wit. It's the second oldest museum in the city, after the Rijkmuseum, and in 2015 was extended into the neighbouring building. It's open for at least four hours every day and is still often used for services. Don't miss it.

Oude Kerk

Hash Marihuana & Hemp Museum

Oudezijds Achterburgwal 148 (020 624 8926, www.hashmuseum.com). Tram 4, 14, 24 or Metro Nieuwmarkt. ***Open*** *10am-10pm daily.* ***Admission*** *€9; free under-13s (must be accompanied by an adult).* ***Map*** *p70 L9.*

Cannabis connoisseurs will lose themselves ogling larger-than-life pictures of perfect plants and gleaming balls of hash in this museum in the Red Light District. But this shrine to skunk is not only for smokers. Strait-laced visitors will be entertained by the detailed history of the plant. There's plenty of pro-cannabis propaganda too, including information about its medicinal uses, the environmental benefits of hemp and the cannabis culture of today. Don't miss the indoor 'grow-op' that showcases plants being lovingly cultivated for their seeds, guarded by a guru of ganja, who offers advice.

❤ Oude Kerk

Oudekerksplein 23 (020 625 8284, www.oudekerk.nl). Tram 4, 14, 24 or Metro Nieuwmarkt. ***Open*** *10am-6pm Mon-Sat; 1-5.30pm Sun.* ***Admission*** *€12, €7 reductions; free under-13s, Iamsterdam, MK. No cards.* ***Map*** *p70 L8*

Built in 1306 as a wooden chapel, and constantly renovated and extended between 1330 and 1571, the Oude Kerk is the city's oldest and most interesting church. One can only imagine the Sunday Mass chaos during its heyday of the mid 1500s, when it contained 38 altars, each with its own guild-sponsored priest. The original furnishings were removed by iconoclasts during the Reformation, but the church has retained its wooden roof, which was painted in the 15th century with figurative images. Look out for the mixed Gothic and Renaissance façade above the northern portal, and the stained-glass windows, parts of which date from the 16th and 17th centuries. Rembrandt's wife, Saskia, who died in 1642, is buried here.

The inscription over the bridal chamber, which translates as 'Marry in haste, mourn at leisure,' is in keeping with the church's location in the heart of the Red Light District, though this is more by accident than design. If you want to be semi-shocked, check out the carvings in the choir benches of men evacuating their bowels – apparently they tell a moralistic tale. Now with a charming café and terrace, **Koffieschenkerij De Oude Kerk**, the church is as much an exhibition centre as anything else, with shows focused on modern and mainly locally created art.

W139

Red Light Secrets Museum of Prostitution

Oudezijds Achterburgwal 60H (020 846 7020, www.redlightsecrets.com). Tram 4, 14, 24 or Metro Nieuwmarkt. ***Open*** *10am-midnight daily.* ***Admission*** *€10 before 1pm, €12.50 all other times. No under-18s.* ***Map*** *p70 L8.*

Set inside a 17th-century canal house, Red Light Secrets allows visitors to step into the intriguing world of Amsterdam's oldest trade. Although it's very much on the tourist trail, Red Light Secrets provides information about the history of the profession along with secrets and stories from the women themselves. Guests can even experience sitting inside a shop window, and it might be the only one in the district which allows you to take photos.

W139

Warmoesstraat 139 (020 622 9434, www.w139.nl). Tram 4, 14, 24 or Metro Nieuwmarkt. ***Open*** *noon-6pm daily.* ***Admission*** *free.* ***Map*** *p70 L8.*

In almost four decades of existence, this contemporary art gallery has never lost its squat aesthetics or sometimes overly conceptual edge, with legendary openings that often spill out on to the street.

Restaurants & cafés

1e Klas €€€

Centraal Station, Platform 2B (020 625 0131, www.restaurant1eklas.nl). Tram 2, 4, 11, 12, 13, 14, 17, 24. ***Open*** *9.30am-11pm daily.* ***Map*** *p166 M7* ❶ *Brasserie/pub*

This former brasserie for first-class commuters is now open to anyone who wants to kill some time in style – with a full meal, snack or drink – while waiting for a train. The art nouveau interior will whisk you straight back to the 1890s. The adjoining pub is also a treat and hosts regular jazz concerts.

A Fusion €€

Zeedijk 130 (020 330 4068, www.a-fusion.nl). Tram 4, 14, 24 or Metro Nieuwmarkt. ***Open*** *12.30-11pm daily.* ***Map*** *p70 M9* ❷ *Asian*

This lounge-style restaurant obviously took notes from the hip side of Chinatown in New York City. The interior is dark and inviting, and you can drink bubble teas (lychee!) and eat some of the tastiest confusion-free pan-Asian dishes in town. The dim sum and satay dishes are particularly recommended.

De Bakkerswinkel €

Warmoesstraat 69 (020 489 8000, www.debakkerswinkel.nl). Tram 2, 4, 11, 12, 13, 14, 17, 24. ***Open*** *8am-5.30pm Mon-Fri; 9am-6pm Sat, Sun.* ***Map*** *p70 L8* ❸ *Café*

A bakery-tearoom where you can indulge in lovingly prepared and hearty sandwiches, soups and the most divine slabs of quiche. **Other locations** Roelof Hartstraat 68, Museum Quarter (020 662 3594); Polonceaukade 1, Westerpark (020 688 0632).

Bird €€

Zeedijk 72-74 & 77 (020 620 1442 restaurant, 020 420 6289 snack bar, www.thai-bird.nl). Tram 2, 4, 11, 12, 13, 14, 17, 24 or Metro Nieuwmarkt. ***Restaurant*** *noon-11pm daily.* ***Snack bar*** *1-10pm Mon-Wed; 1-10.30pm Thur-Sun.* ***Map*** *p70 M8* ❹ *Thai*

The most authentic Thai place in town. As a result, it's also the most crowded, but the food is worth the wait, whether you're dropping by to pick up a pot of tom yam

Chinatown

A small but perfectly formed taste of China

A string of no-frills restaurants on the Zeedijk, winding from Centraal Station towards Nieuwmarkt, makes up what is perhaps the world's smallest Chinatown. Here, you can eat authentic fare for a tenner. Among the top local picks are award-winning Chinese eateries **China Sichuan** (*see below*), **Nam Kee** (*see opposite*) and **New King** (Zeedijk 115-117, 020 625 2180). For dim sum lovers, the Cantonese-style **Hoi Tin** (*see opposite*) is a must do. If you're game, try the dim sum with hot stuffed peppers. **Bird** Thai Restaurant (*see p81*) is also worth a visit, as is its popular **Bird Snackbar** fast-food and takeaway outlet across the street. You'll also find Japanese, Malaysian, Vietnamese and pan-Asian restaurants up and down the street, as well as further east, on Koningsstraat past Nieuwmarkt.

If you want some Asian snacks or plan to cook an Asian meal at home, **Toko Dun Yong** (*see p86*) is the perfect shop. Its shelves, fridges and freezers heave with wonderful products, including frozen dumplings, preserved tofu, handmade noodles, saké and exotic fruit and vegetables, while the basement has kitsch and well-priced Asian crockery. On the southern edge of the square, **Amazing Oriental** (Nieuwmarkt 27, 020 626 2797, www.amazingoriental.com) sells handmade noodles, dumplings and all the Asian veg that you can't find at the Albert Heijn (*see p93*).

And don't miss the Chinese Buddhist temple **Fo Guang Shan He Hua** right next to Hoi Tin (Zeedijk 106-118, 020 420 2357, open noon-5pm Tue-Sat, 10am-5pm Sun), with its bluestone steps, roof tiles and ornaments imported directly from China. Monks and nuns still practise their faith here, but tours are available along with free calligraphy workshops – you'll be asked to remove your shoes as you're guided through the surprisingly spacious complex.

Chinatown is where to experience street celebrations for Chinese New Year (*see p205*), including a traditional lion dance performed with live drumming.

soup or want a full-blown meal. The snack bar is at no.77; the restaurant is across the street at nos.72-74 and is the best choice if you plan to linger.

Blauw aan de Wal €€€

Oudezijds Achterburgwal 99 (020 330 2257, www.blauwaandewal.com). Tram 4, 14, 24 or Metro Nieuwmarkt. ***Open*** *6-11.30pm Mon-Sat.* ***Map*** *p70 L9* 5 *Mediterranean*

The hallmarks of this mainstay in the heart of the Red Light District, complete with a peaceful courtyard, are its tempting Mediterranean tasting menus (four to six courses) and a wine list likely to inspire long bouts of grateful contemplation in visiting oenophiles.

Bridges €€€€

Oudezijds Voorburgwal 197 (020 555 3560, www.bridgesrestaurant.nl). Tram 4, 14, 24. ***Open Open*** *6.30-10pm Mon-Tue; noon-2.30pm, 6.30-10pm Wed-Fri; 1-3pm, 6.30-10pm, Sat, Sun.* ***Map*** *p70 K9* 6 *Fish & seafood*

The Michelin-star winning Bridges restaurant in The Grand Amsterdam hotel (*see p283*) is a committed proponent of slow food. The menu features locally caught, seasonal seafood and five-star ingredients, such as oysters (from the raw bar), Beluga caviar, and Wagyu beef; if you really want to splash out, book the Chef's Table (max 6 ppl).

❤ Café Bern €€

Nieuwmarkt 9 (020 622 0034, www.cafebern.com). Tram 4, 14, 24 or Metro Nieuwmarkt. ***Open*** *4pm-1am (kitchen 6-11pm) daily.* ***No cards. Map*** *p70 M9* 7 *Swiss*

Despite its Swiss origins, the Dutch adopted the cheese fondue as a national dish long ago. Sample its culinary conviviality at this suitably cosy 'brown café', which was established by a nuclear physicist who knew his way around the fusion of cheese with wine – and was also smart enough to know that a menu should be affordable and a bar should be stocked with a generous variety of grease-cutting agents. It's best to book ahead.

China Sichuan €€

Warmoesstraat 17 (020 420 7833, www.sichuanrestaurant.nl). Tram 2, 4, 11, 12, 13, 14, 17, 24 or Metro Centraal. ***Open*** *5-11pm Mon; noon-11pm Tue-Thu, Sun; noon-midnight Fri, Sat.* ***Map*** *p70 L8* 8 *Chinese*

If heat is what you desire, then the lashings of pepper and chilli served up at this authentic Sichuan place is for you. Service can be a little lackadaisical, but the food is more than worth it. Try one of their sizzling dishes, or if you're feeling brave, the Yellow River Chicken.

Hoi Tin €€

Zeedijk 122 (020 625 6451, www.restauranthoitin.com/nl). Tram 4, 14, 24. ***Open*** *noon-10pm daily.* ***Map*** *p70 M9* ⓬ Chinese

Proving that delicious food doesn't need to be complicated, this simple restaurant specialises in traditional Chinese dishes and is known for its delicious dim sum. The restaurant also has an on-site bakery with an array of tempting Asian pastries, so come with an appetite.

❤ Juice by Nature €

Warmoesstraat 108 (www.juicebynature.com). Tram 2, 4, 11, 12, 13, 14, 17, 24. ***Open*** *10am-8pm daily.* ***Map*** *p70 L8* ⓭ Juice bar/café

Providing a stark contrast to the grunge bars in De Wallen, Juice by Nature has set out to 'make healthy delicious'. With a mouth-watering offering of cold-pressed juices, coffee, salads and sandwiches, it's the perfect place to stop in for a recharge before wandering through the Old Centre or to recover after a wild night out.

Latei €

Zeedijk 143 (020 625 7485, www.latei.net). Tram 4, 14, 24 or Metro Nieuwmarkt. ***Open*** *8am-6pm Mon-Wed; 8am-10pm Thur, Fri; 9am-10pm Sat; 10am-6pm Sun.* ***Map*** *p70 M8* ⓯ Café

Packed with kitsch and decorated with funky Finnish wallpaper – all of which, including the wallpaper, is for sale – this little café serves healthy juices and snacks all day long, plus Indonesian dinners (from 6pm Thur-Sat).

❤ Nam Kee €€

Zeedijk 111-113 (020 624 3470, www.namkee.net). Tram 4, 14, 24 or Metro Nieuwmarkt. ***Open*** *noon-11pm daily.* ***Map*** *p70 M8* ⓰ Chinese

Cheap and terrific food has earned this Chinese joint a devoted following: the oysters in black bean sauce has achieved classic status. If it's too crowded, try one of the nearby alternatives (*see opposite* Chinatown).

Oriental City €€

Oudezijds Voorburgwal 177-179 (020 626 8352, www.oriental-city.nl). Tram 4, 14, 24 or Metro Nieuwmarkt. ***Open*** *11.30am-10.30pm daily.* ***Map*** *p70 L9* ⓱ Chinese

The location is simply marvellous, with a view along Damstraat towards the Royal Palace and the canals. But that's not even the best bit: Oriental City serves some of Amsterdam's most authentic dim sum.

Bars

Bierfabriek

Nes 67 (020 528 9910, www.bierfabriek.com). Tram 4, 14, 24 or Metro Rokin. ***Open*** *3pm-1am Mon-Thur; 3pm-2am Fri; 1pm-2am Sat; 1pm-1am Sun.* ***Map*** *p70 K10* ❸

With an industrial look and laid-back attitude, the 'Beer Factory' pulls in a young crowd for its own-brewed beers and excellent free-range roast chicken. Booking for dinner is advisable.

Brouwerij de Prael

Oudezijds Armsteeg 26 & Oudezijds Voorburgwal 30 (bar 020 408 4469, www.deprael.nl, shop 020 408 4470). Tram 2, 4, 11, 12, 13, 14, 17, 24. ***Bar*** *noon-midnight Mon-Wed; noon-1am Thur-Sat; noon-11pm Sun.* ***Shop*** *10am-7pm Mon-Fri; noon-7pm Sat, Sun.* ***Map*** *p70 L8* ❹

An unusual venture: a microbrewery and shop set up to provide employment for people with mental health conditions.

Bubbles & Wines

Nes 37 (020 422 3318, www.bubblesandwines.com). Tram 2, 4, 11, 12, 14, 24 or Metro Rokin. ***Open*** *3.30pm-midnight Mon-Sat; 2-9pm Sun.* ***Map*** *p70 K9* ❺

This long, low-ceilinged room has the feel of a wine cellar, albeit one with mood lighting and banquettes. There are more than 50 wines available by the glass and 180 by the bottle, with accompanying posh nosh (including Osetra caviar, truffle cheese and foie gras). Wine flights are also served.

Café de Jaren

Nieuwe Doelenstraat 20-22 (020 625 5771, www.cafedejaren.nl). Tram 4, 14, 24 or Metro Rokin. ***Open*** *8.30am-1am Mon-Thur; 8.30am-2am Fri, Sat; 8.30am-1am Sun.* ***Map*** *p70 K11* ❽

All of Amsterdam – students, tourists, lesbigays, cinemagoers, the fashion pack – comes to this former bank for lunch, coffee or something stronger, all day long, making it sometimes difficult to bag a seat. Upstairs becomes a restaurant after 5.30pm and booking is advisable – especially if you want to sit on the balcony.

Café 't Mandje

Zeedijk 63 (020 622 5375, www.cafetmandje.amsterdam). Tram 4, 14, 24 or Metro Nieuwmarkt. ***Open*** *4pm-1am Tue-Thur; 3pm-3am Fri, Sat; 3pm-1am Sun.* ***No cards. Map*** *p70 M8* ❾

Launched more than 80 years ago, this historic café was the city's first (moderately)

openly gay and lesbian bar. The original proprietor, Bet van Beeren (who died over 40 years ago), was legendary for her role as (probably) the world's first lesbian biker chick. After years of closure, the café reopened in 2012 to suggest that time can stand still. A replica of the café can be seen at the Amsterdam Museum (*see p87*).

Kapitein Zeppos

*Gebed Zonder End 5 (020 624 2057, www.zeppos.nl). Tram 4, 14, 24 or Metro Rokin. **Open** 11am-1am Mon-Thur, 11am-3am Fri, Sat; noon-1am Sun. **Map** p70 K10* ⑩

Tucked away down the poetically named 'Prayer Without End' alley (a reference to the Santa Clara convent that stood here in the 17th century), this light-drenched, multifaceted music café has an understated Belgian theme: it's named after a 1960s Flemish TV detective, there's Belgian beer on tap, and the most frequently heard soundtrack is *chanson*. Upstairs, Claire's Ballroom features live music and theatre.

Mata Hari

*Oudezijds Achterburgwal 22 (020 205 0919, www.matahari-amsterdam.nl). Tram 4, 14, 24 or Metro Nieuwmarkt. **Open** 11am-1am, Sun-Thu; 11am-3am Fri, Sat. **Map** p70 M8* ⑪

Named after the exotic but tricksy Dutch courtesan, it's appropriate that this bar, restaurant and lounge has brought a touch of comfort and class to the Red Light District. Sympathetic lighting, retro furniture and an open kitchen serving exquisite dishes such as 'chocolate salami with forget-me-not liqueur' make the seduction complete.

Proeflokkal de Ooievaar

*Sint Olofspoort 1 (020 631 586941, www.proeflokkaldeooievaar.nl). Tram 2, 4, 11, 12, 13, 14, 17, 24 or Metro Centraal. **Open** noon-11pm daily. **Map** p70 M7* ⑫

'The Stork' is one of the city's smallest tasting rooms and has been dishing out *jenever* since 1782. Ask the bar staff for help in navigating the many racks of booze – they really know their stuff.

TonTon Club Centrum

*Sint Annendwarsstraat 6 (020 613 300314, www.tontonclub.nl). Tram 4, 14, 24 or Metro Nieuwmarkt. **Open** 4pm-midnight Mon, Tue; noon-midnight Wed-Sun. **No cards**. **Map** p70 L8* ⑬

This arcade bar in the heart of the Red Light District does feature old-school games such as pinball, but most have been hacked to do such things as print out chocolate – making TonTon more of a platform and meeting place for local game designers and artists. Besides offering coffee, beer and snacks, TonTon also regularly brings in local chefs to provide meals – from Korean tacos to Dutch weed burgers.

Nieuwmarkt

❤ Wynand Fockink

Pijlsteeg 31 (020 639 2695, www.wynand-fockink.nl). Tram 4, 14, 24. ***Open*** *2-9pm daily.* ***No cards. Map*** *p70 K9* ⓯

It's standing room only at this historic tasting house. Hidden behind the Grand Hotel Krasnapolsky, and unchanged since 1679, this has been a meeting place for Freemasons since the beginning; past visitors include Churchill and Chagall. The menu of liqueurs and *jenevers* (many available in take-out bottles) reads like a list of unwritten novels: Parrot Soup; The Longer the Better; Rose Without Thorns.

Coffeeshops

Basjoe

Kloveniersburgwal 62 (no phone or website). Metro Nieuwmarkt. ***Open*** *10am-1am daily.* ***No cards. Map*** *p70 L10* ❷

The canal view alone places Basjoe among our favourite coffeeshops in Amsterdam. Candlelit, with a plain decor of terracotta soft vinyl booths, cream walls and wooden tables, it's all about the weed here – but the coffee is also outstanding.

Green House Centrum

Oudezijds Voorburgwal 191 (www.greenhouse.org). Tram 4, 14, 24 or Metro Rokin. ***Open*** *9am-1am daily.* ***No cards. Map*** *p70 L9* ❹

This legendary coffeeshop offers highly potent weed with some fairly strong prices to match – it's won the High Times Cannabis Cup more than 30 times. The Grand Hotel is next door, so the occasional celebrity stops by to get hammered (Rihanna, Snoop Dogg and 50 Cent, for example). The vibe inside has grown quite commercial, but it's still worth a peek, if only to see the beautifully handmade interior with its sunken floors, mosaic stones and blown-glass lamps. **Other locations** Waterlooplein 345, Jodenbuurt; Tolstraat 91, De Pijp.

Greenhouse Effect

Warmoesstraat 53-55 (020 427 7878, greenhouse-effect.business.site). Tram 4, 14, 24 or Metro Nieuwmarkt. ***Open*** *9am-1am daily.* ***Map*** *p70 L8* ❺

Set inside a brick townhouse, this coffeeshop is also a hotel and bar. There's a sister operation across the street (**Hill Street Blues**, Warmoesstraat 52), where you'll discover a full bar and regular DJs. If the drink and dope combination renders you immobile, make a beeline for the hotel upstairs.

Rusland

Rusland 16 (020 845 6434, www.coffeeshop-rusland-amsterdam.com). Tram 4, 14, 24 or Metro Nieuwmarkt. ***Open*** *8am-12.30am daily.* ***No cards. Map*** *p70 L10* ❻

Well known as the longest-running coffeeshop in the city, this 'Russian' den has hardwood floors and colourful cushions that complement an efficient multi-level design. The top-floor bar serves more than 40 different loose teas and healthy fruit shakes, while below there's a decent pipe display. It's off the well-trodden tourist path, which means cheaper prices and smaller crowds.

Shops & services

A Boeken Stoffen & Fournituren

Nieuwe Hoogstraat 31 (020 626 7205, www.aboeken.nl). Tram 4, 14, 24 or Metro Nieuwmarkt. ***Open*** *noon-6pm Mon; 10am-6pm Tue, Wed, Fri; 10am-8pm Thur; 10am-5pm Sat.* ***Map*** *p70 M9* ❶ *Fabric*

The Boeken family has been hawking fabrics since 1920. You'd be hard pushed to find anywhere else with the same range: latex, Lycra, fake fur and sequins abound.

Condomerie

Warmoesstraat 141 (020 627 4174, www.condomerie.com). Tram 4, 14, 24 or Metro Nieuwmarkt. ***Open*** *11am-9pm Mon-Sat; 1pm-6pm Sunday.* ***Map*** *p70 L9* ❻ *Sex shop*

A variety of rubbers of the non-erasing kind, to wrap up trouser snakes of all shapes and sizes, in a store that's equal parts amusing and inspiring.

❤ Droog

Staalstraat 7 (020 523 5059, www.droog.com). Tram 4, 14, 24. ***Open*** *9am-7pm daily.* ***Map*** *p70 L10* ❽ *Homewares*

Dutch design dynamo Droog expanded its HQ into a flagship 'hotel' – a city-centre design mall where you can attend a lecture series or an exhibition, and even spend the night in the single suite. The historic building's rag trade origins continue at ice-cool boutique Kabinet. The Droog shop still sells some of the wittiest ranges around: Jurgen Bey, Richard Hutten, Hella Jongerius and Marcel Wanders.

De Hoed van Tijn

Nieuwe Hoogstraat 15 (020 623 2759, www.dehoedvantijn.nl). Tram 4, 14, 24 or Metro Nieuwmarkt. ***Open*** *noon-6pm Mon; 11am-6pm Tue-Fri; 11am-5.30pm Sat.* ***Map*** *p70 M9* ❿ *Accessories*

Mad hatters will delight in this vast range of bonnets, homburgs, bowlers, sombreros and caps, including second-hand and handmade items.

Lambiek

Koningsstraat 27 (020 626 7543, www.lambiek.nl). Metro Nieuwmarkt. ***Open*** *11am-6pm Mon-Fri; 11am-5pm Sat; 1-5pm Sun.* ***Map*** *p70 M9* ⓫ *Comics*

Lambiek, founded in 1968, claims to be the world's oldest comic shop and has thousands of books from around the world. Its on-site cartoonists' gallery hosts regular exhibitions and the openings bring together the tight-knit local scene.

Nieuwmarkt Antique Market

Nieuwmarkt (no phone or website). Tram 4, 14, 24 or Metro Nieuwmarkt. ***Open*** *May-Oct 9am-5pm Sun.* ***Map*** *p70 M9* ⓭ *Market*

A few streets away from the ladies in the windows, this antiques and bric-a-brac market attracts browsers looking for other kinds of pleasures: old books, furniture and objets d'art.

Oudemanhuis Book Market

Oudemanhuispoort (no phone or website). Tram 2, 4, 11, 12, 14, 24. ***Open*** *9am-5pm Mon-Sat.* ***No cards. Map*** *p70 L10* ⓮ *Books & music*

People have been buying and selling books, prints and sheet music from this indoor row of shops since the 18th century.

Toko Dun Yong

Stormsteeg 9 (020 622 1763, www.dunyong.com). Tram 2, 4, 11, 12, 13, 14, 17, 24 or Metro Nieuwmarkt. ***Open*** *9am-7pm Mon-Fri; 9am-6pm Sat; 11am-6pm Sun.* ***Map*** *p70 M8* ⓯ *Food & drink*

Visit Amsterdam's largest Chinese food emporium for the full spectrum of Asian foods and ingredients, ranging from shrimp- and scallop-flavoured egg noodles to fried tofu balls and fresh veg. You can also seek out a fine range of traditional Chinese cooking appliances and utensils, as well as indulge in Japanese ramen soup.

De Wijnerij

Binnen Bantammerstraat 8 (020 625 6433, www.dewijnerij.com). Tram 2, 4, 11, 12, 13, 14, 17, 24 or Metro Nieuwmarkt. ***Open*** *11am-6.30pm Tue-Fri; 10am-6.30pm Sat.* ***Map*** *p70 M8* ⓰ *Drink*

This friendly and passionate shop specialises in French wine – usually from organic producers – and unique local distillates such as *jenever*. With the relaxed café/terrace **Café Captein en Co** at no.27, this street is a delight for thirsty people.

Amsterdam Museum

THE NEW SIDE

Compared to the Old Side, the New Side is much kinder and gentler. Though it was constructed later, the younger half of the Old Centre still has its roots in the Middle Ages. Historical landmarks including Begijnhof and the Koninklijk Paleis are linked by consumer strip the Kalverstraat. With the University of Amsterdam and Amsterdam Museum to hand, the focus is much more on the mind than the loins.

Around the Dam

Straight up from Centraal Station, just beyond the once watery but now paved and touristy strip named Damrak, lies **Dam Square**, the heart of the city since the first dam was built here back in 1270. Once a hub of social and political activities and protests, today it's a convenient meeting point for throngs of tourists, the majority of whom convene under its mildly phallic centrepiece, the **Nationaal Monument**. The 22-metre (70-foot) white obelisk is dedicated to the Dutch servicemen who died in World War II. Designed by JJP Oud, with sculptures by John Raedecker, it features 12 urns: 11 are filled with earth collected from the (back then) 11 Dutch provinces, while the 12th contains soil taken from war cemeteries in long-time Dutch colony Indonesia.

The New Side of Dam Square is flanked by the **Koninklijk Paleis** (Royal Palace; *see p88*); next to it is the 600-year-old **Nieuwe Kerk** (New Church; *see p89* – so named as it was built a century after the Oude Kerk, or Old Church, in the Red Light District). In kitsch contrast, over on the south side is **Madame Tussaud's** (*see p89*).

Spui and around

Pronounced to rhyme (nearly enough) with 'cow', the **Spui** is a charming square with a Friday book market and numerous bookshops and cafés. It caps the three main arteries that start down near the west end of Centraal Station: the middle-of-the-road walking and retail street **Kalverstraat** (which is called Nieuwendijk before it crosses the Dam), plus **Nieuwezijds Voorburgwal** and the **Spuistraat**.

A quiet backwater accessible via the north side of the Spui square or, when that entrance is closed, via Gedempte Begijnensloot (the alternating entrances were set up to appease residents), the **Begijnhof** (*see p90*) is a group of houses built round a secluded courtyard and garden. It's one of the best known of the city's many *hofjes* (almshouses; *see p118*) and is also very close to one of the several entrances to the **Amsterdam Museum** (*see right*), which in turn is the starting point for the very informal walking tours **Mee in Mokum** (020 625 4450, www.gildeamsterdam.nl).

The Spui square itself plays host to many markets – the most notable being the busy book market on Fridays – and was historically an area where the intelligentsia gathered for some serious alcohol abuse after a day's work on the local papers. The *Lieverdje* (Little Darling) statue in front of the **Athenaeum Nieuwscentrum** store, a small, spindly and guano-smeared statue of a boy in goofy knee socks, was the site for wacky Provo 'happenings' that took place in the mid 1960s.

You can leave Spui by heading up Kalverstraat, Amsterdam's main shopping street, or up Singel past Leidsestraat: both routes lead to the **Munttoren** (Mint Tower) at Muntplein. Just across from the **Bloemenmarkt** (*see p113*), this medieval tower was the western corner of Regulierspoort, a gate in the city wall in the 1480s; in 1620, a spire was added by Hendrick de Keyser, the foremost architect of the period. The tower takes its name from when it minted coins after Amsterdam was cut off from its money supply during a war with England, Munster and France. There's a shop on the ground floor, **Jorrit Heinen Royal Delftware**, but the rest of the tower is closed to visitors. The Munttoren is prettiest when floodlit at night, though daytime visitors may hear its carillon, which often plays for 15 minutes at noon. From here, walk down Nieuwe Doelenstraat past the Hôtel de l'Europe (a mock-up of which featured in Hitchcock's *Foreign Correspondent*). Walk up Staalstraat, across the Ir. B. Bijvoetbrug bridge, and you'll end up at **Waterlooplein** (*see p157*).

Sights & museums

❤ Amsterdam Museum

Kalverstraat 92 (020 523 1822, www.amsterdammuseum.nl). Tram 4, 14, 24 or Metro Rokin. ***Open*** *10am-5pm daily.* ***Admission*** *€15; €12.50 reductions; free under-17s, Iamsterdam, MK.* ***Map*** *p70 J10.*

A note to all those historical museums around the world that struggle to present their exhibits in an engaging fashion: head here to see how it's done. Amsterdam's historical museum is a gem – illuminating, interesting and entertaining.

It starts with the very buildings in which it's housed: a lovely, labyrinthine collection

In the know
On the big screen

The incredibly scenic Staalstraat is the city's most popular film location, having appeared in everything from *The Diary of Anne Frank* to *Ocean's Twelve*.

of 17th-century constructions built on the site of a 1414 nunnery, complete with its own brewery and livestock. The property was turned into an orphanage in 1578, which hundreds of children called home for almost four centuries until 1960. The Amsterdam Museum moved to the location in 1975, having started in De Waag as a branch of the City Museum. You can enter where it all began down Sint Luciensteeg, just off Kalverstraat, or off Spui, walking past the **Begijnhof** (*see p90*) and then through the grand **Civic Guard Gallery**, a small covered street hung with huge 16th- and 17th-century group portraits of wealthy burghers, as well as more modern works.

It continues with a computer-generated map of the area showing how Amsterdam has grown (and shrunk) throughout the last 800 years or so. It then takes a chronological trip through Amsterdam's past, using archaeological finds, works of art and some far quirkier displays to show the city's rise from fishing village to ecstasy capital. One of its most popular recent exhibitions was 100 Years of Schiphol, paying tribute to the progression from muddy pasture to one of Europe's largest high-tech airports, and Amsterdam DNA – the museum's permanent exhibit which gives an hour-long highly engaging overview of Amsterdam's history, based on the city's core values of entrepreneurship, free thinking, citizenship and creativity.

Arti et Amicitiae

Rokin 112 (020 624 5134, www.arti.nl). Tram 4, 14, 24 or Metro Rokin. ***Open*** *noon-6pm Tue-Sun.* ***Map*** *p70 K10.*

This marvellous old building houses a private artists' society, whose initiates regularly gather in the first-floor bar. Members of the public can climb a Berlage-designed staircase to a large exhibition space, home to some great temporary shows.

Body Worlds: The Happiness Project

Damrak 66 (020 2160 601, www.bodyworlds.nl). Tram 4, 14, 24. ***Open*** *9am-8pm Mon-Fri, Sun; 9am-10pm Sat.* ***Admission*** *€22.95; reductions €14, free under-5s.* ***Map*** *p70 K8.*

People seem to love donating their bodies to be plastinated for posterity. German anatomist Dr Gunther von Hagens now has 13,000 such bodies touring the world; since early 2014, 200 of these corpses have been on display in Amsterdam, to illustrate the relationship between anatomy and happiness.

Koninklijk Paleis

Dam (020 522 6161, info@dkh.nl for tours, www.paleisamsterdam.nl). Tram 2, 4, 11, 12, 13, 14, 17, 24. ***Open*** *10am-5pm Tue-Sun.* ***Admission*** *€10; €9 reductions; free under-18s, MK.* ***Map*** *p70 J9.*

Designed along classical lines by Jacob van Campen in the 17th century and built on 13,659 wooden piles that were rammed deep into the sand, the Royal Palace was originally built and used as Amsterdam's city hall. The poet Constantijn Huygens hyped it as 'the world's Eighth Wonder', a monument to the cockiness Amsterdam felt at the dawn of its Golden Age. The city hall was intended as an overtly grand put down to visiting monarchs, the likes of which the people of Amsterdam had thus far happily done without. It was

Body Worlds: The Happiness Project

transformed into a royal palace during harder times, after Napoleon had made his brother, Louis, King of the Netherlands in 1808; this era can be traced through the fine collection of furniture on display inside.

The exterior is only really impressive when viewed from the rear, where Atlas holds his 1,000kg (2,200lb) copper load at a great height. It's even grander inside than out: the Citizens' Hall, with its baroque decoration in marble and bronze that depicts a miniature universe (with Amsterdam as its obvious centre), is meant to make you feel about as worthy as the rats seen carved in stone over the Bankruptcy Chamber's door. The Palace became state property in 1936 and the Dutch royal family still use it when they feel the need to impress international guests.

Madame Tussaud's

Dam 20 (020 522 1010, www.madametussauds.nl). Tram 2, 4, 11, 12, 13, 14, 17, 24. ***Open*** *9.30am-8pm daily.* ***Admission*** *€24.50, discounts available online; €20.50 reductions; free under-4s, Iamsterdam.* ***Map*** *p70 K9.*

Craving some queasy kitsch factor? Waxy cheese-textured representations from Holland's own Golden Age of commerce are depicted alongside the Dutch royal family, local celebs and global superstars. Some of the models look like their subjects; some don't. But while there's much campy fun to be had, it comes at a price.

Nieuwe Kerk

Dam Square (020 626 8168, www.nieuwekerk.nl). Tram 2, 4, 11, 12, 13, 14, 17, 24. ***Open*** *10am-5pm daily, but hrs may vary.* ***Admission*** *Varies from exhibition to exhibition, see website for details. No cards.* ***Map*** *p70 K8.*

While the 'old' Oude Kerk in the Red Light District was built in the 1300s, the sprightly 'new' Nieuwe Kerk dates from 1408. It's not known how much damage was caused by the fires of 1421 and 1452, or even how much rebuilding took place, but most of the pillars and walls were erected after that time. Iconoclasm in 1566 left the church intact, though statue and altars were removed in the Reformation. The sundial on its tower was used to set the time on all the city's clocks until 1890. In 1645, the Nieuwe Kerk was gutted by the Great Fire; the ornate oak pulpit and great organ (the latter designed by Jacob van Campen) are thought to have been constructed shortly after the blaze.

Also of interest here is the tomb of naval hero Admiral de Ruyter (1607-76), who initiated the ending of the Second Anglo-Dutch war – wounding British pride in the process – when he sailed up the Medway in 1667, inspiring a witness, Sir William Batten, to observe: 'I think the Devil shits Dutchmen.' Poets and Amsterdam natives PC Hooft and Joost van den Vondel are also buried here. These days, the Nieuwe Kerk hosts organ recitals, state occasions and consistently excellent exhibitions, including World Press Photo.

Restaurants & cafés

Gartine €

Taksteeg 7 (020 320 4132, www.gartine.nl). Tram 4, 14, 24 or Metro Rokin. ***Open*** *10am-6pm Wed-Sat.* ***No cards. Map*** *p70 J10* 9 Tearoom

Open only for breakfast, lunch and a full-blown high tea, Gartine is a testament to slow food, served by a friendly couple who grow their own veg and herbs in a greenhouse. They've even written their own cookbook. Simple but marvellous.

Gebroeders Niemeijer €

Nieuwendijk 35 (020 707 6752, www.gebroedersniemeijer.nl). Tram 2, 4, 11, 12, 13, 14, 17, 24 or Metro Centraal. ***Open*** *8.15am-5.30pm Tue-Fri; 8.30am-5pm Sat; 9am-5pm Sun.* ***Map*** *p70 L7* 10 Bakery/café

In stark contrast to the rest of the dingy shopping street it's on, Gebroeders Niemeijer is an artisanal French bakery and bright, light tearoom that serves breakfast and lunch. All the breads and pastries are made by hand and baked in a stone oven. Sausages come from local producers Brandt en Levie and cheeses from the city's best French cheese purveyor, **Kef** (Marnixstraat 192, www.abrahamkef.nl). Perfect.

Haesje Claes €€

Spuistraat 275 (020 624 9998). Tram 2, 11, 12, 14, 24 or Metro Rokin. ***Open*** *noon-midnight daily, last food orders at 10pm.* ***Map*** *p70 J10* 11 Dutch

In the heart of the city, between Dam Square and Spui, this beloved landmark is especially popular with tourists, though locals also come flooding in for traditional Dutch food, including *erwtensoep* (split-pea soup) and a great *stamppot* (potato mashed with greens). The service is friendly, available and fast. You can also order from the same menu at the utterly delightful brown bar next door at no.269, **Café de Koningshut**.

Kantjil & de Tijger €€€

Spuistraat 291-293 (020 620 0994, www.kantjil.nl). Tram 2, 4, 11, 12, 14, 24 or Metro Rokin. ***Open*** *noon-10pm, Sun-Thu; noon-11pm Fri, Sat.* ***Map*** *p70 J10* 14 Indonesian

For more than a quarter-century, this Jugendstil-styled brasserie has been serving well-cooked and authentic Indonesian 'rice table' (*rijsttafel, see p41*), though you can also buy à la carte. It's a good place to line one's belly before hitting the bars in the neighbourhood. For a more restrained meal costing less than a tenner, visit its nearby takeaway outlet, **Kantjil To Go** (Nieuwezijds Voorburgwal 342).

d'Vijff Vlieghen €€€

Spuistraat 294-302 (020 530 4060, www.vijffvlieghen.nl). Tram 2, 11, 12. ***Open*** *6-10pm daily.* ***Map*** *p70 J10* ⑱ *Dutch*

'The Five Flies' achieves a rich Golden Age vibe – it even has a Rembrandt room, with etchings – but also works as a purveyor of over-the-top kitsch. The food is best described as poshed-up Dutch, with both à la carte and tasting menus available.

Vleminckx €

Voetboogsteeg 33 (www.vleminckxdesausmeester.nl). Tram 2, 4, 11, 12, 14, 24 or Metro Rokin. ***Open*** *noon-7pm Mon; 11am-7pm Tue-Wed, Fri-Sun; 11am-8pm Thur.* ***Map*** *p70 J11* ⑲ *Chip shop*

Chunky Belgian chips served with your choice of toppings. Opt for the *oorlog* ('war') version, where your chips are accompanied by a spicy peanut sauce, mayo and onions.

Bars

5&33

Martelaarsgracht 5 (020 820 5333, www.5and33.nl). Tram 2, 4, 11, 12, 13, 14, 17, 24 or Metro Centraal. ***Open*** *6.30am-1am Mon-Fri; 6.30am-2am Sat, Sun.* ***Map*** *p70 L7* ❶

Red skull sculptures. Penis lamps. Projection curtains. It's very hard to do over-the-top in a tasteful and welcoming manner, but the insanely arty Art'otel does just that with 5&33, its kitchen/bar/library/lounge/art gallery, located just across from Centraal Station. Drop in for one of their special nights – there's Truffle Tuesday and Lobster Thursday – or just grab a coffee or a Jane's Got Your Gun cocktail and decide how long you want to linger.

Belgique

Gravenstraat 2 (020 625 1974, cafe-belgique.nl). Tram 2, 4, 11, 12, 13, 14, 17, 24. ***Open*** *3pm-1am Mon-Thu; 1pm-3am Fri, Sat; 1pm-1am Sun.* ***No cards. Map*** *p70 K8* ❷

One of the city's smallest bars packs in eight beers on tap, plus another 50 bottled brews – mainly from neighbouring Belgium. It sometimes even manages to squeeze in

Top 20

❤ Begijnhof

Begijnhof 30 (622 19 18, begijnhofkapel amsterdam.nl). Tram 4, 14, 24 or Metro Rokin. ***Courtyard*** *9am-5pm daily.* ***Chapel*** *1pm-6.30pm Mon; 9am-6.30pm Tue, Fri; 9am-6pm Sat, Sun.* ***Map*** *p70 J10.*

Hidden behind the buzzing Spui square is a group of houses with a history as lovely as its pristine courtyard. Established in the 14th century, the Begijnhof originally provided modest homes for the Beguines, a religious and (as was the way in the Middle Ages with religious establishments for women) rather liberated sisterhood of unmarried ladies from good families, who, though not nuns and thus taking no formal vows, lived together in a close community and had to take vows of chastity.

Since they did not have to take vows of poverty, the Beguines were free to dispose of their property as they saw fit, further ensuring their emancipation as a community. They could, however, renounce their vows at any moment and leave – for instance, if they wanted to get married. The last sister died in 1971, while one of

her predecessors never left, despite dying back in 1654. She was buried in a 'grave in the gutter' under a red granite slab that remains visible – and is often adorned with flowers – on the path.

Most of the neat little houses round the courtyard were modernised in the 17th and 18th centuries. In the centre stands the **Engelse Kerk** (English Reformed Church), built as a church around 1400 and given over to Scottish (no, really) Presbyterians living in the city in 1607; many became pilgrims when they decided to travel further to the New World in search of religious freedom. Now one of the principal places of worship for Amsterdam's English community, the church is worth a look primarily to see the pulpit panels, designed by a young Mondrian.

Also in the courtyard is a **Catholic church**, secretly converted from two houses in 1665 following the complete banning of open Catholic worship after the Reformation. It once held the regurgitated Eucharist host that starred in the Miracle of Amsterdam, a story depicted in the church's beautiful stained-glass windows. There's an information centre next door. The house at no.34, known as the **Houten Huis**, dates from 1475 and is the oldest wooden house still standing within the city.

While visiting the Begijnhof, be sure to check out the beautiful painted stones on the wall behind the Houten Huis, each of which depicts a scene from the Bible. Dating from the 17th and 18th centuries, these stones, once housed in the Rijksmuseum's vaults, were restored and installed here in 1961.

In the know
When to visit

The courtyard entrance is easy to miss, but the site is a popular point for tours and is mentioned in various guidebooks so its hidden location doesn't always deter crowds. Visit first thing in the morning or just before it closes for the most room to roam the beautiful courtyard.

Bar Crawl

Follow the roads to oblivion ...

Whether you love them, hate them or secretly want to join them, there's never a shortage of excitable (likely inebriated) bar-hoppers and pub-crawlers pouring onto the streets of Amsterdam. If you fall into the last category or simply want to see what the fuss is about, patrol Spuistraat and Niewezijds Voorburgwal and you're sure to find a bar to match your mood. Starting at the north end of Spuistraat, you'll pass music venue **Bitterzoet** (no.2, *see p225*), straight-friendly gay bar **PRIK** (no.109), arty magnet **Café Schuim** (no.189), squat hole **Vrankrijk** (no.216), punk hole **Café the Minds** (no.245), delightful 'brown bar' **De Koningshut** (no.269), the quite flashy **Dante Kitchen & Bar** (no.320) – which used to be home for the nation's '*troeteljunkie*' (or 'cuddly junkie') Herman Brood – followed by a range of choices around **Café Hoppe** (*see p92*) on Spui square.

Looping back north on Nieuwezijds Voorburgwal, you'll encounter the kitsch and friendly **Café DIEP!** (no.256), American craft-beer joint **Beer Temple** (no.250) not to mention the charming former journo hangout **Scheltema** (no.242).

an eight-piece bluegrass band. A gem of a pub, complete with graffitied walls, dripping candles, and hearty cheer.

Café de Dokter

Rozenboomsteeg 4 (020 626 4427, www.cafe-de-dokter.nl). Tram 2, 4, 11, 12, 14, 24 or Metro Rokin. ***Open*** *4pm-1am Wed-Sat.* ***Map*** *p70 J10* ❻

Definitely the smallest bar in Amsterdam at just a handful of square metres, the Doctor is also one of the oldest, dishing out the cure for whatever ails you since 1798. Centuries of character and all kinds of gewgaws are packed into the extremely compact space. Whisky figures large (there's a monthly special) and snacks include smoked *osseworst* (cured sausage) with gherkins. If it's too cosy, then head one block north to the similarly old-school **De Engelse Reet** (Begijnensteeg 4, 020 623 1777).

Café Hoppe

Spui 18-20 (020 420 4420, cafehoppe.com/nl). Tram 2, 4, 11, 12, 14, 24 or Metro Rokin. ***Open*** *8am-1am Sun-Thu; 8am-2am Fri, Sat.* ***Map*** *p70 K7* ❼

The bonvivant beer magnate Freddy Heineken (1923-2002) spent so much time in this ancient, woody watering hole that he ended up buying it. What appealed to Fred most about the place is that it catered to everyone, from students wanting a cheap *biertje*, through tourists enjoying the terrace, to suits stopping by after work. And nothing much has changed. If you want something more evocative of a classic Parisian brasserie, try handsome **Café Luxembourg** next door.

❤ W Lounge

W Hotel, Spuistraat 175 (020 811 3399, www.mrportersteakhouse.com). Tram 2, 11, 12, 13, 17. ***Open*** *7am-1am Mon-Thur, Sun; 7am-2am Fri, Sat.* ***Map*** *p70 J9* ⓮

There are few vantage points in Amsterdam that are largely undisturbed by hordes of tourists, but the W Lounge definitely makes the cut. Perched at the top of the W Hotel, it has decadent interiors, attentive staff and breathtaking views of the skyline. In the summer, enjoy a Porters Americano – the house cocktail – as you dip your feet into the pool on the terrace. During winter, curl up with an espresso martini by the fire. If you're hankering for a feed, book a table at Mr Porter steakhouse on the same floor. But if you just want to pop up for a drink and some nibbles (and not blow your budget), you're free to do so. There's a sense of exclusivity, but everyone is welcome.

Coffeeshops

Abraxas

Jonge Roelensteeg 12-14 (020 626 1317). Tram 2, 4, 11, 12, 13, 14, 17, 24. ***Open*** *8am-1am daily.* ***No cards. Map*** *p70 J9* ❶

Located down a narrow alley, this lively shop is a tourist hotspot. Staff are friendly, the internet connection is free and chessboards are plentiful – as are the separate rooms connected by spiral staircases. It also has a healthy-sized drug menu, including half a dozen bio weeds and spacecakes.

❤ Dampkring

Handboogstraat 29 (020 638 0705). Tram 2, 11, 12 or Metro Rokin. ***Open*** *10am-1am daily.* ***No cards. Map*** *p70 J11* ❸

Known for its unforgettable (even by stoner standards) interior, the visual experience acquired from Dampkring's decor could make a mushroom trip look grey. Moulded walls and sculpted ceilings are painted deep auburn and laced with caramel-coloured wooden panelling – which made it the perfect location for the movie *Ocean's Twelve*.

Tweede Kamer
Heisteeg 6 (020 422 2236). Tram 2, 11, 12. ***Open** 10am-1am daily.* ***No cards. Map** p70 J10* ❼

Small and intimate, this sister shop of Dampkring embodies the refined look and feel of old-jazz sophistication. Aided by a bakery round the corner, the spacecakes are sweet and lovely. The hash is highly regarded, but seating is extremely limited and the place is notorious for getting very crowded at peak times.

Shops & services

Albert Heijn
Nieuwezijds Voorburgwal 226 (020 421 8344, www.ah.nl). Tram 2, 11, 12, 13, 17. ***Open** 8am-10pm daily.* ***No cards. Map** p70 J9* ❷ *Food & drink*

The Dutch have a very close relationship with this, their biggest supermarket brand. The monopoly it holds on the city means you're always within a stone's throw of a 'Bertie': be it a regular store, an 'AH XL', or small 'AH To Go'. **Other locations** throughout the city.

Copa Football Store

De Bierkoning
Paleisstraat 125 (020 625 2336, www.bierkoning.nl). Tram 2, 11, 12, 13, 17. ***Open** 11am-7pm Mon-Sat; 1-7pm Sun.* ***Map** p70 J9* ❸ *Food & drink*

Named in honour of its location behind the Royal Palace, the 'Beer King' stocks a head-spinning 1,200 brands of beer from around the world, and a range of fine glasses to sup from.

❤ Bij Ons Vintage
Nieuwezijds Voorburgwal 150 (06 1187 1278, www.bijons-vintage.nl). Tram 2, 11, 12, 13, 17. ***Open** 11am-7pm Mon; 10am-7pm Tue-Sat; noon-7pm Sun.* ***Map** p70 J8* ❹ *Fashion*

This place is rammed with leather jackets, woollen hats, old Polaroid cameras and even some authentic 1960s ottomans. There's so much random gear here that you'll be struck with bargain-hunting fever. **Other location** Reestraat 13, Western Grachtengordel.

❤ Book Market at the Spui
Spui (www.deboekenmarktophetspui.nl). Tram 2, 4, 11, 12, 14, 24 or Metro Rokin. ***Open** 10am-6pm Fri.* ***Map** p70 J10* ❺ *Market*

Every Friday, the Spui square is filled with over 25 antiquarian booksellers covering all subjects and languages – it's a browser's paradise.

❤ Copa Football Store
Prins Hendrikkade 20-B (020 620 1660, www.copafootball.com). Tram 2, 4, 11, 12, 13, 14, 17, 24. ***Open** 11am-7pm Mon-Fri; 10am-6pm Sat; 1pm-5pm Sun.* ***Map** p70 L7* ❼ *Gifts & souvenirs*

What happens when a footie obsessive starts a shop? He brings together an expanse of retro shirts, recycled bags, designer footballs, books, DVDs and even some functional football wear.

HEMA
Kalverstraat 212 (020 422 8988, www.hema.nl). Tram 2, 4, 11, 12, 14, 24. ***Open** 9am-7pm Mon-Sat; noon-6.30pm Sun.* ***Map** p70 K11* ❾ *Gifts & souvenirs*

A much-loved high-street institution, HEMA is the place to check out when you need just about anything – clothes, towels, notebooks, soap dispensers, ring binders, those little bike lights – you name it, HEMA's probably got it.

Mark Raven
Nieuwezijds Voorburgwal 174 (020 330 0800, www.markraven.nl). Tram 2, 11, 12, 13, 17. ***Open** 10.30am-6pm daily.* ***Map** p70 J8* ⓬ *Gifts & souvenirs*

This eponymously named artistic hub sells Raven's etchings in many guises – from canvases to T-shirts.

Grachtengordel

Where once there was just water, now there are a series of neat, man-made canals keeping the sea and surrounding bog at bay. Amsterdam's 165 *grachten* (canals) are crossed by 1,400 bridges; they stretch for more than 75 kilometres (47 miles) around the city and are, on average, three metres (ten feet) deep.

At the heart of it all is the Grachtengordel (Canal Belt or Canal Ring), which forms a horseshoe round the historical Old Centre of town. Declared a UNESCO World Heritage Site in 2010, the ring consists of the city's most elegant canals: the original moat, the Singel, along with the Herengracht, Keizergracht and Prinsengracht. Here, you'll find an abundance of places for scenic coffee slurping, quirky shopping, aimless walks and a spot of meditative gable-gazing. But these waterways are more than an attractive crossover between the tourist-laden centre and the artier 'local' neighbourhoods of Jordaan, De Pijp and the Museum District. The Grachtengordel and its radial streets and canals – including Singelgracht and Leidseplein – is where Amsterdam as we know it grew to flourish from its humble beginnings along the river Amstel.

❤ Don't miss

1 Canal cruising *p99*
See how the city came to be, from the best seat in the house.

2 Anne Frank Huis *p102*
An insight into a personal and national history.

3 Nine Streets *p101*
Cluster of cultured streets, where high fashion meets cheese.

4 Paradiso *p227*
One of the world's premier 'music temples'.

5 Foam *p111*
A photography museum worth snapping at.

6 Westerkerk tower *p104*
Marvel at one of the best views the city has to offer.

Museum van Loon *p110*

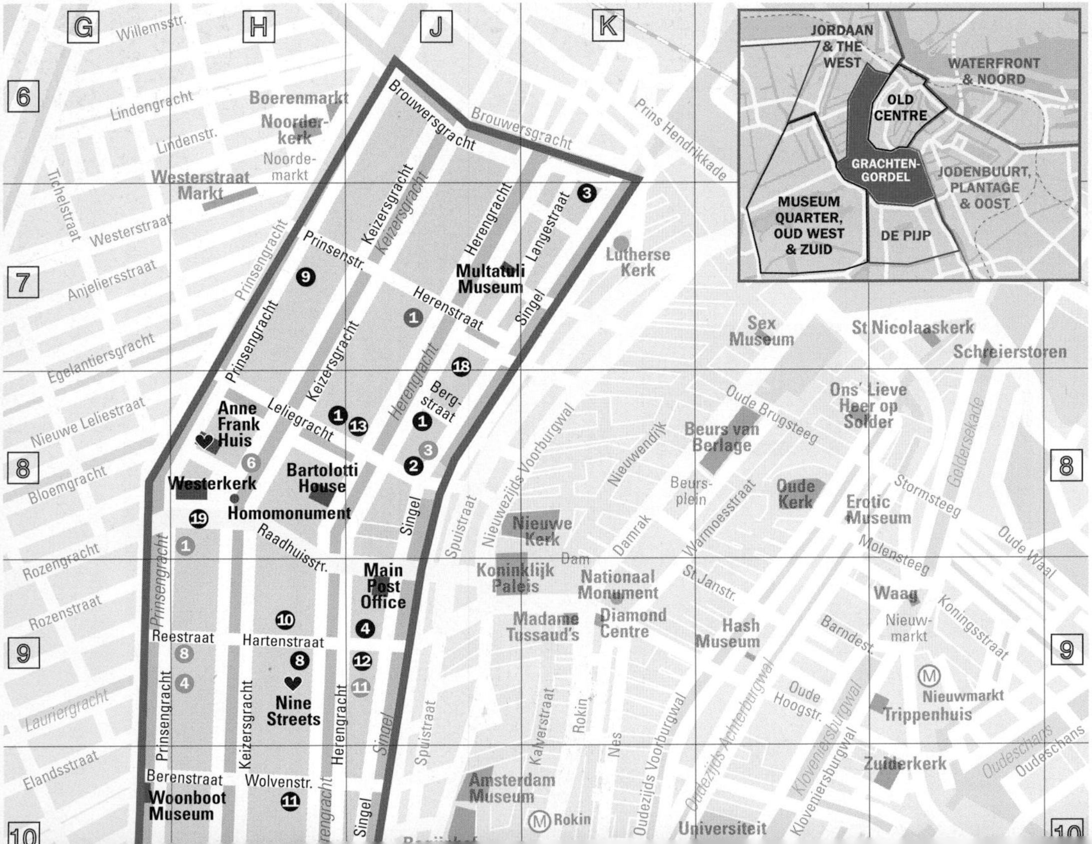

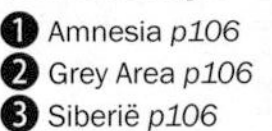

GRACHTENGORDEL

Restaurants & cafés

1. Bistro Bij Ons *p105*
2. Buffet van Odette *p110*
3. Caffé il Momento *p105*
4. Envy *p105*
5. Greenwoods *p110*
6. Gs Brunch Boat *p105*
7. Guts & Glory *p112*
8. Koffiehuis de Hoek *p105*
9. Lion Noir *p112*
10. Los Pilones *p112*
11. Lotti's Café, Bar and Grill *p106*
12. Segugio *p112*
13. Stach Food *p112*
14. Tempo Doeloe *p112*
15. Van Dobben *p112*

Bars

1. Arendsnest *p106*
2. De Balie *p112*
3. Café Brecht *p113*
4. Café Eijlders *p106*
5. Café de Pels *p106*
6. Door 74 *p113*
7. Whisky Café L&B *p113*

Coffeeshops

1. Amnesia *p106*
2. Grey Area *p106*
3. Siberië *p106*

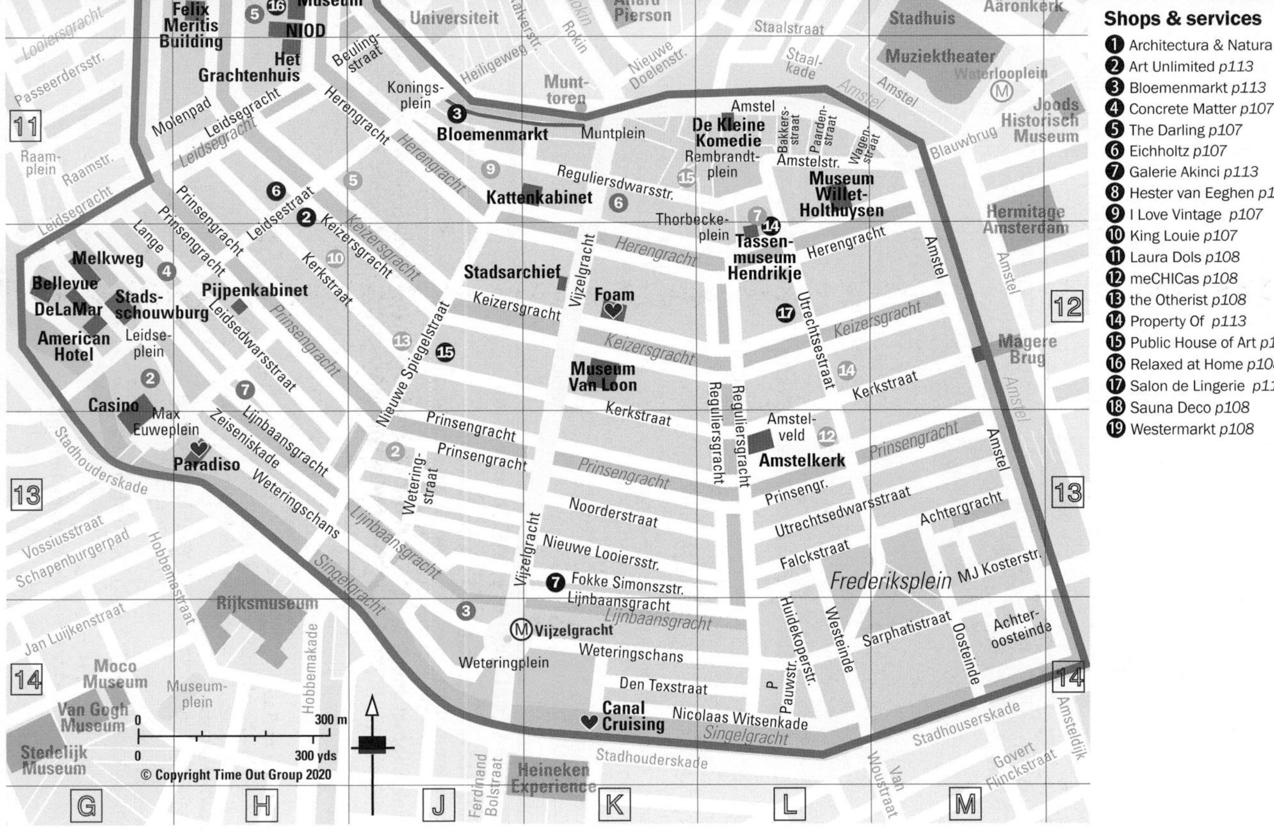

Shops & services

1. Architectura & Natura *p106*
2. Art Unlimited *p113*
3. Bloemenmarkt *p113*
4. Concrete Matter *p107*
5. The Darling *p107*
6. Eichholtz *p107*
7. Galerie Akinci *p113*
8. Hester van Eeghen *p107*
9. I Love Vintage *p107*
10. King Louie *p107*
11. Laura Dols *p108*
12. meCHICas *p108*
13. the Otherist *p108*
14. Property Of *p113*
15. Public House of Art *p113*
16. Relaxed at Home *p108*
17. Salon de Lingerie *p113*
18. Sauna Deco *p108*
19. Westermarkt *p108*

Westerkerk p104

History

From 1600 to 1650, during Amsterdam's Golden Age, the city's population ballooned four-fold, and it was obliged to expand once again. Construction began on the Singel and on the Grachtengordel. Herengracht (Lords' Canal) was where many of the ruling assembly had their homes. So that there would be no misunderstanding about status, Herengracht was followed further out by Keizersgracht (Emperors' Canal) and Prinsengracht (Princes' Canal). Immigrants were housed in the Jordaan.

When the canal belt was declared a UNESCO World Heritage Site, locals began to worry that Amsterdam might meet the same fate as Venice or Bruges, where tourism seems to dominate the city's cultural character. However, except for increased hordes of wobbly tourists on bikes, the vibe remains pretty much the same – whether it's during Gay Pride, the classic Canal Festival or the perhaps ill-advised annual Amsterdam City Swim.

The builders completed the Western Belt before the grander Southern Belt. For ease of use, we have split our listings into these two sections and include the surrounding area of Leidseplein, which borders the Grachtengordel and the Museum Quarter. But when walking about, it's probably easier to just take in one canal at a time – after all, it's very easy to lose your sense of direction in such a circular town.

WESTERN CANAL BELT

Singel

One of the few clues to Singel's past as the protective moat that surrounds the city's wall is the **Torensluis** (Tower Gate) bridge that crosses it at Oude Leliestraat. It did indeed once have a lookout tower, and the space underneath was supposedly used as a lock-up for medieval drunks – but now it's home to very occasional art exhibitions and

❤ Time to eat & drink

Dutch beer specialist
Arendsnest *p106*

Experimental dining
Guts & Glory *p112*

Lavish lunch
Lotti's Café, Bar & Grill *p106*

Morning coffee
Caffe Il Momento *p105*

Quality smokes
Amnesia *p106*

Wee dram
Whisky Café L&B *p113*

❤ Time to shop

Affordable art
Art Unlimited *p113*, Public House of Art *p113*

Alternative gifts
the Otherist *p108*

Bags of fun
Property Of *p113*

Beautiful blooms
Bloemenmarkt *p113*

Fashion for fellas
Concrete Matter *p107*

One-stop shop
Relaxed at Home *p108*

Vintage boutique
The Darling *p107*

In the know
Getting around

Trams 13 and 17 run along Radhuisstraat through the heart of the Western Canal Belt. Canal bikes are available for hire from multiple tourist attractions throughout the Grachtengordel, including Anne Frank Huis; for details of canal cruises, see Canal Cruising, *opposite*. If you prefer to stay on dry land, the Grachtengordel and surrounds is a great area to explore by foot. A stroll from Anne Frank Huis to Bloemenmarkt takes five to ten minutes, give or take a few stops for photo opportunities.

❤ Canal cruising

During a sojourn in the city, Hans Christian Andersen wrote, 'The view from my window, through the elms to the canal outside, is like a fairy tale.'

Canals are what people imagine when they think of Amsterdam, and they continue to enchant visitors today. Like any other city built on water, Amsterdam is best seen from a boat. The larger tourist boats, which can seat between 150 and 200 people and come complete with audio tour guides, are too big to squeeze through all of the narrow waterways connecting the Grachtengordel, but they still provide a doughty service past many of the World Heritage-listed highlights. You'll find the pick-up points for a lot of them along Stadhouderskade, which separates the Southern Canal Belt from the Museum Quarter and De Pijp.

Amsterdam Canal Cruises (no.78, 020 676 0302, www.amsterdamcanalcruises.nl) collects from just outside the Heineken Brewery and offers a range of tours throughout the year, including a candle-lit evening cruise. **The Blue Boat Company** (no. 30, 020 679 1370, www.blueboat.nl) offers a similar service, including seasonal specials like the 'Water Colours Cruise' during the Amsterdam Light Festival (*see p205*). Prices range from €18.50 to €42.50 depending on the cruise type and time of year.

A bit further west along Stadhouderskade, outside the Rijksmuseum, is one of the many pick-up and drop-off points for **Stromma** (020 217 0501, www.stromma.com). Here, you'll be able to jump on a variety of canal cruises, including a hop-on-hop-off canal bus. This service costs €24.50 for a 24-hour ticket, and €33.50 for 48 hours. It takes you past key locations in the city including Anne Frank Huis and A'DAM Toren. Drop off and collection points are also at Rembrandt Square and Albert Cuypmarkt.

If you want to navigate the historical canals for yourself, you can also hire a canal bike for an hour or two at a time for €10.50 per person from Stromma. The bikes hold up to four people and you can pedal your way from Anne Frank Huis, Leidseplein or Rijksmuseum if you want a rest from pounding the pavements. But if you'd prefer something with a bit more horsepower, powerboat rentals provide the best of both worlds. Companies including **Mokum Boot** (020 210 5700, www.mokumbootverhuur.nl), **Kin Boat** (020 261 3466, www.kinboat.com) and **Amsterdam Boat Centre** (020 428 2725, amsterdamboatcenter.com) hire out boats from various locations throughout the city starting from €95 for two hours for up to eight people. No licence is required for boats less than 15 metres (50 foot) in length and some include a mini-fridge and barbecue hire. If you can get a group of four or more together, it's the perfect way to view Amsterdam's finest sights from the best seat in the house.

jazz nights. On the bridge itself, a statue of the 19th-century writer Multatuli depicts his head forming as smoke from a bottle – a reference to the way he let the genie out of the bottle by questioning Dutch imperialism in such novels as *Max Havelaar* (1860). You can learn more about him at the nearby **Multatuli Museum** (*see p104*).

While you're wandering this canal, you may wish to contribute to the debate as to whether Singel 7 or Singel 166 is the smallest house in Amsterdam. In between, opposite Singel 38, is the **Poezenboot** ('Cat Boat', depoezenboot.nl), an asylum for orphaned pussy cats. Always good for a snort is the **House with Noses** at Singel 116, although arty types might be a bit more interested in Singel 140-142. This was once the home of Banning Cocq, the principal figure of Rembrandt's *The Night Watch*.

Herengracht

Starting at the northern end of Herengracht, you'll reach a Vingboons building dating from 1638 at no.168, along with the architectural gem that is De Keyser's **Bartolotti House** (Herengracht 170-172, www.hendrickdekeyser.nl). At Herengracht 366 is the **Bijbels Museum** (*see p102*). A few doors further south is the **Netherlands Institute of War, Holocaust & Genocide Studies** (Herengracht 380, 020 523 3800, www.niod.nl). This copy of a Loire mansion contains three kilometres of archives that include Anne Frank's diary, donated by her father Otto. For gentler thoughts, visit the **KattenKabinet** (Cat Cabinet, Herengracht 497, 020 626 9040, www.kattenkabinet.nl), an art museum devoted to works depicting cats.

Keizersgracht

Walking down Keizersgracht, you'll soon come to the **House with the Heads** (no.123), a pure Dutch Renaissance classic. The official story has these finely chiselled heads representing classical gods, but according to local folklore they are the heads of burglars, chopped off by a lusty maidservant. She decapitated six and married the seventh. It was recently reopened after renovation as a centre for free and contrarian thinking. Another true classic is at **Keizersgracht 174**, an art nouveau masterpiece by Gerrit van Arkels. A few paces down are the pink granite triangular slabs of the **Homomonument** (www.homomonument.nl), the world's first memorial to persecuted gays and lesbians, designed by Karin Daan and unveiled in 1987. Flowers are often left on it for personal remembrance, especially during significant gatherings such as on World AIDS Day.

Another key edifice is the **Felix Meritis Building** (Keizersgracht 324, www.felixmeritis.nl), a neoclassical monolith with the motto 'Happiness through merit' chiselled over its door. Nearby is the equally epic home of the photography foundation **Huis Marseille**. This whole stretch was also the site of the legendary 'slipper parade', where the posh-footed rich strolled about every Sunday both to see and be seen. These days, those in the fashion know spend their time (and cash) in the surrounding stylish **De Negen Straatjes** (Nine Streets; *see opposite*).

Prinsengracht

Named after William, Prince of Orange, Prinsengracht is the most charming of the canals, splitting as it does the smarter ring from the more funky Jordaan. Pompous façades have been mellowed with shady trees, cosy cafés and some of Amsterdam's hipper houseboats. If you find yourself at the weekly **Noordermarkt** or **Boerenmarkt** (for both *see p124*) in the Jordaan, then make sure you stop for coffee at the ever-popular **Papeneiland** (*see p123*). According to local legend, a tunnel used to run under the canal from here to a Catholic church located at Prinsengracht 7 at the time of the Protestant uprising.

On your way up Prinsengracht, you'll pass the **Anne Frank Huis** (*see p102*) and the almost-400-year-old **Westerkerk** (*see p104*). Mari Andriessen's 1977 statue of Anne Frank stands nearby, at the corner with Westermarkt. Meanwhile, René Descartes fans can pay tribute to the great savant by casting an eye on his former house (Westermarkt 6). Further south is the **Woonboot Museum** (*see p105*).

Leidseplein

Leidseplein borders the bottom of the 'U' made by the Canal Belt, and runs south from the end of Leidsestraat to the Amsterdam School-style bridge over Singelgracht and east towards the 'music temple' in a former church, **Paradiso** (*see p227*) to the **Max**

In the know
The scenic route

To avoid the bustle of shopping artery Leidsestraat, take the art and antique gallery route of Spiegelgracht and Nieuwe Spiegelstraat to make your way from the Old Centre to the Museum District. Much more refined, and still delightfully scenic.

❤ Nine Streets

Between Westermarkt and Leidsegracht. Tram 2, 5, 7, 11, 12, 19. ***Map*** *p96 H9*

There are few places in the world that can combine fishnets, cheese and high fashion with seamless, albeit haphazard, ease, but De Negen Straatjes (the Nine Streets) manage to pull it off with picture-perfect charm. Affectionately dubbed 'Negens', these parallel streets connect the city's three main canals between Raadhuisstraat and Leidsegracht. The cobbled streets are steeped in both style and history, constructed in the first half of the 17th century when the canals of the Grachtengordel were dug out around the medieval town to cater for its growing population.

Fast forward over 400 years, the area is a thriving cultural hub of cafés, restaurants, galleries and literally hundreds of retailers, for which De Negen Straatjes is best known. From cheesemongers to doll repairs to designer retailers, the area has something for everyone. First stop has to be that vortex of vintage, **Laura Dols**. Loved by the city's darlings, this fashionable cavern positively glitters. True Dutch style can be cashed in at **Hester van Eeghen**, the shop of the celebrated local shoe designer. Known for her way with leather, Hester loves a geometric shape or two and bold colours (the lime green inlay is a signature). Add a twist of Mexican flavour at **meCHICas**, where local talent Debbie Verhagen designs trinkets 'with Dutch simplicity and South American flair'. **King Louie** is one for women and kids; thick-knit bright scarves adorn the wooden shelves in winter, while dainty frocks and denim will always be a big draw in the summer. Despite its bumbling name, **Relaxed at Home** is a bright and airy store that's the sartorial equivalent of a cuddle – think thick nude scarves by Dutch stalwart Scotch & Soda.

If you have serious shopping stamina and haven't quenched your consumer thirst at the end of peering into every window of the Nine Streets, there are a few other similar streets: connecting Herenstraat and Prinsenstraat in the Western Canal Belt, and Hazenstraat in the Jordaan.

► *For details of the shops mentioned here, see pp106-108.*

Euweplein (a handy passage to Vondelpark; *see p146*) with its **Max Euwe Centrum** (Max Euweplein 30a, 020 625 7017, www.maxeuwe.nl) and giant chess set.

Artists and writers used to congregate on Leidseplein during the 1920s and 1930s, when it was the scene of clashes between communists and fascists. During the war, protests were ruthlessly broken up by the Nazis and there's a commemorative plaque on nearby Kerkstraat. But thanks to the plethora of tourists drinking in pavement cafés, listening to buskers and soaking up the atmosphere – not to mention the huge variety of booze on offer – Leidseplein's latterday persona is more party town than party political.

The area has more theatres, clubs and restaurants than any other part of town. It's dominated by the **Stadsschouwburg**, the municipal theatre (*see p243*), multimedia centre **Melkweg** (*see p230*) just round the corner, and by the cafés that take over the pavements during summer. This is when fire-eaters, jugglers, musicians and small-time con artists and pickpockets fill the square.

The café society associated with Leidseplein began with the opening of the city's first terrace bar, the Café du Théâtre, which, sadly, was demolished in 1877, 20 years before the completion of Kromhout's **Eden Amsterdam American Hotel**. Opposite the American is a building, dating from 1882, that reflects Leidseplein's dramatic transformation: once grand, it's now illuminated by huge adverts and the Apple flagship store, and has been the site of frequent disruptive roadwork in recent years as tram and metro lines are updated. Just off the square, in the Leidsebos, is the more intriguing **Adamant**, a pyramid-like, hologram-effect sculpture that commemorated 400 years of the city's central diamond trade in 1986. It's worth looking out for a tiny 'sawing guy' sculpture by an anonymous artist in one of the trees.

Sights & museums

Bijbels Museum

Herengracht 366 (020 624 2436, www.bijbelsmuseum.nl). Tram 2, 11, 12 or Metro Rokin. ***Open*** *10am-5pm daily.* ***Admission*** *€12.50; €10 reductions; free under-17s, Iamsterdam, MK.* ***Map*** *p96 H10.*

Housed in a restored 17th-century Vingboons canal house, the Bible Museum aims to illustrate life and worship with archaeological finds, models of ancient temples and a splendid collection of Bibles from several centuries (including a rhyming Bible from 1271). You can also admire the splendid

Top 20

❤ Anne Frank Huis

Prinsengracht 267 (020 556 7105, www.annefrank.nl). Tram 13, 17. ***Open*** *Apr-Oct 9am-10pm daily. Nov-Mar, 9am-7pm daily.* ***Admission*** *€10.50; €5.50 reductions, free under-9s. Tickets are only available online, and sell out fast.* ***Map*** *p96 H8.*

During World War II, the young Jewish diarist Anne Frank and her family hid for two years behind a bookcase in the back annexe of this 17th-century canal house. During this time, young Anne kept a vivid diary, which is as confronting as it is emotionally compelling. The diary became a best friend of sorts for Anne, in which she wrote short stories and shared the details of her life in hiding. On 4 August 1944, the occupants were arrested and transported to concentration camps, where Anne died with her sister Margot and their mother. Her father, Otto, was the only one of eight to survive, and decided that Anne's diary should be published.

After the war the secret annex was on the list of buildings to be knocked down, but thanks to a number of campaigners, the house remained. The foundation, now known as the Anne Frank Huis, was set up and the rest is history: Anne's dream of becoming a best-selling author was fulfilled, with tens of millions of copies having since been printed in 70 languages. Today, more than a million visitors every year come to witness these sober unfurnished rooms, which have been delicately preserved throughout the decades. A new wing not only tells the story of Anne's family and the persecution of Jews, but also presents the difficulties of fighting discrimination of all types.

The museum is now one of the most popular in Amsterdam, so much so that tickets can no longer be purchased in person. Tickets are made available online exactly two months in advance, with visitors booking a specific time slot – but beware, they sell out incredibly quickly. If you must be spontaneous, a small number of tickets are released online at 9am everyday.

ANNE
FRANK
HUIS

Het Grachtenhuis

Jacob de Wit paintings, and the grand garden with biblical plants and a sculpture entitled *Apocalypse*.

Het Grachtenhuis

Herengracht 386 (020 421 1656, www.hetgrachtenhuis.nl). Tram 2, 11, 12 or Metro Rokin. ***Open*** *10am-5pm Tue-Sun.* ***Admission*** *€15; €7.50-€12.50 reductions; free under-4s, Iamsterdam, MK.* ***Map*** *p96 H11.*

The building of Amsterdam's Grachtengordel during the 17th-century Golden Age was one of the most ambitious urban expansion projects of all time. At the Canal House Museum, you get the full story through displays and an interactive 40-minute multimedia presentation.

Multatuli Museum

Korsjespoortsteeg 20 (020 638 1938, www.multatuli-museum.nl). Tram 2, 11, 12, 13, 17. ***Open*** *10am-5pm Tue; noon-5pm Wed-Sun.* ***Admission*** *€5; free under-18s, Iamsterdam.* ***Map*** *p96 J7.*

Just off Singel, this museum is dedicated to the satirical and anti-colonialist writer Eduard Douwes-Dekker (1820-87), aka Multatuli (meaning 'I have suffered much' in Latin), set in the house where he was born. The various literary artefacts pay testament to his credo: 'The human calling is to be human.' There's also a small library.

❤ Westerkerk

Prinsengracht 277-279 (020 624 7766, www.westerkerk.nl). Tram 13, 17. ***Open*** *11am-3pm Mon-Sat. Services 10.30am Sun and Christmas Day.* ***Admission*** *free. Guided tour €5; Tower tour €9.* ***Map*** *p96 H8.*

Before noise pollution, it was said that if you heard the bells of Westerkerk's tower, dating from 1631, you were in the Jordaan. The tower also offers a great view of this neighbourhood, provided you don't suffer from vertigo: the 85m (278ft) structure sways by 3cm in a good wind. The tower is emblazoned with a gaudy red, blue and gold 'XXX' crown; this was granted to the city in 1489 by the Holy Roman Emperor Maximillian in gratitude for the treatment he received during a pilgrimage to Amsterdam. The triple-X came to be used by local traders – and later by local pornographers – to denote quality, and is now featured on the city's flag and coat of arms. It's thought that Rembrandt is buried in the church itself, although no one is quite sure where: Rembrandt died a pauper, and, as a result, is commemorated inside the building with a simple plaque. If queues for the tower are long, you can also enjoy expansive views at the Zuidertoren or the Ouderkerkstoren, which are both handled by the same office. Check the concert listings too. The church and the tower underwent extensive restoration during 2019.

Woonboot Museum
Prinsengracht, opposite no.296 (020 427 0750, www.houseboatmuseum.nl). Tram 5, 7, 19. ***Open*** *Sept-June 10am-5pm Tue-Sun; July, Aug 10am-5pm daily.* ***Admission*** *€4.50; €3.50 reductions; free under-5s, Iamsterdam, MK.* ***Map*** *p96 G10.*

Aside from some discreet explanatory panels, a small slide show and a ticket clerk, the Hendrika Maria Houseboat Museum is laid out as a houseboat would be, to help visitors imagine what it's like to live on the water. It's more spacious than you might expect and does a good job of selling the lifestyle afforded by its unique comforts.

Restaurants & cafés

Bistro Bij Ons €€
Prinsengracht 287 (020 627 9016, www.bistrobijons.nl). Tram 13, 17. ***Open*** *11am-midnight (last orders 10pm) Tue-Sun.* ***Map*** *p96 H8* 1 *Dutch*

In the shadow of the Westerkerk, right near the Jordaan, two archetypal Amsterdam hostesses serve typical Dutch fare (think vegetable soup with meatballs, grandma's traditional *stamppot* mash, and warm apple pie) in a canal house restaurant with a living-room vibe and watery views. A fun night out at a friendly price.

❤ Caffé il Momento €
Singel 180 (020 336 652, www.caffeilmomento.nl). Tram 2, 11, 12, 13, 17. ***Open*** *8am-6pm Mon-Fri; 9am-6pm Sat, Sun.* ***Map*** *p96 J8* 3 *Café*

The inside of this quaint café is just as charming as its exterior would have you believe. Grab a quality coffee to go or linger at one of the cosy tables along the exposed brick walls. If you're in need of a bit more sustenance, the croissants are always fresh and the food is delicious. The owner is also super-friendly.

Envy €€€
Prinsengracht 381 (020 344 6407, www.envy.nl). Tram 5, 13, 17, 19. ***Open*** *6pm-1am Mon-Thur; noon-3pm and 6pm-1am Fri-Sun.* ***Map*** *p96 H9* 4 *Italian*

A designer deli-cum-restaurant serving an arsenal of delicacies, which emerge from the streamlined refrigerators that line the walls and from the able kitchen staff. The perfect place for those times when you want to try a bit of everything.

❤ Gs Brunch Boat €€
Keizergracht 177 (www.reallyniceplace.com/brunch-boat). Tram 13, 17. ***Departs*** *10am, noon, 2pm Fri; 10am, 11am, noon, 1pm Sat, Sun.* ***Tickets*** *€42.50 per person.* ***Map*** *p96 H8* 6

Combining one of Amsterdam's finest attributes (the canals) with one of travel's greatest pleasures (food), Gs Brunch Boat guests get to choose from a tempting set menu described as 'an eclectic hot mess of love, lust, hunger and thirst', while enjoying a ride through the city's Grachtengordel. The boat has a retractable roof and runs during weekends throughout the year, come rain, hail or shine. You might get lucky as a walk in, but it's advisable to book in advance.

Koffiehuis de Hoek €
Prinsengracht 341 (020 625 3872). Tram 13, 17. ***Open*** *8.30am-5pm Tue-Fri; 9am-5pm Sat, Mon; 10am-5pm Sun.* ***No cards.*** ***Map*** *p96 H9* 8 *Café*

A traditional Dutch sandwich and lunch (omelettes, pancakes and the like) outlet

Gs Brunch Boat

where all walks of life collide – from construction workers to the advertising folk of nearby agency KesselsKramer.

❤ Lotti's Café, Bar and Grill €€€

Herengracht 255 (020 888 5500, www.lottis.com). Tram 2, 11, 12, 13, 17. ***Open*** *7am-1am daily.* ***Map*** *p96 J9* ⑪ *Bar/restaurant*

Boasting a prime location on the picturesque Herengracht, Lotti's Café, Bar and Grill is an all-day restaurant serving everything from seafood to steak, with various good things in between. Owned by the prestigious Soho House group and part of the Hoxton Hotel, the restaurant is dripping in chic style. By day, you'll spot the city's urban hipsters tapping away on their laptops, but by night it's a buzzing after-work bar. For the ultimate sugar hit, try the brownie – some say it's the best in town.

Bars

❤ Arendsnest

Herengracht 90 (020 421 2057, www.arendsnest.nl). Tram 2, 11, 12, 13, 17. ***Open*** *noon-midnight Sun-Thur; noon-2am Fri, Sat.* ***Map*** *p96 J7* ❶

A temple to the humble hop, and set in a lovely canal house, the 'Eagle's Nest' sells only Dutch beer. Many of the customers are real-ale types, but even amateurs will enjoy the 52 beers on tap and 100 bottled beers, from pale ale to smoked porter. To go with the beer, Arendsnest serves excellent cheese and sausage snacks.

Café Eijlders

Korte Leidsedwarsstraat 47 (020 624 2704, www.cafeeijlders.com). Tram 1, 2, 7, 11, 12, 19. ***Open*** *4.30pm-1am Mon-Wed; noon-2am Fri, Sat; noon-midnight Sun.* ***Map*** *p96 G12* ❹

Neon tat on one side, trendy Wendys on the other; Eijlders on Leidseplein is a cerebral alternative to both. A meeting place for the Resistance during the war, it now has a boho feel, with exhibitions, poetry nights and music – sometimes jazz, sometimes classical. Decor is handsome, with stained glass and dark wood.

Café de Pels

Huidenstraat 25 (020 622 9037, www.cafedepels.nl). Tram 2, 11, 12. ***Open*** *9am-1pm, Sun-Thu; 9am-2am Fri, Sat.* ***No cards. Map*** *p96 H10* ❺

The Nine Streets are littered with characterful bars, and this one is a lovely old-style, tobacco-stained example that has an intellectual bent. In fact, Café de Pels can justifiably claim a prime spot in Amsterdam's literary and political legacy: writers, journalists and social activists often meet at this erstwhile Provo hangout to chew the fat – although it's a nice spot in which to relax, whatever your mood.

Coffeeshops

❤ Amnesia

Herengracht 133 (020 427 7874). Tram 2, 11, 12, 13, 17. ***Open*** *9.30am-1am daily.* ***No cards. Map*** *p96 J8* ❶

You have to wonder at the choice of name, but Amnesia is a shop with swank decor, comfortable cushions and deep red walls. Located off the main tourist routes, it's often cool and quiet – though it occasionally fills up with locals. The pre-rolled joints are strong and smokeable. Summertime brings outdoor seating to the large, quiet canal street.

Grey Area

Oude Leliestraat 2 (020 420 4301, www.greyarea.nl). Tram 2, 11, 12, 13, 17. ***Open*** *noon-8pm daily.* ***No cards. Map*** *p96 J8* ❷

Run by two blokes living the modern American dream: running a thriving Amsterdam coffeeshop that offers some of the best weed and hash on the planet (try the Bubble Gum or Grey Mist Crystals). Also on offer are large glass bongs, a vaporiser and free refills of organic coffee. The owners are very affable and often more baked than the patrons; sometimes they stay in bed and miss the noon opening time.

Siberië

Brouwersgracht 11 (020 623 5909, www.thecoffeeshops.com). Tram 2, 11, 12, 13, 17. ***Open*** *9am-11pm Mon-Thu; 9am-midnight Fri, Sat; 10am-11pm Sun.* ***Map*** *p96 K7* ❸

Friendly and mellow, Siberië offers plenty of board games, making it a cool place to while away any rainy day with great coffee or one of its 40 different loose teas (no nasty bags on a string here). Siberië now has four locations around town; check the website for details.

Shops & services

Architectura & Natura

Leliegracht 22 (020 623 6186, www.architectura.nl). Tram 2, 11, 12, 13, 17. ***Open*** *noon-5pm Mon; 10.30am-6.30pm Tue-Fri; 10.30am-5pm Sat; noon-5pm Sun.* ***Map*** *p96 H8* ❶ *Books*

The stock at 'Architecture & Nature', which includes many works in English for monoglots, is exactly what you'd expect from its name: books on architectural history, landscape architecture, plant life, gardens and animal studies.

❤ Concrete Matter

Gasthuismolensteeg 12 (020 261 0933, www.concrete-matter.com). Tram 2, 11, 12, 13, 17. ***Open*** *1-6pm Mon, Tue; 11am-6pm Wed-Sat; noon-5pm Sun.* ***Map*** *p96 J9* ❹ *Vintage fashion*

A properly curated vintage men's fashion store, this place is hipster heaven. Original US Army flight jackets and old school Hawaiian shirts sit alongside cult grooming products, quirky trinkets, and "mantiques". A veritable treasure trove of stylish goodies, this is the place to source gifts for the bearded dude in your life.

❤ The Darling

Runstraat 4 (020 422 3142, www.thedarlingamsterdam.com). Tram 2, 11, 12. ***Open*** *1-6pm Mon; 11am-6pm Tue-Sat; noon-6pm Sun.* ***Map*** *p96 H10* ❺ *Lifestyle*

Quirky designer Nadine van der Zee set up shop here in 2009, after a friendly fellow patron in her local café tipped her off about the availability of a brilliant space on De Negen Straatjes. The shop offers an eclectic mix of clothing, jewellery, accessories and lifestyle products all 'made with love'. It also hosts monthly mini markets, live expos and shop nights. **Other location** Haarlemmerdijk 43.

Eichholtz

Leidsestraat 48 (020 622 0305, www.eichholtzdeli.nl). Tram 2, 11, 12. ***Open*** *noon-6.30pm Sun, Mon; 9am-6.30pm Tue, Wed, Sat; 9am-9pm Thur.* ***Map*** *p96 H11* ❻ *Food & drink*

Beloved of expats, this is the place where Yanks can get their hands on chocolate chips, homesick Brits can source Christmas puddings and sentimental Australians can score Vegemite.

Hester van Eeghen

Hartenstraat 37 (020 626 9211, https://hestervaneeghen.com). Tram 2, 11, 12, 13, 17. ***Open*** *1-6pm Mon; 11am-6pm Tue-Sat; noon-5pm Sun.* ***Map*** *p96 H9* ❽ *Accessories*

With a dazzling array of accessories, shoes and infamous bags, this shop is a perfect point of call for a special and unique gift you can't replicate in an airport store. The thousands of colours and hundreds of models are the handy work of talented Dutch designer Hester van Eeghen. **Other location** Nieuwe Spiegelstraat 32.

I Love Vintage

Prinsengracht 201 (020 330 1950, www.ilovevintage.nl). Tram 2, 11, 12, 13, 17. ***Open*** *11am-7pm Mon-Sat; noon-5pm Sun.* ***Map*** *p96 H7* ❾ *Fashion*

There are few vintage stores that combine class with affordability and spot-on service. All in all, it's like stepping into your mum's dressing-up box, but everything fits and you won't resemble a bag lady on exiting.

King Louie

Hartenstraat 10-13 (020 344 9390, www.kinglouie.nl). Tram 2, 11, 12, 13, 17. ***Open*** *10am-6.30pm Mon; 9am-6.30pm Tue, Wed, Fri, Sat; 9am-9pm Thu; noon-6.30pm Sun.* ***Map*** *p96 H9* ❿ *Fashion*

King Louie

the Otherist

Owners Ann and George started making their own vintage-oriented knitwear under the King Louie label while running quirky vintage store Exota in this location. The brand is now stocked worldwide, but it began right here in Amsterdam.

Laura Dols

*Wolvenstraat 7 (020 624 9066, www.lauradols.nl). Tram 2, 11, 12. **Open** 11am-6pm Mon-Wed, Sat; 11am-7pm Thu, Fri; noon-6pm Sun. **Map** p96 H10 ⓫ Fashion*

When Jean Paul Gaultier, Viktor & Rolf and Susan Sarandon regularly pop into your store, you know you're on to something good. This place is jam-packed with 1950s-style wedding, ballroom and Hollywood glitter gear.

meCHICas

*Gasthuismolensteeg 11 (020 420 3092, mechicas.com). Tram 2, 11, 12, 13, 17. **Open** 11am-6pm Mon-Wed, Fri, Sat; 11am-7.30pm Thu; noon-6pm Sun. **Map** p96 J9 ⓬ Jewellery*

'Ornaments with soul' is how this unique Mexican-inspired boutique describes its offering, and it's a fitting label. The collections combine different materials – including beads and stones – into handcrafted bracelets, necklaces and earrings. It also sells matchboxes from its own studio.

❤ the Otherist

*Leliegracht 6 (020 320 0420, www.otherist.com). Tram 13, 17. **Open** 11am-6pm Tue-Sat. Closed Mon, Sun. **Map** p96 J8 ⓭ Gifts & souvenirs*

If you are out to stock your own cabinet of curiosities or looking for the ultimate unique gift, the Otherist is alternative-shopping heaven: glass eyeballs, 'vegan mini-skulls', butterfly specimens, amulets, hip flasks, medical posters and an ever-changing selection of other curiosa and handmade design items. Indeed: embrace 'the other'.

❤ Relaxed at Home

*Huidenstraat 19 (020 320 2001). Tram 2, 11, 12. **Open** noon-6pm Mon, Sun; 10am-6pm Tue-Sat. **Map** p96 H10 ⓰ Fashion & furniture*

The versatile store owners of Relaxed at Home have made theirs a true one-stop-shop, stocking everything from clothing and fashion accessories to interior design gems – including furniture and paintings. A great place to indulge in a bit of retail therapy after all of that history-heavy sightseeing.

► *For more on the fabulous Nine Streets, see p101.*

Sauna Deco

*Herengracht 115 (020 623 8215, www.saunadeco.nl). Tram 2, 11, 12, 13, 17. **Open** noon-11pm Mon, Wed-Sat; 3-11pm Tue; 1-7pm Sun. **Admission** from €20 (off peak). **Map** p96 J7 ⓲ Health & beauty*

This beautiful art deco sauna provides facilities for a Turkish bath, Finnish sauna and cold plunge bath. There's also a solarium. Massages, shiatsu and beauty and skincare treatments are all available by appointment. Mixed bathing only.

Westermarkt

*Westerstraat (no phone). Tram 3, 5 or bus 18, 21. **Open** 9am-1pm Mon. **No cards**. **Map** p96 H8 ⓳ Market*

A Monday market selling all sorts of stuff. The people packing the pavement are proof of the reasonable prices and range of goods, including new watches, pretty (and not so pretty) fabrics and cheap clothes.

SOUTHERN CANAL BELT

Around Rembrandtplein

Previously called Reguliersmarkt (Regular Market), this square was renamed in honour of Rembrandt in 1876; his statue – the oldest in the city – stands in the centre of the gardens, surrounded by more recent statues depicting *The Night Watch*, all gazing in the direction of the Jewish quarter. Though there's no longer a market, it's still the centre of commercial activity, with a wild profusion of neon lights, and a cacophony of music blaring out from the cafés, bars, restaurants and clubs on all sides. Unashamedly tacky, the square is home to a variety of establishments, from the faded and fake elegance of the traditional striptease parlours to nondescript cafés, but there are a few exceptions to the air of tawdriness – places such as the grand café **De Kroon** (no.17), the art deco **Schiller** (no.24) and HL de Jong's crazily colourful dream-as-reality masterpiece, cinema **Pathé Tuschinski** (*see p208*).

Head west from here and you'll end up at Muntplein, by the floating flower market, Bloemenmarkt, at the southern tip of Singel. Established in 1862, the **Bloemenmarkt** (*see p113*) sells tulips of every imaginable colour, as well as gaudy gifts and souvenirs. Over on the corner of the Amstel are some lively gay cafés and bars, and on the façade of Amstel 216, the city's freakiest graffiti. The '**House with the Bloodstains**' was home to former mayor Coenraad van Beuningen (1622-93), whose brilliance was eclipsed by insanity. After seeing visions of fireballs and fluorescent coffins above the Reguliersgracht, he scrawled sailing ships, stars, strange symbols, and his and his wife's names – allegedly with his own blood – on the grey stone walls. Subsequent attempts to scrub off the stains have all proved futile.

From Rembrandtplein, walk south along the shopping and eating street Utrechtsestraat, or explore Reguliersgracht and Amstelveld.

The canals

As the first canal to be dug in the glory days, Herengracht (named after the 'gentlemen' who initially invested in it) attracted the richest of merchants, and the southern stretch is where you'll find the most stately and overblown houses on any of Amsterdam's canals. The **Museum Willet-Holthuysen** (*see p110*) is a classic example of such a 17th-century mansion.

However, it's on the 'Golden Bend' – the stretch between Leidsestraat and Vijzelstraat – that things really get out of hand. By then, the rich saw the advantage of buying two adjoining lots so that they could build as wide as they built high. Excess defines the Louis XIV style of Herengracht 475, while tales of pre-rock 'n' roll exuberance are often told about no.527, whose interior was trashed by Peter the Great while he was here learning to be a ship's carpenter and picking up urban ideas for his dream city, St Petersburg.

Home to the **Stadsarchief Amsterdam** (*see p110*), the imposing Gebouw de Bazel building is round the corner on Vijzelstraat. Meanwhile, mischievous types annoy the mayor by mooring up on his personal dock before the official Herengracht 502 residence.

It's a similarly grand story on this southern section of Keizersgracht (named after Holy Roman Emperor Maximilian I). For evidence, pop into the **Museum van Loon** (*see p110*) or photography museum **Foam** (*see p111*). But for an alternative view of this area, head to Kerkstraat, parallel to and directly between Keizersgracht and Prinsengracht. The houses here are less grand, but what they lack in swank they more than make up for in funkiness, with their galleries and shops only adding to the community feel. The pleasant oasis of Amstelveld helps, too, with **Amstelkerk** – the white wooden church that once took a break from sacred duties to act as a stable for Napoleon's horses – worth a look. Also stop for refreshment at **NEL** (Amstelveld 12, 020 626 1199, brasserienel.nl), which has perhaps the most scenic terrace in the city.

Head east along Kerkstraat and you'll find the **Magerebrug** ('Skinny Bridge'), the most photographed bridge in the city and one said to have been built in the 17th century by two sisters living on opposite sides of the Amstel who wanted an easy way to get together for morning coffee. If you cross it and go down Nieuwe Kerkstraat, you'll get to **Plantage** (*see p157*). Alternatively, turn right at Amstel and right again down Prinsengracht to see more grand canal houses and the **Pijpenkabinet** (Pipe Cabinet, Prinsengracht 488, 020 421 1779, www.pijpenkabinet.nl) and its 2,000-plus exhibits of all things tobacco – yes, tobacco.

In the know
Boating about

If you're pressed for time but don't want to forego an authentic Amsterdam experience, use the canal boats to take you from the outskirts of the Grachtengordel near the Rijksmuseum to the Bloemenmarkt or Anne Frank House in the Western Belt. If you can rally a few people to make use of the group discount, all the better.

Sights & museums

Museum van Loon

Keizersgracht 672 (020 624 5255, www. museumvanloon.nl). Tram 24. ***Open*** *10am-5pm daily.* ***Admission*** *€10; €5.50 reductions; free under-6s, Iamsterdam, MK.* ***Map*** *p96 K12.*

Few interiors of Amsterdam's grand canal houses have been preserved in anything approaching their original state, but the former van Loon residence is one that has. Designed by Adriaan Dortsman, it was originally the home of artist Ferdinand Bol. Hendrik van Loon bought it in 1884 and it was opened as a museum in 1973. The terrifically grand mid-18th-century interior and Louis XIV and XV decor is a delight. So is the art. There's a collection of family portraits from the 17th to the 20th centuries; Ram Katzir's striking sculpture *There*; and a modern art show every two years.

Museum Willet-Holthuysen

Herengracht 605 (020 523 1822, www. willetholthuysen.nl). Tram 4, 14. ***Open*** *10am-5pm daily.* ***Admission*** *€12.50; €10 reductions; free under-18s, Iamsterdam, MK.* ***Map*** *p96 L11.*

This 17th-century mansion was purchased in the 1850s by the Willet-Holthuysen family. When Abraham, remembered as 'the Oscar Wilde of Amsterdam', died in 1889, his wife Sandrina Louisa, a hermaphrodite, left the house and its contents to the city on the condition it was preserved and opened as a museum. The family had followed the fashion of the time and decorated it in the neo-Louis XVI style: it's densely furnished, with an impressive collection of rare objets d'art, glassware, silver, fine china and paintings – including a portrait of a rather shocked-looking Abraham (painted on his honeymoon, perhaps?).

Stadsarchief Amsterdam

Vijzelstraat 32 (020 251 1511, www. amsterdam.nl/stadsarchief). Tram 24. ***Open*** *10am-5pm Tue-Fri; noon-5pm Sat, Sun.* ***Admission*** *General admission free. Temporary exhibitions €7.50; €5 reductions; free under-12s, Iamsterdam, MK.* ***Map*** *p96 K12.*

The city archives are located in an epic and decorative 1926 building that's shrouded in esoteric mystery. The highly ornate structure was designed by architect KPC de Bazel, a practitioner of Theosophy – a spiritualist movement founded by the chain-smoking Madame Blavatsky. The grand centrepiece is the Treasure Room. As embellished as Tutankhamun's Tomb, it displays the prizes of the collection. The archives also host exhibitions and film screenings. There is an excellent bookstore and café.

Museum Willet Holthuysen

Tassenmuseum Hendrikje

Herengracht 573 (020 524 6452, www. tassenmuseum.nl). Tram 4, 14, 24. ***Open*** *10am-5pm daily.* ***Admission*** *€13; €4-€10 reductions; free under-6s, Iamsterdam, MK.* ***Map*** *p96 L12.*

The Museum of Bags & Purses is the world's largest collection of its kind, with a total of over 4,500 bags and purses on show: everything from coin purses made of human hair to a Lieber rhinestone collectible named 'Socks' after Hillary Clinton's cat.

Restaurants & cafés

Buffet van Odette €€

Prinsengracht 598 (020 423 6034, www. buffet-amsterdam.nl). Tram 1, 7, 19. ***Open*** *noon-midnight, Wed-Mon.* ***Map*** *p96 J13* ❷ *Café*

A café that's so healthy it's sinful. Service is slow, but the food is worth the wait, whether you choose a hearty sandwich – made with bread from local bakery **Hartog** (Ruyschstraat 56, East, 020 665 1295) – a salad or a homemade cake. For lunch, opt for one of their famous truffle cheese omelettes, or the 'buffet plate' – a fresh selection of vegetable dishes and salads. They've just opened a two-room B&B upstairs as well, should you wish to enjoy their hospitality overnight.

Greenwoods €€

Keizersgracht 465 (020 420 4330, greenwords.eu). Tram 2, 11, 12. ***Open*** *9.30am-4pm, Mon-Thu; 9.30am-4.30pm Fri, Sat.* ***Map*** *p96 J11* ❺ *Café*

Top 20

❤ Foam

Keizersgracht 609 (020 551 6500, www.foam.org). Tram 24. ***Open*** *10am-6pm Mon-Wed, Sat, Sun; 10am-9pm Thur, Fri.* ***Admission*** *€12.50; €8.50-€9.50 reductions; free under-12s, Iamsterdam, MK.* ***Map*** *p96 K12.*

In comparison to the big tourist magnets Rijksmuseum (*see p140*) and the Van Gogh Museum (*see p142*), which welcome millions of visitors through their doors every year, the photography museum – which has 200,000 annual visitors – is relatively small. But what it lacks in size it certainly makes up for with the high quality of its exhibited talent.

Located in a tightly renovated 150-year-old canal house, the progressive museum displays everything from still photography to interactive and immersive installations. And don't be fooled by its narrow exterior, Foam's interior is characterised by an effortless combination of original architecture and modern chrome and glass, which exudes space and calm. Large white walls highlight the power of the exhibits over the jam-packed three floors.

Foam's programme rotates on a fairly regular basis – typically every two to four months – and features a comprehensive array of talent, from rising local stars such as Viviane Sassen to big names including Diane Arbus and Chinese contemporary artist and activist Ai Weiwei, who captured the reality of modern-day refugees with an iPhone for his 2016 #SafePassage exhibition.

The museum sells limited-edition photographs, organises workshops and also publishes its own magazine. It collaborates with MTV each year to champion burgeoning creative talent. If you're feeling peckish, the basement café's food is a feast for the eyes as well as the stomach.

► *Check the website for details of exhibitions, free guided tours and pop-ups in other locations.*

Service at this English tearoom is friendly but can be slow. Everything is freshly made, though – cakes, scones, muffins and their famous Irish soda bread are baked daily on the premises – so it's understandable. In summer, sit on the terrace by the canal for the ultimate alfresco eating experience. **Other location** Singel 103 (020 623 7071).

❤ Guts & Glory €€€€

Utrechtsestraat 6 (020 362 0030, www.bredagroup-amsterdam.com/guts). Tram 4, 14. ***Open*** *noon-3pm, 6-10pm daily.* ***Map*** *p96 L11* ⑦ *International*

If you fancy a meal with a side of surprise, Guts & Glory should be your first point of call. The versatile bar/restaurant offers a set dinner menu with either five or seven 'chapters', each inspired by a different culture or country. The chapters cover chicken, fish, vegetables, beef and pork – so bring an appetite. Its sister restaurant at Singel 210, **Breda** (020 622 5233, www.breda-amsterdam.com) serves innovative menus for serious foodies.

Lion Noir €€€

Reguliersdwarsstraat 28 (020 627 6603, www.lionnoir.nl). Tram 2, 11, 12, 24. ***Open*** *6pm-1am Mon; noon-2.30pm, 6pm-1am Tue-Thur; noon-2.30pm, 6pm-3am Fri, Sat; noon-2.30pm, 6pm-1am Sun. Kitchen closes at 10pm* ***Map*** *p96 J11* ⑨ *French*

The emphasis at Lion Noir is firmly on meat and seafood, with hearty but not overwhelming mains, including guinea fowl with truffle gnocchi and sea bass fillet with paella. The velvet and artfully weather-beaten leather furnishings, stuffed birds and (yes) ornamental dog skeletons, combined with the genetically perfect staff, give the impression of an Abercrombie & Fitch shoot curated by Tim Burton.

Los Pilones €€

Kerkstraat 63 (020 320 4651, www.lospilones.com). Tram 2, 11, 12. ***Open*** *4-10pm Mon; noon-10pm Tue-Sun.* ***Map*** *p96 H12* ⑩ *Mexican*

A splendid Mexican cantina with an anarchic bent, Los Pilones is run by three young and friendly Mexican brothers, one of whom does the cooking, so expect authentic food rather than standard Tex-Mex fare. **Other locations** Kerkstraat 59 (020 331 3780); Geldersekade 111, Old Centre (020 776 0210).

Segugio €€€

Utrechtsestraat 96 (020 330 1503, www.segugio.nl). Tram 4. ***Open*** *6-10pm Tue-Sat.* ***Map*** *p96 L13* ⑫ *Italian*

Best. Risotto. Ever. A delightful variety of fresh ingredients and flavour combinations embellish and embolden this most comforting of dishes. There are pastas, soups, meat and fish dishes on offer too. In fact, this Italian restaurant has all the elements to make the perfect lingering meal for both foodies and romantics.

Stach Food €

Nieuwe Spiegelstraat 52 (020 737 2679, www.stach-food.nl). Tram 1, 7, 19. ***Open*** *8am-9pm daily.* ***Map*** *p96 J12* ⑬ *Sandwiches*

A healthy takeaway shop on the antique and art gallery strip. Sandwiches, salads and full meals – with a tiny coffee bar in the back. **Other locations** throughout the city.

Tempo Doeloe €€€

Utrechtsestraat 75 (020 625 6718, www.tempodoeloerestaurant.nl). Tram 4. ***Open*** *6pm-midnight Mon-Sat.* ***Map*** *p96 L12* ⑭ *Indonesian*

This cosy and rather classy Indonesian restaurant (heck, it even has white linen) is widely thought to serve the city's best and spiciest *rijsttafel* ('rice table'), a local speciality, and not without good reason. It's best to book ahead, but if you want to go spontaneously, try Friday or Saturday lunchtime – just bring a healthy appetite.

Van Dobben €

Korte Reguliersdwarsstraat 5-9 (020 624 4200, www.eetsalonvandobben.nl). Tram 4, 14, 24. ***Open*** *10am-9pm Mon-Wed; 10am-1am Thur; 10am-2am Fri, Sat; 10.30am-8pm Sun.* ***No cards.*** ***Map*** *p96 K11* ⑮ *Dutch*

A *kroket* is the national version of a croquette: a melange of meat and potato with a crusty, deep-fried skin, best served on a bun with lots of hot mustard. This 1945-era late-nighter is the uncontested champion of *kroket* shops.

Bars

De Balie

Kleine Gartmanplantsoen 10 (020 553 5151, www.debalie.nl). Tram 1, 2, 5, 11, 12. ***Open*** *9am-midnight Mon-Thu; 9am-2am Fri; 10am-2am Sat; 10am-11pm Sun.* ***Map*** *p96 G12* ❷

Theatre, new media, photography, cinema and literary events sit alongside lectures, debates and discussions about social and political issues at this influential centre – which was formerly a 19th-century courthouse – for the local intelligentsia. Throw in a café too, and you've got healthy food for both mind and body.

Café Brecht

Weteringschans 157 (020 627 2211, www.cafebrecht.nl). Tram 1, 7, 19 or Metro Vijzelgracht. ***Open*** *11am-1am Mon-Thur, Sun; 11am-3am Fri, sat.* ***Map*** *p96 J14* ❸

Café Brecht is designed to look like a Berlin living room from the 1970s; the shabby, mismatched sofas and antique lamps are all part of the charm. The constantly changing selection of German beers is great, as are the huge pretzels, freshly baked and hung over the bar to tempt hungry drinkers.

Door 74

Reguilersdwarsstraat 741 (020 63 404 5122, www.door-74.com). Tram 24. ***Open*** *8pm-3am Mon-Thur, Sun; 8pm-4am Fri, Sat.* ***Map*** *p96 K11* ❻

'Exclusivity' may be a dirty word in Amsterdam's strenuously egalitarian bar scene, but rather than using inflated prices, long queues or grumpy doormen as its filter, Door 74 employs secrecy – and rewards in-the-know trendies with excellent cocktails mixed by some of the best barmen in the business. Make a reservation via text or online to guarantee entry into the unassuming-looking bar.

❤ Whisky Café L&B

Korte Leidsedwarsstraat 82-84 (020 625 2387, www.lbwhiskyproeverijen.nl). Tram 1, 7, 19. ***Open*** *8pm-3am Mon-Thu; 5pm-4am Fri, Sat; 5pm-3am Sun.* ***Map*** *p96 H12* ❼

If a whisky exists, chances are Léon Elshoff has procured a bottle for his charming little bar a few minutes walk from Leidseplein. There are over 2,100 to choose from, with a particularly good range of Japanese whiskies and some super-rare Scottish malts. A fine selection of other booze is available for those not seduced by the water of life.

Shops & services

❤ Art Unlimited

Keizersgracht 510 (020 624 8419, www.artnl.com). Tram 2, 11, 12. ***Open*** *noon-6pm Mon, Sun; 10.15am-6pm Tue-Sat.* ***Map*** *p96 H11* ❷ *Gifts & souvenirs*

The most comprehensive collection of international photographs and posters in the Netherlands, and the largest collection of postcards in Western Europe. The typography posters are good for tourists seeking a unique memento.

❤ Bloemenmarkt

Singel, between Muntplein & Koningsplein. Tram 2, 4, 11, 12, 14, 24. ***Open*** *9am-5.30pm Mon-Sat; 11am-5.30pm Sun.* ***No cards. Map*** *p96 J11* ❸ *Market*

This fascinating collage of colour is the world's only floating flower market, with 15 florists and garden shops (although many also hawk cheesy souvenirs these days) permanently ensconced on barges along the southern side of Singel. The plants and flowers usually last well and are good value.

Galerie Akinci

Lijnbaansgracht 317 (020 638 0480, www.akinci.nl). Tram 1, 4, 7, 14, 19, 24 or Metro Vijzelgracht ***Open*** *1-6pm Tue-Sat.* ***Map*** *p96 K13* ❼ *Gallery*

Part of a row of connected galleries on Lijnbaansgracht, Akinci thrives on surprising its visitors, hosting five or six exhibitions a year that employ every contemporary art medium, with a slightly political aesthetic and a bent towards feminist interpretations.

❤ Property Of

Utrechtsestraat 18a (020 845 5372, www.thepropertyof.com). Tram 4, 14. ***Open*** *11am-6.30pm Mon-Sat; noon-6pm Sun.* ***Map*** *p96 L12* ⓮ *Leather goods*

Founded in 2006 as an alternative to boring leather briefcases and hiking backpacks, Property Of makes bags, wallets and leather goods for contemporary urban workers. Endlessly stylish, their clean, timeless aesthetic is an antidote to the endless Fjällräven and Herschel bags you see draped over young urbanites' shoulders.

❤ Public House of Art

Nieuwe Spiegelstraat 39 (020 221 3680, www.publichouseofart.com). Tram 1, 4, 7, 14, 19. ***Open*** *noon-6pm Mon, Sun; 10am-6pm Tue-Sat.* ***Map*** *p96 J12* ⓯ *Art*

Art enthusiasts eat your hearts out. The makers of this creative paradise believe 'art is for all – to disrupt not bankrupt'. Remarkable photography, digital art and paintings are available here, starting at €100 per print. It works in three price tiers – Villa, Mansion, and Castle – to suit all preferences (and budgets). Artworks are curated and based on bi-annual themes.

Salon de Lingerie

Utrechtsestraat 38 (020 623 9857, www.salondelingerie.nl). Tram 4, 14. ***Open*** *10am-6pm Tue-Sat.* ***Map*** *p96 L12* ⓱ *Accessories*

Find sultry lingerie brands such as Andres Sarda, Empreinte, Marie Jo and Freyja, and the kind of staff who can determine if you've been wearing the wrong-sized bra for a decade.

Jordaan & the West

Charming narrow streets and flower-lined canals make Jordaan, in many ways, the quintessential Amsterdam neighbourhood. Atmospheric and bohemian, the area is a higgledy-piggledy mix of old buildings, densely packed housing and the occasional eyesore, which combine to create an eclectic and chilled-out feel that is hard to resist. Artists, students and young entrepreneurs have long gravitated here, establishing the area's reputation as a centre for art and the creative industries and slowly diluting its working-class roots. Such gentrification has, of course, left its mark; quaint boutiques, stylish restaurants, hip cafes, and modern gallery spaces abound, and property here is highly desirable. But despite the changes, the folk of Jordaan maintain their laid-back lifestyle and jealously guard their quirky sense of identity.

Northwest of the Jordaan, the Westerpark has been wholly reinvigorated by the conversion of an old gasworks into cultural hotspot Westergasfabriek, whose clubs, restaurants and performance venues have breathed creative energy into the area.

❤ Don't miss

1 A stroll through the Jordaan *p120*
Get your creative juices flowing with a wander through the back streets.

2 Westergasfabriek *p132*
Industrial past and an artistic future.

3 Noordermarkt *p124*
Old-world flea market held every Monday morning.

4 Haarlemmerdijk *p130*
Quirky and cool shopping opportunities galore.

5 Winkel 43 *p122*
Sample the best apple pie in the city.

Bloemgracht

❤ Time to eat & drink

Arty coffee
Cloud Gallery Amsterdam *p127*

Beer from a brown café
Café Nol *p123*, 't Smalle *p123*

Ethiopian spice
Semhar *p122*

Fishy feast
Pesca *p127*

Sweet treat
Winkel 43 *p122*

❤ Time to shop

Funky fashion
Tenue de Nimes *p128*

High-end design
Moooi *p124*

Quirky collectables
Antiekcentrum Amsterdam *p128*, Noordermarkt *p124*, Westermarkt *p126*

Vintage clothes
Jutka & Riska *p133*, Lena the Fashion Library *p124*

Vinyl and veg
Flesch Records *p124*

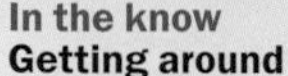

In the know
Getting around

Public transport through the Jordaan itself is limited due to the narrow streets. The area is best accessed on foot from the Rozengracht, which is reached via tram 13, 17, or bus 284. Get to Westerpark via tram 5 or bus 21 from Centraal.

Noordermarkt

JORDAAN & THE WEST

Restaurants & cafés

1. De Aardige Pers *p118*
2. Balthazar's Keuken *p127*
3. 't Blaauwhooft *p130*
4. Café-Restaurant Amsterdam *p131*
5. Cloud Gallery Amsterdam *p127*
6. Comestibles Kinders *p118*
7. Duende *p119*
8. De Gouden Reael *p131*
9. Gs Really Nice Place *p119*
10. Moeders *p127*
11. Mossel & Gin *p131*
12. La Oliva Pintxos y Vinos *p119*
13. Pesca *p127*
14. REM Island *p131*
15. Semhar *p122*
16. SLA *p122*
17. Small World Catering
18. Toscanini *p122*
19. WestergasTerras *p131*
20. Winkel 43 *p122*
21. YamYam Trattoria Pizzeria *p122*

Bars

1. Café Hegeraad *p122*
2. Café Kobalt *p131*
3. Café Nol *p123*
4. Café Sound Garden *p127*
5. De Nieuwe Anita *p123*
6. Papeneiland *p123*
7. 't Smalle *p123*
8. Struik *p127*
9. De Twee Zwaantjes *p123*
10. Vesper Bar *p131*
11. Waterkant *p127*

Coffeeshops

1. Barney's *p133*
2. La Tertulia *p128*

Shops & services

1. Antiekcentrum Amsterdam *p128*
2. Chocolátl *p128*
3. Delicious Food *p123*
4. Les Deux Frères *p128*
5. Distortion Records *p123*
6. Flesch Records *p124*
7. HJ van de Kerkhof *p128*
8. Jutka & Riska *p133*
9. KochxBos Gallery *p124*
10. Lena the Fashion Library *p124*
11. Moooi *p124*
12. Noordermarkt *p124*
13. Papabubble *p133*
14. Store Without A Home *p133*
15. Tenue de Nîmes *p128*
16. Wegewijs *p130*
17. Westerstraat markt *p126*

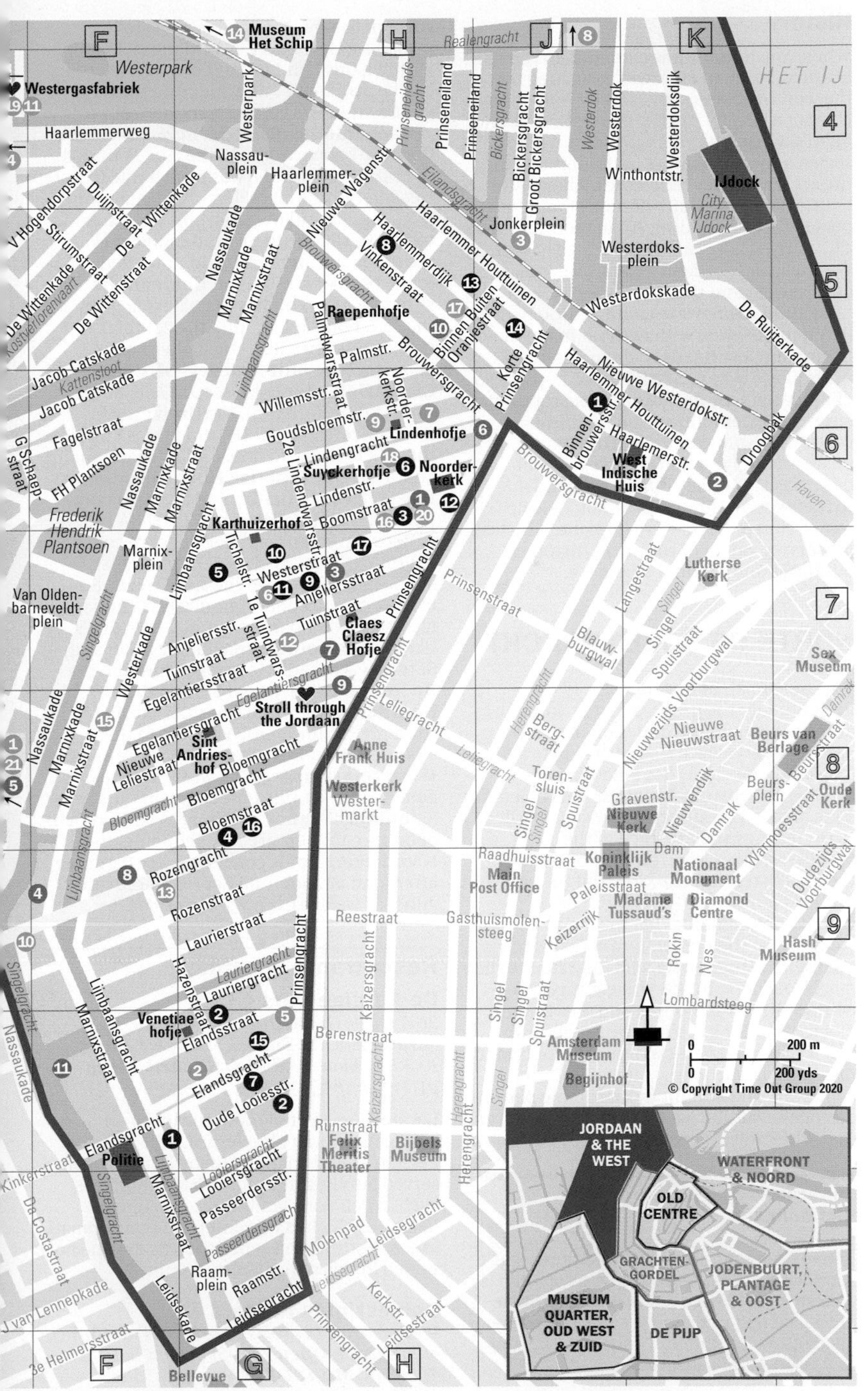

Museum Het Schip
Westerpark
Westergasfabriek
Haarlemmerweg
Nassauplein
Haarlemmerplein
Realengracht
HET IJ
IJdock
City Marina IJdock
Westerdoksplein
Westerdokskade
De Ruijterkade
Jonkerplein
Raepenhofje
Lindenhofje
Suyckerhofje
Noorderkerk
Karthuizerhof
West Indische Huis
Claes Claesz Hofje
Stroll through the Jordaan
Sint Andrieshof
Anne Frank Huis
Westerkerk
Westermarkt
Lutherse Kerk
Sex Museum
Beurs van Berlage
Oude Kerk
Nieuwe Kerk
Koninklijk Paleis
Nationaal Monument
Madame Tussaud's
Diamond Centre
Main Post Office
Hash Museum
Venetiae hofje
Politie
Amsterdam Museum
Begijnhof
Felix Meritis Theater
Bijbels Museum
Bellevue
Prinsengracht
Keizersgracht
Herengracht
Singel
Rozengracht
Bloemgracht
Egelantiersgracht
Lijnbaansgracht
Marnixstraat
Leidsegracht
Leidseplein
200 m
200 yds
© Copyright Time Out Group 2020
JORDAAN & THE WEST
WATERFRONT & NOORD
OLD CENTRE
GRACHTENGORDEL
JODENBUURT, PLANTAGE & OOST
MUSEUM QUARTER, OUD WEST & ZUID
DE PIJP

History

When Amsterdam was extended in the 17th century, Jordaan emerged as an area for the working classes and smelly industries, characterised by its tiny houses, slums and open sewers. The years to follow would see an enormous influx of immigrants to the area, as it grew to provide a haven for political refugees and victims of religious persecution, including Huguenots and Jews. The narrow houses were overloaded with big families, and Jordaan's canals were used as both sewers and thoroughfares.

By 1900, there were about 80,000 people living in the area, with the vast majority having modest financial circumstances. After World War II, Jordaan had become so dilapidated that the authorities proposed large-scale demolition and rebuilding as the only solution, a measure that, unsurprisingly, its feisty, independent denizens vigorously opposed. Thanks to their successful protests, small-scale renovation projects were implanted instead, preserving much of the area's historical buildings and original character.

NORTH OF ROZENGRACHT

The area north of Rozengracht is undoubtedly the prettiest in the Jordaan and an excellent introduction to the neighbourhood as it's so easy to get pleasantly lost in. Little lanes and alleys link the already quiet main streets in a mazy haze, and it's no surprise that such chilled surroundings shelter some of the city's best cafés. For a leisurely tour of some of the area's streets, *see p120* Stroll through the Jordaan.

It's widely claimed that the name 'Jordaan' comes from the French *jardin* (garden) via the French Huguenots who migrated to the neighbourhood in the 17th century. Peek behind the grand houses and apartment blocks that flank the nearby canals and you'll see why: there's a multitude of tranquil residential courtyards, known in Dutch as *hofjes*. Originally built by charitable patrons during the Middle Ages for elderly women and the vulnerable, these almshouses now form some of the most desirable spots to live, providing the luxury of verdant seclusion within a busy and vibrant city. Private tours can be arranged, but wandering them on your own preserves the tranquil feel.

Raepenhofje (Palmgracht 28-38) is one of the best-known *hofjes* in the city. Founded in 1648, Raepenhofje was once home to the treasurer of the city, Pieter Adriaanszoon Raep, and is still owned by his descendants today. To the south on Lindengracht is the gorgeous **Suyckerhofje**, squeezed at the back of no.149, and **Lindenhofje** at nos.94-112, which is the oldest *hofje* in the city. Founded in 1616, the complex is now a children's hospital. Other notable *hofjes* include **Sint-Andrieshof**, **Claes ClaeszHofje** (for both, *see p120* Stroll through the Jordaan), **Karthuizerhof** (Karthuizerstraat 21-31), which was built in the 17th century to house widows and their children, and **Venetiae Hofje** (Elandsstraat 104-142), which lies behind a simple door marked with large letters 'VENETIA'.

Between scenic sightseeing or decadent daytime beers, check out the specialist shops tucked away in the side streets. Some of the city's best outdoor markets can also be found nearby: Monday morning's bargainous **Noordermarkt** (*see p124*) and Saturday's paradise of organic produce, **Boerenmarkt**, are held around the **Noorderkerk** church (*see p121*, Stroll through the Jordaan). Adjacent to the Noordermarkt is the equally bargain-packed **Westermarkt** (*see p126*), while another general market fills Lindengracht on Saturdays. For those wishing to add a pinch of culture to their grocery shopping, the Noorderkerk holds concerts every Saturday afternoon at 2pm (mid September to mid June) as well as evening performances.

In the know
Hofje-hopping

Remember that the art of *hofje*-hopping is a gamble, because entrances are sometimes locked in deference to the residents. Take a chance and you may be surprised by the delights inside, but don't peer through the windows – that's just rude.

Restaurants & cafés

De Aardige Pers €€

2e Hugo de Grootstraat 13 (400 3107, www.aardigepers.nl). Tram 3, 5. ***Open*** *4.30-10.30pm Mon, Wed-Sun.* ***No cards. Map*** *p117 off map* ❶ Persian

Located just west of the Jordaan, on an emerging culinary boulevard, 'The Nice Persian' is aptly named. Enjoy Iranian cuisine served family-style and with family grace, such as delicious lamb with *sabzi* (green herbs), or chicken in walnut and pomegranate sauce. A surprising experience for anyone not versed in this rich culinary culture.

Comestibles Kinders €

Westerstraat 189 (020 622 7983). Tram 3, 5 or bus 18, 21. ***Open*** *7am-5pm Mon-Sat; 9am-4pm Sun.* ***Map*** *p117 G7* ❻ Sandwiches

Brienenhofje, Prinsengracht 133

The best sandwich shop in the Jordaan? Decide over a *bolgeri* with chicken fillet, bacon, pesto, lettuce, mayo and some secret herbs for less than a fiver. There's also a tempting spread of other options.

Duende €€

Lindengracht 62 (020 420 6692, www.cafe-duende.nl). Tram 3. ***Open*** *4pm-midnight Mon-Fri; noon-midnight Sat; 2pm-midnight Sun.* ***Map*** *p117 H6* 7 *Spanish*

Get a real taste of Andalucía with fine tapas at Duende, the city's oldest tapas bar. Be prepared to share your table with an amorous couple or, perhaps, one of the flamenco dancers who might offer you a free lesson before getting up to stamp and strut. It exercises a strict 'always welcome' policy, so doesn't take bookings.

Gs Really Nice Place €€

Goudsbloemstraat 91 (www.reallyniceplace.com). Tram 3. ***Open*** *10am-4pm Thur-Sun.* ***Map*** *p117 H6* 9 *Café*

Resembling a Hipstamatic version of a 'brown café' (all letterpress fonts and vintage crockery), Gs is a bar that serves a first-rate brunch on weekends and hosts quirky pop-up events. It also happens to mix a cracking Bloody Mary – a food group in itself, according to the owner. Hours can vary and extra events can happen spontaneously, so check ahead on the website and book via email. Gs has a branch in De Pijp and also runs a brunch boat, for breakfast with a canal-side view (*see p105*).

La Oliva Pintxos y Vinos €€€

Egelantiersstraat 122-124 (020 320 4316, www.laoliva.nl). Tram 3, 10. ***Open*** *noon-10pm Mon-Wed, Sun; noon-11pm Thur-Sat.* ***Map*** *p117 G7* 12 *Spanish*

From yuppies to genuine Spaniards, many praise La Oliva's authentic Cantabrian-Basque food and tapas, as well as the rich selection of wines by the glass. If it's too busy (and there's a good chance it will be, so book ahead), there are plenty of other restaurants along this strip, nicknamed 'Little Italy'.

❤ Stroll through the Jordaan

True to form as an artistic neighbourhood, the Jordaan is hailed as one of the most charming and romantic parts of the city. Whether it's the flowers in window boxes, the intriguing street art, the seemingly infinite number of brown bars or the colourful history, the area lures both locals and curious tourists to its enticing streets all year round.

For a walk that takes in a selection of interesting local landmarks, shops and cafés, as well as the most scenic streets and canals, start at **Bloemgracht** and follow what is arguably the most beautiful canal in the Jordaan. Take in its varied façades and well-maintained canal houses. The three houses that make up nos.87-91 (on the south side of the canal) date back to 1642 and are an excellent example of 17th-century Amsterdam architecture. They are known as **De Drie Hendricken** (the Three Hendricken) because of their three gable stones depicting a city-dweller, farmer and sailor.

Cross the canal at Tweede Leliedwarsstraat, heading north for some full-on Amsterdam weirdness at **Electric Ladyland** (Tweede Leliedwarsstraat 5, 020 420 3776, www.electric-lady-land.com). It's the first museum in the world dedicated to the art, science and history of fluorescent colours. Just round the corner at nos.107-145 Egelantiersgracht, there's the altogether more peaceful **Sint-Andrieshof**, a good example of the Jordaan's secret courtyards (*see p118* Hofje Hopping). Push hard on the door to open and take a seat on one of the benches to absorb the silence away from the bustle outside.

Continue east up Egelantiersgracht as far as the picturesque **Hilletjesbrug**. Cross and continue up the canal on the opposite side until you reach **'t Smalle** (*see p123*). Set on a small canal, it's where Peter Hoppe (of Hoppe & Jenever, the world's first makers of gin) founded his distillery in 1780. It's so charming that the Japanese have built an exact replica of 't Smalle in Nagasaki's Holland Village. Further on you'll find an unassuming red-brick building which houses **Claes ClaeszHofje** (Egelantiersdwarsstraat 1-5). The complex, which covers a large part of the block, hides four charming courtyards behind its walls. The first garden has a fountain with a lion's head. These courtyards date to 1626 and are always open to the public.

Carry on past pretty boutiques, cosy cafés and quirky galleries, including **KochxBos**

Bloemgracht

Noorderkerk

Gallery (*see p124*), taking a right on to Westerstraat. For an energy boost stop off at **Winkel 43** (*see p122*) – it's famous for its apple pie, which is reportedly the best in town. This should set you up to explore **Noorderkerk** (North Church), opposite. The Protestant church was built in 1623 and its plain exterior matches the traditionally working-class Jordaan parishioners. Outside the main entrance there's a sculpture of three figures bound together with the inscription '*Eenheid de sterkste keten*' ('the strongest chains are those of unity'). The statue commemorates the bloody Jordaan riots of 1934 against government austerity measures. On the east exterior wall of the church there's a plaque commemorating the February 1941 labour strikes, protesting the deportation of Jews by the occupying Nazis. Every Saturday the church square (**Noordermarkt**) hosts Boerenmarkt, the largest market of organic produce in Amsterdam, and on Monday there's a wonderful flea market.

A ten-minute stroll down Prinsengracht will take you back to where you started on Bloemgracht. If you're curious about the Dutch national symbol, stop in en route at the **Tulip Museum** (Prinsengracht 116, 020 421 0095, www.amsterdamtulipmuseum.com). It tells the fascinating story of tulip mania, which gripped the city in the 17th-century.

Egelantiersgracht

Winkel 43

❤ Semhar €€
Marnixstraat 259-261 (020 638 1634, www.semhar.nl). Tram 5. ***Open*** *4-10pm Tue-Sun.* ***Map*** *p117 F8* ⓯ *Ethiopian*

A great spot to sample the spicy, vegetarian-friendly food of Ethiopia, including *enjera* (a type of sourdough pancake), best accompanied by a beer. Ideal after an afternoon spent wandering the Jordaan.

SLA €
Westerstraat 34 (020 370 2733, www.ilovesla.com). Tram 3. ***Open*** *11am-9pm daily.* ***No cash. Map*** *p117 H6* ⓰ *Salads*

'Sla' means salad. And, indeed, they are organic health freaks here – but in a relaxed and tasty way. Try one of the house 'favourites' (grilled organic chicken with cauliflower, broccoli and red quinoa, perhaps) or create your own personalised salad. To maintain balance, forgo the juices and opt for a locally produced beer from Brouwerij 't IJ. **Other locations** throughout the city.

Toscanini €€€
Lindengracht 75 (020 623 2813, www.restauranttoscanini.nl). Tram 3, 5. ***Open*** *noon-2.30pm, 6-10.30pm Mon-Sat.* ***Map*** *p117 H6* ⓲ *Italian*

The invariably excellent food at this popular spot is prepared in an open kitchen. Expect the likes of Sardinian sheep's cheese with chestnut honey and black pepper, or beef tenderloin with rosemary and *lardo di colonnata*. Book in advance if you want to ensure a table. If you don't want to make an evening of it, or are looking for something cheaper, nearby **Capri** (Lindengracht 63, 020 624 4940) has fine pizza.

❤ Winkel 43 €€
Noordermarkt 43 (020 623 0223, winkel43.nl). Tram 3, 5 or bus 18, 21, 22. ***Open*** *7am-1am Mon; 8am-1am Tues-Thur; 8am-3am Fri; 7am-3am Sat; 10am-1am Sun.* ***Map*** *p117 H6* ⓴ *Dutch*

Hailed for having the best apple pie in all of Amsterdam – quite a claim to fame – Winkel 43 is well worth a visit. Nestled on the corner near the city's scenic Brouwersgracht, look for the green and white shutters and you won't miss it. It also serves other food, including quiche and a delicious brioche burger, but make sure you leave room for the famous apple pie. It lives up to the hype.

YamYam Trattoria Pizzeria €
Frederik Hendrikstraat 88-90 (020 681 5097, www.yamyam.nl). Tram 3, 5 or bus 18, 21. ***Open*** *5.30pm-9.30pm Wed , Sun; 5.30-10pm Thu-Sat.* ***Map*** *p117 off map* ㉑ *Italian*

Unequalled and inexpensive pastas and pizzas (cooked in a wood oven) in a hip and casual atmosphere: no wonder YamYam is a local favourite. It's certainly worth the trip west of the Jordaan, but be sure to book in advance.

Bars

Café Hegeraad
Noordermarkt 34 (020 624 5565). Tram 3, 5 or bus 18, 21. ***Open*** *8am-1am Mon-Thur; 8am-3am Fri, Sat; 11am-1am Sun.* ***No cards. Map*** *p117 H6* ❶

This gabled building with leaded windows has probably been a café for as long as the Noorderkerk church opposite has been standing. Be careful not to spill your drink on the carpeted tables.

❤ Café Nol

Westerstraat 109 (020 624 5380, www.cafenol-amsterdam.nl). Tram 3, 5 or bus 18, 21. ***Open*** *9pm-3am Wed, Thur, Sun; 9pm-4am Fri, Sat.* ***Map*** *p117 H7* ❸

At a glance, it looks like just another one of the many brown bars the Jordaan is known for. But by night, Café Nol transforms into the neon-lit site of Dutch folk singalongs for locals and tourists alike. Self-proclaimed as the 'most famous café in the Jordaan', its red shuttered doors hold 50 years of stories, which the older patrons will be more than happy to share with you after a beer or two.

De Nieuwe Anita

Frederik Hendrikstraat 111 (020 774 4922, www.denieuweanita.nl). Tram 3, 5. ***Open*** *8pm-1am Mon-Thu, Sun; 8pm-2am Fri, Sat.* ***Map*** *p117 off map* ❺

Stuffed full of vintage furniture and shabby charm, there's a lot going on at Anita's. Live music and DJs in the tiny, downstairs basement are common, as is comedy, theatre and movie nights. Ignore the extensive beer menu though and head to the cocktail bar at the back on the right for some delicious – and deadly – concoctions; they'll keep you dancing all night.

Papeneiland

Prinsengracht 2 (020 624 1989, www.papeneiland.nl). Tram 3 or bus 18, 21, 22. ***Open*** *10am-1am Mon-Thu; 10am-3am Fri, Sat; noon-1am Sun.* ***Map*** *p117 J6* ❻

't Smalle

This beautiful Delft-tiled bar is a wonderful spot for a drink and a chinwag. A definite talking point is the café's fascinating history: apparently, a tunnel runs under the canal, which, when Catholicism was outlawed in the 17th century, secretly delivered worshippers to their church opposite. It certainly explains the bar's name: Pope's Island.

❤ 't Smalle

Egelantiersgracht 12 (020 623 9617). Tram 3, 5. ***Open*** *10am-1am Mon-Thur, Sun; 10am-2am Fri, Sat.* ***Map*** *p117 H7* ❼

This is one of the most scenic terraces on one of the prettiest canals, so it's no surprise that waterside seats are snared early in the day – patience is essential. It's very cute inside too, with gleaming brass fixtures harking back to the heady drinking days of the 18th century, when it was the Hoppe distillery.

De Twee Zwaantjes

Prinsengracht 114 (020 625 2729, www.cafedetweezwaantjes.nl). Tram 3, 5, 13, 17. ***Open*** *noon-1am Mon-Thu, Sun; 11am-3am Fri, Sat.* ***Map*** *p117 H7* ❾

Oom-pah-pah, oom-pah-pah: that's how it goes at this salt-of-the-earth bar on the Jordaan side of the Prinsengracht. It's relatively quiet during the week, but weekends are real swinging singalong affairs, with revellers booming out tearjerkers about love, sweat and the Westerkerk. All together now: 'Op de Amster-dam-se grachten ...'

Shops & services

Delicious Food

Westerstraat 24 (020 320 3070, www.deliciousfood.nl).Tram 3, 5 or bus 18, 21, 22. ***Open*** *9.30am-6.30pm Mon-Fri; 9am-6pm Sat.* **No cards.** ***Map*** *p117 H6* ❸ *Food & drink*

Organic produce has reached the pinnacle of urban chic at this fancy health-food store – a useful place if you're buying in bulk.

Distortion Records

Westerstraat 244 (020 627 0004, www.distortion.nl). Tram 3, 5. ***Open*** *11am-6pm Tue, Wed, Fri; 11am-9pm Thur; 10am-6pm Sat.* **No cards.** ***Map*** *p117 G7* ❺ *Books & music*

A tiny store with a chaos of vinyl (and some CDs), from 1970s punk rock, jazz, funk, soul, Latin and soundtracks, through lo-fi, indie, noise, garage and industrial, to 1980s and 1990s indie, electro, hip hop and reggae, ending up in break beats and house for those with more dancefloor-oriented interests.

❤ Flesch Records

Noorderkerkstraat 16 (06 5265 7669 mobile). Tram 3 or bus 18, 21. ***Open*** *11am-3pm Mon; 1-5pm Wed-Fri; 10am-6pm Sat.* ***Map*** *p117 H6* ❻ *Music & food*

Sheer genius: if sales lag in the world of rare vinyl, antique radios and classic record players and needles, don't whine – just start selling a selection of fruit and veg on the side.

KochxBos Gallery

Eerste Anjeliersdwarsstraat 36 (020 681 4567, www.kochxbos.nl). Tram 3, 5. ***Open*** *1-6pm Wed-Sat.* ***Map*** *p117 G7* ❾ *Art*

With a sister studio in New York City, KochxBos Gallery is the first independent low-brow pop-surrealist gallery in Amsterdam. It celebrates contemporary underground art, and has exhibited the up-and-coming likes of Ray Caesar and Meryl Donoghue.

❤ Lena the Fashion Library

Westerstraat 174h (020 789 1781, www.lena-library.com). Tram 3, 5. ***Open*** *10am-7pm Mon; 11am-7pm Wed, Fri; 11am-8pm Thur; 11am-5pm Sat.* ***Map*** *p117 G7* ❿ *Fashion*

As the name would imply, Lena takes its lead from an old-fashioned library. Instead of borrowing books, visitors can borrow pre-loved clothing. The founders aim to raise awareness of the negative effects of consumerism – including worker exploitation and textile waste – with their initiative. But there is such a thing as no returns; if you decide you can't part with an item after borrowing it you'll receive a 10 per cent discount on purchase price.

❤ Moooi

Westerstraat 187 (020 528 7760, www.moooi.com). Tram 3, 5. ***Open*** *10am-6pm Tue-Sat.* ***Map*** *p117 G7* ⓫ *Homewares*

A former school has been transformed into a Dutch design hub and the studio of design star Marcel Wanders – inventor of the iconic Knotted Chair, and also responsible for the Andaz Amsterdam hotel. On the ground floor, step into his stylish store, Moooi, the showroom for his work and the portfolios of other creatives such as Studio Job, Piet Boon and Jurgen Bey. Just don't come here expecting to find any bargains.

❤ Noordermarkt

Noordermarkt (no phone, www.noordermarkt-amsterdam.nl). Tram 3, 5 or bus 18, 21, 22. ***Open*** *9am-2pm Mon; 9am-4pm Sat.* ***No cards. Map*** *p117 H6* ⓬ *Market*

North of Westermarkt, Noordermarkt is frequented by the serious shopper. The huge stacks of (mainly second-hand) clothes, shoes, jewellery, hats and bric-a-brac need

Gallery Spaces

Tap into the Jordaan's rich art scene

You could easily spend a whole holiday trawling the 40-odd galleries in the Jordaan. Occupying former homes or shops, they're pleasantly compact spaces, best visited in the afternoon from Wednesday to Saturday. Hazenstraat contains many galleries and is an excellent artery from which to dart left and right to visit others.

Wouter van Leeuwen (Hazenstraat 27, www.woutervanleeuwen.com) is a great starting point. This simple, white-walled gallery presents some of the biggest names in contemporary portrait and landscape photography. Just round the corner, **Stigter van Doesburg** (Elandstraat 90, 020 624 2361, www.stigtervandoesburg.com) has an impressive roster of artists, including Helen Verhoeven and miniaturist Saskia Olde Wolbers.

Cross a bridge and turn right to find canalside **Torch** (Lauriergracht 94, 020 626 0284, www.torchgallery.com), which has built a quirky reputation by exhibiting the likes of Terry Rodgers and Chicago-based photographer Sandro Miller.

Returning to Hazenstraat, the next left leads to **Annet Gelink Gallery** (Laurierstraat 187-189, 020 330 2066, www.annetgelink.com) – she's seen by many artists as the most desired contemporary-art dealer of the moment. Why? Simple: her stable of hot, young international up-and-comers, including Anya Gallaccio, Carla Klein, David Maljkovic and

KochxBos Gallery

Yael Bartana. And she has plenty of space and light to lavish on them.

Paul Andriesse (Leliegracht 47, 020 623 6237, www.paulandriesse.nl) is one of the area's original gallerists, but has relocated more than once during the last decade. Currently he's just over the Prinsengracht in the Western Canal Belt, where he shows top-tier artists such as Jan van de Pavert and Marlene Dumas along with newcomers.

Then there's the even more curious **KochxBos Gallery** (*see opposite*), back in the Jordaan and further north. It specialises in work from the dark sides of 'low-brow' artists such as Ray Caesar, Meryl Donoghue and SauerKids – art for those who like their hot rods ablaze, their punk snotty and their films in the Lynchian tradition.

On the north side of Rozengracht is **Galerie Fons Welters** (Bloemstraat 140, 020 423 3046, www.fonswelters.nl). Doyen of the Amsterdam art scene, Fons Welters likes to 'discover' local talent and has shown remarkable taste in the fields of photography and installation, providing a home for artists Eylem Aladogan and Dutch Berend Strik. A visit here is worth it for the Atelier van Lieshout entrance alone.

If you are fascinated by what lies behind closed doors, then visit **Open Ateliers Jordaan** (www.openateliersjordaan.nl) in mid to late May, when around 60 artists' studios open their doors to the public.

KochxBos Gallery

Galerie Fons Welters

Lena the Fashion Library *p124*

Moooi *p124*

to be sorted with a grim determination, but there are real bargains to be had if you delve deeply enough. Arrive early or the best stuff will have been nabbed. On Monday mornings there is also furniture.

Every Saturday, the Noordermarkt turns into an organic farmers' market. Singers or medieval musicians sometimes perform alfresco, making the whole experience feel more like a cultural day trip than a grocery run.

❤ Westermarkt

Westerstraat (www.amsterdam.info/markets/westermarkt). Tram 3. ***Open*** *9am-1pm Mon.* ***Map*** *p117 H7* ⓱

As one of the biggest streets in the Jordaan, Westerstraat is always busy with locals or in-the-know tourists escaping the confines of the Old Centre. But the street truly comes alive on Monday mornings, when it transforms into the Westermarkt. Boasting almost 200 stands, the weekly market has evolved from a humble textile trading area to a dynamic hub for pre-loved clothing, delicious street food and unique art. Perusing it makes for a perfect way to spend a sunny morning before popping over to its neighbour, **Noordermarkt** (*see p124*).

ROZENGRACHT & SOUTH

Once a canal, the now filled-in Rozengracht scythes through the heart of the Jordaan in unappealing fashion. Rembrandt lived at no.184 from 1659 until his death a decade later – there is a plaque on the first floor. While you're here, look up at the gable of Rozengracht 204 to spy an iron stickman wall anchor, or consider visiting some of the many galleries (*see p125* Gallery Spaces).

The area is notable for the **Antiek-centrum Amsterdam** antiques market (*see p128*). Elandsgracht 71-77 is where the labyrinthine **Sjako's Fort** was said to have once stood. Sjako is often referred to as the 'Robin Hood of Amsterdam', though while he was happy stealing from the rich, he usually neglected to give to the poor. Still, he had style: not many burglars go about their business dressed in white and accompanied by henchmen clad in black. In 1718, his 24-year-old head ended up spiked on a pole where the Shell Building now stands, but local anarchist bookstore **Fort van Sjako** (Jodenbreestraat 24, Jodenbuurt, 020 625 8979, www.sjakoo.nl) and a shrine in the window of the building that replaced his fort keep his name alive – though, sadly, a local historian recently proved the story of Sjako was almost completely myth.

Restaurants & cafés

Balthazar's Keuken €€

Elandsgracht 108 (020 420 2114, www.balthazarskeuken.nl). Tram 5, 7, 19. ***Open*** *6-10.30pm Tue-Sun.* ***Map*** *p117 G10* ❷
Mediterranean

This tiny restaurant is always packed tight, so you need to book ahead if you want to enjoy its excellent set menu of meat or fish dishes.

❤ Cloud Gallery Amsterdam €

Prinsengracht 276 (020 358 3574, www.cloudamsterdam.com). Tram 5, 17, 19. ***Open*** *8am-6pm Mon-Fri; 9am-6pm Sat; 10am-6pm Sun.* ***Map*** *p117 G10* ❺ *Café*

You'll find stimulants for the mind, body and soul at this art gallery-meets-coffee shop. Frequented by freelancers, art enthusiasts and local coffee lovers, the gallery showcases a variety of temporary photography and painted exhibits.

Moeders €€

Rozengracht 251 (020 626 7957, www.moeders.com). Tram 13, 14, 17. ***Open*** *5pm-midnight Mon-Fri; noon-midnight Sat, Sun. Last orders 10.30pm.* ***Map*** *p117 E9* ❿
Dutch

It's all about the *stamppot* at 'Mothers', a quirky city-centre restaurant that's decorated with photographs of customers' actual mothers. The closest thing the Dutch have to a national dish, the combination of mashed potato, cabbage, bacon and sausage is quite a plateful, especially when it comes with an extra meatball. There's plenty else to choose from, but bring a hearty appetite and don't bother with starters – portions are huge.

❤ Pesca €€

Rozengracht 133 (020 334 5136, pesca.restaurant). Tram 5, 17, 19. ***Open*** *6-10pm Mon-Thu; 6-10.30pm Fri; noon-10.30pm Sat; noon-10pm Sun.* ***Map*** *p117 F9* ⓭
Seafood

Pesca – 'Theatre of Fish' – offers a unique concept for seafood lovers. The restaurant is set up like a fancy fish market. As you enter, you're greeted by a host who will offer a glass of champagne while you peruse a selection of fresh catch – including mussels, cod, scallops and octopus. Once you've chosen, you progress to the next stage of the restaurant where you tell a different staff member what you'd like to drink and order your sides. Finally, you arrive in the eating hall. The service is fast, the music is loud and the atmosphere is buzzing. A great place to kickstart an evening out before enjoying a cocktail or two in **Struik** (*see below*) across the road.

Bars

Café Sound Garden

Marnixstraat 164-166 (020 620 2853, www.cafesoundgarden.nl). Tram 3, 5, 13, 17, 19. ***Open*** *1pm-1am Mon-Thur; 1pm-3am Fri; 3pm-3am Sat; 3pm-1am Sun.* ***Map*** *p117 F9* ❹

A dirty old rockers' bar where musos, journos and everyone else who refuses to grow up gets smashed in one big, sloppy mêlée. The soundtrack is composed from the entire back catalogue of classic alternative pop, often from DJs and bands, and sometimes accompanied by (inexpert) dancing. At the back is a surprisingly restful terrace, where boats can moor when it's time for a break from touring the canals. Sound Garden also has pool, pinball and a good range of beer.

Struik

Rozengracht 160 (06 5260 8837). Tram 5, 13, 17. ***Open*** *5pm-1am Tue-Thu, Sun; 5pm- 3am Fri, Sat.* ***Map*** *p117 F9* ❽

A chilled bar for hipsters who like their music cool and their design street. The friendly neighbourhood café vibe is enhanced by budget-priced daily dinner specials. Later on, the DJ kicks in. There's also a larger sister operation up the street, **Brandstof** (Marnixstraat 341, 020 422 0813, www.bar-brandstof.nl).

Waterkant

Marnixstraat 246 (020 737 1126, www.waterkantamsterdam.nl). Tram 5, 17, 19. ***Open*** *11am-1am Mon-Thu, Sun; 11am-3am Fri, Sat.* ***Map*** *p117 F10* ⓫

Don't be fooled by Waterkant's location under a car park. When the sun is shining, there are few better spots for some alfresco booze and food than this canal-side establishment; in the summer, the terrace is permanently packed. The food veers towards Surinamese: the gado gado is good and the chicken roti roll is legendary. There's also a fun pub quiz (in Dutch) every Monday night.

Coffeeshops

La Tertulia

Prinsengracht 312 (www.coffeeshoptertulia.com). Tram 5, 7, 19. ***Open*** *11am-7pm Tue-Sat.* ***No cards. Map*** *p117 G10* ❷

This mellow mother-and-daughter-run joint is decorated with plenty of plants, a little waterfall and lots of sunlight, which balances harmoniously with the all-bio buds and scrumptious weed brownies. Two floors provide space for relaxation, quiet reading or gazing at the canal. Look for the seriously stoned Van Gogh painted outside.

Shops & services

❤ Antiekcentrum Amsterdam

Elandsgracht 109 (020 624 9038, www.antiekcentrumamsterdam.nl). Tram 5, 7, 17, 19. ***Open*** *11am-6pm Mon, Wed-Fri; 11am-5pm Sat, Sun.* ***Map*** *p117 F10* ❶ *Antiques*

The 70-plus stalls here deal mainly in antiques, with plenty of collectors' items; you'll find everything from pewter to paintings, and glassware to gold. It's easy to get lost in the quiet premises and find yourself standing alone by a stall crammed with antiquated clocks ticking eerily away.

Chocolátl

Hazenstraat 25a (020 789 3670, www.chocolatl.nl). Tram 5, 17, 19. ***Open*** *noon-6.30pm Tue-Sat; 1-5pm Sun. Hours may vary in winter.* ***Map*** *p117 G10* ❷ *Food & drink*

Regarding their shop as a 'chocolate gallery', the folks behind Chocolátl are evangelical about artisanal, single-origin chocolate from around the globe – along with chocolate-friendly teas, coffees and beer. All in all, a very sweet operation.

Les Deux Frères

Rozengracht 58HS (020 846 4613, www.lesdeuxfreres.nl). Tram 13, 17. ***Open*** *noon-6.30pm Mon; 10.30am-6.30pm Tue-Fri; 10.30am-6pm Sat; noon-5pm Sun.* ***Map*** *p117 G8* ❹ *Clothing*

The brainchild of brothers Alain and Matthieu, Les Deux Frères is a lifestyle-based clothing store for men, selling a range of quality brands. Designed for males who aren't so fond of shopping, the store also sells coffee. Enough said.

HJ van de Kerkhof

Elandsgracht 43 (020 623 4084, www.kerkhofpassementen.com). Tram 5, 7, 19. ***Open*** *11am-5.30pm Tue-Sat.* ***No cards. Map*** *p117 G10* ❼ *Accessories*

Tassel maniacs go wild at this well-stocked haberdashery. A sea of shakeable frilly things, lace and rhinestone banding, and much more besides.

❤ Tenue de Nîmes

Elandsgracht 60 (020 320 4012, www.tenuedenimes.com). Tram 5, 7, 19. ***Open*** *noon-7pm Mon; 11am-7pm Tue-Fri; 10am-6pm Sat; noon-6pm Sun.* ***Map*** *p117 G10* ⓯ *Fashion*

Pesca *p127*

Street Art

From graffiti to galleries

Amsterdam has an active street-art scene, visible on almost every corner, in many shapes and sizes, from free-hand graffiti to stencils, sculptures, tags and stickers. Although it's illegal to mark public and private buildings, the city's famous liberalism makes it somewhere that 'writers' (as they're called in graff parlance) love to tag. The city spends around €400,000 a year on cleaning monuments and municipal buildings, but that's a pittance compared to other cities. And there are plenty of legal walls – aka 'Halls of Fame' – where artists collaborate on a stretch of concrete or an entire building.

Initiatives such as **Street Art Museum Amsterdam** (www.streetartmuseum amsterdam.com), founded by a local non-profit NGO, help to protect these creative works by offering tours for €20 a head. Social media has also enabled graffiti artists to preserve and promote their creations: you could easily spend hours scrolling through the Instagram feeds of @graffitiamsterdam and @dutchgraffiti_com.

Street artists who have made their distinctive mark throughout Amsterdam include C215, Stinkfish and Space Invader (just look for the small digital characters, which take you back to the 1990s at a glance). Swiss-born local Bustart specialises in paper posters depicting introspective animals, while British-born duo The London Police (TLP) have put their own stamp on the streets of the world with deceptively simple-looking, black and white blob 'lads', which first appeared on electricity boxes around town, but later found their way into galleries. Another prolific practitioner is Laser 3.14. Dubbed Amsterdam's very own 'guerrilla poet', his words of wisdom are dotted all over town. No building site is safe from his aerosol and post-modern one-liners (in English). 'Swallowed by your own introspective vortex' and 'She fears the ghouls that reside in her shadow' are just two cryptic examples. His work now also appears for sale in the **Original Dampkring Gallery** (Handboogstraat 29, dampkring-coffeeshop-amsterdam.nl), which hosts regular street-art exhibitions. Many other old-school graffiti artists – such as Morcky, Boghe, Hugo Mulder (DHM), Ottograph, Juice, Delta and Shoe – have also crossed over to creating design work and/or exhibiting in galleries worldwide.

There's more street art on show at graffiti shop **Henxs** (St Antoniebreestraat 136-138, 0631 094 886 mobile, henxs.amsterdam), where you might also come face to face with the artists themselves, as this is where they stock up on spray cans and markers (when they're not buying them from the spray paint stand at nearby Waterlooplein flea market). Henxs is hard to miss: the sticker-covered front porch is a kind of who's who of the Amsterdam street scene. Meanwhile, bar **Hannekes Boom** (*see p172*) hosts painting events in the summer, and there's of course plenty to see at the former shipyard-turned-artists' playground **NDSM** (*see p176*), the go-to place for street artists to practise their trade.

Fatherhood, Stinkfish

Aptly named after the spiritual home of denim (a French town called Nîmes), this boutique-cum-photography-gallery features bare brick walls adorned with denim-covered beams, antiquated Singer sewing machines and limited-edition Raw Cannondale bicycles. The shop's selection of edgier brands, including Momotaro, Acne and Rag & Bone, is second to none. **Other locations** Haarlemmerstraat 92-94, Western Canal Belt (020 331 2778).

Wegewijs

Rozengracht 32 (020 624 4093, www.wegewijs.nl). Tram 13, 17. ***Open*** *8.30am-5.30pm Mon-Fri; 9am-4pm Sat.* ***Map*** *p117 G8* ⓰ *Food & drink*

The Wegewijs family opened this shop more than a century ago. On offer are around 50 foreign and more than 100 domestic varieties of cheese, including *graskaas*, a grassy-tasting cheese that's available in summer. You're allowed to try the Dutch varieties before you buy, and they also do a delicious range of homemade soups and sandwiches.

BEYOND THE JORDAAN

Between **Brouwersgracht** and the impossibly scenic **Westelijke Eilanden**, more quirky shopping opportunities can be found on Haarlemmerstraat and its westerly extension, **Haarlemmerdijk**. Though not officially part of the Jordaan, this strip and its alleys share an ambience. Head east towards Centraal Station past the **West Indische Huis** (Herenmarkt 93-97), where the West Indies Trading Company (WIC) stored the silver that Piet Hein took from the Spanish after a sea battle in 1628. The house was the setting for such dubious decisions as selling all of Manhattan for 60 guilders, and running the slave trade between Africa and the Caribbean. Today, it's a popular venue for events and wedding receptions.

Heading west, Haarlemmerdijk ends at **Haarlemmerplein**, where you'll see the imposing Haarlemmerpoort city gate, built in 1840. Beyond it is **Westerpark**, location of monumental **Westergasfabriek**, a former gas works turned cultural centre (*see p132*). The area around the energy plant is now a thriving park with walking and running trails, a babbling brook, a wading pool for kids, sports fields, tennis courts and outdoor gym equipment.There are also some standout eateries in the adjoining neighbourhood, including **Café-Restaurant Amsterdam** (*see p131*).

Just north of the Jordaan are the **Westelijke Eilanden** ('Western Islands'). Realeneiland, Prinseneiland and Bickerseiland are artificial islands that were created in the 17th century to sustain maritime activity. Shipyards, tar distillers, and fish salters and smokers have been replaced by trendy warehouse flats, artists' studios and a yacht basin, but the area still remains the best place for a scenic stroll evocative of seafaring times. After admiring the yellow submarine moored on Bickerseiland, unwind at **'t Blaauwhooft** or **De Gouden Reael** (*see p131*).

Sights & museums

Museum Het Schip

Oostzaanstraat 45 (020 686 8595, www.hetschip.nl). Bus 22, 48. ***Open*** *11am-5pm Tue-Sun. Guided tours every hr, but only 3pm tour is guaranteed in English.* ***Admission*** *€15; €5-€7.50 reductions; free under-5s, Iamsterdam, MK.* ***Map*** *p117 off map.*

Just north of Westerpark, Spaarndammerplantsoen features three monumental public housing blocks designed by Michel de Klerk, the most expressionist of which is known as Het Schip (The Ship). Museum Het Schip is one of the finest examples of the Amsterdam School architectural movement and a must-see for architecture students the world over. The carefully designed interior is quite an experience to behold, and exhibitions investigate the importance of public housing in Amsterdam, and the cultural-historical value of the Amsterdam School (*see p266* Amsterdam School).

Restaurants & cafés

't Blaauwhooft €€

Hendrik Jonker Plein 1 (020 623 8721, www.blaauwhooft.nl). Tram 3 or bus 18, 21, 22. ***Open*** *3am-1pm daily. Kitchen 6-10pm daily.* ***Map*** *p117 J5* ❸ *Dutch.*

Museum Het Schip

Boasting a large outdoor terrace, the Bickerseiland's picturesque Blaauwhooft has been luring locals and tourists for years. On the menu you'll find traditional Dutch pub favourites, including cheese fondue – the best in the city according to *Het Parool* – chicken satay, and mussels.

Café-Restaurant Amsterdam €€

Watertorenplein 6 (020 682 2666, www.cradam.nl). Tram 5 or bus 21. ***Open*** *10.30am-midnight (kitchen closes 10.30pm) Mon-Thur, Sun; 10.30am-1am, Fri, Sat (kitchen closes 11.30pm).* ***Map*** *p117 off map* 4 Dutch

This spacious monument to industry just west of the Jordaan pumped water from the coast's dunes for around a century. Now it pumps out honest Dutch and French dishes, from *kroketten* to caviar, under a mammoth ceiling and floodlights rescued from the old Ajax stadium. It's a truly unique – and child-friendly – experience.

De Gouden Reael €€

Zandhoek 14 (020 623 3883, www.goudenreael.nl). Bus 48. ***Open*** *noon-11pm daily.* ***Map*** *p117 off map* 8 Dutch/Global

If you're in the market for a wide variety of flavour, De Gouden Reael certainly won't disappoint. Guests can choose from dozens of sharing plates, which range from sherry rib-eye to hazelnut mackerel, for just €9 a pop. The wine menu is just as impressive. A great way to treat yourself after a day of sightseeing.

Mossel & Gin €€€

Gosschalklaan 12 (020 486 5869, www.mosselengin.nl). Bus 21. ***Open*** *4pm-midnight Tue-Thu; 2pm-1am Fri; 1pm-1am Sat; 1pm-midnight Sun. Kitchen closes at 10.30pm.* ***No cash. Map*** *p117 off map* 11

Mossel & Gin does exactly what it says on the tin, and does it very well indeed. The former comes with frites and a choice of six different sauces; the latter is infused with all manner of herbs, fruits and spices, and can be served in liver-friendly half sizes.

In the know
City farm

Just a few minutes by bicycle from Westergasfabriek, you'll come across a friendly neighbourhood farm in the middle of a sheep field. The volunteer-run **Buurtboerderij Ons Genoegen** (Spaarndammerdijk 319, 020 337 6820, www.buurtboerderij.nl) has a lovely café and organises assorted events throughout the year. Perfect for when the big bad city just gets too much.

REM Eiland €€

Haparandadam 45-2, Houthavens (020 688 5501, www.remeiland.com). Bus 48. ***Open*** *noon-10pm daily.* ***Map*** *p117 off map* 14 Modern French

A former pirate TV station in the North Sea, this striking red and white ocean platform was brought to the outer reaches of the western industrial waterfront area to be reborn as a posh restaurant with compelling 360° views and excellent seafood. Ascend the steep metal steps for an Amsterdam Negroni on the old helipad.

Small World Catering €

Binnen Oranjestraat 14 (020 420 2774, www.smallworldcatering.nl). Bus 18, 19, 21. ***Open*** *10.30am-7pm Tue-Fri; 10.30-6pm Sat; noon-6pm Sun.* ***No cards. Map*** *p117 H5* 17 Café

The home base for this catering company is this tiny deli with a lovely proprietor. As well as superlative coffee and fresh juices, there are salads, a weekly pasta bake, and excellent sandwiches.

WestergasTerras €€

Klönneplein 4-6 (020 684 84 96, www.westergasterras.nl). Tram 5 or bus 21. ***Open*** *11am-1am Mon-Thur; 11am-3am Fri; 10am-3am Sat; 10am-1am Sun.* ***Map*** *p117 off map* 19 Modern Dutch

During summer months WestergasTerras is a hugely popular spot because of its expansive terrace looking out on the former gasworks and water gardens. In winter the *hygge* factor is cranked up with a cosy open fire and comfortable sofas. Based in an attractive conservatory, the restaurant serves up seasonal produce with an always-changing menu.

Bars

Café Kobalt

Singel 2A (020 320 1559, www.cafekobalt.nl). Tram 2, 4, 11, 12, 13, 14, 17, 24. ***Open*** *8am-1am Mon-Thu; 8am-3am Fri, Sat; 10am-1am Sun.* ***Map*** *p117 K6* 2

This rather sophisticated bar near Centraal Station is a great way to beat the train-delay blues, especially since its 2019 makeover. It has free Wi-Fi, round-the-clock food – from breakfast to tapas to dinner – and any drink that you can name, from ristretto to champagne. DJs spin on Friday nights, while Sunday afternoons are dedicated to slinky live jazz shows.

Vesper Bar

Vinkenstraat 57 (www.vesperbar.nl). Bus 18, 21, 22. ***Open*** *6pm-1am, Tue-Thu; 5pm-3am Fri, Sat.* ***Map*** *p117 H5* 10

You know you're in the hands of a good bartender when, instead of offering you a

Top 20

❤ Westergasfabriek

Pazzanistraat 37 (020 586 0710, westergas.nl). Tram 5 or bus 21. ***Open*** *daily, hours vary.* ***Admission*** *Free, unless ticketed event.* ***Map*** *p117 E4.*

Lying west of the Jordaan within the Westerpark is a cultural hub for film, theatre, music and art. Whether you've got the itch to wash down some *bitterballen* with a craft beer, immerse yourself in the latest art exhibition or dance to the latest sounds, chances are Westergasfabriek is the place to scratch it. But this local hotspot wasn't always thriving with the creativity it effortlessly exudes today. From 1885 to 1967, the Westergasfabriek (which translates to Western Gasworks) pumped coal gas into the homes of Amsterdam. When the Netherlands switched over to natural gas, the 45,000-square metre (36-acre) site became obsolete.

The heavily polluted site was left largely untouched for decades until the early 1990s, when creative and cultural pioneers used the space for temporary showcases. In 2002, the site was redeveloped with an entirely new kind of energy. Designed by American landscape architect Kathryn Gustafson, it's a clever example of urban reuse. The 19th-century factory buildings now house dance clubs, performance venues and other cultural destinations, including the intimate art-house cinema, **Het Ketelhuis** (*see p210*) and **Pacific Parc** (Polonceaukade 23, 020 488 7778, www.pacificparc.nl), which regularly features nasty-but-nice rock 'n' roll bands. The giant gas tank in the middle of the complex is a rentable events location called the **Gashouder**. There are office spaces for creative entrepreneurs, and various high-profile events and art exhibits are held here, such as **Unseen** (*see p204*) and **Rollende Keukens** (*see p201*). There are also excellent cafés, bars and restaurants on site, including **WestergasTerras** (*see p131*), microbrewery and bar **Troost Brewery** (020 737 1028, brouwerijtroost.nl/westergas-amsterdam) and seafood restaurant **Mossel & Gin** (*see p131*).

cocktail menu, he simply asks, 'What do you feel like?' Vesper's talented team serve old-fashioned classics and modern interpretations, or anything you fancy, in classy and charming surroundings. Wine and beer take a back seat to the hard stuff, but, like everything at this intimate bar, both are sourced from small-scale and carefully selected producers.

Coffeeshops

Barney's

Haarlemmerstraat 102 (020 625 9761, www.barneys.biz). Bus 18, 21, 22. ***Open*** *8.30am-1am daily.* **No cards.** ***Map*** *p117 J6* ❶

Renovated with some lovely old-fashioned apothecary paraphernalia, media screens showing specially filmed information videos and a vaporiser on every table, Barney's serves excellent organic bud.

Shops & services

❤ Jutka & Riska

Haarlemmerdijk 143 (06 2466 8593 mobile, www.jutkaenriska.nl). Tram 3 or bus 18, 21, 22. ***Open*** *10.30am-7pm Mon-Wed; 10am-9pm Thu; 10am-7pm Fri, Sat; noon-6.30pm Sun.* ***Map*** *p117 H5* ❽ *Fashion*

This kooky store (there are Barbie dolls lurking all over the place) stocks a mix of 'old, new, borrowed and blue' fashion and prides itself on its extensive range of reasonably priced 1950s, 1960s and 1970s frocks. Most cost under €50. There's also second-hand Sonia Rykiel, vintage Yves Saint Laurent blazers and some colourful one-off pieces from the store's Jutka & Riska label. **Other locations** Bilderdijkstraat 194, Oud West (020 618 8021).

Papabubble

Haarlemmerdijk 70 (020 626 2662, www.papabubble.nl). Bus 18, 21, 22. ***Open*** *noon-6pm Wed, Sat only.* ***Map*** *p117 H5* ⓭ *Food & drink*

Touch, smell and ask about the world of freestyle swirly candy making. You can even purchase a customised business card made out of water, sugar and glucose. **Other location** Staalstraat 16, Old Centre.

Store Without A Home

Haarlemmerdijk 26 (020 416 2027, www.storewithoutahome.nl). Bus 18, 21, 22. ***Open*** *10am-6pm Wed-Sat.* **No cash.** ***Map*** *p117 J5* ⓮ *Homewares*

It must bode well for the local economy: pop-ups are putting down permanent roots. From cloud-shaped lights to cushions embroidered with birds, everything in this interiors trove is guaranteed to make your living environment happier.

Museum Quarter, Oud West & Zuid

Over a century ago, the area now known as the Museum Quarter was still outside the city limits and an undistinguished marshy meadow. But the completion of the Rijksmuseum in 1885 was the catalyst for construction that would transform the area into one of the plushest parts of town. The Rijksmuseum has since been joined by the Stedelijk and Van Gogh museums, as well as one of Amsterdam's most famous and expensive shopping streets to create a hub of high culture and haute couture.

Zuid, Amsterdam's own monument to the good life, is located south of the city's iconic Vondelpark. Stretching out in a ring beneath it is Nieuw Zuid (New South); further south is Amstelveen with the beautiful Amsterdamse Bos forest. To the north of Vondelpark is Oud West. Now abuzz with cafés, high-end restaurants, daily markets and quaint boutiques, this leafy and lively suburb once housed the city's smelly industries and plague victims but was developed in the 19th century to make way for working-class families. Since then it has flourished into a charming – and impeccably clean – area, conveniently located close to the city centre.

❤ Don't miss

1 Rijksmuseum *p140*
Get your fill of Old Masters in the nation's treasure house.

2 Vondelpark *p146*
Take a break from trams and bikes in Amsterdam's green lung.

3 Van Gogh Museum *p142*
A lifetime's body of work by the post-Impressionist genius.

4 Stedelijk Museum *p139*
Modern art galore, giant 'bath tub' included.

5 Concertgebouw *p237*
Take in the acoustics at one of the world's best classical venues.

't Blauwe Theehuis *p146*

MUSEUM QUARTER, OUD WEST & ZUID

Restaurants & cafés

Bars

Shops & services

❤ Time to eat, drink & shop

Communal street food
Foodhallen *p144*

Craft beer
Butcher's Tears *p149*, Gollem's Proeflokaal *p148*

Designer wear
Azzurro Due *p144*

Hangover-busting brunch
Staring at Jacob *p146*

Hipster coffee
Lot Sixty One *p145*

Laid-back bar
Café Welling *p143*

Perfect pasta
Spaghetteria West *p146*

In the know
Getting around

Trams 2, 11, and 12, and Metro 52 run from Centraal Station through the Museum Quarter and Oud West towards Zuid. Bike paths are established throughout the area.

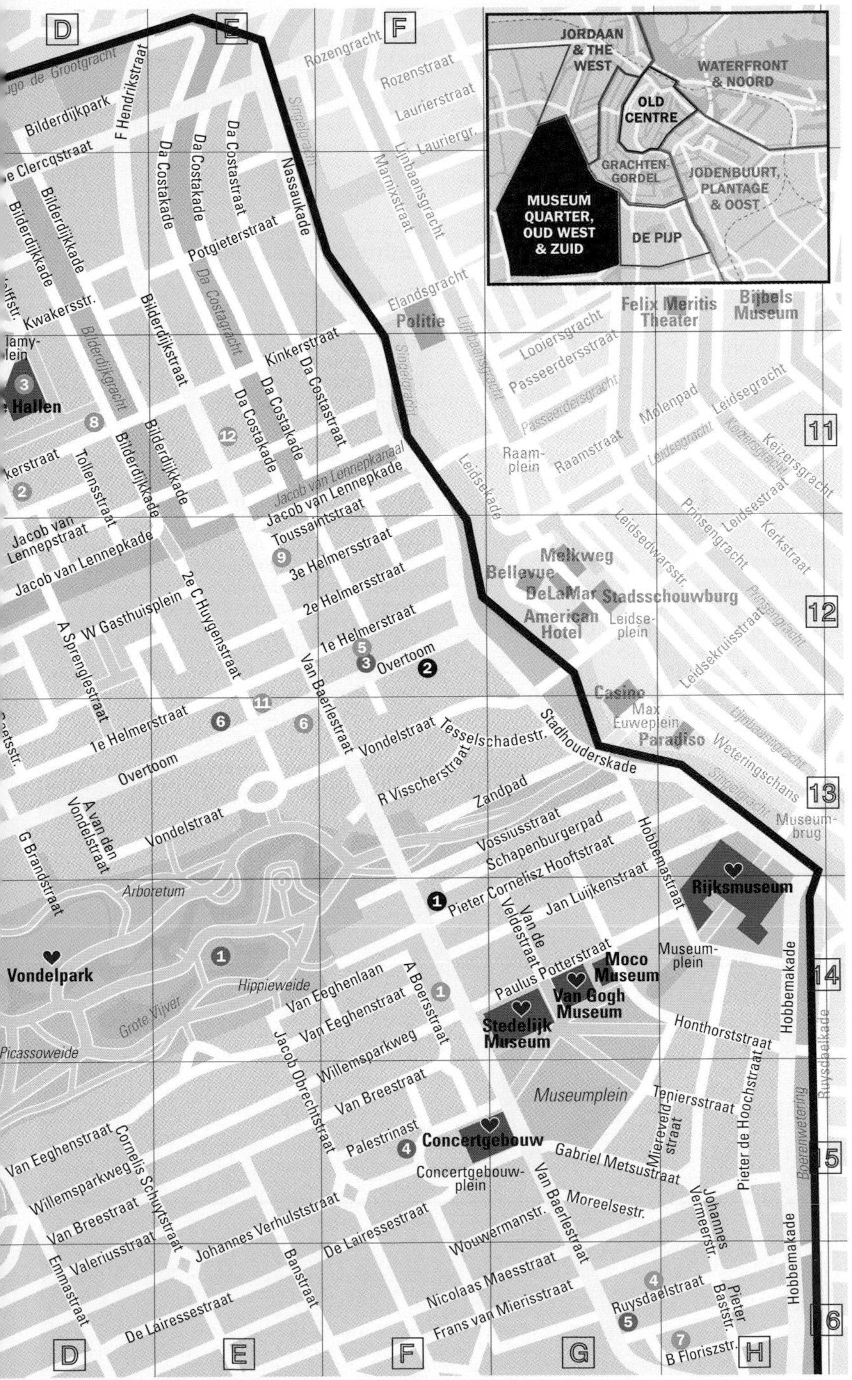

THE MUSEUM QUARTER

The centre of the Museum Quarter is **Museumplein**, the city's largest square, bordered by the **Rijksmuseum** *(see p140)*, the **Stedelijk Museum** *(see p139)*, the **Van Gogh Museum** *(see p142)* and the **Concertgebouw** *(see p237)*. Developed in 1872, Museumplein served as the location for the World Exhibition of 1883, and was then rented out to the Amsterdam ice-skating club between 1900 and 1936. During the Depression, the field was put to use as a sports ground, and during World War II, the Germans built bunkers on it. In 1953, the country's 'shortest motorway', Museumstraat, cut it in two. The more recent additions of grass, a wading pool (that gets transformed into an ice-skating rink in winter), a skate ramp, café and a wacky extension to the Van Gogh Museum have improved the surroundings, and now the square is back to being an essential destination for visitors.

As you might expect in such seriously highfalutin cultural surroundings, property in this area doesn't come cheap – and the affluence is apparent. **Van Baerlestraat** and, especially, **PC Hooftstraat** are as close as Amsterdam gets to Rodeo Drive, offering solace to the kind of ladies who would otherwise be lunching.

While you're in the area, it's worth visiting nearby **Roemer Visscherstraat**. This road, which leads to Vondelpark, is notable not for its labels but for its buildings. Each of the houses from nos.20 to 30 represents a different country and all are built in the appropriate 'national' architectural style: thus Russia comes with a miniature dome; Italy has been painted pastel pink; and Spain's candy stripes have made it one of the street's favourites.

Sights & museums

Moco Museum

Honthorststraat 20 (020 370 1997, www.mocomuseum.com). Tram 2, 5, 12. ***Open*** *9am-7pm Mon-Thu, Sun; 9am-8pm Fri, Sat.* ***Admission*** *€15; €12.50 reductions; €9.50 under-15s; free under-10s, Iamsterdam, MK.* ***Map*** *p136 G14.*

Once you've had your fill of Old Masters, try some modern masterpieces from the 'rockstars of modern art' instead. The Modern Contemporary (Moco) Museum Amsterdam is located on the Museumplein at Villa Alsberg, a townhouse designed in 1904 by Eduard Cuypers, cousin of PJH Cuypers, architect of the nearby Rijksmuseum. Moco opened its doors in April 2016 with acclaimed Warhol and Banksy exhibitions – many of the pieces borrowed from private collections – and followed with shows by Os Gemeos, KAWS and Maya Hayuk.

Museumplein

❤ Stedelijk Museum

Museumplein 10 (020 573 2911, www.stedelijk.nl). Tram 2, 3, 5, 12. ***Open*** *10am-6pm Mon-Thur, Sat, Sun; 10am-10pm Fri.* ***Admission*** *€18.50; €10 reductions; free under-18s, Iamsterdam, MK. Temporary exhibitions may vary. No cards (except shop).* ***Map*** *p136 G14.*

With a world-class, diverse collection, the Stedelijk Museum holds its own on the international modern art stage. Pre-war highlights include works by Cézanne, Picasso, Matisse and Chagall, plus a collection of paintings and drawings by the Russian constructivist Kasimir Malevich. Among post-1945 artists in the collection are minimalists Donald Judd, Barnett Newman and Frank Stella, pop artists Roy Lichtenstein, Sigmar Polke and Andy Warhol, abstract expressionists Karel Appel and Willem De Kooning, and conceptual artists Jan Dibbets, Jeff Koons and Bruce Nauman. You'll also find work by local heroes such as video artist Aernout Mik and painter Marlene Dumas. And there is also an excellent display of 2,000 design objects – including a complete bedroom by Gerrit Rietveld from 1926 – which provide evidence of why the Netherlands remains at the vanguard internationally in this field. On the ground floor, you'll find a historic display of visual art and design dating back to 1850, while the top floor boasts an awe-inspiring permanent collection spanning Warhol and more recent acquisitions by Flavin and Dumas.

After roaming homeless for years, the Stedelijk Museum returned to its revamped building in 2012 following an eight-year wait. The extension, aptly dubbed the 'bathtub' by locals, is made of shiny composite fibre more commonly used for the hulls of yachts. Architect Benthem Crowel created the extension, which hulks over the rather ho-hum original 1895 building. It also provides a very grand entrance that faces Museumplein square instead of the street. Inside, the contrasts come together in presenting the best of the Stedelijk's collection of 90,000 objects.

Peak times are weekends and holiday periods, when you can wait up to an hour in line. If you're no good with crowds, a Monday or a Friday night visit is always a good option. If you decide on the latter and want to make a date of it, **Restaurant Stedelijk** provides a delicious three-course meal. Call 020 573 2651 for reservations.

❤ Don't miss

1 Formes Circulaires, Soleil et Lune
Gallery 0.12, Ground floor
A much-reproduced abstract piece by Robert Delaunay that captures warmth and sunlight (1912).

2 TV As A Fireplace
The Base, Basement
Jan Dibbets' looping video of an actual fireplace is a wry take on how the TV replaced the hearth as the focal point of our living rooms (1968).

3 Cathedra
Gallery 0.4, Ground floor
Is a single-colour canvas art or not? Witness intellectualist art at its finest by Barnett Newman (1951).

Bella Dressed in Green, Marc Chagall

❤ Rijksmuseum

Museumstraat 1 (020 674 7000, www. rijksmuseum.nl). Tram 1, 2, 5, 7, 12, 19. ***Open*** *9am-5pm daily.* ***Admission*** *€20; €10 reductions; free under-19s, Iamsterdam, MK.* ***Map*** *p136 H14.*

Originally designed by PJH Cuypers and opened in 1885, the nation's 'treasure house' is home to 40 Rembrandt and four Vermeer paintings – and holds up a mirror to Centraal Station, also built by Cuypers. The collection was started when William V began to acquire pieces just for the hell of it, and has been growing ever since. Besides Rembrandt's *The Night Watch* plus Vermeer's *The Milkmaid* and *Woman Reading a Letter*, it also has works by the likes of Frans Hals, Jacob de Wit and Ferdinand Bol, as well as a 1917 biplane hanging from the ceiling. There's also a wealth of Asian and decorative arts on display, including 17th-century furniture, intricate silver and porcelain, and 17th- and early 18th-century dolls' houses. All this, plus temporary exhibitions and the museum's freely accessible garden, filled with Dutch Golden Age gateways and architectural fragments.

In the early 21st century, the Rijksmuseum was closed for a decade and a €375 million renovation. It reopened to much fanfare in 2013, and Spanish architect firm Cruz y Ortiz was awarded the prestigious Abe Bonnema Prize for its masterful work, recreating the museum's original clear layout. Minimal alternations were made to the building itself, but the redesign transformed the 19th-century building into the bright, spacious and awe-inspiring 21st-century museum it is today. British historian Simon Schama called the design 'an inauguration of a curatorial revolution'. He said: 'When you see those early Rembrandts or the great mannerist *Massacre of the Innocents* of Cornelis van Haarlem with its ballet of twisting rumps, you will also encounter, as would those who would first have seen them, the silver, weapons and cabinets that were the furniture of the culture that made those pictures possible.'

It's easy to be completely consumed by a museum of this stature, and it's certainly a worthy way to spend the best part of a day. The museum is laid out over four floors numbered from zero to three, but the collections aren't laid out chronologically. If you want to take a walk through the ages, start in the basement (where the main entrance is) for the Middle Ages and the Renaissance, then head up to the 17th-century rooms on Floor 2. Eighteenth- and 19th-century artefacts (plus a few Van Goghs) are housed back down on Floor 1, and there is a limited 20th-century collection on Floor 3. However, if you can't spare a full day to devour the museum's historical delights, head straight to Floor 2, where you'll find the finest works of the Dutch Golden Age on show in the Gallery of Honour, culminating with Rembrandt's *The Night Watch* (officially titled *Militia Company of District II under the Command of Captain Frans Banninck Cocq*; 1642). The Asia Pavilion, a new addition courtesy of Cruz y Ortiz, is separate to the main museum and accessed from the entrance foyer. If you want to avoid the crowds, visit between Monday and Thursday, either right on opening or after 3pm.

There is also a vaulted cycle passage that goes through the museum. The museum's original plan was to close the tunnel to bicycles, but the local government stepped in (after much goading by the Dutch Bicycling Union and the public) to keep it open. So enjoy the art, but do keep an eye out for those passing cyclists while you're standing in line. Don't miss the museum's excellent website; book tickets online to avoid the queues.

▶ *Visit the Rembrandthuis to see the world's largest collection of Rembrandt's sketches;* *see p155.*

❤ Don't miss

1 Gallery of Honour *Floor 2*
All the big hitters of the Dutch Golden Age: Hals, Steen, Vermeer and, of course, Rembrandt.

2 The Cuypers Library *Floor 1*
The Netherlands' biggest and oldest art library restored to its stunning original glory.

3 Dolls' houses *Room 2.20*
Marvel at these miniature delights among the many 17th-century treasures on Floor 2.

4 Asia Pavilion
A beautiful setting for the museum's collection of exquisite Asian artefacts.

Model of the William Rex

The Night Watch

❤ Van Gogh Museum

Museumplein 6 (020 570 5200, www.vangoghmuseum.nl). Tram 2, 3, 5, 12. ***Open*** *9am-5pm Mon-Thu, Sat, Sun; 9am-9pm Fri.* ***Admission*** *€19; free under-18s, Iamsterdam, MK. Temporary exhibitions vary.* ***Map*** *p136 G14.*

The Van Gogh Museum lures art enthusiasts, historians and curious tourists year-round, and is the second most visited museum in the Netherlands with good reason. As well as the bright colours of his palette, Vincent van Gogh is best known for his productivity, and this is reflected in the sheer volume of work permanently exhibited here. With more than 200 paintings, 500 drawings and 700 hand-written letters, the museum houses the world's largest collection of works by the artist.

The Van Gogh Museum first opened in Museumplein in 1973, and has since evolved to become a cutting-edge exhibition space consisting of two buildings: the main Rietveld Building and the Kurokawa Wing – a new glass and steel entrance hall opened in 2015 to connect the two. The main building exhibits everything Van Gogh, with each section dedicated to a different era. To follow the timeline of his tragic life, start at the bottom then make your way up to the third floor. The second floor provides background information about Van Gogh's life, family and friends, including the original letters he wrote to his brother and other relatives. The exhibition wing serves to add perspective to Van Gogh's artistic efforts, with examples of Japanese prints and work by the likes of Manet, Monet and Toulouse-Lautrec. Temporary exhibitions focusing on Van Gogh's contemporaries and his influence on other artists are assembled from both the museum's own extensive archives and private collections.

► *To avoid the queues book online, or try visiting either between 9am and 11am or late afternoon. A walk through the museum will only take an hour or two. It's worth noting that Friday evenings often feature lectures, concerts and films.*

❤ Don't miss

1 The Potato Eaters *First floor*
The emerging artist's first major work, depicting peasants eating at a table (1885).

2 The Yellow House *First floor*
The house Van Gogh temporarily shared with Gauguin in Arles (1888).

3 Sunflowers *First floor*
A master study in yellow, described by Gauguin as 'completely Vincent' (1889).

4 Wheatfield with Crows *Top floor*
Dead-end path under a menacing sky – was this 1890 work Van Gogh's final painting?

Van Gogh's colour palette

Child's Play

Family-friendly museum visits

Visiting a museum with kids is not always a peaceful or inspiring experience. To keep boredom or tantrums at bay, ask about any children-specific activities. Many of the museums offer treasure hunts, audio tours and special children's trails.

CoBrA Museum of Modern Art *p149*
Every Sunday between 11am and 2pm, the CoBrA hosts its popular Kinderatelier (Children's Studio), where kids can paint and draw under the guidance of a teacher. This includes a special tour of the museum.

Rijksmuseum *p140*
The museum offers a variety of workshops related to colour, etching, digital cartooning, photography and even stop-motion animation. There's also a kids' highlights tour and family multimedia tour with a number of museum mysteries to solve. The Picnic Room on the ground floor provides a space for families to relax, draw and eat.

Stedelijk Museum *p139*
Amsterdam's main modern art museum offers kids' workshops, trails and family tours, as well as a Family Lab related to the current temporary exhibition – for example, build a useless machine or moving artwork à la Jean Tinguely.

Van Gogh Museum *p142*
This popular museum hosts a bevy of children's activities, such as a weekend workshop themed to a current exhibition, including a tour and painting time. English tours are available with advance group bookings. There's also a children's audio tour and a treasure hunt.

► *For kids' activities at other museums and attractions throughout the city, check individual websites and consult the 'Families and children' section of iamsterdam.com.*

Restaurants & cafés

Bagels & Beans €

Van Baerlestraat 40 (020 675 7050, www.bagelsbeans.nl).Tram 2, 5, 12. ***Open*** *8am-5.30pm Mon-Fri; 8.30am-5.30pm Sat, Sun.* ***Map*** *p136 F14* ❶ *Café*

An Amsterdam success story, this branch of B&B has a wonderfully peaceful back patio. It's perfect for an economical breakfast, lunch or snack, elevating the humble bagel to the status of something far more sublime and satisfying. **Other locations** throughout the city.

Le Garage €€€€

Ruysdaelstraat 54-56 (020 679 7176, www.restaurantlegarage.nl). Tram 3, 5, 12, 24. ***Open*** *noon-3pm, 6-11pm Mon-Fri; 6-11pm Sat.* ***Map*** *p136 G16* ❹ *French*

Don your glad rags to blend in at this fashionable brasserie, which is great for emptying your wallet while you watch a selection of ageing Dutch glitterati do exactly the same. The authentic French regional cuisine – and 'worldly' versions thereof – is pretty good.

I Kriti €€

Balthasar Floriszstraat 3 (020 664 1445). Tram 3, 5, 12, 24. ***Open*** *5-10.30pm daily.* ***Map*** *p136 H16* ❼ *Greek*

Eat and party Greek-style in this evocation of Crete, where a standard choice of dishes is lovingly prepared. Bouzouki-picking legends drop in on occasion and pump up the frenzied atmosphere, further boosted by plate-lobbing antics. Nearby, **De Greikse Taverna** (Hobbemakade 64-65, 020 671 7923, www.degrieksetaverna.nl) may lack plate-smashing atmosphere but competes on taste.

Bars

❤ Café Welling

Jan Willem Brouwerstraat 32 (020 662 0155, www.cafewelling.nl). Tram 3, 5, 12. ***Open*** *4pm-1am Mon-Fri; 3pm-2am Sat; 3pm-1am Sun.* ***Map*** *p136 F15* ❹

Just behind the Concertgebouw, brownish Welling offers plenty of choice in the beer department – plus excellent, locally produced *jenever*. The welcoming atmosphere is in contrast to many of the other overpriced, posh spots near here. Be charmed by the regulars, who often come in carrying their instruments.

Café Wildschut

Roelof Hartplein 1-3 (020 676 8220, www.cafewildschut.nl). Tram 3, 5, 12. ***Open*** *9am-midnight Mon; 9am-1am Tue-Thu; 9am-2am Fri; 10am-2am Sat; 10am-midnight Sun.* ***Map*** *p136 G16* ❺

A stunning example of Amsterdam School architecture (*see p266*), this elegant semi-circular place puts the 'grand' into grand café and drips with nouveau detail. Drink and food choices mirror the upmarket surroundings, as do the clientele, which include flush locals, loud yuppies and art-weary tourists in desperate need of refuelling.

Shops & services

PC Hooftstraat may be known as the high-end shopping street, but it's not the only place. Head further south, around Cornelius Schuytstraat and Jacob Obrechtstraat, to really give your wallet a bashing.

❤ Azzurro Due

Van Baerlestraat 3 (020 671 9708, www.azzurrodue.com). Tram 2, 5, 12. ***Open*** *noon-6pm Mon; 10am-6pm Tue-Sat; noon-5pm Sun.* ***Map*** *p136 F14* ❶ *Fashion*

If you have the urge to splurge, this is as good a spot as any, with saucy picks from Balenciaga, Vetements, Jade Jagger and Chloé.

Azzurro Due

OUD WEST

Between Westerpark and the Museum Quarter and Vondelpark lies Oud West. While mostly a residential area, the shopping streets De Clercqstraat, Kinkerstraat and, especially, hipster strip Jan Pieter Heijestraat are all worth a wander. Outdoor market **Ten Katemarkt** (Ten Katestraat 97-99. 9am-5pm Mon-Sat) provides the district's heart – along with food, clothes and cafés. One of the market's cross-streets, Bellamystraat, is regarded by many as one of the cuter streets in the city, with its tiny but lush front yards. In recent years, Oud West has developed into more of a going-out destination, with the opening of various bars, hipster cafés and creative hubs, notably **De Hallen** (Hannie Dankbaarpassage 47, dehallen-amsterdam.nl) in 2014. This former tram depot and 19th-century monument has been turned into a centre for media, fashion, craft and culture, complete with hotel, shops, cinema (*see p208* Film Hallen), TV studios, library, food court (Foodhallen) and daycare.

Restaurants & cafés

Café Panache €€€

Ten Katestraat 117 (cafepanache.nl). Tram 3, 7, 17. ***Open*** *5pm-1am Mon-Thur, Sun; 5pm-3am Sat, Sun.* ***Map*** *p136 D11* ❷ *American*

The perfect place to take cover from Amsterdam's unpredictable weather, Café Panache makes you feel at ease the second you walk in. Exposed wood walls are decorated with forest-green plants to create the sense of an urban saloon. Guests can sit down for a meal (be sure to book in advance) or sip on a cocktail at the bar. Just ask the waiter what the specials are.

❤ Foodhallen €€

Bellamyplein 51 (www.foodhallen.nl). Tram 7, 17. ***Open*** *11am-11pm Mon-Thu, Sun; 11am-1 am Fri, Sat.* ***Map*** *p136 D11* ❸ *Eclectic*

Located in the tram-depot-turned-cultural complex De Hallen (*see above*), the Foodhallen is an indoor food market with something to satisfy just about every hankering. Serving a delicious array of high-end street food and both traditional and imported beers, the Foodhallen is often full of locals enjoying a casual meal or drink with friends. On a cold winter's night you can't go past the wood-fired pizzas and if you're visiting in the warmer months the Vietnamese summer rolls never disappoint. It tends to get busy around peak times, so if you're with a big group it's worth heading there a bit earlier to nab a seat.

Hap Hmm €€

1e Helmerstraat 33 (020 618 1884, www.hap-hmm.nl). Tram 1, 2, 3, 5, 11, 12. ***Open*** *5-9.15pm Mon-Fri.* ***No cards. Map*** *p136 F12* 5 Dutch

Hungry but hard up? You need some of the Dutch grandma cooking served in this canteen with a living-room feel. 'Yummy Bite', as the name translates, will happily fill your empty insides with meat and potatoes for not much more than €12. Bookings are not possible.

Koffie Academie €€

Overtoom 95 (020 370 7981, www.koffie-academie.nl). Tram 1, 3, 11. ***Open*** *8.30am-5pm Mon-Fri; 9am-5pm Sat, Sun.* ***Map*** *p136 E13* 6 Global

Freelancers and creative types abound in this cosy Dutch coffee-bar. Centrally located on the north of bustling Overtoom, Koffie Acadamie provides a tranquil oasis from the buzz of the outside world. The prices are high but the experience is lovely. A great place to relax or people watch from the window seats.

❤ Lot Sixty One €€

Kinkerstraat 112 (020 1605 4227, lotsixtyonecoffee.com). Tram 3, 7, 17. ***Open*** *8am-6pm Mon-Fri; 9am-6pm Sat, Sun.* ***Map*** *p136 D11* 8 Café

It's a hipster coffee snob's paradise. Australian-born Adam Craig brought his barista expertise to Amsterdam and opened Lot Sixty One with roaster pal Paul (also Aussie) in 2013. It has fast become one of the biggest players in Amsterdam's caffeine scene, supplying beautiful beans to cafés and restaurants across the city. The tiny café is often overflowing with coffee-lovers, but it's worth the wait: coffee here is among the best in the city.

Pastis €€€

1e Constantijn Huygensstraat 15 (020 616 6166, www.pastisamsterdam.nl). Tram 3, 7, 17. ***Open*** *5-10pm Mon-Thu; 3-10.30pm Sat, Sun.* ***Map*** *p136 E12* 9 Brasserie

This Pastis may not be in New York's meatpacking district, but the neighbourhood favourite sure packs a punch when it comes to brasserie classics, from caesar salad to crème brûlée. Generous opening hours make it the perfect choice for a very easy Sunday afternoon.

De Peper €

Overtoom 301 (020 412 2954, www.depeper.org). Tram 1, 11. ***Open*** *6pm-1am Tue, Thu; 6pm-3am Fri (kitchen 7-8.30pm). Closed Mon, Wed, Sat, Sun.* ***No cards. Map*** *p136 C13* 10 Vegetarian

The cheapest and best vegan food in town is to be found within the artistic 'breeding ground' OT301 (ot301.nl), a legalised squat with a wide range of cultural activities and

Lot Sixty One

spaces. De Peper is a collectively organised, non-profit project combining culture with cooking – and there's usually a DJ to aid digestion. But do book ahead on the day that you plan to visit (call 3-7pm).

De Peperwortel €
Overtoom 140 (020 685 1053, www.peperwortel.nl). Tram 1, 3, 11. ***Open*** *noon-9pm daily.* ***No cards. Map*** *p136 E13* ⑪
Global

One could survive for weeks eating nothing except takeaways from **Riaz** (*see below*) and this *traiteur*, the fabulous 'Pepper Root'. It serves a wide range of dishes, embracing Dutch, Mexican, Asian and Spanish cuisines.

Riaz €
Bilderdijkstraat 193 (020 683 6453, www.riaz.nl). Tram 3, 7, 17. ***Open*** *4pm-10pm Tue-Sun.* ***No cards. Map*** *p136 E11* ⑫ *Surinamese*

A household name in these parts, Riaz is one of Amsterdam's finest Surinamese restaurants. Since 1981, the chefs have been cooking their exclusive and authentic recipes. You have to taste it to believe it.

❤ Spaghetteria West €€
Jan Hanzenstraat 32 (spaghetteria-pastabar.nl). Tram 7, 17. ***Open*** *5-10pm daily.* ***Map*** *p136 C11* ⑭ *Italian*

Nestled cosily on the corner of Jan Hanzenstraat, Spaghetteria has the warm, inviting feel of a family living room, with the addition of expertly prepared pasta. The menu changes daily, with all six pasta dishes prepared freshly that day according to age old recipes. Wander over after a pre-dinner cocktail at **Café Panache** (*see p144*) and you won't be disappointed.

❤ Staring at Jacob €€
Jacob van Lennepkade 215 (020 223 7498, www.staringatjacob.nl). Tram 7, 17. ***Open*** *9.30am-4.30pm daily.* ***Map*** *p136 B13* ⑮
American

This New York-style brunch spot and diner is the perfect place to go for hearty hangover food. With fried chicken waffles, fluffy butternut pancakes, and BLTs to make you salivate – there's also a mean Dirty Bloody Mary if you require some hair of the dog – you'll be rolling home regardless of whether you arrive by bike.

Bars

't Blauwe Theehuis
Vondelpark 5 (020 662 0254, www.blauwetheehuis.nl). Tram 2, 5, 12. ***Open*** *9am-11pm daily (hours extended on sunny weekends).* ***Map*** *p136 E14* ❶

Top 20

❤ Vondelpark

Vondelpark is named after the city's best-known poet, Joost van den Vondel, whose controversial play *Lucifer* caused the religious powers of the 17th century to crack down hard on those who engaged in what was termed 'notorious living'. This is the most central of the city's major parks. Its creation was inspired by the redevelopment of Plantage, which, until the 19th century, had provided green surroundings for the leisurely walks of the rich. The original ten acres opened in 1865 and were designed in the 'English style' by Jan David Zocher, with the emphasis on natural landscaping. The park has actually sunk some two to three metres since it was first built – some larger trees are either 'floating' on blocks of styrofoam or reinforced with underground poles.

There are several ponds and lakes in the park plus a number of play areas and cafés, including **'t Blauwe Theehuis** (*see p146*) and the **Groot Melkhuis** (020 612 9674, www.

grootmelkhuis.nl), a chalet-style café by the water with a terrace and kids' playground.

Keep your eye out for a huge Picasso sculpture in the middle of the park, and for the wild parakeets that were accidentally released in 1976 and have spread across the city. Round the corner – and providing a unique place for coffee – is the **Hollandsche Manege** (Vondelstraat 140, 020 618 0942, www.dehollandschemanege.nl), a wooden version of the Spanish Riding School in Vienna. It has been teaching people to ride for well over 100 years.

Vondelpark gets insanely busy on sunny days and Sundays, when bongos abound, dope is toked and football games take up any space that happens to be left over. Hundreds of avid runners and cyclists use it for their daily dose of exercise. The **Vondelpark Openluchttheater** (www.openluchttheater.nl), a long-running programme of free open-air films, plays and concerts, takes place throughout the summer.

The south-western end of the park runs along Amstelveenseweg, a varying culinary strip very much worth cruising. Head to **Ron Gastrobar** (*see p149*), but if that's busy, there are lots of other options.

For decades, Vondelpark, and especially its rose garden, has also been a notorious midnight meet-up spot for gay men looking for some frisky risk-taking, but it wasn't until 2008 that the Amsterdam district council, in a display of typical Dutch pragmatism, proclaimed a new set of rules announcing the official 'toleration' of public sex in the park. 'As long as other people in the park don't feel disturbed, then there is no problem with it,' said one politician at the time. According to the 'house rules', enjoying a garden romp is only permitted after dark, and condoms must be cleared away to keep the surrounds tidy. Police officers cannot interrupt the fun unless participants are causing a public nuisance, such as broadcasting their enjoyment too noisily or appearing too close to a public path.

One of the few local landmarks that allows you to nestle inside with a beer, HAJ Baanders' extraordinary 1930s teahouse – a sort of UFO/hat hybrid in the middle of Vondelpark – is a choice spot for fair-weather drinking, with its huge surrounding terrace. In summer, there are DJs and barbecues, although it's a romantic spot for dinner and drinks all year round.

Café Ebeling

Overtoom 52 (020 777 2005, www.de-ebeling.nl). Tram 1, 2, 3, 5, 11, 12. ***Open*** *10am-1am Sun-Wed; 10am-3am Thu; 10am-4am Fri, Sat.* ***Map*** *p136 F12* ❸

Don't be surprised if you have to swerve to avoid the crowds of people piling out of Café Ebeling on your way home at night. The bar is a favourite among locals, who are known to carve up the dancefloor on any given evening. If you decide to go on a weekend, brace yourself for the immense number of people looking to blow off some steam – rain, hail or shine. It's far more low key during the day, however – with a reasonably priced menu.

❤ Gollem's Proeflokaal

Overtoom 160-162 (020 612 9444, www.cafegollem.nl). Tram 1, 3, 11. ***Open*** *1pm-1am Mon-Thur; noon-3am Fri, Sat; noon-1am Sun.* ***No cards. Map*** *p136 E13* ❻

A simply outstanding place to get sozzled, this dark and cosy Belgian beer specialist offers more than 150 bottled brews – including 42 abbey beers and 14 trappist – and 21 on tap, from easy-drinkers to demonic head-pounders such as Delirium Tremens. The helpful menu lists the strengths of the suds for those erring on the side of caution. There's also a pubby food menu. Another more elfish and ancient branch is at Raamsteeg 4, on the New Side.

Shops & services

Marqt

Overtoom 21 (020 820 8292, www.marqt.com). Tram 1, 2, 5, 11, 12. ***Open*** *9am-9pm daily.* ***No cash. Map*** *p136 F12* ❷ *Food & drink*

Amsterdam's newest organics market focuses on fresh produce, meat and fish sourced from local and regional farmers and independent producers. It also sells great fresh bread from Brood bakery and pizzas from De Pizza Bakker. Products are predominately fair trade too. **Other locations** Utrechtsestraat 17; Haarlemmerstraat 165; Wolvenstraat 32, Western Canal Belt; all in the Grachtengordel.

NIEUW ZUID

Nieuw Zuid (New South) is bordered to the north by Vondelpark, to the east by the Amstel and to the west by the **Olympisch Stadion** (www.olympischstadion.nl), constructed for the 1928 Olympic Games. The area is noted for its Amsterdam School glory (*see p266*). The New South was planned by Hendrik Berlage and put into action by a variety of Amsterdam School architects, who designed both private and public housing for the area. It's the former that's given the New South what character it has, most notably around Apollolaan and Beethovenstraat.

The few visitors tend to be here on business, especially around the **World Trade Center** and the steadily rising modern architecture neighbourhood of **Zuidas**. The controversial Noord/Zuidlijn metro is designed to link this district with the centre of town and Amsterdam Noord (*see p32*). East of here is another staple of Amsterdam business life: the ugly **RAI Exhibition & Congress Centre**, which holds numerous trade fairs, conventions and public exhibitions throughout the year.

However, in between the RAI and the WTC lies one of Amsterdam's most beautiful parks. Extended and renovated in 1994, **Beatrixpark** is a wonderfully peaceful place, very handy if you want to avoid the crowds in town on a summer's day. The Victorian walled garden is worth a visit, as is the pond, complete with geese, black swans and herons. Amenities include a wading pool and play area for kids. Nearby, housed in a circular ex-church, is the highly regarded **Restaurant As** (Prinses Irenestraat 19, 020 644 0100, www.restaurantas.nl); it's known for rearing its own pigs.

Further south still, **Amstelpark** was created for a garden festival in 1972, and today offers recreation and respite to locals in the suburb of Buitenveldert. A formal rose garden and rhododendron walk are among the seasonal spectacles, and there's also a labyrinth, pony rides, mini golf, and a children's farm, plus tours on a miniature train.

Sights & museums

Electrische Museumtramlijn Amsterdam

Amstelveenseweg 264 (020 673 7538, www.museumtramlijn.org). Tram 2 or bus 15, 62. ***Open*** *Easter-Oct 11am-5pm Sun only; trams depart every 20-30 mins.* ***Tickets*** *(return) Line 20 €7, €4 reductions; Line 30 €5.50, €3.50 reductions. No cards.* ***Map*** *p136 off map.*

Both the pride and raison d'être of the Electric Tramline Museum, based in a beautiful 1915 railway station, is its rolling stock. Colourful antique streetcars, gathered from several cities, make their way along the special 7km (4-mile) Line 30 that heads south from the station through the surprisingly rural Amsterdamse Bos, and Line 20, which takes you on a loop round the central canal ring. The station also houses a fine café called **Macy's**.

Restaurants & cafés

Ron Gastrobar €€

Sophialaan 55 (020 496 1943, www.rongastrobar.nl). Tram 2. ***Open*** *noon-2.30pm every day; 5.30-10.20pm Mon-Sun; 5-10.30pm Sun.* ***Map*** *p136 A16* ⓭ Modern Dutch

Ron Gastrobar is named after local entrepreneurial celebrity chef Ron Blaauw, who put his two Michelin stars on the line by coming up with a simpler, more affordable menu of 12 classic, back-to-basics mains costing €17.50 each (there's also a specials menu and a steak list).

Bars

❤ Butcher's Tears

Karperweg 45 (www.butchers-tears.com). Tram 2, 24 or bus 15, 62. ***Open*** *4-9pm, Wed, Thur; 4-11pm Fri, Sat; 2-7pm Sun.* ***No cards.*** ***Map*** *p136 off map* ❷

This small brewery opened a 'tasting local' in 2013. A self-proclaimed 'haven to clear your senses from the blur', it has eight beers on draft ranging from a hoppy table ales to a 7% double stout. It has also started doing events and small gigs too.

AMSTELVEEN

Of all the southern suburbs, Amstelveen is the most welcoming to the casual visitor. Though the **CoBrA Museum** helps, the main attraction here is the **Amsterdamse Bos**, a mammoth planned wood that's treasured by locals yet neglected by visitors. Providing work for 20,000 unemployed people during the Depression, this forestation project started in 1934, and the last tree was planted in 1967. With its 137 kilometres (85 miles) of footpaths, 51 kilometres (32 miles) of cycle paths, 50 bridges, 150 indigenous species of trees and over 200 species of birds, the Amsterdamse Bos is one of the largest city parks in Europe. The eight-square-kilometre (three-square-mile) site sprawls beautifully and comes with a great many attractions in case the tranquillity isn't enough.

The man-made **Bosbaan** lake is used for rowing, fishing and, in freezing winters, a spot of ice-skating. Other attractions include a visitor centre (**Bezoekerscentrum Amsterdamse Bos**), play areas, a horticultural museum, jogging routes, a buffalo and bison reserve, the Fun Forest tree-top climbing park (Apr-Nov), a bike-hire centre (Apr-Oct), a watersports centre, stables and a picnic area. There's also the free **Ridammerhoeve Goat Farm** (Nieuwe Meerlaan 4, Amsterdamse Bos, 020 645 5034, www.geitenboerderij.nl), where you can pet and feed goats, pigs, hens and horses, and purchase some excellent-quality cheese.

Sights & museums

Bezoekerscentrum Amsterdamse Bos

Bosbaanweg 5, near Amstelveenseweg (545 6100, www.amsterdamsebos.nl). Bus 463. ***Open*** *10am-5pm Tue-Sun.* ***Admission*** *free.* ***Map*** *p136 off map.*

The visitor centre recounts the history and use of the Amsterdamse Bos. Its mock woodland grotto, which can turn from day to night at the flick of a switch, is wonderful for kids.

CoBrA Museum of Modern Art

Sandbergplein 1 (020 547 5050, www.cobra-museum.nl). Tram 5, 6 or Metro 51 or bus 347, 357. ***Open*** *11am-5pm Tue-Sun.* ***Admission*** *€15; reductions €8.50; free under-6s, Iamsterdam, MK. No cards (except shop).* ***Map*** *p136 off map.*

An acronym for Copenhagen, Brussels and Amsterdam – the cities from which the key artists of the movement hailed – the marvellous CoBrA Museum of Modern Art includes masterpieces by the avant-garde artists of the original CoBrA movement, as well as new work by contemporary artists. It was the northern European artistic response to the destruction and chaos of World War II. The CoBrA artists created a style unimpeded by academic traditions, marked by vibrant colours and typically created with a sense of spontaneity. The museum itself, a beautiful airy space with an abundance of natural light and a view over a swan-dotted canal bordered by weeping willows, was founded in 1995 with a mission to become the definitive exhibition space and archive for artwork and documentation about the movement. Its permanent collection contains about 300 paintings, sculptures and works on paper, as well as archived documents from the CoBrA era.

Jodenbuurt, Plantage & Oost

Starting east of the Old Centre and bordered by the IJ harbour to the north, the area now known as Jodenbuurt is the city's old Jewish quarter. Evidence of this history remains at the Jewish Historical Museum and the Portugese Synagogue. The area is also known as the home of Rembrandt, who relocated from Leiden in 1631 to what is now the Rembrandthuis museum. To the south-east, Plantage is characterised by verdant spaces and 19th-century residences, with the city's royal zoo, founded in 1838, at its heart. Cross Singelgracht from here to reach Oost, a working-class and immigrant district that has since become one of the city's hippest and buzziest areas. Oosterpark and Flevopark are pleasant green oases here, or you can head north and east to the Eastern Docklands and the IJ islands (*see p168*).

❤ Don't miss

1 Rembrandthuis *p155*
Walk in Rembrandt's footsteps at his original place of work.

2 Nationale Opera & Ballet *p238*
The custom-built home of high culture.

3 Verzetsmuseum *p159*
The moving story of the Dutch Resistance in World War II.

4 Brouwerij 't IJ *p163*
Beer brewed in the shadow of a windmill.

5 Tropenmuseum *p161*
Dig deep into world cultures.

Tropenmuseum

JODENBUURT, PLANTAGE & OOST

Restaurants & cafés

1. Alex + Pinard *p161*
2. Beter & Leuk *p161*
3. Café Bakhuys *p159*
4. Café Waterlooplein 77 *p155*
5. Canvas *p161*
6. Coffee Bru *p161*
7. De Kas *p163*
8. Louie Louie *p163*
9. De Plantage *p159*
10. Rijsel *p163*
11. La Rive *p157*

Bars

1. De Biertuin *p163*
2. Brouwerij 't IJ *p163*
3. Café de Sluyswacht *p157*
4. Café Eik & Linde *p159*
5. Hiding in Plain Sight *p157*

Shops & services

1. Dappermarkt *p163*
2. Hartje Oost *p163*
3. Waterlooplein Market *p157*

❤ Time to eat, drink & shop

Coffee on the terrace
Coffee Bru *p161*

Dangerous cocktails
Hiding in Plain Sight *p157*

Endless beer list
De Biertuin *p163*, Brouwerij 't IJ *p163*

Fine dining
La Rive *p157*

Local market
Dappermarkt *p163*

Neighbourhood boutique
Hartje Oost *p163*

Sundowner with a view
Canvas *p161*

In the know
Getting around

Jodenbuurt is centrally located to the east of the Old Centre, walking distance from Nieuwmarkt. Tram 14 runs through Jodenbuurt to Plantage. Waterlooplein is served by metro lines 51, 53 and 54.

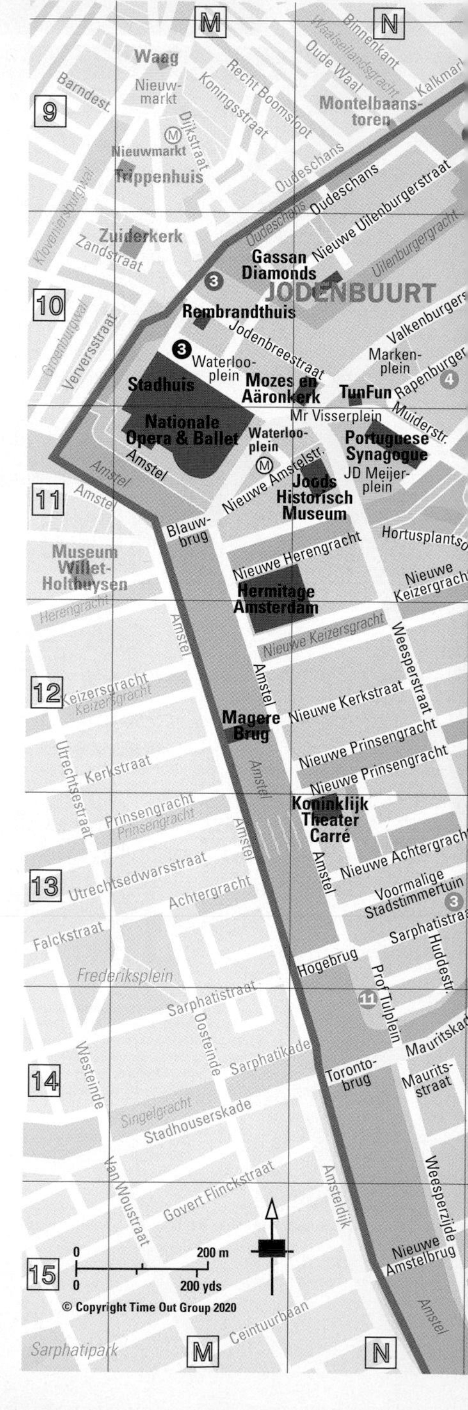

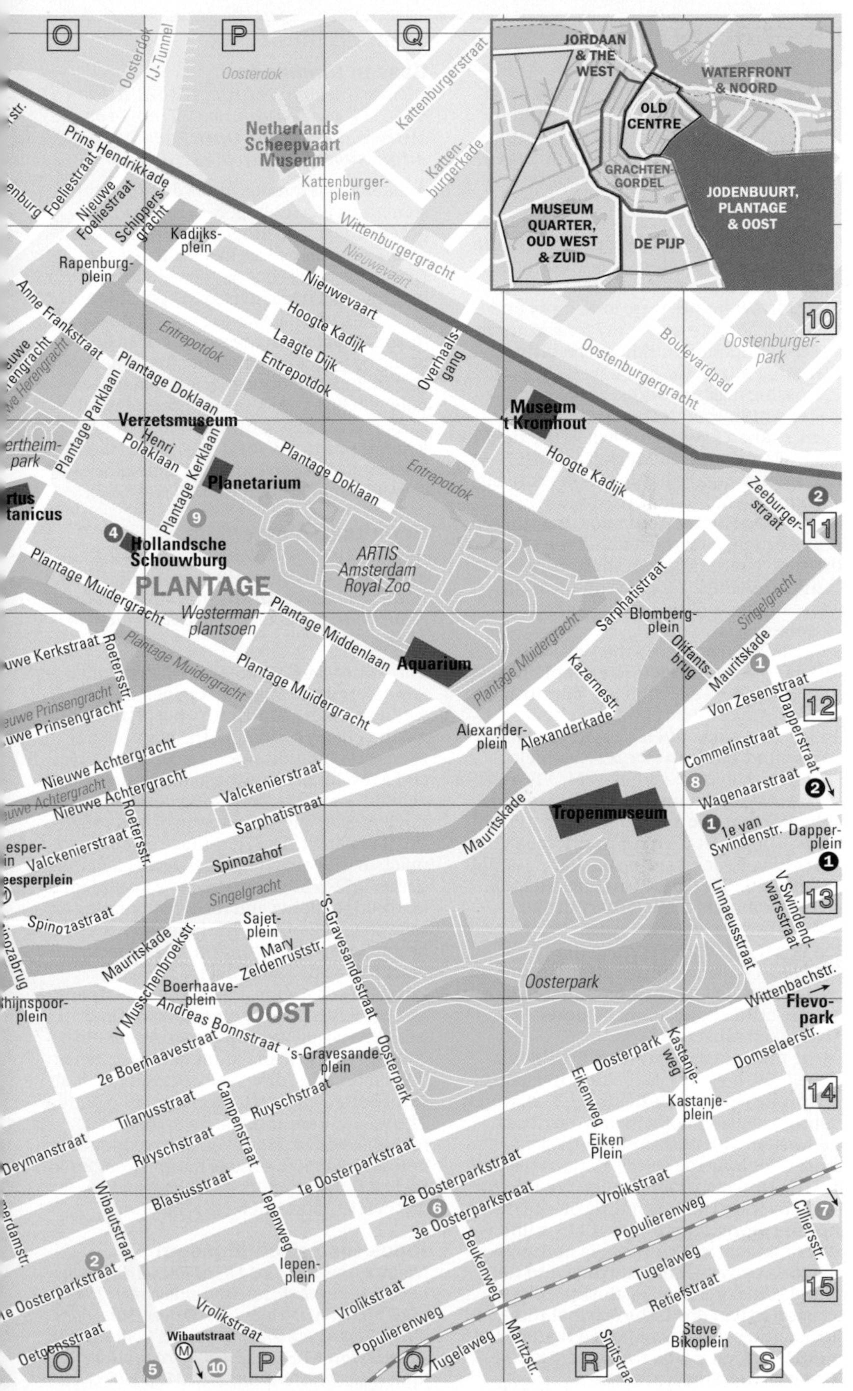

Netherlands Scheepvaart Museum
Verzetsmuseum
Planetarium
Hollandsche Schouwburg
PLANTAGE
ARTIS Amsterdam Royal Zoo
Aquarium
Museum 't Kromhout
Tropenmuseum
Oosterpark
OOST
Flevo-park
JORDAAN & THE WEST
OLD CENTRE
WATERFRONT & NOORD
GRACHTENGORDEL
MUSEUM QUARTER, OUD WEST & ZUID
DE PIJP
JODENBUURT, PLANTAGE & OOST

JODENBUURT

Jodenbuurt's Jewish heritage dates back to the 1600s, when Jews were lured from other parts of Europe by the comparative freedom that life in Amsterdam provided. The centuries to follow saw the district develop into a lively Jewish hub; this lasted until World War II, when the Nazis concentrated the Jewish population of the Netherlands here before deportation. Not many Jews returned alive after the war. Their former homes were left empty and then torn down to make way for the metro and contemporary buildings, resulting in an intriguing mix of old and new architecture.

Crossing over the bridge at the end of Sint Antoniesbreestraat from the Old Centre, take a few steps down to the right to reach **Waterlooplein Market** (*see p157*) – a magnet for bargain-hunters. Alternatively, continuing onto Jodenbreestraat you'll arrive at **De Hogeschool voor de Kunsten** (Arts Academy) on the left and see the distinctive red and green shutters of **Rembrandthuis** (*see p155*) on the right, where Rembrandt lived and worked for 20 years.

Further along, there's the 19th-century **Mozes en Ääronkerk** (Waterlooplein 205), built on Spinoza's birthplace. This former clandestine Catholic church is situated almost above the much chirpier children's playground **TunFun** (*see p157*), which occupies an underpass below Mr Visserplein square. Above ground on Mr Visserplein is the **Portuguese Synagogue** (*see p155*). Outside, look out for Mari Andriessen's bronze *Dockworker* statue on Jonas Daniël Meijerplein. The statue was erected in 1952 to commemorate the February Strike of 1941 – a protest against Jewish deportations that began among workers in the city's shipyards. Also nearby are the museum and concert hall **Hermitage Amsterdam** and the critically acclaimed **Joods Historisch Museum**.

One of the biggest cultural highlights of the area, however, is the multipurpose **Nationale Opera & Ballet** (*see p238*), which dominates Waterlooplein and overlooks the Amstel. This custom-built theatre houses not only the Dutch National Opera and the Dutch National Ballet, but also the Stadhuis (City Hall). Standing on the site of a former Jewish ghetto, this €136 million civic headquarters-cum-opera house was designed by Wilhelm Holzbauer and Cees Dam. Locals protested against the city's decision to tear down the original 16th- and 17th-century residences, and a riot ensued in 1982 – which is why the theatre is still known as the 'Stopera'.

Sights & museums

Gassan Diamonds

Nieuwe Uilenburgerstraat 173-175, (020 622 5333, www.gassan.com). Tram 14 or Metro Waterlooplein. ***Open*** *9am-5pm daily.* ***Admission*** *free.* ***Map*** *p153 N10.*

Amsterdam is famous for its diamond trade, something it owes largely to the Jewish population in and around the Jodenbuurt area. Of the many sparkler shops, Gassan Diamonds comes out on top with an epic building that once housed 357 polishing machines, when it was the biggest diamond processing plant in the world. Get in the mood by upgrading from the free tour to one that includes champagne. But remember: falling in love with a piece of compressed carbon is the easy part – working out how you're going to pay for it may prove trickier. There's also a showroom on Dam Square in the Old Centre (Rokin 1-5, 020 624 5787).

Hermitage Amsterdam

Amstel 51 (020 530 8758, www.hermitage.nl). Tram 14 or Metro Waterlooplein. ***Open*** *10am-5pm daily.* ***Admission*** *€25; €2.50-€15 reductions; free under-11s, Iamsterdam, MK.* ***Map*** *p153 M11.*

The Amsterdam outpost of St Petersburg's State Hermitage Museum opened in 2009. Set in a former 19th-century hospital with a 17th-century courtyard, the building has two vast exhibition spaces, a concert hall and a restaurant. The museum mounts two exhibitions a year, borrowing items from the three-million-strong collection of its prestigious Russian parent. The Hermitage's riches owe much to the collecting obsession of Peter the Great (1672-1725), who came to Amsterdam to learn shipbuilding and the art of building on waterlogged ground – the latter knowledge he applied to his pet project, St Petersburg. Peter befriended local doctor Frederik Ruysch, perhaps the greatest ever anatomist and preserver of body parts and mutants in jars. Ruysch enjoyed constructing ghoulish collages with gall and kidney stones piled up into landscapes; dried veins woven into lush shrubberies, and testicles crafted into pottery. The scenes were animated with dancing foetus skeletons. However, most exhibitions here are of a more genteel nature: Rembrandt, French Impressionists or archaeological discoveries found along the Silk Route.

Joods Historisch Museum

Nieuwe Amstelstraat 1 (020 531 0310, jck.nl/nl/locatie/joods-historisch-museum). Tram 14 or Metro Waterlooplein. ***Open*** *11am-5pm daily. Closed Jewish New Year & Yom Kippur.* ***Admission*** *€17; €4.25-€8.50 reductions; free under-6s, Iamsterdam, MK.* ***Map*** *p153 N11.*

Rembrandthuis

Located in the heart of Amsterdam's historical Jewish quarter, the Jewish Historical Museum is housed in four former synagogues dating back to the 17th and 18th centuries. The museum is packed with religious items, photographs and paintings detailing the rich history of Jews and Judaism in the Netherlands throughout the centuries. It features both permanent and rotating exhibits. The former focuses on the dynamic nature of Judaism in both the past and the present with interactive exhibits on different aspects of Jewish culture. Temporary exhibitions often use interviews, film footage and photos to bring their themes to life.

The museum has received much critical acclaim thanks to its informative displays and programming, and attracts thousands of tourists all year round. The special children's wing allows youngsters to follow the life of a Jewish family, partake in Hebrew workshops and get creative with special activities.

► *For an intimate insight into a Jewish family's life in hiding, visit the Anne Frank Huis; see p102.*

Portuguese Synagogue

Mr Visserplein 3 (020 624 5351, www.esnoga.com). Tram 9, 14 or Metro Waterlooplein. ***Open*** *10am-5pm Mon-Fri, Sun. Closed Sat. Hours may change in different seasons. Closed Yom Kippur.* ***Admission*** *€17; €4.25-€8.50 reductions; free under-6s, Iamsterdam, MK.* ***Map*** *p153 N11.*

Inaugurated in 1675, architect Elias Bouwman's mammoth synagogue is one of the largest in the world and was reputedly inspired by the Temple of Solomon. It is built on wooden piles and surrounded by smaller annexes (including offices, archives and one of the world's oldest libraries). The synagogue holds occasional concerts and candlelit events.

❤ Rembrandthuis

Jodenbreestraat 4 (020 520 0400, www.rembrandthuis.nl). Tram 14 or Metro Waterlooplein. ***Open*** *10am-6pm daily.* ***Admission*** *€14; €5-€10 reductions; free under-6s, Iamsterdam, MK.* ***Map*** *p153 M10.*

Rembrandt (*see p156*) bought this house in 1639 for 13,000 guilders (then a massive sum), at the height of his career. Sadly, the free-spending artist went bankrupt in 1656 and was forced to move to a smaller house (Rozengracht 184). The house on Jodenbreestraat is now a museum, whose faithfully reconstructed interiors are based on the room-by-room inventory of his possessions that was made when he went bankrupt. Knowing it's a mock-up does add a slightly unreal air to proceedings, though. The museum also contains a remarkable collection of Rembrandt's etchings, which show him at his most experimental.

► *If it's Rembrandt's paintings you're interested in, the Rijksmuseum holds one of the largest collections of his work in the world; see p140.*

Restaurants & cafés

Café Waterlooplein 77 €€

Rapenburgerstraat 169 (020 627 9918, www.cafewaterloo.nl) Metro Waterlooplein. Tram 14 or Metro Waterlooplein. ***Open*** *2pm-1am Mon-Sat.* ***No cards.*** ***Map*** *p153 N10* ④ *Café*

Rembrandt van Rijn

Jodenbuurt's artist in residence

One of Jodenbuurt's greatest claims to fame is that it was once home to Rembrandt van Rijn (1606-1669). Though he was born in Leiden, 35 kilometres (22 miles) away, Rembrandt's professional career began and ended here. Jodenbuurt is where the artistic icon became a true Amsterdammer: broadminded, largely secular and rather prone to speculating wildly on treasures from abroad.

Rembrandt got his first taste of the city as a teenager, when, in 1623, he took a brief apprenticeship under the painter Pieter Lastman. Lastman's studio was in the then-artists' quarter of the city, which surrounded Sint Antoniesbreestraat from the Nieuwmarkt to Waterlooplein. The area, now known as Jodenbuurt, was crammed with art dealers, antiques shops, writers and map-makers, and was peopled by recent immigrants, Sephardic Jews and prostitutes – a perfect spot for a young artist to find resources and plenty of models for sketches and biblical paintings.

When Rembrandt officially settled in Amsterdam in 1631, he returned to Jodenbuurt to head up a painting academy established by art dealer Hendrick van Uylenburgh. Among Rembrandt's early works was *The Anatomy Lesson of Dr Nicolaes Tulp* (1632), now in the Mauritshuis museum in the Hague, which depicted the famous surgeon's annual dissection in the anatomy theatre in De Waag (*see p76*).

Almost immediately, the young artist became hot property, selling his portraits for hundreds of guilders and running a highly productive studio of his own, with scores of pupils and apprentices. He married his dealer's cousin, Saskia van Uylenburgh, and bought a grand mansion (now the **Rembrandthuis**; *see right*), filling it with art and collectibles. High-profile commissions flooded in, including the colossal, shadowy painting of the Arquebusiers militia group, *The Night Watch* (1642), which now hangs in the Rijksmuseum; the *Portrait of Jan Six* (a local burgher; 1654); and a group portrait of the *Syndics of the Drapers' Guild* (1662), also held by the **Rijksmuseum** (*see p140*).

Despite his professional success, Rembrandt suffered increasing personal misfortunes over the years: his wife and three of his four children died, and relationships with his two mistresses ended badly. Eventually, the commissions dried up as he fell out of favour. He went bankrupt in 1656 and was consequently forced to sell most of his art collection. He died in 1669, a year after his one remaining son, Titus, and was buried in an unmarked grave in the **Westerkerk** (*see p104*).

Nestled into a cosy space just three minutes' walk from the Jewish Historical Museum, Café Waterlooplein is the perfect place to grab a quick and easy bite to fuel up for wandering the area's streets.

❤ La Rive €€€€

InterContinental Amstel Amsterdam, Professor Tulpplein 1 (020 520 3264, www.restaurantlarive.com). Tram 1, 7, 19 or Metro Wesperplein. ***Open*** *6.30-10pm daily.* ***Map*** *p153 N14* ⑪ *French*

Here you'll find superb regional French cuisine without the excessive formality that can too often mar such places. For the perfect meal when money is no object.

Bars

Café de Sluyswacht

Jodenbreestraat 1 (020 625 7611, www.sluyswacht.nl). Tram 14 or Metro Waterlooplein. ***Open*** *12.30pm-1am Mon-Thur; 12.30pm-3am Fri, Sat; 12.30-7pm Sun.* ***Map*** *p153 M10* ❸

Listing crazily, this wooden-framed bar has been pleasing drinkers for decades, though the building itself has been around since 1695, when it began life as a lock-keeper's cottage. It's snug and warm inside, while outside commands great views of Oude Schans – making it suitable for boozing in both balmy and inclement weather. An excellent place for a sneaky sundowner.

❤ Hiding in Plain Sight

Rapenburg 18 (06 2529 3620 mobile, www.hpsamsterdam.com). Bus 22, 48. ***Open*** *6pm-1am Mon-Thur, Sun; 6pm-3am Fri, Sat.* ***Map*** *p153 N9* ❺

Given this speakeasy-style cocktail bar's proximity to the ancient docks where sailors would snog their goodbyes before embarking on treacherous journeys, it's appropriate that it offers liquid danger in the form of a concoction called 'the Walking Dead'. Based on the potent zombie, HPS's secret recipe is served (and then set on fire) in a giant glass skull. Bar-imposed limit: one per night. Reservations are recommended and are essential for groups.

Shops & services

Waterlooplein Market

Waterlooplein (no phone). Tram 14 or Metro Waterlooplein. ***Open*** *9am-5.30pm Mon-Fri; 8.30am-5.30pm Sat.* ***No cards. Map*** *p153 M10* ❸ *Market*

Amsterdam's top tourist market is basically an enormous flea market with the added attraction of loads of new clothes (although gear can be a bit pricey and, at many stalls, a bit naff). Bargains can be found, but they may well be hidden under piles of cheap 'n' nasty toasters and down-at-heel (literally) shoes. Be prepared to dig around.

In the know

Indoor playground

Located in a former underpass at Mr Visserplein, **TunFun** (020 689 4300, www.tunfun.nl, closed Mon, Tue) is a cavernous indoor playground and an excellent example of creative urban regeneration. Huge soft-play constructions provide endless joy for those under 12, with ball pools for tiny tots and full-on jungle gyms for more adventurous older kids. Prices are €4.25 for toddlers and €8.50 for 3-12s; accompanying adults pay €2.50.

PLANTAGE

South-east of Mr Visserplein lies the largely residential area known as Plantage. Located between Jodenbuurt and Oost, 'The Plantation' began as leisure gardens for Amsterdam's citizens. The area came within the city limits in the late 1600s, but the government couldn't find enough buyers for the land. It wasn't urbanised until the city expanded in the 1800s, when it became one of Amsterdam's first suburban developments for the wealthier residents of Amsterdam, with elegant villas and wide streets. The attractive Plantage Middenlaan winds past the **Hortus Botanicus** (*see p158*), passes close to the **Verzetsmuseum** (*see p159*) and runs along the edge of **ARTIS Amsterdam Royal Zoo** (*see p158*) before heading towards the marvellous **Tropenmuseum** (*see p161*).

In the late 19th and early 20th centuries, Amsterdam was a major world diamond centre, and most of the rocks were cut and sold in and around this area. The headquarters of the diamond cutters' union, designed by Hendrik Berlage as a far more outward expression of socialism than his Stock Exchange (aka **Beurs van Berlage**, *see p78*), still exists on Henri Polaklaan as **De Burcht** (www.deburcht.nl), an events location that also runs occasional tours of the epic interior. Other extant buildings – such as the **Gassan** (*see p154*) back on Nieuwe Uilenburgerstraat– also act as reminders that the town's most profitable trade was once based here. However, the spectre of World War II reappears at the **Hollandse Schouwburg** (*see p158*), while the **Verzetsmuseum** (*see p159*) documents the Dutch Resistance. Look out too for Van Eyck's **Moederhuis** (Plantage Middenlaan 33), built as a refuge for young, pregnant women.

Plantage is still a wealthy part of town, with graceful buildings and tree-lined streets, although its charm has somewhat faded over the years. The area has seen extensive redevelopment; if you wander down Entrepotdok, you can admire the delicate balancing act between the new and the old, with post-hippie houseboats and good views of ARTIS providing a charming contrast to the new apartment buildings.

Sights & museums

ARTIS Amsterdam Royal Zoo

Plantage Kerklaan 38-40 (020 523 3670, www.artis.nl). Tram 14. ***Open*** *Summer 9am-6pm daily. Winter 9am-5pm daily.* ***Admission*** *€24; €20.50 reductions; free under-3s. €2 discount for online tickets.* ***Map*** *p153 P11.*

Founded in 1838, ARTIS was the first zoo in mainland Europe and is the third oldest in the world. Exhibiting both live and mounted specimens, it was established by nature-lovers Gerard Westerman, JWH Werlemann and JJ Wijsmuller in what was then the outskirts of a much smaller Amsterdam. ARTIS was open exclusively to members only until 1851, when the general public was able to visit during the month of September. It wasn't until the early 20th century that the public could visit all year round.

Today, the zoo is home to more than 750 species of animals, including giraffes, elephants and zebras. It is an active member of the European Endangered Species breeding programme and is heavily oriented towards scientific research, with close affiliations with the Zoological Museum Amsterdam.

Along with the usual animals, ARTIS has an indoor 'rainforest' for nocturnal creatures and a 120-year-old aquarium with a simulated canal, complete with eels and bike wrecks. Further attractions include a planetarium, a geological museum and, for kids, a petting zooand playground. Next door you'll find Micropia, the world's only museum dedicated to micro-organisms. From June to August, the zoo stays open until sunset every Saturday. Known as 'ZOOmeravonden', these extended summer evenings bring a roster of free activities, such as face-painting for kids, live music and zookeeper talks (in Dutch, but worth watching nevertheless).

> **In the know**
> **What's in a name?**
>
> ARTIS Amsterdam Royal Zoo got its nickname by mistake. When the zoo was opened to the public in the 1800s, the words '*Natura*', '*Artis*' and '*Magistra*' (Latin for 'Nature is the teacher of art') were written above three separate gates within its grounds. Often, only the middle gate was opened, so visitors thought the zoo was simply called 'Artis'.

Hollandsche Schouwburg

Plantage Middenlaan 24 (020 531 0310, www.hollandscheschouwburg.nl). Tram 14 or Metro Waterlooplein. ***Open*** *11am-5pm daily.* ***Admission*** *donations accepted (or as part of admission to Joods Historish Museum or Portuguese Synagogue).* ***Map*** *p153 O11.*

In 1942, this grand theatre became a main point of assembly for around 80,000 of the city's Jews before they were taken to the transit camp at Westerbork. It is now a monument with a small but impressive exhibition and a memorial hall displaying 6,700 surnames by way of tribute to the 104,000 Dutch Jews who were exterminated.

Hortus Botanicus

Plantage Middenlaan 2A (020 625 9021, www.dehortus.nl). Tram 14 or Metro Waterlooplein. ***Open*** *10am-5pm daily.* ***Admission*** *€9.75; €5.50 reductions; free under-5s, Iamsterdam.* ***Map*** *p153 O11.*

The Hortus has been a peaceful oasis since 1682, although it was set up more than 50 years earlier when East India Company ships brought back tropical plants and seeds to supply doctors with medicinal herbs (as well as coffee plant cuttings, one specimen of which continued to Brazil to kickstart the South American coffee industry). Highlights include a massive water lily, the *Victoria amazonica*, which blooms only once a year, and the oldest potted plant in the world, a 350-year-old cycad, on display in the 1912 palm greenhouse. Other conservatories maintain desert, tropical and subtropical climates, and a butterfly greenhouse sets hearts of all ages aflutter. Round out your visit in the organic café.

Regular tours of the garden and greenhouses at Hortus Botanicus are given every Sunday at 2pm. No reservation is required; just keep an eye out for the two guides standing under the large oak tree near the entrance.

Museum 't Kromhout

Hoogte Kadijk 147 (020 627 6777, www.kromhoutmuseum.nl). Tram 7 or bus 22. ***Open*** *varies seasonally.* ***Admission*** *€7. Free under-15s.* ***Map*** *p153 R10.*

Dating from the 18th century, this is the oldest remaining original shipyard still in use. The nostalgic museum is full of old ship engines – some of which can still burst into life – and an original 19th-century workshop.

❤ Verzetsmuseum

Plantage Kerklaan 61 (020 620 2535, www. verzetsmuseum.org). Tram 14. ***Open*** *10am-5pm Mon-Fri; 11am-5pm Sat, Sun.* ***Admission*** *€11; €6 reductions; free under-7s, Iamsterdam, MK.* ***Map*** *p153 P11.*

The Verzetsmuseum is one of Amsterdam's most illuminating museums, and quite possibly its most moving. It tells the story of the Dutch Resistance through a wealth of artefacts: false ID papers, clandestine printing presses, illegal newspapers, spy gadgets and an authentic secret door behind which Jews once hid. The engaging presentation is enhanced by the constant use of personal testimonies. Regularly changing temporary exhibitions explore various wartime themes and modern-day forms of oppression, and there's a small research room as well. All in all, an excellent enterprise.

Restaurants & cafés

Café Bakhuys €€

Sarphatistraat 61 (020 370 4861, www. bakhuys-amsterdam.nl). Tram 1, 7, 19 or Metro Weesperplein. ***Open*** *7am-8pm Mon-Fri; 7.30am-6pm Sat; 8am-6pm Sun.* ***Map*** *p153 N13* ③

The delicious smells emanating from this huge, open-plan bakery are enough to tempt even the hardened dieter. All manner of cakes, buns, breads and sweet treats are prepared daily, as are pizzas, fresh soups, and a range of sandwiches. The coffee is damn good too.

De Plantage €€€

Plantage Kerklaan 36 (020 760 6800, www. caferestaurantdeplantage.nl). Tram 14. ***Open*** *9am-1am Mon-Fri; 10am-1am Sat, Sun.* ***Map*** *p153 P11* ⑨

Housed in an orangery dating from 1870 and formerly part of ARTIS Zoo, this airy room oozes understated class – all bleached-wood flooring and tan leather banquettes. The food by Koen van Brunschot is just as good; classic Mediterranean with a modern twist, such as wild boar ravioli. A great place if you want to impress.

Bars

Café Eik & Linde

Plantage Middenlaan 22 (020 622 5716, www. eikenlinde.nl). Tram 14. ***Open*** *11am-1am Mon-Thur; 11am-2am Fri; 2pm-2am Sat.* ***No cards. Map*** *p153 O11* ④

'The Oak & Lime Tree' is an old-fashioned, family-run neighbourhood café-bar. Local memorabilia on the walls, including posters from radio shows that were held on the premises, give it historical appeal. Low prices, Dutch snacks, soups and sandwiches, and a laid-back air make it user-friendly.

Verzetmuseum

OOST

South of Mauritskade, Amsterdam Oost (East) is bordered by the Amstel river in the west and the IJ in the east and north. This area was developed in the late 19th century to provide housing for the city's lower-income families; many immigrants from Morocco, Suriname and Turkey settled in Oost during the 1960s and 1970s, and the low rents lured students and artists to the area in the decades to follow. After several years of gentrification, this multicultural neighbourhood is now known for its picturesque wide streets, culinary hotspots and buzzing atmosphere.

The hotel complex **Arena** (*see p284*) is located along the edge of a former graveyard that was long ago transformed into **Oosterpark**. Wild ducks swim on the lake, grey herons nest here, and the park also has a Speaker's Corner for anyone wishing to have a rant. Near the corner of Oosterpark and Linneausstraat is the spot where filmmaker Theo van Gogh was murdered by an Islamic extremist in 2004, after making a film deemed to be offensive to Muslims. A sculpture, *The Scream*, was unveiled in the park in 2007 in his memory.

The **Tropenmuseum** and **Dappermarkt** (*see p163*) are the area's main tourist draws, while popular hotel/club **Volkshotel** (*see p286*) lures locals. Here too, the famous **Studio/K** (Timor plein 62, 020 692 0422, studio-k.nu) – one of the city council's biggest baits for artists and creative types considering the area – offers hip parties, savvy films and a terrific café with an expansive terrace. This approach follows tried-and-tested urban development logic: artists improve the profile of an area, then the yuppies rush in. Nearby, the Javastraat is dotted with ethnic shops, cute boutiques and hip bars, and Linnaeusstraat should satisfy all your café-lingering needs – if you dare, venture into the wildly over-the-top brown café **Ruk & Pluk** (no.48, 020 665 3248) for some real local flavour.

Further north, the **Brouwerij 't IJ** (*see p163*), a brewery beside a windmill in the Indische Buurt (Indonesian neighbourhood), is a good place to stop and sip a beer.

► *For details of the Eastern Docklands and IJburg, see p168 and p170.*

Sights & museums

Flevopark

Flevoweg (020 624 1111). Tram 3, 14, or train to Amsterdam Science Park. ***Map*** *p153 off map.*

Head to the eastern reaches of Oost and you'll find Flevopark, a green gem with a large lake connected to the IJ. This rural-feeling park is home to an ancient Jewish cemetery and the stellar **Distilleerderij 't Nieuwe Diep** (Flevopark 13 (06 2537 8104 mobile, www.nwediep.nl), an old mill house and now a

National Monument to Slavery Past, Oosterpark

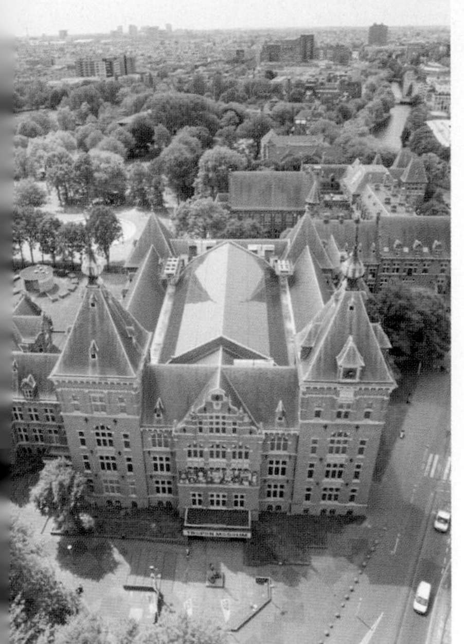

distillery and tasting-house pumping out Dutch *jenever* and other liquors. With views over a pond from the picnic tables and a nice selection of bar snacks, this is the perfect place to stop and smell the flowers – and the fermenting grains. The park also has an outdoor swimming pool and several running trails for the more actively inclined.

❤ Tropenmuseum

Linnaeusstraat 2 (088 0042 800, www.tropenmuseum.nl). Tram 19. ***Open*** *10am-5pm Tue-Sun.* ***Admission*** *€19; €7-€10 reductions; free under-4s, Iamsterdam, MK.* ***Map*** *p153 R12.*

Visitors to this handsome building get a vivid glimpse of daily life in the tropical and subtropical parts of the world – a strange evolution for a museum that was originally erected in the 1920s to glorify Dutch colonialism. Exhibits (which range from religious items and jewellery to washing powder and vehicles) are divided by region, including South-east Asia, Africa, Netherlands East Indies and New Guinea, and a series called Travelling Tales. Temporary shows, covering everything from Buddhism to Rhythm and Roots, are also consistently excellent. There's an engaging array of books and souvenirs in the shop, and the restaurant offers tasty global eats and a terrace with a view. Children are made welcome too: a special branch of the museum, the Tropenmuseum Junior, is aimed at six- to 13-year-olds and has some inspired exhibitions of its own.

Restaurants & cafés

Alex + Pinard €€€

Dapperstraat 10 (020 891 5528, www.alexpinard.nl). Tram 7, 14. ***Open*** *4-11pm Mon-Thu, Sun; 4pm-midnight Fri, Sat.* ***Map*** *p153 S12* ❶ *Wine bar*

Built around ingredients from small, artisanal producers, the sharing plates at this hip, cosy hangout are homely and moreish. And with all wines available by the glass, it's all too easy to work one's way through the drinks menu as well.

Beter & Leuk €€

Eerste Oosterparkstraat 91 (020 767 0029, www.beterenleuk.nl). Tram 3 or Metro Wibaustraat. ***Open*** *8.30am-5pm Mon-Fri; 9.30am-5pm Sat, Sun.* ***Map*** *p153 O15* ❷ *Café*

A breakfast-slash-lunch-slash-boutique café with a mission summed up by its name: 'Better & Nice'. Decoration is minimal and the kitchen open to view. The menu – including eggs, croissants, homemade granola, sandwiches, salads and cakes – is scribbled on a blackboard and handwritten on brown paper. The monthly Sunday vegan brunch is popular.

❤ Canvas €€

Volkshotel, Wibautstraat 150 (020 261 2110, www.volkshotel.nl/en/canvas). Metro Wibautstraat. ***Open*** *7am-1am daily. Food served noon-10.30pm daily.* ***Map*** *p153 P15* ❺ *International*

The arrival of Canvas, a versatile all-in-one rooftop café/restaurant/cocktail bar/club was the icing on the cake for the culturally revived Oost. Located on the seventh floor of the Volkshotel, the complex reopened in 2014 after extensive renovations. What was once a go-to for journalists on their lunch break has now become a hub for foodies, party-goers, cocktail connoisseurs and clued-up visitors. With generous opening hours year-round and a location outside the centre, Canvas offers unrivalled views of the 17th-century skyline morning, afternoon and night. You can't reserve tables on the roof terrace, so visit during off-peak hours for a view unspoiled by hordes of people.

❤ Coffee Bru €

Beukenplein 14 (020 751 9956, www.coffeebru.nl). Tram 1, 3. ***Open*** *8am-5pm Mon-Thu; 9am-5pm Fri, Sat.* ***Map*** *p153 Q15* ❻ *Café*

What's Brewing?

Amsterdam's craft beer scene shows no sign of going flat

For decades, **Brouwerij 't IJ** (*see opposite*) in Oost ruled the roost when it came to locally brewed golden elixirs. While it still reigns supreme as one of the largest breweries in Amsterdam, recent years have seen an influx in competition from other home-grown microbreweries. In the Old Centre, **Bierfabriek** (*see p83*) offers home-brewed beers, including red ale Rosso and dark porter Nero, as well as some of the finest roast chicken in town. Just be wary on Friday nights when the joint gets taken over by the post-work crowd attracted to the 'tap tables' (booking essential), where you can pour your own beer.

For more hipster-flavoured brews, try **Butcher's Tears** (*see p149*) in Nieuw Zuid (Amsterdam South), where you can indulge in the rather strong and evocatively named beers, which rotate seasonally. Popular drafts have included Old Geezer, Monster Soup and Spiral Scratch. There are also coffees, Dutch ciders, international beers and wines and, on occasion, snacks. It's also a good spot for concerts, hot-sauce tastings and other special events.

If you want to spice up your brewery experience, **Brouwerij De 7 Deugden** in Amsterdam's West (Akersluis 8D, 020 667 3221, www.de7deugden.nl) is the place to go. Its speciality beers are brewed using a variety of herbs and spices for a subtle hint of fiery flavour. Unsurprisingly, given their chosen brand name, the four friends behind **Oedipus Brewing** in Noord (Gedempt Hamerkanaal 85, 020 244 1673, www.oedipus.com) don't take themselves too seriously. The brewery is all about 'energy, fun, and doing things differently', a philosophy that extends to their taproom (they have a beer called 'Mama'). Don't miss FreshBeerFriday: from 4 to 8pm, enjoy one of 14 brews, served straight from the bottling line for only €3. Oedipus hosts all manner of live music and special events too.

And who says that psychiatric patients and alcohol shouldn't mix? Brewery and shop **De Prael** (*see p83)* in the heart of the Red Light District is proving all the critics wrong. The owner combined his experience in mental healthcare with a love of both brewing and quirky local music to create a company that provides employment opportunities for those who otherwise struggle to find work. Many of them have a mental health condition, from schizophrenia to borderline personality disorders. Yes, there are plenty of jokes, but the rules are simple: no drinking on the job and be on time.

Oedipus Brewing

A local favourite for unbeatable beans, Coffee Bru is often crowded with friends catching up and freelancers with their heads down. If you pop by in summer, order an iced latte and head out to the charming terrace (if you can manage to get a seat).

De Kas €€€

*Kamerlingh Onneslaan 3 (020 462 4562, www.restaurantdekas.nl). Tram 9 or bus 41. **Open** noon-2pm, 6.30-10pm Mon-Fri; 6.30-10pm Sat. **Map** p153 off map* 7 *Global*

In Park Frankendael, way out to the east, is this renovated 1926 greenhouse. It's now a posh and peaceful restaurant that inspires much fevered talk among local foodies. The international menu changes daily, based on whatever goodies were harvested that morning from their own field, greenhouses and herb garden.

Louie Louie €€

*Linnaeusstraat 11A (020 370 2981, www.louielouie.nl). Tram 19. **Open** 9am-1am Mon-Thur, Sun; 9am-3am Fri, Sat. **Map** p153 S12* 8 *European*

Boasting a prime location right near the lush Oosterpark, Louie Louie is the perfect place for a spot of unashamed people-watching. In summer, the windows are opened so the cocktail-sipping patrons can spill out onto the large terrace. The brunch menu is delicious, and if you're dropping by for a pre-dinner drink be sure to try the beef tacos.

Rijsel €€

*Marcusstraat 52b (020 463 2142, www.rijsel.com). Tram 3, 12 or Metro Wibaustraat. **Open** 6pm-1am Mon-Sat (kitchen closes at 10pm). **Map** p153 off map* 10 *French/Belgian*

Housed in a former *huishoudschool*, one of the domestic science institutions blamed for the general decline of the Dutch kitchen, you'll find frugality only in terms of the decor at Rijsel. The busy dining room is overseen by amiable staff. Specialising in the best rotisserie chicken, like, ever, Rijsel has established itself as another delicious reason to head east.

Bars

❤ De Biertuin

*Linnaeusstraat 29 (020 665 0956, www.debiertuin. nl). Tram 19. **Open** 11am-1am Mon-Thur, Sun; 11am-3am Fri, Sat. **Map** p153 S13* 1

The 'Beer Garden' does indeed have a wide selection of beers, as well as some of the city's most highly regarded roast chicken and a fantastic burger. The proprietors also run other student- and hipster-friendly restaurant-bars in Oost, including the more appropriately liquor-soaked **Bukowski** (Oosterpark 10, 370 1685, www.barbukowski.nl). **Other location** Prinsengracht 494, Grachtengordel.

❤ Brouwerij 't IJ

*Funenkade 7 (020 528 6237, www.brouwerijhetij.nl). Tram 7, 14. **Open** 2-8pm daily. **Map** p153 S11* 2

Amsterdam is known for its thriving microbrewery scene, which continues to evolve to this day (*see left*, What's Brewing?). There are dozens dotted throughout the city, but most locals will argue Brouwerij 't IJ sets the standard, with tours and tastings and its very own famous pub adjoining, where wares can be sampled. The award-winning local brewery is located in a former bath-house named Funen at the base of the Gooyer windmill. Former musician Kaspar Peterson opened Brouwerij 't IJ in 1985, after Dutch consumers complained about 'generic' beer brewed by larger companies. Among the draft and bottled beers, classic favourites include Ijwit, Zatte and Natte, while Summer Wheat Ale and Clel Bleu Imperial Stout are among the more exotic brews. The standard range includes pale Plzen, British-style IPA and darker, stronger Colombus. The pub's interior still reflects its former function as the municipal baths, and while a recent refurbishment has increased the amount of seating, the best place to sit (weather permitting) is outside at the pavement tables or on the huge terrace. You'll recognise the brewery's label and logo – which features an ostrich with an egg and a distant windmill – from bars and restaurants around town.

Shops & services

❤ Dappermarkt

*Dapperstraat (no phone). Tram 1, 3. **Open** 9am-5pm Mon-Sat. **No cards. Map** p153 S13* 1 *Market*

Dappermarkt is a locals' market at heart: prices don't rise to match the number of visitors. It sells all the usual market fodder, along with piles and piles of cheap clothes.

❤ Hartje Oost

*Javastraat 23 (020 233 2137, www.hartjeoost.nl). Tram 14. **Open** 9am-6.30pm Mon-Fri; 9am-6pm Sat, Sun. **Map** p153 off map* 2 *Boutique*

This wonderful little boutique is a great place to while away an hour or two if you're in Oost. Not only are the coffee and homemade cakes great, but they have a charming selection of clothes, jewelery, homeware and accessories.

Waterfront & Noord

Amsterdam's historic wealth owes much to the city's waterfront, where goods were unloaded, weighed and prepared for storage in the area's warehouses. During the 17th century, maritime activity was centred east of Centraal Station, along Prins Hendrikkade and on the artificial islands east of Kattenburgerstraat, and there was nothing to be found north across the IJ except gallows, where prisoners were executed with a view across the river. But during the 18th and early 19th centuries, Amsterdam's industrial sites spilled north, and the district quickly became a maritime and trading hub. Industrial and petrochemical giant Royal Dutch Shell, among others, also settled in Noord.

Shipbuilding declined in the late 1900s, and the trading boom well and truly ended following World War II, leaving the industrial part of Noord as a wasteland of derelict docks and decrepit buildings. But the turn of the 21st century saw students, young creatives and families lured to the region by its low rent and easy access to open fields beyond the city limits.

Since then, Noord's popularity and its population have continued to grow, helped by the opening of the North-South metro line in 2018.

❤ Don't miss

1 A'DAM Toren *p174*
Swing from the rooftop at the 'King of the Noord'.

2 NDSM *p176*
A post-industrial cultural hub.

3 EYE *p173*
This film institute typifies the Noord's revival.

4 Nederlands Scheepvaartmuseum *p169*
One of the world's finest nautical museums.

5 Eastern Docklands *p168 and p170*
A showcase of modern Dutch architecture.

Hannekes Boom *p172*

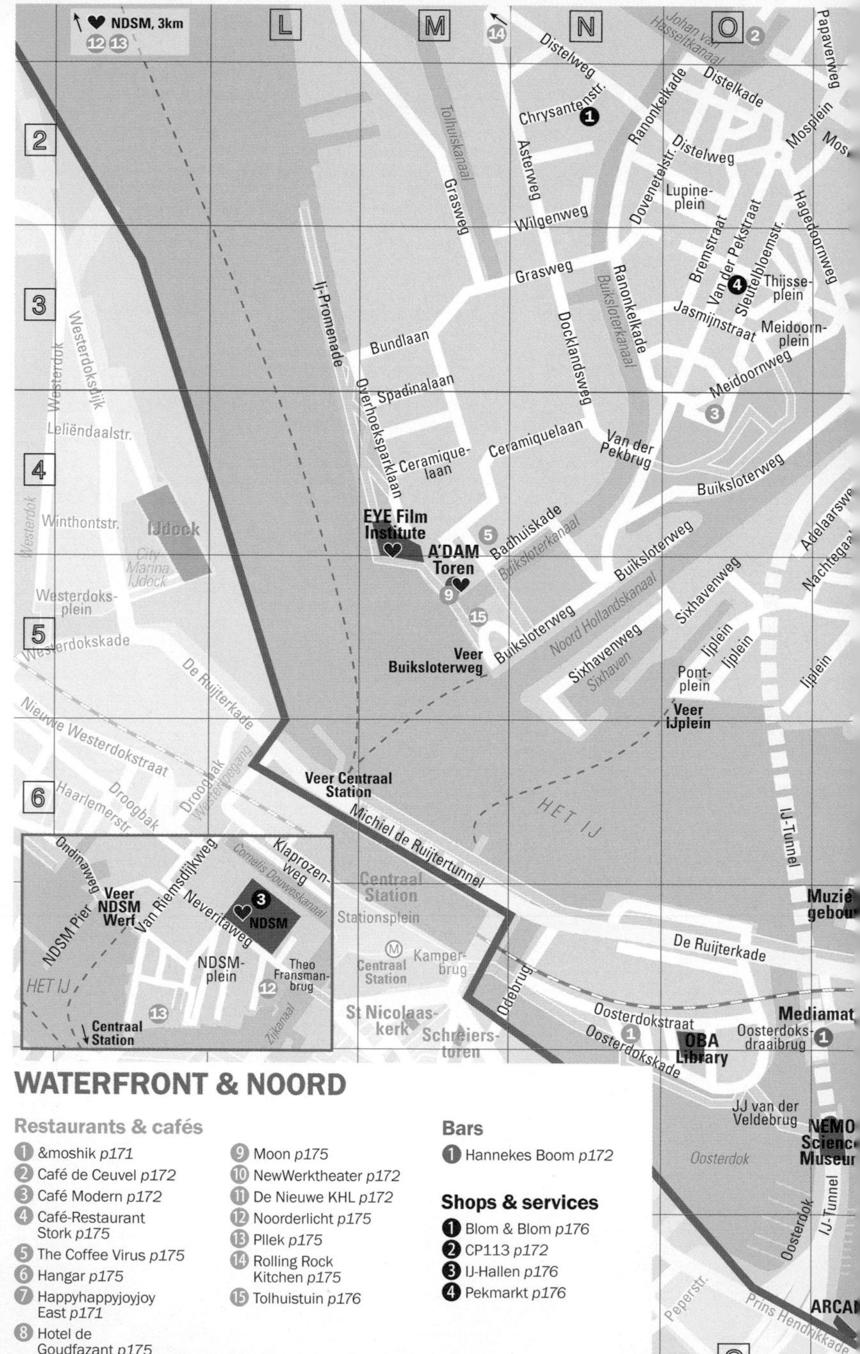

WATERFRONT & NOORD

Restaurants & cafés

1 &moshik *p171*
2 Café de Ceuvel *p172*
3 Café Modern *p172*
4 Café-Restaurant Stork *p175*
5 The Coffee Virus *p175*
6 Hangar *p175*
7 Happyhappyjoyjoy East *p171*
8 Hotel de Goudfazant *p175*
9 Moon *p175*
10 NewWerktheater *p172*
11 De Nieuwe KHL *p172*
12 Noorderlicht *p175*
13 Pllek *p175*
14 Rolling Rock Kitchen *p175*
15 Tolhuistuin *p176*

Bars

1 Hannekes Boom *p172*

Shops & services

1 Blom & Blom *p176*
2 CP113 *p172*
3 IJ-Hallen *p176*
4 Pekmarkt *p176*

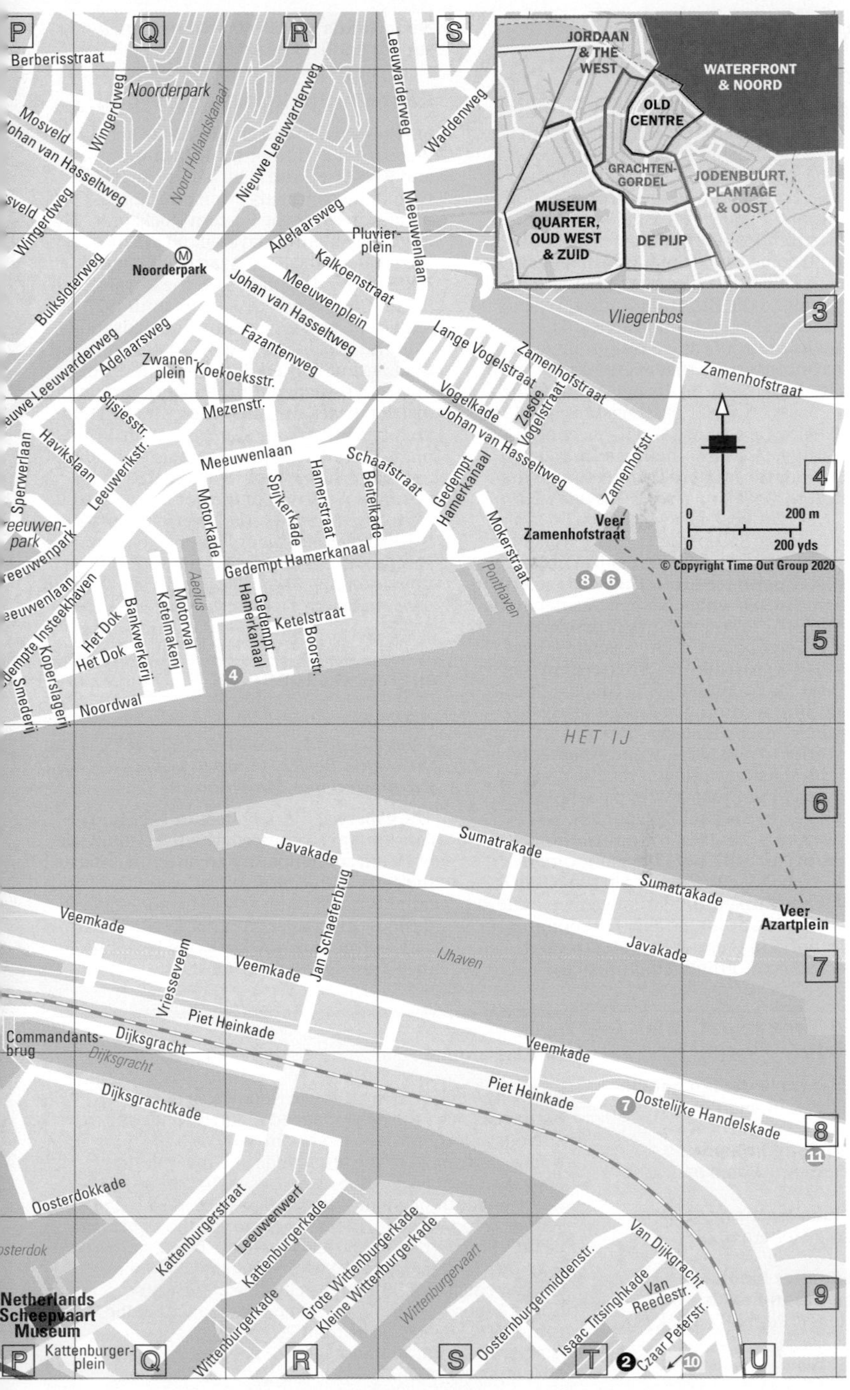
P
Q
R
S
Berberisstraat
Noorderpark
Mosveld
Johan van Hasseltweg
Wingerdweg
Noord Hollandskanaal
Nieuwe Leeuwarderweg
Leeuwarderweg
Waddenweg
Meeuwenlaan
Adelaarsweg
Pluvier-
plein
Kalkoenstraat
Noorderpark
Buiksloterweg
Johan van Hasseltweg
Meeuwenplein
Fazantenweg
Lange Vogelstraat
Zamenhofstraat
Vliegenbos
Zamenhofstraat
Adelaarsweg
Zwanen-
plein
Koekoeksstr.
Nieuwe Leeuwarderweg
Slijsjesstr.
Mezenstr.
Vogelkade
Zesde Vogelstraat
Johan van Hasseltweg
Havikslaan
Sperwerlaan
Leeuwerikstr.
Meeuwenlaan
Schaafstraat
Hamerstraat
Beitelkade
Spijkerkade
Motorkade
Gedempt Hamerkanaal
Mokerstraat
Zamenhofstr.
Veer
Zamenhofstraat
Leeuwenpark
Gedempt Hamerkanaal
Aeolus
Ponthaven
Meeuwenlaan
Gedempte Insteekhaven
Het Dok
Het Dok
Bankwerkerij
Ketelmakerij
Motorwal
Gedempt Hamerkanaal
Ketelstraat
Boorstr.
Koperslagerij
Smederij
Noordwal
HET IJ
Sumatrakade
Javakade
Sumatrakade
Veer
Azartplein
Jan Schaeferbrug
Javakade
IJhaven
Veemkade
Vriesseveem
Veemkade
Piet Heinkade
Commandantsbrug
Dijksgracht
Dijksgracht
Veemkade
Piet Heinkade
Oostelijke Handelskade
Dijksgrachtkade
Oosterdokkade
Oosterdok
Kattenburgerstraat
Leeuwenwerf
Kattenburgerkade
Grote Wittenburgerkade
Kleine Wittenburgerkade
Wittenburgervaart
Wittenburgerkade
Oostenburgermiddenstr.
Van Dijkgracht
Isaac Titsinghkade
Van Reedestr.
Czaar Peterstr.
Netherlands
Scheepvaart
Museum
Kattenburger-
plein
T
U
3
4
5
6
7
8
9
JORDAAN & THE WEST
WATERFRONT & NOORD
OLD CENTRE
GRACHTENGORDEL
JODENBUURT, PLANTAGE & OOST
MUSEUM QUARTER, OUD WEST & ZUID
DE PIJP
0 200 m
0 200 yds
© Copyright Time Out Group 2020

WATERFRONT

Oosterdok & around

The entire eastern waterfront, all the way from Centraal to the Verbindingsdam bridge that connects the Eastern Docklands to Java-eiland and KNSM-eiland, was redeveloped around the turn of the 20th century. If you walk east along the IJ riverfront from *behind* Centraal Station, you'll come to the famous **Muziekgebouw** (*see p236*). This epicentre of modern music is home to the **Bimhuis** studios, rehearsal spaces and exhibition galleries. There's also a grand café and a restaurant with a charming terrace that overlooks the scenic wateriness of the IJ. Its neighbour is the glass wave-shaped passenger terminal for luxury cruise ships. And if you continue heading eastwards along the IJ, you will discover the modern architecture of the Eastern Docklands (*see below and p170*).

Alternatively, head east from the *front* of Centraal Station on Oosterdoksgade to reach Amsterdam's vast central library, **OBA** (**Openbare Bibliotheek Amsterdam**; *see opposite*), which has spectacular views from its restaurant. Equally ambitious is its neighbour, the city's music school, **Conservatorium van Amsterdam** (*see p236*). De Architekten Cie designed the building according to Japanese *engawa* principles: the hallways are on the exterior to maximise soundproofing for the practising students, yet also create a transparency that invites passers-by in to listen to a recital. To your left, you'll spy trendy summer hotspot **Hannekes Boom** (*see p172*) but if you fancy more views, head to the rooftop of the **NEMO Science Museum**, a striking green building resembling a sinking ship that dominates the horizon. Across the water from NEMO is the grand structure of the **Nederlands Scheepvaartmuseum**, a superb nautical museum.

Eastern Docklands & beyond

Further east, in the middle of the IJ between Waterfront and Noord, are **Java-eiland** and **KNSM-eiland**. The pair make up a manmade peninsula originally built as breakwaters for the Eastern Docklands. The largely residential Java-eiland is a nice spot for a watery stroll. At Azartplein it meets KNSM-eiland, named after the Royal Dutch Steam Company located here until 1977. Squatters, artists and urban nomads took over the area in the 1980s, but were ordered to move out in the 1990s when the entire area was reshaped into a modern residential district, based on a 1988 blueprint by Dutch architect/urban planner Jo Coenen. While plans initially called for a rather exclusive neighbourhood, the city mandated that a significant portion of the homes were to be rented to attract a more diverse population. Nevertheless, with its waterside bars and eateries, the area is looked upon as an upmarket neighbourhood and a showcase of modern Dutch architecture (*see p170*).

Sights & museums

ARCAM

Prins Hendrikkade 600 (020 620 4878, www.arcam.nl). Bus 22, 48. ***Open*** *1-5pm Tue-Sun.* ***Admission*** *free.* ***Map*** *p166 P9.*

The gallery at the Architecture Centrum Amsterdam is obsessed with the promotion of Dutch contemporary architecture, from the early 20th-century creations of the world-famous Amsterdam School to more modern designs. It organises forums, lectures, its own series of architecture books, and exhibitions in its fresh 'silver snail' location.

❤ Time to eat, drink & shop

Covetable design goodies
Blom & Blom *p176*

Drinking hotspot
Hannekes Boom *p172*

Globe-trotting set menu
Café Modern *p172*

Summer lunch on an urban beach
Haas & Popi *p171*, Pllek *p175*

In the know
Getting around

Buses 314 and 316 run through Noord from Centraal Station, as does the newly opened Metro 52 line, with stations at Noorderpark and Noord, but beware – from Nooderpark, most of the attractions and the waterfront area are a further bus ride away. Buses 34, 35, 36, and 38 meander throughout Noord and pass by most of the venues listed. As such, the best way to see the sights is by bicycle. Free ferries, which accommodate bikes, run 24/7 from Centraal across to NDSM and Tolhuistuin (where you can catch bus 38). On the city side of the waterfront, tram 14 runs from Centraal Station to the heart of the Eastern Docklands, while tram 26 connects several islands on its way to IJburg; bus 22 goes via Zeeburg to Muiderpoortstation.

Mediamatic

Dijksgracht 6 (020 638 9901, www.mediamatic.net). Tram 26. ***Open*** *varies.* ***Admission*** *varies.* ***Map*** *p166 P7.*

Mediamatic is a project/exhibition space and hydroponic farm in an ancient warehouse. It's home to an inspired multimedia team, who pop up all over the place with all sorts of inspired projects. From an interactive urinal installation that creates fertilizer for its park to an exhibition of pimped-up pig hearts, it's almost impossible to guess what's next up the Mediamatic sleeve.

❤ Nederlands Scheepvaartmuseum

Kattenburgerplein 1 (020 523 2222, www.hetscheepvaartmuseum.nl). Bus 22, 48. ***Open*** *9am-5pm daily.* ***Admission*** *€16.50; €8 reductions; free under-4s, Iamsterdam, MK. €1 discount for online booking.* ***Map*** *p166 P9.*

Dutch nautical history is rich and fascinating, so it follows that the country should boast one of the world's finest maritime museums – second only, say experts, to London's National Maritime Museum. Marvel at the models, portraits, boat parts and other naval ephemera, housed in a wonderful building built 350 years ago by Daniel Stalpaert. Don't miss the large replica of an 18th-century East India Trading Company (VOC) ship, with costumed 'sailors'.

NEMO Science Museum

Oosterdok 2 (020 531 3233, www.nemosciencemuseum.nl). Bus 22, 48. ***Open*** *10am-5.30pm daily.* ***Admission*** *€17.50; €8.75 reductions; free under-4s, Iamsterdam, MK.* ***Map*** *p166 P8.*

NEMO has built a strong reputation as a child-friendly science museum. It eschews exhibits in favour of all manner of hands-on trickery, gadgetry and tomfoolery: you can play DNA detective games, blow mega soap bubbles or explode things in a 'wonderlab'. The building itself, designed by Renzo Piano to look like a mammoth copper-green ship's hull, is a true eye-pleaser. The rooftop café is a lovely place in which to while away an afternoon reading and relaxing – that is, if it's not being used as a virtual beach or for a jazz festival.

OBA (Openbare Bibliotheek Amsterdam)

Oosterdokskade 143 (020 523 0900, www.oba.nl). Tram 2, 4, 11, 12, 13, 14, 17, 24, 26 or Metro Centraal. ***Open*** *10am-10pm daily.* ***Admission*** *free.* ***Map*** *p166 O7.*

One of Europe's largest public libraries, this big city landmark ceremoniously opened on 07-07-07 and has since become one of Amsterdam's most treasured architectural gems. Designed by Jo Coenen, the former state architect of the Netherlands, OBA is sprawled over seven floors of pioneering ecological design. The building treats arriving visitors to a soaring view up to its top floor café-restaurant, which, in turn, offers a spectacular view over Amsterdam. The interior, with walnut floors and white walls and shelves, is eminently low-key; colour comes from the books and the mixed bag of people using the free Wi-Fi – or the polyester study 'pods' (an ideal spot for a nap).

Visitors can take their pick from 600 internet-connected computers, 50 multimedia workplaces, 110 catalogue reference terminals and almost a dozen fully equipped print and copy stations. Going above and beyond the expectations for a typical public library, its unique collections are accompanied by a theatre, conference rooms, exhibition space and a music department. OBA also houses a radio station.

Nederlands Scheepvaartmuseum

Waterfront Walk

An open-air display of architectural ingenuity

Amsterdam's Eastern Docklands area is one of the city's premier eating and entertainment hotspots. It's also a fantastic showcase for the Netherlands' daring experiments in residential living. If you want to see Amsterdam's inventive ingenuity, set aside a few hours to explore.

Take tram 26 from Centraal to **Pakhuis de Zwijger**, an old cocoa storage warehouse reinvented as a new-media centre. It has a charming café – ideal to grab a coffee before you set off.

Walk across the airy **Jan Schaefer** bridge, which will take you to the tip of **Java-eiland**. At first glance it may look like a dense, designer confinement, but it's not hard to be charmed by the island's central pedestrian and cycle path, which will have you crossing canals on funky bridges and walking past a startling variety of architecture. On a warm, sunny day, you'll be hard pressed to spot a glimpse of grass among the picnic baskets and young locals who sprawl out to soak up the all-too-rare rays.

At Azartplein, the island suddenly changes its name to **KNSM-eiland**, in honour of the Royal Dutch Steam Company (KNSM), once based here. Here, you can visit the excellent local bookshop **Van Pampus** (KNSM-laan 303, 020 419 3023, www.boekhandelvanpampus.nl) or **De Kompaszaal** (KNSM-laan 311, 020 419 9596, www.kompaszaal.nl), a café and restaurant in the former KNSM arrivals and departures hall, which has the feel of a 1950s cruise ship, complete with watery views from the terrace. Otherwise, stop off at hipster-approved **Bar & Kitchen De Zuid** (Azartplein 2a, 020 362 8776, www.dezuid.amsterdam), then veer north and follow Surinamekade east, with houseboats on one side and artists' studios on the other. Pass the 'Black Widow' tower and loop round the island's tip and back west along KNSM-laan, turning left into Barcelonaplein, and then right when you pass through the abstract sculpted steel archway. Linger and look at the imposing residential Piraeus building by German architect Hans Kollhoff, if only for its eye-twisting inner court.

The two peninsulas to the south of KNSM-eiland are **Borneo** and **Sporenburg**, the work of urban-planning and landscape architecture firm West 8. Cross over to Sporenburg via the Verbindingsdam to the mighty silver Whale residential complex, designed by architect Frits van Dongen, over on Baron GA Tindalplein. From here, cross over to Borneo on the swooping red bridge. Turn left up Stuurmankade – past a still more violently undulating pedestrian bridge – and pause to enjoy the view at the end. Then return west along Scheepstimmermanstraat, easily Amsterdam's most eccentric architectural street, where every single façade on show – from twisting steel to haphazard plywood – manages to be more bizarre than the next.

From Scheepstimmermanstraat it's a brisk ten-minute walk to Oostelijk Handelskade, where you'll find **De Nieuwe KHL** *(see*

IJburg

p172), the **Lloyd Hotel** (see p286) and neighbouring **Puerto Pata Negra** (Oostelijke Handelskade 999, 419 1793, puertopatanegra.nl). Or head up Czaar Peterstraat, a once dangerous street that's now a pleasant area with quirky shops and cafés, to go for a home-brewed beer at **Brouwerij 't IJ** (*see p163*). Alternatively, from the Rietlandpark tram stop, you can extend your exploration by heading on tram 26 further east to **IJburg**.

More energetic types might even prefer to take the 20-minute bike ride to IJburg, heading south via C van Eesterenlaan and Veelaan, then left down Zeeburgerdijk. This in turn connects up with Zuiderzeeweg, which then merges into a bridge that ends at a set of traffic lights. Here, follow the cycle path to the right, to IJburg. Originally intended to be completed in 2012, seven artificial islands were to be home to 45,000 people inhabiting more than 18,000 units, many floating on the water. Economic problems may have delayed its completion and resulted in a subdued version of what was hyped as a showcase for Dutch landscaping and architecture, but there's still plenty to look at. When you've had your fill of innovative floating buildings, head to the artificial Blijburg beach to relax at **Haas & Popi** (*see right*).

▶ *For more detailed information on architectural tours of all these areas and more, contact ARCAM (see p168).*

Restaurants & cafés

&moshik €€€€

Oosterdokskade 5 (020 260 2094, moshik restaurant.com). Tram 2, 4, 11, 12, 13, 14, 17, 24 or Metro Centraal. ***Open*** *7-9.30pm Wed, Thu; noon-2pm, 7-9.30pm Fri; 7-9.30pm Sat; noon-2pm, 7-8.30pm Sun.* ***Map*** *p166 N7* ❶ *Global*

Bringing gastronomy to Amsterdam, &moshik is the delectable collaboration between entrepreneur Salem Samhoud and chef Moshik Roth – a super-popular TV chef in Israel. This is one of the most insanely popular (and expensive) high-end restaurants in town – complete with two Michelin stars. If your budget won't stretch that far, you can settle in the lounge for a cocktail and a rather more affordable tomato burger.

❤ Haas & Popi €€

Pampulsaan 501, IJburg (06 1129 6214, wwwhaasenpopi.nl). Tram 26. ***Open*** *10am-6pm Mon-Wed; 10am-11pm Thu; 10am-midnight Sat, Sun; 10am-8pm Sun. Fish/Dutch*

Being 25km (15 miles) from the sea, Amsterdam was no-one's choice for a beach holiday – until sand was tipped on the artificial islands of IJburg. The vast expanse of sand and adjoining freshwater lake are being exploited for their surreal beach-like properties by restaurant/bar Haas & Popi. There's a short but sweet menu, a cultural centre, and the third Friday of every month is 'Fishing Friday', complete with €1 oysters and DJs.

Happyhappyjoyjoy East €€

Oostelijke Handelskade 4, (020 344 6424, www.happyhappyjoyjoy.asia). Tram 7. ***Open*** *noon-11.30pm daily.* ***Map*** *p166 T8* ❼ *Thai*

When the first Happyhappyjoyjoy opened in Oud West several years ago, it was the hottest restaurant in town for months, and it's easy to see why. The cheerful takes on Asian street food are heavy on flavour and spice, but easy on the wallet. On this side of the city, there's no better place to indulge in dim sum, bao buns or pad thai. **Other locations** Ceintuurbaan 256, De Pijp (020 344 6406); Bilderdijkstraat 158hs, Oud West (020 344 6433).

The Harbour Club €€€

Cruquiusweg 67, Zeeburg (020 767 0421, www.theharbourclub.nl). Tram 7, 14. ***Open*** *11am-1am Mon-Thur, Sun; 11am-2am Fri, Sat. Meals served noon-11pm daily. Modern European*

Thousands of square metres of pure glam, contained in a former wine warehouse on the IJ riverfront, Harbour Club brings Ibiza to these rainy climes. Featuring a restaurant with sushi room, bar, club and terrace, this is the place to see and be seen.

NewWerktheater €€

Oostenburgergracht 75 (020 572 1380, www.newwerktheater.com). Tram 7. ***Open*** *8am-5pm Mon-Fri; 9am-5pm Sat, Sun.* ***Map*** *p153 S10* ⑩

There's an eclectic flavour to this ultra hip joint's breakfast and lunch offerings which sets it apart from standard brunch destinations. Lovingly brewed coffee, a quirky cocktail list, and a huge communal table laden with magazines in the back make it a great place to work, or just while away a few lazy hours.

De Nieuwe KHL €€

Oostelijke Handelskade 44 (020 779 1575, www.khl.nl). Tram 7. ***Open*** *4-11pm daily.* ***Map*** *p166 U8* ⑪ *European*

The beautiful, light-flooded interior harks back to the days in the early 20th century when this was a canteen serving staff of the Royal Holland Lloyd shipping line. Now it's a café-cum-restaurant-cum-meeting space serving the local community, with plenty to attract new visitors. There's art on the walls and regular live music to lift the spirits.

Bars

❤ Hannekes Boom

Dijksgracht 4 (020 419 9820, www.hannekesboom.nl). Tram 26. ***Open*** *10am-1am Mon-Thu; 10am-3am Fri, Sat.* ***Map*** *p166 P7* ❶

With a huge terrace and a view of the harbour, the shack-style Boom rates as one of the city's hottest hangouts – even though it is made of scrap lumber. Not only street-art friendly, it also has live music and DJ nights.

Shops & services

CP113

Czaar Peterstraat 113 (020 223 1976, www.cp113.com). Tram 7. ***Open*** *11am-6pm Tue-Sat.* ***Map*** *p166 T9* ❷ *Fashion*

Founded in 2014 by Stefanie Derks and Kris Hartman, CP113 was Oost's first concept store. The on-trend collection offers unique pieces for men and women from the likes of Won Hundred, Mads Norgaard and Dawn x Dare. It also stocks some super-cool jewellery and things to make your house beautiful.

NOORD

Once the city's engine house, the industrial expanse of Noord is now one of Amsterdam's hippest enclaves. After a few hours in this now-thriving district, you'll find it hard to believe there was a time when it was right off the map.

Since the opening of the much delayed Noord/Zuidlijn metro link – Metro 52 – in 2018, the development of this area has accelerated and its appeal as a place to live and work has continued to grow. Dubbed the 'Williamsburg of Amsterdam' by property asset managers, it's now a booming bastion of alternative culture and a creative incubator, with music festivals, sustainable restaurants and unrivalled views of the city. Have a meal at culture venue **Tolhuistuin** (*see p176*), now home to Paradiso Noord (*see p229*), before climbing the King of the Noord **A'DAM Toren** (*see p174*) or immersing yourself in film history at the futuristic **EYE Film Institute** (*see p173*). And don't miss **NDSM** (*see p176*), ground zero for cool and cutting-edge initiatives.

Restaurants & cafés

Café de Ceuvel €€

Korte Papaverweg 4 (020 229 6210, www.deceuvel.nl). Bus 34, 35 or Buiksloterweg ferry. ***Open*** *11am-midnight Tue-Thur, Sun; 11am-2am Fri, Sat.* ***Map*** *p166 O1* ❷ *Dutch*

Amsterdam's sustainable culture extends beyond architectural developments and – with a menu based entirely on locally sourced, seasonal produce – Café de Ceuvel is the perfect example. The restaurant is part of the award-winning De Ceuvel complex, a former shipyard revived using only recycled materials. It even sells fresh produce from its rooftop farm.

❤ Café Modern €€

Meidoornweg 2 (020 494 0684, www.modernamsterdam.nl). Bus 38 or Buiksloterweg ferry. ***Open*** *noon-3pm, 6pm-midnight Mon-Sat.* ***Map*** *p166 O4* ❸ *Global*

By day, this old bank building is brunch spot **Jacques Jour**. By night, under the name Café Modern, this roomy and wittily designed space is a globe-trotting restaurant serving a set menu (one easily adapted for vegetarians); book in advance. Upstairs is boutique hotel **Hotel Café Modern** (hotelcafemodern.nl).

In the know
Lock stop

If you're exploring Noord via bike, it's always worth stopping at the ancient **Café 't Sluisje** (Nieuwendammerdijk 297, 020 636 1712, www.hetsluisje.nl), with its terrace straddling a lock system in Nieuwendam, the oldest part of Noord.

❤ EYE Film Institute

IJPromenade 1 (020 589 1400, www.eyefilm.nl). Bus 38 or Buiksloterweg ferry. ***Open*** *Exhibitions 10am-7pm daily. Box office 10am-10pm Mon-Thur, Sun; 10am-11pm Fri, Sat.* ***Tickets*** *€7.50-€11. No cash.* ***Map*** *p166 M4.*

It doesn't take visitors to the city centre very long to spot the EYE Film Institute. With a futuristic angular design, the origami-like structure – which looks as though it might take flight at any moment – is pretty hard to miss, dominating the northern bank of the IJ alongside the A'DAM Toren (*see p174*). Completed in 2012, it was the first major cultural institution to settle in Noord and was a key element in the area's regeneration and development.

Formerly known as the Nederlands Filmmuseum, the Institute is actually an amalgamation of four distinct entities. Holland Film, the Filmbank, the Netherlands Institute for Film Education and the Filmmuseum itself were formally merged in 2009, and the decision was taken to relocate from the Vondelpark Pavillion, the Filmmuseum's longstanding and much-loved home. National and international film fans alike had flocked there since 1975 to see the cream of cinematic history. The new building, while honouring that rich heritage, delivers on its promise to provide a world-class, 21st-century platform for film and cinematography.

Visually stunning, the building's raw statistics are too. Nearly 1,200-square-metres of exhibition space complements the four screens, a quirky gift shop, and plethora of workspaces and meeting rooms, not to mention the huge bar-restaurant with wrap-around waterfront terrace – truly, there is no better spot for a beer on a sunny day. And alongside everything cinema, EYE plays host to various art and music events all year round; small wonder visitor numbers have grown year after year.

EYE specialises in major retrospectives and edgier contemporary fare, something that's reflected in its exhibitions – legendary Russian director Andrei Tarkovsky, Danish artist Jesper Just, and master animator Jan Švankmajer have all been the subject of recent shows. The annual summer programme typically features an exhaustive array of screenings and talks dedicated to the celebration and reassessment of showbiz lynchpins, and it even squeezes in a few festivals.

❤ A'DAM Toren

Overhoeksplein 1 (020 237 6310, www.adamtoren.nl). Bus 38 or Buiksloterweg ferry. ***Open*** *10am-1am Mon-Thur, Sun; 10am-3am Fri, Sat (hours vary for restaurant, bar and Lookout – check website for details).* ***Tickets*** *Lookout €13.50; €7.50 reductions; free under-4s.* ***Map*** *p166 M5.*

You can spot it from a mile (or more) away. Standing tall in Amsterdam's trendiest neighbourhood, the A'DAM Toren has been hailed the 'King of the Noord'. Perched directly across the IJ from Centraal Station, it is the pinnacle of the area's post-industrial revival in every sense of the word. It opened in 2016 as a cultural hub for creatives, culinary enthusiasts and clubbers. And while it may look shiny and new, the tower's 22 storeys have decades of tales to tell.

The landmark dates back to 1971 as the home of multinational oil company Royal Dutch Shell. Designed by architect Arthur Staal, it was known as Shelltoren by Amsterdammers until 2009, when the company's headquarters relocated.

Almost a decade and a multi-million-euro refit later, the building reopened. The very existence of A'DAM Toren is a big nod to how much the city values art and culture. There were much higher bids placed for the building, but the municipality chose the vision for a vertical city with a 'wow' factor over standard accounting, investment and law firms.

On the top floor, at almost 100 metres (330 feet) above ground, its 360° observation deck offers panoramic views of the city. For daredevils, **A'DAM Lookout** (020 242 0100, www.adamlookout.com) has the highest swing in Europe, which lets riders swoop dramatically over the 17th-century skyline. The tower is also home to **Moon**, the high-end restaurant which revolves as you eat (*see opposite*); **MA'DAM** (020 237 6310, www.madamamsterdam.com) skybar on the top floor; **A'DAM Music School** for locals to brush up on their talents; **A'DAM&Co** (020 237 6312, www.adamand.co), a swanky members club for creatives; and **Shelter** – a 24-hour club in the basement (*see p228*). Want to try it all? Spend a night or two in **Sir Adam** (020 215 9510, www.sirhotels.com/en/adam), the Tower's urban boutique hotel.

Café-Restaurant Stork €€

Gedempt Hamerkanaal 201 (020 634 4000, www.restaurantstork.nl). Bus 35, 38. ***Open*** *11am-midnight daily.* ***Map*** *p166 R5* 4 Seafood

Oyster lovers, eat your heart out. Scenically set upon the IJ with an all-encompassing view of Amsterdam, Stork was one of the trendsetters in the revived Noord district and its menu is perfect for seafood fans. If you fall into this category be sure to try the Plateau Fruits de Mer; a mouth-watering combination of oysters, crab, cockles, scallops and shrimps (to name but a few).

The Coffee Virus €€

Overhoeksplein 2 (020 2870 9872, www.thecoffeevirus.nl). Bus 38 or Buiksloterweg ferry. ***Open*** *9am-4.30pm Mon-Fri.* ***Map*** *p166 M4* 5 Café

Creative types flock to this lunch and coffee canteen, which has two espresso roasts and three filter coffee roasts that rotate regularly. The menu also features delicious sandwiches and salads, so come with an appetite and a couple of hours to sit back and take in the buzzing atmosphere. **Other locations** throughout the city.

Hangar €€

Aambeeldstraat 36 (020 363 8657, www.hangar.amsterdam). Bus 35, 38 or Zamenhofstraat ferry. ***Open*** *10am-1pm Mon-Thur, Sun; 10am-3am Fri, Sat.* ***Map*** *p166 T5* 6 International

A self-described 'beautiful mess', the aptly named Hangar has warmed up an old hangar with a tropical-inspired interior. The brainchild of Jop Pollmann, Koen Schippers and Tim Immers, the restaurant has been a raging success since it opened several years ago.

Hotel de Goudfazant €€

Aambeeldstraat 10h (020 636 5170, www.hoteldegoudfazant.nl). Bus 35, 38 or Zamenhofstraat ferry. ***Open*** *6pm-late Tue-Sun.* ***Map*** *p166 T5* 8 Global

Deep within a warehouse, this is post-industrial dining at its best. Yes, it's about the location, but the food – from French dishes to pizza – is excellent and affordable.

Moon €€€€

A'DAM Toren, Overhoeksplein 1 (020 237 6310, restaurantmoon.nl). Bus 38 or Buiksloterweg ferry. ***Open*** *noon-2pm, 6-9pm daily.* ***Map*** *p166 M5* 9 Global

If you're willing and able to splash out on one memorable experience during your stay, Moon will undoubtedly deliver. Perched proudly on the 19th-floor of the A'DAM Toren, Moon promises guests 360° views of the city, without having to leave the dinner table. How? The entire floor revolves, of course. It's fine dining with a twist. Literally.

Noorderlicht €€

NDSM Plein 102 (020 492 2770, www.noorderlichtcafe.nl). Bus 35, 36, 38 or NDSM ferry. ***Open*** *11am-10pm daily. Nov-Feb closed Mon.* ***Map*** *p166 inset* 12 Global

Set inside a greenhouse with an inbuilt fireplace, this cultural café-restaurant is the perfect place for a spot of cosy stargazing. The dynamic menu has excellent vegetarian options, including 'Viking bread', white cabbage rendang, and a mean Aloo Gobi Mutter.

❤ Pllek €€

Neveritaweg 59 (020 290 0020, www.pllek.nl). Bus 35, 36, 38 or NDSM ferry. ***Open*** *9.30am-1am Mon-Thur, Sun; 9.30am-3am Fri, Sat. Kitchen closes 10pm daily.* ***Map*** *p166 inset* 13 Global

Surrounded by the cultural melting pot that is NDSM, Pllek is the picture of innovative sustainability. The product of a recycled warehouse and shipping containers, the venue has been a popular go-to for locals since opening earlier in the decade. The set menu rotates frequently, and prides itself on being surprising and always featuring exclusively seasonal and sustainable products. Chef Dimitry Mulder works his magic to produce affordable three-course set menus for €35.

If you'd rather just pop by for a drink and nibbles, you're more than welcome to do so. During summer, the man-made urban beach – which overlooks Amsterdam from across the IJ – is inundated with sun-seekers, and in the winter a huge bonfire keeps patrons warm. The venue also hosts DJs and major music events, including the city's notorious ADE (Amsterdam Dance Event), and has opened the hall next to the restaurant as a live music venue, **Pllek Live Stage**, to cater for the 'curious music lover'. Every first Thursday of the month, the room, which is fully equipped with sound and lighting, welcomes around 300 partygoers to discover contemporary and up-and-coming artists.

Rolling Rock Kitchen €€

Distelweg 113 (020 5320 5853, rollingrockkitchen.com). Bus 38 or ferry 900. ***Open*** *hours vary weekly.* ***Map*** *p166 off map* 14 Dutch/Belgian

Lunch with a side of rock'n'roll? Why not? Complete with piano and wall-hanging guitar on the inside, the Rolling Rock Kitchen has its own terrace with lovely views of the IJ and a special summer BBQ menu (check their website for dates and details). The creative menu includes Dutch- and Belgian-inspired weekly dishes that are both vegetarian and meat-lover friendly.

Tolhuistuin €€

IJ Promenade 2 (020 763 0650, www.tolhuistuin.nl). Ferry 901. ***Open*** *10am-10pm daily (kitchen 11am-4pm, 5.30-10pm).* ***No cash.*** ***Map*** *p166 M5* ⓯ *World cuisine*

A former Shell-site-turned-cultural-playground, Tolhuistuin (Toll House) definitely fits Noord's achingly trendy bill. With prime real estate directly across the IJ from Centraal Station, Tolhuistuin is the perfect hangout spot on a warm sunny day. Within the precinct is a concert hall, exhibition space and café-restaurant complete with outdoor terrace and hammocks.

Shops & services

❤ Blom & Blom

Chrysantenstraat 20 (020 737 2691, www.blomandblom.com). Bus 34, 35 or ferry 901 or Metro Nooderpark. ***Open*** *10am-5pm Mon-Fri.* ***Map*** *p166 N2* ❶ *Homewares*

Industrial home deco at its finest – interior fanatics with no space in their suitcase should approach Blom & Blom with caution. The minimalist white-space interior is decorated with exposed industrial lamps and wooden furnishings, all of which are available for purchase, along with cooler-than-cool accessories. If you're looking for a special gift (or an excuse to splurge on a new lamp) you've found the right place.

IJ-Hallen

Neveritaweg 15, NDSM, (020 2958 1598, www.ijhallen.nl). Bus 35, 36 or ferry 906. ***Open*** *9am-4.30pm one weekend each month.* ***Admission*** *€5.* ***Map*** *p166 inset* ❸ *Market*

If your visit happens to coincide with the monthly IJ-Hallen, you'd be remiss not to check it out. Regarded by locals as the best flea market in Amsterdam, savvy shoppers can score vintage clothing, homeware, instruments and just about everything else from the 800-plus vendors that flood the halls.

Pekmarkt

EC Van der Pekstraat (020 737 1412). Bus 34, 35 or Buiksloterweg ferry or Metro Nooderpark. ***Open*** *9am-5pm Wed, Fri, Sat.* ***Map*** *p166 O3* ❹ *Market*

Make the trip to Pekmarkt if strolling through a market, warm coffee in hand, is your idea of a perfect morning. With an array of fresh produce and unique trinkets, it's a veritable treasure trove. There's a special organic market on Fridays, and on Saturdays vintage sellers come out to play.

Top 20

❤ NDSM

Neveritaweg 61 (020 493 1070, www.NDSM.nl). Bus 35, 36, or ferry 906. ***Open*** *9am-5pm Mon-Fri.* ***Map*** *p166 inset.*

A 20-minute free ferry ride from Centraal Station, the former shipyard NDSM-werf sports a wonderful and unique post-apocalyptic vibe that's ideal for parties, concerts and wacky theatre festivals. One hall forms the country's largest cultural incubator, with over 100 studios for artists, theatre companies and other creative professionals. The interior walls of this Kunststad ('Art City', as it's now known) give the feeling of an expressionist film set, with parts covered in Banksy-like graffiti and an LED McDonald's sign hanging beside a large-scale chalk drawing of a child crying.

As ground zero for Dutch subculture, NDSM has attracted some big players. TV network MTV set up its Benelux headquarters in a wildly revamped former woodwork factory; Greenpeace moved its offices here (handy for parking its boat *Sirius*); and even the iconic Dutch department store HEMA is headquartered here, complete with a flagship shop (NDSM-straat 12) to test new products and services. One of NDSM's most impressive assets is **Crane Hotel Faralda** (*see p283*): the high-end mini hotel is situated in a crane once used to drag ships to dry dock; it's now a private hotspot for DJs, VIPs and even royals.

To complete the picture of an alternative area where hippie ideals meet high tech, visit **Noorderlicht** (*see p175*), a café that offers a rustic vibe: there's a campfire, lounge music, strings of colourful lights and a terrace. Two minutes away is urban beach hotspot **Pllek**, which is built, appropriately enough, out of shipping containers (*see p175*). There's also conceptual club **Sexyland** (Ms van Riemsdijkweg 39, www.sexyland.amsterdam) – which has a different 'owner' every day, all year round, and hosts everything from rap nights to sporting events and themed dinner parties – and **IJ-Hallen** (*see left*), Europe's largest fleamarket. Recycling has indeed come a long way – what's described above is only the tip of the post-industrial iceberg.

Pllek

De Pijp

De Pijp may not be a treasure trove of cultural sights compared to its neighbour the Museum Quarter, but what it lacks in prestige, it makes up for with culinary delights, buzzing cafés and interesting shops. Well over 150 different nationalities keep its global-village atmosphere alive, and the last decade has seen many niche restaurants and bars flourishing here – so much so that when Starbucks arrived in the area it was met by local protest. The wide streets underwent frequent upheaval during the construction of the metro's controversial and much delayed Noord/Zuidlijn, which turned the normally bustling Ferdinand Bolstraat into a construction site.

Originally a late 19th-century working-class neighbourhood, today De Pijp is home to a mix of halal butchers, Surinamese, Spanish and Turkish delicatessens, and restaurants offering authentic Syrian, Moroccan, Thai, Pakistani, Chinese and Indian cuisines. This makes it one of the best areas in town to buy snacks and street food, the many ingredients for which are almost always bought fresh from the single largest daily market anywhere in the Netherlands: Albert Cuypmarkt – the hub around which De Pijp turns.

❤ Don't miss

1 Albert Cuypmarkt *p184*
A neighbourhood-defining street market.

2 Hutspot Amsterdam *p187*
Hipster department store with ultra cool brands, local art and a barber shop.

3 Sarphatipark *p182*
Have a picnic in this friendly local park.

4 Gerard Douplein *p180*
Eat, drink and people-watch.

Huis met de Kabouters, Ceintuurbaan Street

EXPLORING DE PIJP

The socially mobile De Pijp of today has come a long way from its 19th-century working-class beginnings. Back then, harsh economics saw the construction of long, narrow streets lined with tenement blocks, which probably inspired the change in name from the official, double-yawn-inducing 'Area YY' to its appropriate nickname, 'the Pipe'. Because rents were high, many tenants were forced to sublet rooms to students, who then gave the area its bohemian character.

Several Dutch writers and painters lived here in the late 19th and early 20th centuries, including such luminaries as Heijermans, De Haan, Bordewijk and Piet Mondrian. And, of course, the area was packed with brothels and drinking dens. In the basement of Quellijnstraat 64 (now a neighbourhood centre), the Dutch cabaret style – distinguished by witty songs with cutting social commentary for lyrics – was formulated by Eduard Jacobs.

From the corner of Ferdinand Bolstraat and Albert Cuypstraat, head west past a cluster of cheap and cheerful Chinese, Surinamese and Indonesian restaurants, and past the former-diamond-factory-turned-boutique-hotel **Sir Albert** (*see p284*) to Ruysdaelkade, De Pijp's very own mini red-light district. The windows here may not look as impressive as those in De Wallen, but it is still a place of business for the sex workers, which means the same rules apply: strictly no photos or video footage. Despite the hooter-happy motorists caught in a traffic gridlock, Ruysdaelkade is worth a wander for its carefully planned 19th-century architecture and its canalside setting. The artist Piet Mondrian once lived in the attic of Ruysdaelkade 75, where he began formulating De Stijl art movement (*see p275*) while enjoying a view of the decidedly old-school Rijksmuseum.

Head away from the water (and the red lights) a few blocks along 1e Jan Steenstraat and you'll soon reach De Pijp's little green oasis: **Sarphatipark**, named after the slightly mad genius Samuel Sarphati (1813-66). After a stroll in the park, wander north up 1e Van der Helststraat. Veer east to browse the stalls and soak up the atmosphere at the unmissable **Albert Cuypmarkt** (*see p184*). Amsterdam's largest general market sells everything from pillows to prawns at great prices, although the clothes tend to be run-of-the-mill cheapies. Then continue towards **Gerard Douplein**. This little square, with its cafés, coffeeshops, chip shops and authentic Italian ice-cream parlour, turns into one big terrace during the summer and is hugely popular with locals. Just beyond is Heinekenplein, the U-shaped open-air gathering of cafés, Indian restaurants and Irish pubs next to the **Heineken Experience**. It's another favoured suntrap in summer months, and often hosts one-off cinema screenings and the occasional music festival.

In the know
Street artists

Take a look at the street signs in De Pijp, and you'll notice that most of the blocks are named after famous 17th-century painters: Jan Steen, Ferdinand Bol, Gerard Dou and Frans Hals. Frans Halsstraat is very pretty and has plenty of cafés and bars.

❤ Time to eat & drink

Burgers with attitude
The Butcher *p183*

Lounging in style
CT Coffee & Coconuts *p185*

Scandi chic
Scandinavian Embassy *p185*

Top-floor cocktails
Twenty Third Bar *p186*

Wholesome brunch
Little Collins *p185*

Wind-down wines
Boca's Park *p186*

❤ Time to shop

Covetable homewares
Anna + Nina *p187*

Mini hipster department store
Hutspot Amsterdam *p187*

Vintage and new fashion
Things I Like Things I Love *p187*

In the know
Getting around

Tram 24 runs from Centraal Station to Albert Cuypstraat in the heart of De Pijp, as does Metro 52 (stop De Pijp). Tram 4 runs through the area's eastern fringe; tram 3 runs between the eastern and western sides of the city through the neighbourhood, and tram 12 takes you to the south-west corner, next to the new metro stop. Key destinations in the area are easily walkable: Albert Cuypmarkt is a five-minute walk from the Heineken Experience.

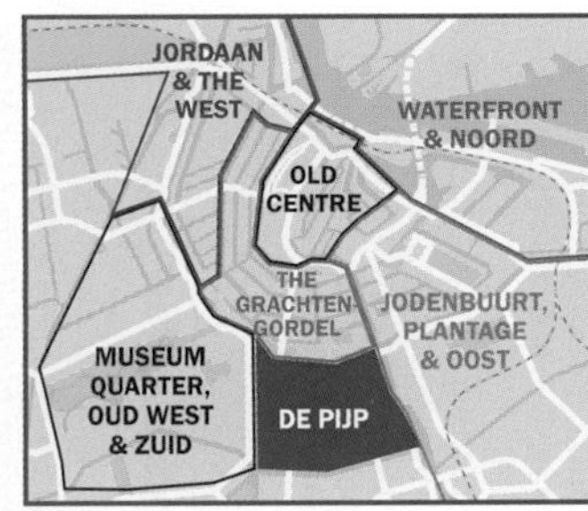

DE PIJP

Restaurants & cafés

1. Albina *p182*
2. Bakers & Roasters *p183*
3. Bazar *p183*
4. Brut de Mer *p183*
5. The Butcher *p183*
6. Cannibale Royale *p183*
7. CT Coffee & Coconuts *p185*
8. Firma Pekelhaaring *p185*
9. Little Collins *p185*
10. Mamouche *p185*
11. Scandinavian Embassy *p185*
12. De Taart van m'n Tante *p185*
13. VOLT *p185*
14. Warung Spang-Makandra *p186*

Bars

1. Boca's Park *p186*
2. Brouwerij Troost *p186*
3. Kingfisher *p186*
4. Twenty Third Bar *p186*
5. Wijnbar Boelen *p186*

Coffeeshops

1. Katsu *p186*
2. Yo-Yo *p187*

Shops & services

1. Anna + Nina *p187*
2. Duikelman *p187*
3. Hutspot Amsterdam *p187*
4. Things I Like Things I Love *p187*

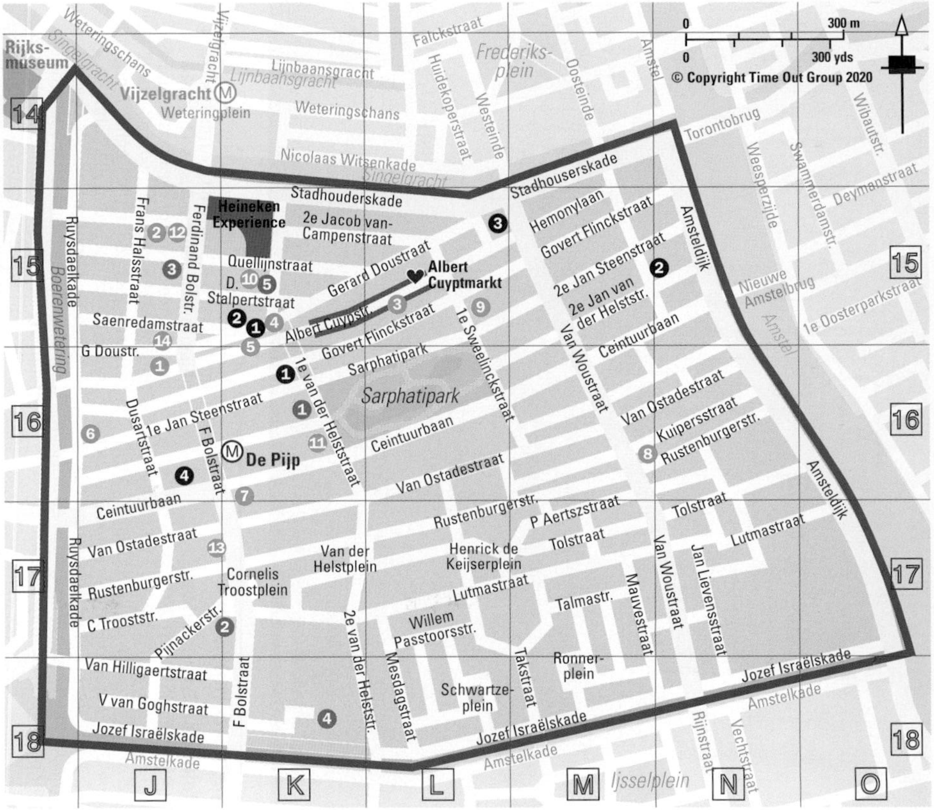

Heineken Experience

Sights & museums

Heineken Experience

Stadhouderskade 78 (020 523 9666, www.heinekenexperience.com). Tram 1, 7, 19, 24 or Metro Vijzelgracht. ***Open*** *10.30am-7.30pm Mon-Thur; 10.30am-9pm Fri-Sun. Last ticket sale 2hrs before closing.* ***Admission*** *€21; €17.50 reductions; free under-11s. €3 discount for booking online.* ***Map*** *p181 K15.*

Heineken stopped brewing here in 1988, but kept the building open for tours and marketing. The 'experience' is spread across four levels and multiple interactions, including lots of interactive displays, a mini brewery and a stable walk, where visitors can see Heineken's iconic shire horses. And where else could you take a virtual reality ride from the perspective of a Heineken bottle? Plus you get two cold ones at the end – best enjoyed on the roof terrace, of course.

❤ Sarphatipark

Sarphatipark (www.sarphatipark.wordpress.com). Tram 3, 4. ***Open*** *daily.* ***Admission*** *free.* ***Map*** *p181 L16.*

Sarphatipark occupies two blocks in the middle of the thriving district. It is named after the doctor and philanthropist Samuel Sarphati, who is remembered with a monument and centrepiece fountain. Aside from building the Amstel hotel and the Paleis voor Volksvlijt, Sarphati showed philanthropic tendencies as a baker of inexpensive bread for the masses, and as initiator of the city's rubbish collection. The park was designed in the English landscape style and was opened in 1886, almost two decades after its namesake's death. Construction included the installation of a pumping station to manage groundwater levels. During the German occupation in World War II, Sarphati's monument was removed due to his Jewish ancestry and the park was temporarily renamed. But in 1945 when Amsterdam was liberated the changes were overturned.

Today, the picturesque space is populated by young families, picnicking locals and cycling tourists escaping the buzz of the district. The park is the ideal place to relax after a busy morning of sightseeing or shopping at nearby Albert Cuypmarkt.

Restaurants & cafés

Albina €

Albert Cuypstraat 69 (020 675 5135, www.albina-amsterdam.nl/en). Tram 24 or Metro De Pijp. ***Open*** *11am-10pm Tue-Sat; noon-10pm Sun.* ***No cards. Map*** *p181 J16* ①
Asian

One in a whole row of cheap Suri-Chin-Indo spots located in De Pijp, Albina – where a Chinese influence predominates – gets top marks for its lightning service and reliable vegetarian or meat meals with roti, rice or noodles. If you need a fix on a Monday, sister restaurant **New Albina**, a few doors down at no.49, is open seven days a week.

Bakers & Roasters €€

Eerste Jacob van Campenstraat 54 (020 772 2627, www.bakersandroasters.com). Tram 24 or Metro De Pijp. ***Open*** *8.30am-4pm daily.* ***Map*** *p181 J15* ❷ *Café*

The brainchild of a Brazilian and New Zealander who met while backpacking in South America, Bakers & Roasters delivers brunch favourites in generous quantities. The café has had such success over the last couple of years it has opened another branch at Kadjiksplein 16 in Centrum. Come with enough room for a main course and a peanut butter smoothie, but be warned, it doesn't take bookings and the waiting list can be up to an hour long. It's best to visit between Monday and Wednesday, and get there early.

Bazar €

Albert Cuypstraat 182 (020 675 0544, www.bazaramsterdam.nl). Tram 3, 4 or Metro De Pijp. ***Open*** *4-11pm Mon-Thur, Sun; 4pm-midnight Fri, Sat.* ***Map*** *p181 L15* ❸ *North African*

This former church, now an Arabic-kitsch café, is one of the glories of Albert Cuypmarkt. Sticking to the winning formula set by its Rotterdam mothership, the delicious menu lingers in North Africa.

Brut de Mer €€

Gerard Douplein 811 (020 471 4099, www.brutdemer.nl). Tram 3, 12, 24 or Metro De Pijp. ***Open*** *4-11pm Mon-Thur; 1-11pm Fri-Sun.* ***Map*** *p181 K15* ❹ *Seafood*

The gentrification of De Pijp saw an influx of trendy restaurant and café concepts popping up next to street food vendors. One of these is Brut de Mer, which was the first seafood joint in the area when it opened in the spring of 2015. Unsurprisingly, it's been a raging success ever since. You can't go wrong with oysters and bubbles.

❤ The Butcher €€

Albert Cuypstraat 129 (020 470 7875, www.the-butcher.com). Tram 3, 12, 124 or Metro De Pijp. ***Open*** *noon-11pm Mon-Wed, Sun; noon-1am Thur; noon-3am Fri, Sat.* ***Map*** *p181 K15* ❺ *Burgers*

Never mind the hush-hush 'invite only' club upstairs, it's all about the burgers at this chic-but-spare joint. About a dozen versions are on offer, from aptly titled The Daddy (230g prime Aberdeen Angus beef) to the Veggie Delight. Note closing time is subject to change. **Other locations** throughout the city.

Cannibale Royale €€€

Ruysdaelkade 149 (020 233 5860, www.cannibaleroyale.nl). Tram 3, 12, 24. ***Open*** *noon-1am Mon-Thur, Sun; noon-3am Fri, Sat. Kitchen closes at 11pm Sun-Thur; midnight Fri, Sat.* ***Map*** *p181 J16* ❻ *Meat*

Meat-lovers rejoice, for this is your happy place. Home of the city's best ribs, jerk-style whole roast chicken, killer burgers and a steak

Bakers & Roasters

❤ Albert Cuypmarkt

Albert Cuypstraat (no phone). Tram 4, 24, or Metro De Pijp. ***Open*** *9.30am-5.30pm Mon-Sat.* ***No cards. Map*** *p181 L15.*

This vast and busy street market is definitely one for the locals or visitors keen to break free of the *grachts*. Once a 19th-century development for the working class, it's now populated by Dutch, Moroccan, Surinamese, Vietnamese and Turkish stallholders. You'll find everything from walls of veg, fresh *stroopwafels* (the gooey, syrupy Dutch treat) and Edam cheese to Vietnamese *loempias* (spring rolls) and Turkish flatbreads all being hawked loudly by enthusiastic vendors. Besides the food and the regular market tat – nylon lingerie that errs on the porno side, knock-off perfumes (Guggi Envy, anyone?), and a whole spectrum of textiles, from faux Andy Warhol prints to tan-coloured corduroy – one of the biggest draws to dear old Albert are the florists selling ten white roses for €5 or bunches of tulips for €1.50. If you go at the end of the day, you may even score some for free before marketeers discard them. Attracting thousands of customers six days a week, Albert Cuypmarkt spills merrily into the adjoining roads: the junctions of Sweelinckstraat, Ferdinand Bolstraat and 1e Van der Helststraat, north into the lively Gerard Douplein, and south towards Sarphatipark.

While it's easy to get distracted by all the stalls, it's worth checking out the nearby shops and cafés. For example, the charming and helpful **Fourniturenwinkel Jan De Grote Kleinvakman** (Albert Cuypstraat 203a, 020 673 8247) – which translates as 'Haberdashery Shop Jan the Big Small Craftsman' – has everything you need to keep your wardrobe in good repair.

► *For other shopping options in the area, see p187 Shops & services.*

menu that includes bavette, rib roast and the 1kg L'Absurde (which has to be ordered 24 hours in advance), there is no greater temple for carnivores. They have other locations in Noord, the Red Light district and Jordaan.

❤ CT Coffee & Coconuts €€

Ceintuurbaan 282 (020 354 1104, www.ctamsterdam.nl). Tram 3, 4, 12, 16. ***Open*** *8am-11pm daily.* ***Map*** *p181 K16* 7 Café

A former movie cinema, this four-storey loft café retains its classic exterior. Inside, sofas line exposed-brick walls and rope suspends candlelit tables from the high ceiling. It's a buzzing spot, where the city's urban creatives come to caffeinate. CT's menu is a reflection of its vacation-inspired atmosphere. The coconut coffee is a decadent must for anyone with a sweet tooth, and the scrambled eggs avo is its perfect savoury accompaniment. Or opt for The Harry Nilsson – a whole fresh coconut served with a straw and lots of lime. On arrival, steal away to the third floor and perch yourself on a plush corner beanbag for some privacy. Come with an appetite and time: you won't be rushed through your first feed, or your second.

Firma Pekelhaaring €€

Van Woustraat 127 (020 679 0460, www.pekelhaaring.nl). Tram 3, 4. ***Open*** *10am-midnight daily.* ***Map*** *p181 M16* 8 *European*

Meat and fish dominate the menu here – the baked plaice is recommended – although vegetarians will be happy with the creative pasta dishes. Desserts are also exemplary: the chocolate mousse with wild peach and mille feuille makes a trip here worthwhile.

❤ Little Collins €€

Eerste Sweelinckstraat 19 (020 753 9636, www.littlecollins.nl). Tram 3, 4. ***Open*** *10.30am-4pm Mon; 10.30am-10pm Wed-Fri; 9am-10pm Sat, Sun.* ***Map*** *p181 L15* 9 *Brasserie*

This Aussie-run bar-restaurant has one of the most inventive brunch menus in town; dishes range from peach brioche toast to hot smoked salmon, plus a variety of other homemade delights. Whatever you choose, wash it down with a spicy Bloody Mary. **Other location** Bilderdijkstraat 140, Jordaan.

Mamouche €€

Quellijnstraat 104 (020 670 0736, www.restaurantmamouche.nl). Tram 24 or Metro De Pijp. ***Open*** *5-11pm Wed-Sun.* ***Map*** *p181 K15* 10 *North African*

In the heart of multicultural De Pijp, this is a Moroccan-French restaurant with a difference: it's posh, stylish (in a sexy, minimalist sort of way) and provides background music that's best described as 'North African lounge'.

The Butcher *p183*

❤ Scandinavian Embassy €€€

Sarphatipark 34 (020 61951 8199, scandinavianembassy.nl). Tram 3, 12, 24 or Metro De Pijp. ***Open*** *8am-6pm Mon-Fri; 9am-6pm Fri, Sat.* ***Map*** *p181 K16* 11 *Scandinavian*

Scandinavians know how to master the finer things in life, including food, design and coffee. This place combines all three, and very well at that. Set inside a cosy space overlooking Sarphatipark, the menu features delicious breakfast and lunch options, which you can eat while browsing the books and coffee paraphernalia.

De Taart van m'n Tante €

Ferdinand Bolstraat 10 (020 776 4600, www.detaart.com). Tram 3, 12, 24 or Metro De Pijp. ***Open*** *11am-6pm Mon-Fri, Sun; 11am-7pm Sat.* ***No cards. Map*** *p181 J15* 12 *Tearoom*

'My Aunt's Cake' started life as a purveyor of over-the-top cakes (which it still makes) before becoming the campest tearoom in town. In a glowing pink space filled with mismatched furniture, it's particularly gay-friendly (note the Tom of Finland cake).

VOLT €€€

Ferdinand Bolstraat 178 (020 471 5544, www.restaurantvolt.nl). Tram 3, 12, 24 or Metro De Pijp. ***Open*** *4pm-1am Mon-Thur; 4pm-3am Fri; 11am-3am Sat; 11am-1am Sun. Kitchen closes at 10pm.* ***Map*** *p181 K17* 13 *French*

This hip, buzzy gastrobar is exactly what every neighbourhood needs: a modern local that is all things to all people. The French-leaning menu is fresh, inventive and changes regularly; the bar is open late, and the service is unfussy and friendly.

Little Collins p185

Warung Spang-Makandra €

Gerard Doustraat 39 (020 670 5081, www.spangmakandra.nl). Tram 3, 12, 24 or Metro De Pijp. ***Open*** *11am-10pm Mon-Sat; 1-10pm Sun.* ***No cards. Map*** *p181 J15* ⑭
Indonesian

An Indonesian-Surinamese restaurant where the Indonesian influence always comes up trumps in the excellent Javanese rice platter. It is great for a takeaway, but its relaxed vibe and beautiful dishes may encourage you to linger.

Bars

❤ Boca's Park

Sarphatipark 4 (020 675 9945, www.barbocas.nl). Tram 3, 12, 24 or Metro De Pijp. ***Open*** *noon-1am Mon-Wed; 10am-1am Thur; 10am-3am Fri, Sat; 11am-1am Sun.* ***Map*** *p181 K16* ❶

Following the success of its first location on Westerstraat, Boca's Park perfects the bar-meets-mixed-dining concept. The varied plates are designed for sharing, and complement the extensive wine list with thirst-inducing precision.

Brouwerij Troost

Cornelis Trootsplein 21 (020 737 1028, www.brouwerijtroost.nl). Tram 3, 12, 24 or Metro De Pijp. ***Open*** *4pm-midnight Mon-Thur; 4pm-3am Fri; 2pm-3am Sat; 2pm-midnight Sun.* ***Map*** *p181 K17* ❷

If you don't have the time or energy to battle crowds at the Heineken Experience, why not visit De Pijp's first official brewery instead? Troost opened its doors in 2014, much to the delight of locals. With a tasting room and pub on site, the beers are brewed right before your eyes.

Kingfisher

Ferdinand Bolstraat 24 (020 671 2395, www.kingfishercafe.nl). Tram 24. ***Open*** *10am-1am Mon-Thur; 10am-3am Fri, Sat; noon-1am Sun.* ***No cards. Map*** *p181 J15* ❸

The bar that kick-started the gentrification of De Pijp is now one of the old guard, but its sleek-with-a-twist-of-kitsch chic (glossy red walls, American fridges) still sets the agenda for other young pretenders in the area, as does its loungey feel, cocktails and world-fusion snack menu. The hip clientele have aged gracefully along with the watering hole, but make room for a dash of new blood.

❤ Twenty Third Bar

Hotel Okura, Ferdinand Bolstraat 333 (020 678 7111, www.okura.nl). Tram 12. ***Open*** *6pm-1am Mon-Thur, Sun; 6pm-2am Fri, Sat.* ***Map*** *p181 K18* ❹

On the 23rd floor of Hotel Okura this international cocktail and champagne bar offers fantastic views of De Pijp and the compact Amsterdam School architecture of the Rivierenbuurt. Be prepared to pay for the view – cocktails start at €15 a pop and the sommelier-selected champagne and wine don't come cheap either. But if you want to splash out, you won't be disappointed, particularly at sunset when you'll get a spectacular shot of the skyline. If you're feeling particularly flush, try the hotel's excellent (but expensive) Japanese restaurant **Yamazato** (020 678 7450).

Wijnbar Boelen

1e Van der Helststraat 50 (020 671 2242, www.wijnbar.nl). Tram 3, 12, 24 or Metro De Pijp. ***Open*** *4pm-midnight Tue-Thur, Sun; 4pm-1am Fri; 3pm-1am Sat.* ***Map*** *p181 K15* ❺

Many people come here for the Frenchified food, but, as the name implies, the wine is the star at this compact yet airy bar on the edge of De Pijp's main nightlife strip. Dozens are available by the glass, more by the bottle, and prices range from pocket-friendly to splurge. The emphasis is on Old World wine, but there are also good selections from the Antipodes and the Americas.

Coffeeshops

Katsu

Eerste van der Helststraat 70 (020 675 2617, www.katsu.nl). Tram 3, 12, 24 or Metro De Pijp. ***Open*** *10am-midnight Mon-Thur; 10am-1am Fri, Sat; 11am-midnight.* ***No cards. Map*** *p181 K16* ❶

This little treasure offers a giant selection of various strains of hash and weed at a wide and fair range of prices – quite possibly the best selection in town, in fact. The interior is pleasantly green, with plenty of leafy potted plants, and a crowd of older locals.

Yo-Yo
2e Jan van der Heijdenstraat 79 (020 233 9800, coffeeshopyoyo.nl). Tram 3, 4. ***Open*** *noon-7pm Mon-Thur, Sun; noon-8pm Fri, Sat.* ***No cards. Map*** *p181 N15* ❷

Located on a leafy street near Sarphatipark and the Albert Cuypmarkt, this relaxed spot lacks the commercialism and crowds found in more central shops. The herb is all-organic, as is the coffee.

Shops & services

❤ Anna + Nina
Gerard Doustraat 94 (020 204 4532, www.anna-nina.nl). Tram 3, 12, 24 or Metro De Pijp. ***Open*** *noon-6pm Mon; 10am-6pm Tue-Fri; 11am-6pm Sat, Sun.* ***Map*** *p181 K15* ❶ *Homewares*

If you needed another reminder that homeware is better bought from boutiques than generic outlets, Anna + Nina will certainly sort you out. The charming concept store provides a variety of quirky and unique pieces for the home. Specialising in botanical-inspired and rustic collections, Anna + Nina is definitely a cut above other interior stores.

Duikelman
Ferdinand Bolstraat 66-68 (020 671 2230, www.duikelman.nl). Tram 3, 12, 24 or Metro De Pijp. ***Open*** *9.30am-6pm Mon-Fri; 9.30am-5pm Sat.* ***Map*** *p181 K15* ❷ *Homewares*

Offering over 10,000 culinary tools – from ladles to truffle raspers – Duikelman is *the* place for professional cooks. It also runs a couple of other spaces across the street: head to Gerard Doustraat 54 for cookbooks and porcelain, or next door to that if you want to admire the stoves.

❤ Hutspot Amsterdam
Van Woustraat 4 (020 223 1331, www.hutspot.com). Tram 1, 4, 7, 19. ***Open*** *10am-7pm Mon-Sat; noon-6pm Sun.* ***Map*** *p181 L15* ❸ *Market*

What started as a permanent place for hipster pop ups has morphed into a shop stocking ultra cool brands, innovative design and local art. Young designers and artists in particular are given a platform to exhibit their wares alongside favourites such as WEARECPH and Ontour – Hutspot has even branched out with its own label. True to dynamic Dutch form, the 800sqm building also encompasses a photo booth and a barber, should you be in need of a quick trim. The shop also hosts events, such as book launches or creative workshops. The concept proved such a success that a second, larger location has opened in the Jordaan (Rozengracht) as well as one in the Magna Plaza shopping centre (Nieuwezijds Voorburgwal 182, 020 333 24 04).

❤ Things I Like Things I Love
Ceintuurbaan 69 (020 846 4142, www.thingsilikethingsilove.com). Tram 3, 4, 12, 16. ***Open*** *1-6pm Mon; 11am-6pm Tue, Wed, Fri, Sat; 11am-8pm Thur; noon-6pm Sun.* ***Map*** *p181 J16* ❹ *Fashion*

An undisputed favourite for local fashionistas, the boutique boasts a unique combination of brand new collections, second-hand treasures and vintage pieces. An excellent place to nab something you won't discard as soon as you return to normality. The prices aren't as high as you might expect, either. **Other locations** throughout the city.

CT Coffee & Coconuts *p185*

Day Trips

Amsterdam is part of one of the world's most densely populated areas: 40 per cent of the country's population inhabits the built-up sprawl known as the Randstad or 'Edge City', which encompasses the cities of Amsterdam, Rotterdam, Delft, Haarlem, the Hague, Leiden and Utrecht. (The Randstad takes its name from its coastal location on the Netherlands' western edge.) However, despite the urban spread, the area's road, rail and waterway networks are impressive, making for pleasant and straightforward journeys from the city to the countryside. You'll find rivers, beaches, windmills and castles all within easy reach of Amsterdam. The destinations and excursions mentioned here can be visited on day trips, but they also stand up to more leisurely and sustained exploration.

❤ Don't miss

1 Keukenhof *p192*
Few sights are as spectacular as these gardens in full bloom.

2 Muiderslot *p193*
Photo-friendly fairy-tale castle.

3 Haarlem *p194*
Genteel and laid-back medieval city.

4 Wijk aan Zee *p194*
Wide, sandy beach and North Sea surfing.

5 Durgerdam *p190*
Flat fields, neat houses and big skies.

6 De Zaanse Schans *p191*
History in 3D.

In the know
Getting around

There's much to see within an hour's travel of Amsterdam. There are car hire options (*see p289*) or, for hardier souls, bike hire (*see p290*). Alternatively, the public transport network is comprehensive and good value. Discover Amsterdam and the surrounding area with the Amsterdam & Region Travel Ticket – a public transport pass valid on bus, tram, metro and train operated by GVB, Connexxion, EBS, AllGo and NS. The ticket costs €19.50 for one day, €28 for two days and €36.50 for three days. It is available from the Iamsterdam Visitor Centres in Amsterdam, selected hotels and campsites, and ticket offices of the participating public transport companies. For more transport options from Amsterdam, *see p287* Getting Around.

Grote Kerk, Haarlem

WATERLAND

Until the IJ Tunnel opened in 1956, the canal-laced peat meadows of Waterland, lying north-east of Amsterdam, were only accessible to the public by ferry and steam railway. This isolation meant that much of the area's traditional fishing and farming heritage and associated architecture were preserved. Today, the picturesque villages draw plenty of visitors from the city and can be easily reached by bus or, better, by bike. The eastern Waterland region is just 20 minutes' cycle away from the city centre, but it's another world: at points, it feels as if you've arrived in a 17th-century Dutch landscape painting. From the Buiksloterweg ferry stop in Amsterdam Noord, signposts mark the cycle route to **Durgerdam**. Riding into this tiny former fishing village, you'll find a tranquil scene: old painted wooden houses line the cobbled street and hundreds of masts pierce the IJmeer skyline. Two kilometres from Durgerdam is **Vuurtoreneiland** (020 362 1664, www.vuurtoreneiland.nl, €€€), an organic restaurant that is the sole occupant of 'Lighthouse Island'. Back in 2013, a contest for how to best use the island produced 300 ideas (including a brothel). But the winner was this restaurant, housed in a greenhouse in summer and in a 'fort' in the colder months, complete with fire, blankets and a *gezellig* atmosphere. The five-course meal changes seasonally and uses locally sourced ingredients. Reservations, complete with ferry arrangements, can be made online; just be sure to book well in advance.

From Durgerdam, the route north passes numerous inlets, home to scores of bird colonies. Shortly after the village of **Uitdam** is the start of the **Zeedijk**, a two-kilometre long causeway that has joined the former island of **Marken** to the mainland since 1957. Marken itself is chocolate-box quaint, with clusters of traditional green houses built on mounds to protect against flooding. It's awash with tourists, especially in summer, but you can cycle lazily around the perimeter, taking in the sturdy lighthouse (nicknamed *de paard* – 'the horse' – for its shape) dating from 1700. You can also enjoy uninterrupted views across the IJmeer towards Almere and back towards the mainland to Volendam. Visit the cutesy **Marker Museum** (Kerkbuurt 44-47, 0299 601904, www.markermuseum.nl), which provides an overview of the island's history, or sample one of the myriad cafés, bars and restaurants – try fish and chips with a view at **De Visscher** (0299 601304, www.tavernevisscher.nl).

Back on the mainland, **Broek in Waterland** can be reached by bus from Centraal Station in just 15 minutes. It is characterised by immaculate wooden buildings, some of which date from the 17th and 18th centuries. The surrounding watercourses can be explored by canoe or electric motor boat, both of which can be rented from **Waterland Recreatie** (Stal Baco, Belmermeer 5, 06 3752 5640, www.fluisterbootvaren.nl). A four-hour return trip will allow you to visit **Monnickendam**, with its collection of well-preserved historic buildings, from Golden Age merchants' dwellings to herring-smokehouses. Also listen out for the fine carillon from the belltower of the old town hall.

Further north is **Volendam**, a fishing port turned theme park. It's said that

De Zaanse Schans

Living history

Located about 20 kilometres north-west of Amsterdam, De Zaanse Schans (www.dezaanseschans.nl) is not your typical museum village: people still live here. One of the world's first industrial zones, Zaan was once crowded with 800 windmills, which powered the production of paint, flour and lumber. Today, amid the gabled green-and-white houses, attractions include an old-fashioned Albert Heijn store. In nearby Zaandam, you can visit Czaar Peterhuisje, the tiny wooden house where Peter the Great stayed in 1697 while he was honing his shipbuilding skills and preparing for the foundation of St Petersburg.

To get to De Zaanse Schans, from Centraal Station catch R-net bus 391 or the train to Zaandijk-Zaanse Schans.

the town flag was flown at half-mast when the Zuider Zee was enclosed in 1932, cutting off Vollendam's access to the sea, but the village applied its enterprising spirit to devising a tourist attraction from its fascinating historic features. Sadly, the cheerily garbed locals can barely be seen for the coachloads of tourists dumped here every day. One 'attraction' is the world's biggest collection of cigar bands (11 million in total), all of them on view at the **Volendams Museum** (Zeestraat 41, 029 936 9258, www.volendamsmuseum.nl).

Just inland from Volendam is **Edam**, famous for its cheese (*see p194* Say Cheese) but also worth a visit for the Golden Age architecture of its town centre.

Essential information

Tourist information

VVV i-Point Broek in Waterland *Kerkplein 13 (02 9982 0046, www.vvvwaterland.nl).* ***Open*** *10am-4pm Tue-Sat; 1-4pm Sun, Mon.*

VVV Tourist Office Volendam *Zeestraat 37 (02 99 31 5125, www.vvv-volendam.nl).* ***Open*** *Apr-Oct 10am-5pm Mon-Sat; 11am-4pm Sun. Nov-Mar noon-4pm Mon; 11am-4pm Tue-Sat; closed Sun.*

Getting there

If you're not cycling, from Centraal Station you can get to Durgerdam on bus 37, then bus 30; bus 315 goes to Marken; bus 314 goes to Broek in Waterland and Edam; bus 316 goes to Volendam.

Durgerdam

Flower Power

Tulips from Amsterdam, but also carnations, daffodils, gladioli ...

The Netherlands might produce a staggering 70 per cent of the world's commercial flower output, but it still has enough blooms left to fill up its own markets, botanical gardens, auctions and parades all year round.

The co-operative flower auction **FloraHolland** (www.florahollland.com) handles more than 12 billion cut flowers and over half a million plants a year, mostly for export, through a network of marketplaces. The most impressive of these is in **Aalsmeer**, in the world's biggest trading building (120 football fields' worth; Legmeerdijk 313, 029 739 0697). It's a 15-kilometre (9-mile) drive south-west of Amsterdam; take the train from Centraal Station to Hoofddorp then catch bus 340.

Aalsmeer's unusual sales method gave rise to the phrase 'Dutch auction'. Dealers bid by pushing a button to stop a 'clock' that counts from 100 down to one; thus, the price is lowered – rather than raised – until a buyer is found. Bidders risk either overpaying for the goods or not getting them if time runs out. The auction is open to the public between 7am and 11am, Monday to Friday (Thursday until 9am). The earlier you get there, the better.

Broeker Veiling (Museumweg 2, Broek-op-Langerdijk, 022 631 3807, www.broekerveiling.nl, hours vary by season) is the oldest flower and vegetable auction in the world and therefore a bit of a tourist trap, but nonetheless includes a museum of old farming artefacts, plus a boat trip. It's 36 kilometres (22 miles) north of Amsterdam; if you're not driving, take a train from Centraal Station to Alkmaar, then catch bus 169.

Nowhere is the Dutch cult of the tulip celebrated in more glorious fashion than at the **Keukenhof** (025 246 5555, www.keukenhof.nl), located in South Holland's 'dune and bulb' region. Open for eight weeks each year (from mid March to mid May), this former royal 'kitchen garden' has been a showcase since 1949 for local bulb growers, who still donate the staggering seven million bulbs planted by hand each year. There are other flowers, of course – crocuses, hyacinths and narcissi from late March; lilies and roses in early summer – but the tulip is the star, standing to attention in rows of glorious colour. It's 43 kilometres (26 miles) north of Amsterdam; driving is your best option, as the nearest public transport (bus) stop is 2 kilometres away at Lisse, De Nachtegaal.

Keukenhof

CASTLE DISTRICT

Many important events in Dutch history took place in the legendary stronghold of **Muiderslot** (029 425 6262, www.muiderslot.nl), located in Muiden, about 12 kilometres (7 miles) south-east of Amsterdam. This formidable moated castle at the mouth of the River Vecht looks as though it belongs in a fairytale and is a great place to visit with children. It was built in 1280 for Count Floris V, who was murdered in 1296. Rebuilt in the 14th century, it has since been through many sieges and renovations. Meandering up the River Vecht from the picturesque harbour at Muiden towards Utrecht, boat passengers and cyclists can glimpse some of the homes built in the 17th and 18th centuries by rich Amsterdam merchants.

Further east, the town of **Naarden** is a striking example of a star-fort, with a moat and arrowhead-shaped bastions; it was in active service as recently as 1926. All is explained in the **Vestingmuseum** (Turfpoortbastion Westwalstraat 6, 035 694 5459, www.vestingmuseum.nl). The fortifications date from 1675, after the inhabitants were massacred by the Duke of Alva's son in 1572; the slaughter is depicted above the door of the Spaanse Huis (Spanish House). Today, Naarden is the perfect setting for a leisurely Sunday stroll.

Both Muiderslot and Naarden are part of the **Stelling van Amsterdam**, a defensive ring of forts and dykes that were constructed between 1874 to 1914 to protect the city and are now a UNESCO World Heritage Site. Visit www.stellingvanamsterdam.nl, if you're interested in exploring the defensive line further.

Essential information

Getting there

In summer, a tourist ferry runs from IJburg in Amsterdam to Muiden via the man-made fortified island of Pampus. Otherwise, buses 320, 322 or 327 go from Amsterdam's Amstel station to Muiden; bus 320 goes to Naarden.

Say Cheese

In search of the yellow stuff

Few things are held in higher national esteem in the Netherlands than cheese. When they're not munching on it or exporting more than 400,000 tonnes of it every year, the Dutch are making a tourist industry of it. So it shouldn't be a surprise that the Dutch have been known as 'cheeseheads' since medieval times, when they sported wooden cheese moulds on their heads in battle.

Alkmaar, a 40-minute train ride north of Amsterdam, hosts the oldest and biggest cheese market in the world from 10am to 1pm every Friday between the end of March and the end of September (www.kaasmarkt.nl). You'll also find craft stalls and a cheese museum, **Het Hollands Kaas Museum** (Waagplein 2, 072 515 5516, www.kaasmuseum.nl).

The Netherlands' famous red-skinned cheese is sold at **Edam**'s cheese market, every Wednesday in July and August from 10.30am until 12.30pm. The town is 20 kilometres (12.5 miles) north-east of Amsterdam and was a prosperous port during the Golden Age, but even its exquisite façades and bridges can't compete with the cheese. Take bus 314 from Centraal Station.

Meanwhile, over in **Gouda** (less than an hour by train from Amsterdam), golden wheels of cheese go on sale at the market every Thursday from 10am in July and August. Near the town there are also many *kaasboerderijen* (cheese farms); look out for *kaas te koop* (cheese for sale) signs.

Cheese market, Alkmaar

HAARLEM & THE BEACHES

Lying between Amsterdam and the west coast, **Haarlem** is a smaller, gentler and older version of Amsterdam, with canals and Golden Age architecture.

Haarlem's **Grote Markt** is one of the loveliest squares in the Netherlands and hosts one of the country's best Saturday markets. The square is dominated by the imposing **Grote Kerk** (also known as **St-Bavo Kerk**), whose spire defines the Haarlem skyline. It was built around 1313 but suffered fire damage in 1328; rebuilding and expansion lasted another 150 years. The highlight of the ornate interior is the famous Müller organ (1738), with an amazing 5,068 pipes, which was played by Handel and the young Mozart.

Also on the square, **De Hallen** (Grote Markt 16, 023 511 5775) is administered by the Frans Hals Museum (*see below*) and extends through two buildings, the Verweyhal and the Vleeshal (meat market). It houses an extensive range of modern and contemporary art.

Not far away is the **Teylers Museum** (Spaarne 16, 023 516 0960, www.teylersmuseum.nl). Founded in 1784, it's one of the oldest public museums in the world and retains its period interior. The collection is eclectic: fossils and minerals sit beside antique scientific instruments and 16th- to 19th-century drawings by such eminent artists as Rembrandt, Michelangelo and Raphael. To the south is a former almshouse and orphanage which houses the **Frans Hals Museum** (Groot Heiligland 62, 023 511 5775, www.franshalsmuseum.nl). Hals was the most famous Haarlem painter of the Golden Age, and this museum has the largest collection of his work in the world, plus paintings by his predecessors and contemporaries.

If you've time to spare, visit the **Corrie ten Boomhuis** (Barteljoristraat 19, 23 531 0823, www.corrietenboom.com), where victims of Nazi persecution were hidden by a local family during World War II, or enjoy the varied retail opportunities on **De Gouden Straatjes** (Golden Streets).

In summer, don't forget that Haarlem is a mere stone's throw from the coast; a cycle ride will take you through the dunes to the sea, where the family resort beach of **Zandvoort** and party beach **Bloemendaal aan Zee** (*see opposite* Beach Bars) attract flocks of sand-seeking Amsterdammers and Germans every summer. Further north up the coast, **Wijk aan Zee** (www.visitwijkaanzee.nl) rates as the country's

Beach Bars

Head out of the city for fun at the seaside

Once a wonderful secret, the beach clubs at Bloemendaal aan Zee (*see opposite*) – less than an hour's train and bus ride from Amsterdam – lure clubbers by the thousands each summer weekend. Several different bars (open May to October) offer music, fashion and fabulous fixtures and fittings. There's a venue to suit everyone, from kooky **Woodstock 69** (woodstock69.nl) to chic **Republiek** (023 573 0730, republiekbloemendaal.nl) to the Ibiza-like **Bloomingdale** (023 573 7580, bloomingdalebeach.com). Bloemendaal aan Zee also hosts the three-day **Luminosity Beach Festival** (luminosity-events.nl) in June, with some of the biggest trance DJs from around the world. To get to Bloemendaal beach from Centraal Station, take the train to Haarlem and then the 81 bus from Haarlem station.

Republiek

only authentic surfing beach. And it's a surreal one: the North Sea on one side, transporter ships exiting and entering the North Sea Canal on another, and refinery chimneys jutting up above the dunes on yet another.

Essential information

Tourist information

VVV Haarlem *Grote Markt 2 (02 3531 7325, www.visithaarlem.com).* ***Open*** *Apr-Sept 9.30am-5.30pm Mon-Fri; 9.30am-5pm Sat; 11am-3pm Sun. Oct-March 1-5pm Mon; 9.30am-5.30pm Tue-Fri; 10am-5pm Sat.*

Getting there

There are trains from Centraal Station to Haarlem every 15 minutes; change here for Zandvoort aan Zee. In summer a sprinter service runs direct to Zandvoort, taking around 25 minutes. Bloemendaal is a 20-minute walk from Zandvoort from Centraal or take bus 81 from Haarlem. You can reach Wijk aan Zee in an hour from Amsterdam by catching a Sprinter from Centraal to Beverwijk, followed by a 15-minute bus (78) ride.

Wijk aan Zee

Experience

Giselle, Nationale Ballet *p238*

Events

A run-down of Amsterdam's packed calendar

The Dutch have a reputation for being a fairly reserved bunch, but when they shed their inhibitions and dive into a fun-seeking frenzy, they dive deep. On the likes of Oudejaarsavond (New Year's Eve) and Koningsdag (King's Day) – and whenever AFC Ajax wins a big game – the city falls into a joyous, orange-tinted psychosis of song, drink and dance. Happily, orange is yet to play a leading role during Fashion Week, but that's not to say it won't become the new black next year.

Dance music is a big deal in Amsterdam, and the city's annual electronic music festivals, including Amsterdam Dance Event in October, are a major draw. If you prefer your culture more genteel, there's plenty more to choose from, including Open Monuments Day (which sees the city's historical buildings throw their doors open free of charge), the ever-popular Museum Night, and the world's largest documentary film festival. Or there's a dedicated cello biennale, a curate-it-yourself festival and – no joke – a National Windmill Day.

► *For a sense of seasonal Amsterdam and advice on when to visit, see p26 When to Visit.*

N8 (Museum Night) *p205*

❤ Best events

Amsterdam Gay Pride *p203*
Few parties can compare to the annual madness that takes over the Prinsengracht.

Amsterdam Light Festival *p205*
Marvel at the creativity of light installations by some of the world's top artists.

Dekmantel *p203*
An exceptionally well-curated electronic festival for true ravers, purists and techno heads.

London Calling *p201*
An indie showcase at the legendary Paradiso, featuring up-and-coming UK and US bands.

N8 (Museum Night) *p205*
One of the most unique ways to explore the city's many museums: late into the night with a host of special events.

Over het IJ *p202*
Ten days of large-scale avant-garde theatre in the suitably vast environs of NDSM.

Rollende Keukens *p201*
Bring an appetite to this huge international food-truck festival.

World Press Photo *p200*
An exhibition of photojournalism at its finest.

Spring

Amsterdam Restaurant Week

Various venues (www.restaurantweek.nl). ***Date*** *Mar, Sept.*

A three-course gourmet dinner in a top restaurant for only €28.50? Possibly only during Amsterdam Restaurant Week (in fact, it lasts two weeks). Just as in New York, where the idea originated, restaurant owners think this is a great way to promote their businesses. The food isn't fast, but your reservation really needs to be, especially for the high-end restaurants where bookings start as early as a month before.

Stille Omgang

Old Centre (www.stille-omgang.nl). ***Map*** *p70.* ***Date*** *mid Mar.*

The candlelit night-time Silent Procession, a key event for Catholics, commemorates the 14th-century Miracle of Amsterdam. It follows a circular route from the Spui, north on Nieuwendijk and back on Warmoesstraat and Nes, between midnight on Saturday and 4am on Sunday. It's a sight that becomes particularly surreal as the procession snakes through the Red Light District.

King's Day

Tulip Festival

Throughout the city (www.tulpfestival.com). ***Date*** *Apr.*

What better way to ring in spring than a celebration of the iconic Dutch flower? The Netherlands has a relationship with the beautiful bloom dating back to the 17th century, and every April Amsterdam celebrates its beloved tulip with a display of over 500,000 of the most colourful and rare specimens throughout the city.

National Museum Weekend

Throughout the Netherlands (www.museumweekend.nl). ***Date*** *Apr.*

Around a million visitors flock to the country's 500 or so state-funded museums, which offer free or discounted admission and special activities for this one weekend.

❤ World Press Photo

Nieuwe Kerk, Dam Square, Old Centre (www.worldpressphoto.org). Tram 2, 4, 11, 12, 13, 14, 17, 24. ***Map*** *p70 K8.* ***Date*** *mid Apr-July.*

Launched in 1955, this is the world's largest photography competition, with exhibits from thousands of photojournalists. The show is held in the Nieuwe Kerk (*see p89*); after kicking off in Amsterdam, it then tours another 100 cities around the world.

Koningsdag (King's Day)

Throughout the city. ***Date*** *27 Apr.*

Formerly known as Queen's Day, the most popular event in the city actually starts the night before, with street parties and late-night drinking sessions in cafés. By day, the canals become a sea of orange as they are overrun with party boats and floats. Party-lovers and students of the surreal should make sure their visit coincides with this date, when up to a million extra people pour into the city. You're as likely to happen upon a leather-boy disco party on one side street or an old-school crooner on the other, as you are to witness a boat bellowing out heavy metal. It's all quite insane.

Herdenkingsdag & Bevrijdingsdag

Throughout the city. ***Date*** *4 & 5 May.*

At 7.30pm on 4 May, in the presence of the King and many dignitaries, those who lost their lives during World War II are remembered at the Nationaal Monument on Dam Square. The LGBTQ community has its own ceremony, with a remembrance service at the Homomonument, and there are also other events in various quarters of the city. The two-minute silence is usually observed in the city's bars and restaurants.

Liberation Day (to mark the end of Nazi occupation in World War II) is celebrated the following day, with music and speeches. The best places for visitors to see what's going on are Museumplein, Leidseplein and Westermarkt (the focal point of the gay commemorations).

❤ London Calling

Paradiso, Weteringschans 6-8, Grachtengordel (www.londoncalling.nl). Tram 1, 2, 7, 11, 12, 19. ***Map*** *p96 H13.* ***Date*** *May & Oct.*

Taking place twice a year, this two-day indie music festival at Paradiso (*see p227*) is a showcase for new bands, with special focus on the UK and USA. The festival started in 1992, and since then has welcomed the likes of Bloc Party, White Lies, Florence + the Machine, The xx, Hudson Mohawke and Franz Ferdinand.

Kunstvlaai

Various venues (www.kunstvlaai.nl). ***Date*** *May & Nov.*

This biennial art market is the very much hipper twin to KunstRAI (*see below*), focusing on new and more original artists, groups and galleries.

KunstRAI

RAI Convention Centre, Europaplein, Zuid (www.kunstrai.nl). Tram 4 or Metro Europaplein or RAI rail. ***Date*** *mid May-early June.*

A hundred or so galleries, both national and international, present their artists' work at this huge commercial five-day exhibition. For a few years, it was known as Art Amsterdam, in an attempt to piggyback on the much more successful and inspired Art Rotterdam, which takes place in February.

National Windmill Day

Throughout the Netherlands (020 623 8703, www.molens.nl/event/nationale-molendagen). ***Date*** *mid May.*

On the second Saturday and Sunday in May, about 600 state-subsidised windmills open their doors and spin their sails. Most have demonstrations and activities, and you can buy flour and bread made the traditional way. The best place near Amsterdam to see windmills in action is De Zaanse Schans (*see p191*).

❤ Rollende Keukens

Westergasfabriek, Westerpark (www.rollendekeukens.nl). Tram 5 or bus 21, 288. ***Map*** *p117 off map.* ***Date*** *late May.*

Street food festival 'Rolling Kitchens', with its massive serving of food trucks, is a much-loved event at Westergasfabriek (*see p132*). Bands and DJs provide a musical backdrop to the gastronomic weirdness.

Summer

Open Ateliers: Kunstroute de Westelijke Eilanden

Prinseneiland, Bickerseiland & Realeneiland, West (www.oawe.nl). Tram 3 or bus 18, 21, 22. ***Map*** *p117 H4.* ***Date*** *late May-early June.*

Most neighbourhoods with a significant number of artists' studios hold an annual open weekend, when artists open their doors to the general public. The Westelijke Eilanden event, covering the picturesque and peaceful islands around Prinseneiland, is the most popular.

► *The Jordaan also hosts an Open Ateliers in late spring; details on www.openateliersjordaan.nl.*

ArtZuid

Various venues (www.artzuid.com). ***Date*** *late May-late Sept.*

An installation of modern sculptures that snakes through Amsterdam South every other year. In the past, ArtZuid has included work by such heavy hitters as Ai Weiwei, Richard Serra and Atelier Van Lieshout.

Vondelpark Openluchttheater

Vondelpark, Museums Quarter (www.openluchttheater.nl). Tram 1, 2, 3, 11. ***Map*** *p136 E14.* ***Date*** *early May-early Sept.*

The big open-air stage in this popular park is used to the max, with a free programme that ranges from classical music to stand-up to pop. There are dance nights and kids' afternoons, too. Few places capture the laid-back vibe of Amsterdam in the summer with quite such conviction.

Bacchus Wine Festival

Amsterdamse Bos, Amstelveen (www.bacchuswijnfestival.nl). Tram 5, 6. ***Date*** *early June.*

Sail Amsterdam

Named after the Roman god of wine, this festival is heaven for oenophiles. Over 300 wines are available by the glass – each a reasonable €3 – and all manner of grape varieties and vineyards are represented, from the classics to the new world. Cheers!

Holland Festival

Throughout the city (020 523 7787, www.hollandfestival.nl). ***Date*** *June.*

This hugely popular month-long event (established in 1947) is the Netherlands' leading performing arts festival. It takes a refreshing approach to dance, literature, visual arts, theatre and film, but there's no doubting that music is its central theme, particularly in the realms of contemporary classical, experimental and electronic music. It attracts international stars and composers each year, and you're guaranteed a series of groundbreaking premieres and reworkings that'll move on to make waves in other cultural capitals around the world. Tickets go on sale several months beforehand; check the website for details of the programme and to book.

Open Garden Days

Various venues (www.opentuinendagen.nl). ***Date*** *late June.*

On the third weekend in June, the owners of the beautiful, hidden gardens behind the city's posh canal houses open their doors, giving the public a chance to have a peek at these stunning secret gems. Sadly, dogs and prams are not allowed, and wheelchair access is almost impossible.

Amsterdam Roots Festival

Various venues (www.amsterdamroots.nl). ***Date*** *early July.*

World music acts from around the globe flock to Amsterdam for this four-day shindig. The event is held at various indoor and outdoor venues across the city. It culminates in a free open-air extravaganza in Oosterpark, which starts at noon and goes on until late.

❤ Over het IJ

NDSM, Noord (www.overhetij.nl). NDSM ferry. ***Map*** *p166 inset.* ***Date*** *early-mid July.*

This ten-day international festival celebrates adventurous theatre on a large scale, with a series of avant-garde theatrical projects, which take over the former NDSM shipyard (*see p176*).

Sensation

Amsterdam ArenA, Zuidoost (www.sensation.com). Metro 50, 54 or Metro/rail Bijlmer ArenA. ***Date*** *July.*

A spectacle in every sense of the word, Sensation combines major DJs with mesmerising acrobatic dancers and pyrotechnic displays. A highlight of Amsterdam's dance music calendar, if you want to experience one Dutch dance event and can handle a heavy bass – look no further. Tickets go fast; check the website well in advance for details of programming and ticket sales.

Julidans

Various venues (www.julidans.nl). ***Date*** *July.*

This international contemporary dance festival provides a taster of what's going on – and what's to come – in the field of dance theatre. It features internationally renowned dance artists as well as newcomers that now rank among the greatest in their fields. Know nothing about dance? No problem. The 'poetry of the purest kind' won't fail to entertain.

Kwaku

Nelson Mandelapark, Zuidoost (www.kwakufestival.nl). Metro 50, 54 or Metro/rail Bijlmer ArenA. ***Date*** *mid July-mid Aug.*

'Kwaku' is the word that symbolises the emancipation of the people of Suriname and is also the name of this family-oriented festival, which takes place every weekend throughout the summer in the multicultural 'hood around ArenA stadium. Come for excellent ass-shaking music, plus theatre, film, literature, sport and Caribbean food.

❤ Amsterdam Gay Pride

Prinsengracht, Grachtengordel (www.amsterdamgaypride.nl). ***Map*** *p96.* ***Date*** *early Aug.*

Although Gay Pride is always surrounded by drama and controversy to do with money, politics and big egos, the atmosphere during the spectacular boat parade on the first Saturday in August is simply fabulous and utterly infectious. Over half a million spectators line the Prinsengracht to watch the boats, each with garish decorations, a loud sound system and a crew of bare-chested sailors.

❤ Dekmantel

Amsterdamse Bos, Amstelveen (www.dekmantelfestival.nl). Tram 5, 6. ***Date*** *early Aug.*

Centred around five stages in Amsterdamse Bos, this five-day event is a hit with seasoned ravers who claim that it might just be unrivalled when it comes to electronic music. With a very selective booking policy and a cap on numbers, it's all about the experience and musical diversity.

Loveland Festival

Sloterpark, Nieuw West (www.loveland.nl). Tram 13 or Metro Postjesweg or bus 18. ***Date*** *Aug.*

Loveland celebrates its 25th anniversary in 2020. It's a multi-genre electronic music festival that specialises in hard house and techno. Known for its epic sound system and wonderful location in Sloterpark, it attracts the likes of Carl Cox and Maya Jane Coles to keep attendees dancing way beyond the small hours.

De Parade

Martin Luther Kingpark, Zuid (033 465 4555, www.deparade.nl). Tram 4, 12 or bus 62 or Amstel rail. ***Date*** *Aug.*

When this touring show lands in Amsterdam (Rotterdam, The Hague and Utrecht are also on the route), locals flock to eat, drink, be merry and to catch an act – cabaret, music, comedy or drama – outside or in one of the many kitschly decorated tents that give the vibe of an old-fashioned carnival. Afternoons are child-friendly.

Appelsap

Flevopark, Oost (www.appelsap.net). Tram 7, 14. ***Date*** *mid Aug.*

The atmosphere at this outdoor hip hop festival is always hot. Attracting around 15,000 visitors, the programme takes hip hop back to its roots and includes up-and-coming artists as well as local favourites. Kids under 12 can attend the festival for free, but must be accompanied by an adult.

Grachtenfestival

Various venues (020 421 4542, www.grachtenfestival.nl). ***Date*** *mid Aug.*

What started out in 1997 as a single free concert from an orchestra floating on a pontoon in front of the Hotel Pulitzer has grown into the 'Canal Festival'. Handel would be delighted to hear that this modern water music has expanded to offer almost 100 classical music concerts, each set somewhere near or on the water.

Sail Amsterdam

Waterfront (www.sail.nl). ***Map*** *p166.* ***Date*** *late Aug 2020.*

Every five years, dozens of tall ships and hundreds of modern boats sail into Amsterdam, and huge crowds gather along the harbour to admire them. The event runs for five days in late August and lures maritime enthusiasts from across the globe.

Uitmarkt

Museumplein & Leidseplein (www.uitmarkt.nl). ***Map*** *p96 G12 & H14.* ***Date*** *end Aug.*

Over the last weekend in August, the chaotic Uitmarkt whets appetites for the coming cultural season with previews of theatre, opera, dance and music events. Everything is free and, as a result, it all gets very crowded.

Autumn

Netherlands Theater Festival

Various venues (www.tf.nl). ***Date*** *early Sept.*

This ten-day festival showcases an edited selection of the best Dutch and Belgian theatre of the previous year. As at the Edinburgh Festival, the accompanying Amsterdam Fringe event is uncurated and brings a heady mix of more experimental productions.

Amsterdam Beer Festival

Marrineterrein, Kattenburgerstraat 5, Waterfrront (020 723 2555, www.tabfestival.com). ***Map*** *p166 P9.* ***Date*** *Sept.*

Just €5 gives you access to this three-day beer jamboree by the docks, and you even get your own special glass to boot. Twelve Dutch breweries showcase all manner of brews alongside talks, barbecues and live music. There's even a special, four-course beer-themed Sunday dinner for the hardcore aficionados.

Amsterdam City Swim

Marine Etablissement Amsterdam, Kattenburgerstraat, Waterfront (www.amsterdamcityswim.nl). ***Map*** *p166 Q9.* ***Date*** *Sept.*

The temperature may be plummeting but that doesn't discourage about 2,500 brave swimmers from jumping into the canals to raise funds for motor neurone disease (known as ALS in the Netherlands). Canal boats and other vessels make way for the hordes of game paddlers who swim a gruelling 2,000m (6,560ft) course through Amsterdam city centre.

Open Monuments Day

Various venues (033 209 1000, www.openmonumentendag.nl). ***Date*** *mid Sept.*

On the second weekend in September, you get the chance to visit buildings that are normally closed to the public. Some are breathtaking historic buildings from the Golden Age; others are schools, farms or ex-industrial buildings. Look out for the Open Monumentendag flag, check the website or pick up a booklet. It's all part of European Heritage Days, involving around 5,000 sites across the Netherlands.

Dam tot Damloop

Amsterdam to Zaandam (www.damloop.nl). ***Date*** *late Sept.*

Taking place on the third Sunday in September, the Dam to Dam Run stretches 16.1km from Amsterdam to the town of Zaandam. Up to 250,000 people gather to watch almost 100,000 participants trying to finish within the two-hour limit. Bands line the route and a circus in Zaandam keeps the little ones amused. There's also a 6.5km course and an opportunity for 15,000 runners to complete an 8km run the night before.

In the know
24 hours in ...

Visit www.Iamsterdam.com to see if your visit coincides with '24h in...' when shops, clubs and cultural institutions in a chosen area of town throw open their doors with some 'special surprises'. It's a great way to immerse yourself in the city's culture and get a feel for a particular neighbourhood.

Unseen

Westergasfabriek, Westerpark (www.unseenamsterdam.com). Tram 5 or bus 21, 22. ***Map*** *p117 off map.* ***Date*** *late Sept.*

This multi-day 'photo fair with a festival flair' is based in Westergasfabriek (*see p132*) but expands to various locations throughout the city. It not only includes exhibitions of up-and-coming photography work, but also books, talks, city-wide projects and a lot of parties.

Amsterdam Tattoo Convention

RAI Convention Centre, Europaplein, Zuid (www.tattooexpo.eu). Tram 4, Metro Europaplein or RAI rail. ***Date*** *Oct.*

All the big names from the global tattoo scene swoop down on to Amsterdam for a weekend inking up everyone from needy bikers to housewives.

Amsterdam Dance Event

Various venues (www.amsterdam-dance-event.nl). ***Date*** *mid Oct.*

The organisers claim this five-day event is the world's largest festival of clubbing, involving more than 2,200 artists. It combines business with pleasure: during the day, there are conferences and workshops, while at night, roughly 400 international acts and DJs (professional and non-professional) make sure your feet keep moving with mind-blowing performances across the city. Amsterdam Music Festival (AMF) runs at the same time, showcasing the world's biggest DJs at the biggest venues in Amsterdam.

Amsterdamse Cello Biennale

Muziekgebouw, Piet Heinkade 1, Waterfront (020 519 1808, www.cellobiennale.nl). Tram 26. ***Map*** *p166 P7.* ***Date*** *late Oct.*

Muziekgebouw (*see p236*) plays host to this nine-day festival of daytime and evening concerts, masterclasses and presentations. Spanning generations and genres, it shows off the cello as a virtuosic and versatile instrument. Musicians and ensembles come from around the world.

Amsterdam Spook Halloween Festival

Various venues (www.halloweenamsterdam.com). ***Date*** *end Oct.*

During the last decade, Amsterdam has embraced Halloween as a new celebration. While there are many imitators, Amsterdam

Amsterdam Light Festival

Spook has spent years bringing buckets of blood to the masses. An over-the-top party in a scary location is the main attraction, but the festival also includes make-up workshops, boat cruises and plenty of other ghoul-infested activities.

❤ N8 (Museum Night)

Various venues (020 527 0785, www.n8.nl). ***Date*** *early Nov.*

The success of Museum Night shows that Amsterdammers like to mix art with entertainment. On the first Saturday in November every year, almost every museum and gallery in town opens late and organises something special to complement the regular exhibits. You might see a take on Rembrandt's *The Night Watch* made out of Chupa Chups lollies, or dance the night away in the Anne Frank Huis. Tickets sell fast.

Sinterklaas

Throughout the city. ***Date*** *mid Nov-early Dec.*

Sinterklaas (St Nicholas) marks the start of three weeks of festivities by sailing down the Amstel into town on his steamboat in mid November. With a white beard, red robe and mitre, he parades around the centre of town on his horse, ending up at the Scheepvaartmuseum (*see p169*), while his dubious sidekicks, the Zwarte Pieten (Black Petes), hand out sweets. The celebrations continue, with little gifts being left in children's shoes at night, until Pakjesavond ('gift evening') on 5 December, when families celebrate by exchanging presents and poems.

Winter

❤ Amsterdam Light Festival

Various venues (www.amsterdamlight festival.com). ***Date*** *early Dec-mid Jan.*

Some 30 light sculptures and projections by the world's best light artists brighten up town in this annual festival, which started in 2012. Follow the special route from Amstel to the Maritime Museum to see Amsterdam in a whole new shiny way.

Oudejaarsavond (New Year's Eve)

Various venues. ***Date*** *31 Dec.*

New Year's Eve (or literally 'old year's evening') is a riot of champagne, *oliebollen* (deep-fried blobs of dough, apple and raisins), and tons and tons of scary fireworks that officially only go on sale the day before. Come midnight, people take to the streets to celebrate. The loudest and liveliest areas are Nieuwmarkt and Dam Square; the latter often stages a big council-sponsored concert, with Dutch acts and DJs to help keep things moving. Not for the faint-hearted.

FashionWeek Amsterdam

Various venues (www.fashionweek.nl). ***Date*** *mid Jan.*

Even with such home-grown talent as Viktor & Rolf, Amsterdam has never been a cutting-edge fashion centre. But FashionWeek is out to change this, with catwalk shows in unique locations, plus exhibitions and readings.

Chinese New Year

Nieuwmarkt, Old Centre. Tram 4, 9, 14 or Metro Nieuwmarkt. ***Map*** *p70 M9.* ***Date*** *late Jan/early Feb.*

Nieuwmarkt is a focal point for Amsterdam's Chinese community and for the festivities to mark Chinese New Year. Expect lion dances, firecrackers, Chinese drums and gongs.

► *For details of film festivals, see p209 Screen Time; for music festivals, see p231 Best of the Fests.*

Film

Mainstream multiplexes, quirky art houses and film festivals galore

The Netherlands may not be a major global player when it comes to film, but things have been looking up for Dutch cinema in the last few years. Cinema revenue from Dutch-made films still hovers around ten per cent, but the local industry is experiencing near record levels of inward investment as a location and post-production hub. The Netherlands Film Fund has also expanded its support schemes to invest in high-profile international projects from Dutch directors, among them Paul Verhoeven's *Benedetta* and Paula van der Oest's *Bay Of Silence*. Dutch film professionals that have reached an international audience include *Game of Thrones* actors Carice van Houten and Michiel Huisman; acclaimed photographer and director Anton Corbijn, as well as Dutch transplants, such as directors Steve McQueen (*12 Years a Slave*) and Peter Greenaway (*Nightwatching*).

❤ Best cinemas

EYE Film Institute *p173*
Stunning film institute at the heart of Noord.

De FilmHallen *p208*
Dinner and a movie has never been so trendy.

The Movies *p210*
Old-world atmosphere for films old and new.

Pathé Tuschinski *p208*
Deco architecture to rival anything on the screen.

CINEMAS

Multiplexes

Pathé ArenA

ArenA Boulevard 600, Zuidoost (0900 1458 premium rate, www.pathe.nl). Metro Bijlmer ArenA. ***Screens*** *14.* ***Tickets*** *€6-€16.50.*

This multi-screen complex is one of the best places to enjoy those guilty-pleasure blockbusters with little chance of bumping into someone you know, because of its peripheral location out by the Ajax stadium. Styled with all the finesse of a big brick house, it nonetheless has comfortable seating and the only IMAX screen in Amsterdam – unquestionably the best place to catch 3D movies.

Pathé City

Kleine-Gartmanplantsoen 15-19, Grachtengordel (0900 1458 premium rate, www.pathe.nl). Tram 1, 2, 5, 7, 11, 12, 19. ***Screens*** *7.* ***Tickets*** *€10-€12.50.* ***Map*** *p96 H12.*

Once the cinematic equivalent of a used-car salesman, this former multiplex received a long-overdue reinvention in 2010 as an art house/mainstream hybrid, with the emphasis firmly on quality programming. It's perfect for a date, with a grown-up theatrical vibe (think velvet curtains) and a wine bar.

Pathé de Munt

Vijzelstraat 15, Grachtengordel (0900 1458 premium rate, www.pathe.nl). Tram 4, 14, 24. ***Screens*** *13.* ***Tickets*** *€5.50-€14.50.* ***Map*** *p96 K11.*

This is central Amsterdam's monster multiplex. In its favour are huge screens and comfortable seating, making it the best choice in the city centre for big-budget Hollywood kicks.

❤ Pathé Tuschinski

Reguliersbreestraat 26-34, Grachtengordel (0900 1458 premium rate, www.pathe.nl). Tram 4, 14, 24. ***Screens*** *6.* ***Tickets*** *€5-€12.50.* ***Map*** *p96 K11.*

This extraordinary cinema is named after Abraham Icek Tuschinski, who was Amsterdam's most illustrious cinematic entrepreneur. Built in 1921 as a 'world theatre palace', the decor is an arresting clash of rococo, art deco and Jugendstil, which can make it hard to keep your eyes on the silver screen. Glittering premieres take place to road-blocking effect. If you're more 'in the red' than red carpet-ready, check out the morning screenings, but if you're feeling flush, there are balcony seats and even private boxes.

Art houses

► *For full details of the fabulous EYE Film Institute, see p173.*

Cinecenter

Lijnbaansgracht 236, Grachtengordel (020 623 6615, www.cinecenter.nl). Tram 2, 5, 7, 11, 12, 19. ***Screens*** *4.* ***Tickets*** *€8-€11.50, €0.50 discount for online purchases. Cineville. No cash.* ***Map*** *p96 G12.*

Tucked discreetly away from the madding bustle of nearby Leidseplein, this snug, artsy and student-friendly cinema is home to a cosmopolitan array of films. The trendy yet welcoming bar is the perfect arena for a little post-film debate, should you emerge from the screening to find it's raining. That's if you even need an excuse.

❤ De FilmHallen

Hannie Dankbaarpassage 12, Oud West (020 820 8122, www.filmhallen.nl). Tram 7, 17. ***Screens*** *9.* ***Tickets*** *€8-€11.50, €0.50 discount for online purchases. Cineville.* ***Map*** *p136 D11.*

Set inside the train-depot-turned-trendy-spot De Hallen (*see p144*), De FilmHallen is the sister to Amsterdam's oldest cinema, The Movies (*see p210*) and one of the largest cinemas in the city. It shows an eclectic mix of movies, from Hollywood blockbusters to quirky art-house films. For a real treat, grab some streetfood from nearby Foodhallen beforehand and make a night of it.

Filmhuis Cavia

Van Hallstraat 51-52, West (020 681 1419, www.filmhuiscavia.nl). Tram 10 or bus 21. ***Screens*** *1.* ***Tickets*** *€4-€5. Cineville.* ***Map*** *p117 D5.*

Blink and you'll miss this one. Housed in the amiable seclusion of a once-squatted school above a gym, the left-of-mainstream Filmhuis Cavia specialises in obscure, queer and/or political pictures. You can also rent the place out for a film-themed party of your own; ideal if you consider yourself an armchair

Screen Time

A year of film festivals

Amsterdam's bulging calendar of film festivals offers plenty of intriguing alternatives to the regular mainstream offerings. The festival season kicks into gear at the end of January with the annual **International Film Festival Rotterdam** (www.iffr.com) – the largest film festival, and one of the largest cultural events, in the country. Lasting 12 days and using venues across nearby Rotterdam, IFFR specialises in art house fare and exotic films, with a traditionally strong helping of esoteric Asian flicks, and plenty of directors showing up for Q&As.

A couple of months later is **Roze Filmdagen** (www.rozefilmdagen.nl), literally Amsterdam's 'pink film days', a ten-day showcase of queer-minded flicks from around the world. It's been held in the wonderful Westergasfabriek (*see p132*) in recent years, but look out for witty promo posters all around town. Also in March is **Cinedans** (www.cinedans.nl), an international dance and movie festival held at the iconic EYE Film Institute.

April brings the **Imagine Film Festival** (www.imaginefilmfestival.nl), also held at EYE, which caters to both gorehounds and those with a predilection for fantasy and sci-fi. Gory and ghoulish appearances notwithstanding, the crowds and crew are a good-natured bunch and the festival has grown large enough to offer some intriguing flicks while maintaining a cosy atmosphere.

In August, the popular **Pluk de Nacht** (*see p211* Beyond the Mainstream) takes over an old pier in Amsterdam West for a week, while the **World Cinema Amsterdam** (www.worldcinemaamsterdam.nl) shows both indoor and outdoor screenings at the charming Rialto Cinema and De Balie (for both these venues, *see p210*).

The kids are all right during October's autumn holiday, when the five-day **Cinekid** (www.cinekid.nl), the largest child-oriented film festival on the planet, has its annual play date. It involves over 500 productions, from feature films to TV series to interactive installations. MediaLAB lets four- to 14-year-olds experience movie-making through play, workshops and installations, guided by industry experts. Key venues are The Movies cinema (*see p210*) and Westergasfabriek.

For five fun-packed days at the end of the year, Amsterdam becomes the animated capital of Europe, courtesy of the brilliant **Kaboom Animation Festival** (www.klik.amsterdam/festival), geared towards the young, the old and every cartoon-lover in between. The event is jointly held between Utrecht and Amsterdam – in the latter, the action takes place at Westergasfabriek's Het Ketelhuis in November.

The biggest documentary festival in the world also touches down at the end of November in the form of the **International Documentary Filmfestival Amsterdam** (www.idfa.nl), with intimate Q&As and workshops from the best in the biz, and screenings throughout the city.

World Cinema Amsterdam

revolutionary. And fittingly, given their political leanings, it's the first cinema in the world to accept Bitcoin for payment. Tickets and entrance can be reserved via email.

Het Ketelhuis

Pazzanistraat 4, Westerpark (020 684 0090, www.ketelhuis.nl). Tram 5 or bus 21. ***Screens*** *3.* ***Tickets*** *Feature films €7.50-€10.50, €0.50 discount for online purchases. Short films €6. Cineville.* ***Map*** *p117 off map.*

Once of little interest to non-Dutch-speaking film fans (it used to specialise in un-subtitled homegrown movies), the Ketelhuis now screens interesting international art films alongside the Netherlands' finest flicks. The revival of the Westergasfabriek and regular festivals haven't hurt its popularity among cinematically minded Amsterdammers, and the staff here are among the friendliest in town.

Kriterion

Roetersstraat 170, Oost (020 623 1708, www.kriterion.nl). Tram 1, 7, 19 or Metro Weesperplein. ***Screens*** *3.* ***Tickets*** *€5-€10. Cineville.* ***Map*** *p153 O13.*

Founded in 1945 by a group of Resistance-fighter undergraduates, this cinema continues to be run by a bunch of students – to great success. The programme is made up of quality films, first-runs as well as contemporary classics, while the Movies that Matter series guarantees thought-provoking discussions. Cult films make up the bulk of the weekend Midnight Movies too. The Kriterion's sneak previews are almost always sold out, and the convivial bar usually facilitates much post-film analysis.

❤ The Movies

Haarlemmerdijk 161, Jordaan (020 638 6016, www.themovies.nl). Tram 3 or bus 18, 21, 22. ***Screens*** *4.* ***Tickets*** *€10.50, €1 discount for online purchases. Cineville. No cash.* ***Map*** *p117 H5.*

The oldest cinema in Amsterdam to remain in regular use, The Movies has been circulating celluloid since way back in 1912 and still exudes a genteel atmosphere of sophisticated elegance.

► *The Movies is one of the hosts of the brilliant annual Cinekid film festival* *(see Screen Time, p209).*

Rialto

Ceintuurbaan 338, De Pijp (020 662 3488, www.rialtofilm.nl). Tram 3, 12, 24 or Metro De Pijp. ***Screens*** *3.* ***Tickets*** *€7-€11.50; €2.50 reductions. Cineville.* ***Map*** *p181 K16.*

De Pijp's neighbourhood cinema, the Rialto offers an eclectic mix of arty features, documentaries, classics, festivals and kids' fare. It broadens the mix with frequent avant-garde film premieres, as well as regular introductory talks about films chosen by guest speakers. Disabled access is good too. Be warned, though: the foreign films screened here usually only have Dutch subtitles.

De Uitkijk

Prinsengracht 452, Grachtengordel (020 223 2416, www.uitkijk.nl). Tram 2, 11, 12. ***Screens*** *1.* ***Tickets*** *€9-€11. Cineville.* ***Map*** *p96 H12.*

This charming hole-in-the-wall cinema shows select art-house flicks for a discerning audience, plus a smattering of mainstream and foreign-language gems that may have escaped your attention first time around.

Cultural centres

De Balie

Kleine-Gartmanplantsoen 10, Grachtengordel (020 553 5100, www.debalie.nl). Tram 1, 2, 7, 11, 12, 19. ***Screens*** *2.* ***Tickets*** *€8.50-€11.50. Cineville.* ***Map*** *p96 G12.*

A temple to high culture, De Balie is a bar, theatre and debating ground, and plays host to several leftfield film festivals and expertly curated cinematic curiosities. Look out for Cineville Talkshow, often your first chance

In the know
Access all areas

A fictional town called **Cineville** (www.cineville.nl) brings together 17 art-house and repertory cinemas in Amsterdam, including EYE and De FilmHallen, and more than 43 cinemas across the country. A pass costing €21 – €17.50 if you're under 30 – a month provides access to them all.

Beyond the Mainstream

Alternative movie venues

The trend for showing films any place but in the buildings specifically designed for that purpose is very popular in Amsterdam. The underground film scene has been booming for a decade, thanks largely to film buff Jeffrey Babcock, an American-born long-term Amsterdam resident who curates a host of indie nights. His weekly **Cinemanita** gatherings in the cavernous space at the back of hipster hangout **De Nieuwe Anita** (*see below*) often showcase films that have never been screened in the Netherlands before. **Shortcutz** (www.shortcutznetwork.com/shortcutz-amsterdam) takes place in the rather rarefied surrounds of **De Kring** (Kleine Gartmanplantsoen 7-9, Grachtengordel, 020 623 6985, www.kring.nl), a private members' club for artists. At free weekly screenings on Tuesdays, local filmmakers, both amateur and professional, can show their latest short-film creations and receive critical feedback.

There are also various squat initiatives, such as former bomb shelter **Vondelbunker** (www.vondelbunker.nl), which screens everything from weird B-movies to documentaries that inspire activism. **Joe's Garage** (www.joesgarage.nl) in Oost has regular Sunday 'Movie Nights' and even asks people to make contact if they have a film they want to share with an audience.

In summer, the underground scene is supplemented by a plethora of open-air cinema events. These include **Films with a View** at shipyard-turned-faux-beach **Pllek** (*see p175*) and **Pluk de Nacht** ('Seize the Night', www.plukdenacht.nl), the city's annual open-air film festival, which screens yet-to-be-released international films at a dockside location in Amsterdam West. Those who don't mind braving the cold can also enjoy flicks in the fresh air at the **Pluk De Winternacht**, held in December.

to see an upcoming release, with a little heated (quite often Dutch) debate thrown in for good measure.

Filmhuis Griffioen

Uilenstede 106, Amstelveen (020 598 5100, www.griffioen.vu.nl). Tram 5, 6. ***Screens*** *1.* ***Tickets*** *€5.15-€9.30. Cineville.*

A small student-run cinema on the campus of the Free University, this is a cheap and eminently enjoyable place in which to check out the films you didn't see on their first run – even if you missed them by a decade or so.

Melkweg

Lijnbaansgracht 234a, Grachtengordel (020 531 8181, www.melkweg.nl). Tram 2, 5, 7, 11, 12, 19. ***Screens*** *1.* ***Tickets*** *€10.50-€15. Cineville.* ***Map*** *p96 G12.*

For a venue famed primarily for its musical appeal (*see p230*), Melkweg hosts a surprisingly broad array of quality cinema, from foreign-language festival fodder to music-video nights, although the racket that comes through the floor when there's a band playing elsewhere in the building might distract you from your flick. Rather than grumbling about noise pollution, it helps if you go with the flow and consider this a free sample.

In the know
The reel deal

If you come across 'OV' at the end of a film title when looking at cinema listings (especially for animated and children's movies), it means the film is showing in its original language, usually with Dutch subtitles. If you see 'NL', it means the movie will be shown in Dutch.

De Nieuwe Anita

Frederik Hendrikstraat 111, West (www.denieuweanita.nl). Tram 3, 5. ***Screens*** *1.* ***Tickets*** *€3.* ***Map*** *p117 E8.*

This former squat is a buzzing hive of hipster activity. Aside from the live performances, laid-back lounging nights and (but of course!) impromptu hair salons that crowd the eclectic schedule here, Monday evenings feature staggeringly obscure but highly enjoyable films, often with a lengthy intro from the Anita's voluble curator.

Studio/K

Timorplein 62, Oost (020 692 0422, www.studio-k.nu). Tram 14. ***Screens*** *2.* ***Tickets*** *€5-€10.50. Cineville. No cash.*

The 'K' here might stand for 'kooky', sometimes veering into the realms of the pleasantly 'kitsch'. Screening mostly alternative and non-commercial films, the venue also has a theatre, club and a café/gallery, which makes it the ideal venue for festivals. The restaurant, with good vegetarian options, offers a dinner and film deal for €17.

LGBTQ

The original gay capital where anything goes

Amsterdam's standing as a gay capital of Europe seemed to be on the slide in the decade after it held the world's first same sex wedding in 2001, but playing host to EuroPride in 2016 reaffirmed the city's place on the LGBTQ+ map. Today, Amsterdam remains keen to broadcast its credentials as a haven for liberalism and open-mindedness. It has an impressive track record when it comes to gay rights: homosexuality was decriminalised in 1811, the first gay/lesbian bar opened in 1927 (Café 't Mandje, still open today), and one of the first gay rights organisations, COC Nederland, was founded in Amsterdam in 1946, at a time when much of the rest of the world considered homosexuality an illness. A renewed focus on LGBTQ+ rights and freedoms means there's still plenty to party about.

Gay Pride Canal Parade 2019 *p203*

Gay Pride *p203*

The scene today

After a number of years during which Amsterdam's gay scene was somewhat taken for granted, the city is once again investing in its credentials and recognising the importance of its history of acceptance and worldwide legacy in this regard. Local political parties have tried hard to make Amsterdam gay-friendly and, in 2016, King Willem-Alexander visited COC Nederland to help celebrate the 70th anniversary of the gay liberation movement. In the same year, Amsterdam opened its first LGBTQ-only nursing home and launched a monument to countdown the days until the world is AIDS free. The abacus, called 'Living by Numbers', was designed as both a memorial to those who have passed away and a beacon of hope for those living with the disease. Amsterdam was chosen to host the monument as the city is seen as a sanctuary for many people with HIV from across the globe.

Amsterdam Gay Pride (*see p203*) has gone the way of many other Gay Prides worldwide by embracing corporate sponsorship – some major companies and banks even have their own floats to make sure spectators get the message (the main message being that they're keen to emphasise their employee diversity).

Some gay clubs have shut down in recent years but, in general, the gay clubbing scene is thriving, reinvigorated by a wealth of young talent and plenty of fresh faces. Many of the venues are still concentrated in a handful of areas in the Old Centre (*see p216*), so moving between them is easy and quick. There's another gay hub in the Southern Canal Belt around Reguliersdwarsstraat and Rembrandtplein (*see p218*), not to mention a series of gay party nights that take-over various venues around town (*see p220* Big Night Out).

The nightlife scene for lesbians is not quite as exciting or as varied as the men's scene and strictly lesbian events are still relatively few, but there's still a variety of bars (**Bar Buka** and **Saarein**; *see p221*) and club nights (**Femmazing**; *see p220*) to choose from.

Until recently, the scenes for gay men and women were quite separate and they'd only get together on big occasions such as King's Day, Pride or one-off parties like the mighty Love Dance. During recent years, however, the number of mixed bars and club nights has increased somewhat. Many lesbians will also venture along to men's bars and will be happily admitted, although they will, of course, be in the minority – in fact, women are welcome in all but a few strictly men-only places (generally sex clubs).

Finally, a word of warning: free condoms aren't universal on the scene, and a range of STDs – including HIV – are on the rise, with barebacking as popular and controversial here as in any other big city.

INFORMATION & RESOURCES

Most gay printed matter is in Dutch, but it's good to know that a fair chunk is bilingual, including *Gay News* (www.gaynews.nl) and *Amsterdam Gay Map* (www.guide.gayamsterdam.com/maps), both of which are published monthly. The standard of English varies, but they're free and available both online and in selected bars around the city. There's also the Amsterdam-published *Butt* (www.buttmagazine.com), which pulls off some of the most interesting interviews in the gay press, and *Fantastic Man* (www.fantasticman.com) from the same stable, a very influential gentleman's style journal' that, while not strictly gay, is doused in homosexual sensibility.

If you can read some Dutch, check out the local edition of *Winq* (www.winq.com), the global gay glossy with brains, published quarterly from a canal house in the Red Light District. If you prefer it in English, the content is also available on the website.

Also in Dutch is *Zij aan Zij* (www.zijaanzij.nl), 'Side by Side', a general lesbian glossy (back copies of the mag are available online). And then there's *Girls Like Us* (*GLU*, www.glumagazine.com), an English-language quarterly with a side order of parties that delivers a mixture of chatty interviews, fashion-driven shoots and ephemera dug from dusty old archives.

Online-only resources include *ExpresZo* (www.expreszo.nl), a great website for young LGBTQs that aims to be informative, entertaining and educational. It's run completely by volunteers and even offers a 'non-judgemental' dating service. *Geen Flikker Te Doen* (www.geenflikkertodoen.nl) provides the most comprehensive run down of gay and lesbian parties in Amsterdam and beyond. If it's worth going to, it'll be listed here.

The lesbian and gay community broadcast company **MVS Gay Station** (www.mvs.nl) covers all aspects of gay life, from visiting porn stars to retired hairdressers, and all points in between. It broadcasts on Salto TV (channels 39+, 616MHz, 11-11.30pm Sat; 9-10pm Sun), on the radio on Stads FM (106.8 FM, 103.3 on cable 7-8pm Fri, Sat) and, of course, online. Programmes are usually in Dutch but with English-language items.

Organisations

COC Amsterdam

www.cocamsterdam.nl

COC has been advocating for LGBTQ rights in Amsterdam since 1946, and is often the first port of call for those looking for support. It aims to empower people to make changes from within their own community, and campaigns for emancipation, social acceptance, and equal rights, with particular emphasis on youth and education.

Gay & Lesbian Switchboard

020 623 6565, www.switchboard.nl.

Affiliated with the umbrella organisation Schorer, this band of sympathetic and knowledgeable volunteers has been giving advice for years. You can ask them about anything, from HIV risk factors to the best new bars, and they speak perfect English. The switchboard is manned on Monday, Thursday and Saturday for a few hours in the afternoon or evening; check the website for further info.

IHLIA

6th floor, Openbare Bibliotheek Amsterdam, Oosterdokskade 143, Waterfront (020 523 0837, www.ihlia.nl). Tram 1, 2, 4, 11, 12, 13, 14, 17, 24 or Metro Centraal. ***Open*** *exhibitions 10am-10pm daily. Information noon-5pm Mon-Thur.* ***Map*** *p166 O8.*

The spectacular view is reason enough for journeying up to the sixth floor of Amsterdam's amazing public library, but this archive of LGBTQ-related materials, from biographies to condom packets, is Europe's largest.

Pink Point

Westermarkt, Western Canal Belt (020 428 1070). Tram 13, 17. ***Open*** *10am-6pm Mon-Sat; noon-6pm Sun.* ***Map*** *p96 H8.*

Queer queries? Need to know which party to go to? Looking for political pamphlets, or just a gay postcard or a street map? Head to this kiosk near the Homomonument and speak to its friendly and chatty staff.

Accommodation

The **Gay & Lesbian Switchboard** has details of gay- and lesbian-friendly hotels. Those listed below are mostly gay-run. For more hotel options, *see p280*.

Amistad €€

Kerkstraat 42, Grachtengordel (020 624 8074, www.amistad.nl). Tram 1, 2, 11, 12. ***Map*** *p96 H11.*

Self-described as the 'most popular gay hotel in Amsterdam', this hip hotel shines like the pages of a trendy magazine. Rooms are cosy, and the breakfast area on the ground floor doubles as a gay internet lounge every day after 1pm. The lounge is also open to non-residents.

Anco Hotel €€

Oudezijds Voorburgwal 55, Old Centre (020 624 1126, www.ancohotel.nl). Tram 4, 9, 14, 16. ***Map*** *p70 L8.*

Minutes away from the Zeedijk and Warmoesstraat, the Anco has double, single and three- to four-bed dorm rooms, and a studio. All come with TV, free gay adult channel and free Wi-Fi. The renovated rooms are set inside a 17th-century canal home.

Golden Bear €€

Kerkstraat 37, Grachtengordel (020 624 4785, www.quentingoldenbear.com). Tram 1, 2, 11, 12. ***Map*** *p96 H11.*

The first gay hotel in town, the Golden Bear has spacious and comfortable rooms, though not all are en suite. Single rooms have double beds.

ITC Hotel €€

Prinsengracht 1051, Grachtengordel (020 623 0230, www.itc-hotel.com). Tram 4. ***Map*** *p96 L13.*

Situated on a quiet stretch of Prinsengracht that's convenient for the gay hotspots, the ITC Hotel has 20 charming rooms. Free internet access and friendly staff help ensure guests have a pleasant stay.

OLD CENTRE

The long and narrow **Warmoesstraat** is the oldest street in town. It's just round the corner from the red-lit headquarters of the oldest profession. Packed in the tourist season, it's full of cheap hostels and eateries, coffeeshops, bars and sex shops aimed at backpackers. It's also the street with leather/sex bars, a gay porn cinema/shop, and a gay hotel, the **Anco** (*see p215*), just minutes away. Once-notorious **Zeedijk** runs from Nieuwmarkt all the way to Centraal Station. It is now full of Asian eateries, bars and restaurants, but a residual seediness means you should take care of yourself and your possessions. Be aware that junkies and drug sellers regard tourists as easy prey, so act streetwise.

Bars & clubs

Eagle Amsterdam

Warmoesstraat 90 (020 808 5283, www.theeagleamsterdam.com). Tram 2, 4, 11, 12, 13, 14, 17, 24. ***Open*** *11pm-4am Mon-Thur, Sun; 11pm-5am Fri, Sat.* ***Map*** *p70 L8.*

Known for its reputation – sexy and friendly punters, but dirty toilets and unfriendly staff – this men-only cruise bar with 35 years of history can get absolutely packed. The downstairs darkroom is always action-filled, as is the upstairs area late at night; it has some cosy benches should you want to get intimate and a pool table complete with adjustable sling above it.

In the know
Sex parties

Visitors looking specifically for sex parties may find it a bit difficult, largely thanks to the opening of **Club Church** (*see p219*), a multi-level, cavernous venue hosting everything from regular FF parties to the occasional Twink Sex Orgy. Meanwhile, 'erotic café' **Sameplace** (Nassaukade 120, Oud West, 020 475 1981, www.sameplace.nl) goes gay every Monday night between 7pm and midnight.

PRIK

Spuistraat 109 (020 320 0002, www.prikamsterdam.nl). Tram 1, 2, 11, 12, 13, 17. ***Open*** *4pm-1am Mon-Thu; 4pm-3am Fri; 3pm-3am Sat; 3pm-1am Sun.* ***Map*** *p70 J8.*

This popular meeting point succeeds in attracting a diverse bunch, who enjoy Prik's 'lovely liquids, sexy snacks and twisted tunes'. The sporadic speed-dating events held here are a particularly fun way to infiltrate the local scene. After a night here you might be tempted to squeeze yourself into one of those saucy T-shirts.

Queen's Head

Zeedijk 20 (020 420 2475, www.queenshead.nl). Tram 1, 2, 4, 11, 12, 13, 14, 17, 24 or Metro Centraal. ***Open*** *4pm-1am Mon-Thur, Sun; 4pm-3am Fri, Sat.* ***Map*** *p70 M8.*

Zeedijk

Gay Pride *p203*

A fun, attitude-free bar (and clientele), with a great view over the canal at the back. Tuesday is bingo night and Sundays are for Netherbears. It also hosts special parties, for example on King's Day, plus skin nights, football nights, Eurovision Song Contest night and so on.

The Web

Sint Jacobsstraat 6 (020 623 6758, www.thewebamsterdam.com). Tram 1, 2, 11, 12, 13, 17. ***Open*** *1pm-1am Mon-Thur, Sun; 1pm-2am Fri, Sat.* ***Map*** *p70 L7.*

Cheap booze and sexy bartenders, cheesy/classic dance tracks, Wednesday sex-shop vouchers lottery, Sunday snack afternoon – such ingredients make this men-only leather/cruise bar heave with a crowd of all ages. The upstairs darkroom is hygienic, and the numerous cubicles almost resemble those at a gym – perfect to act out the locker-room fantasy you've always dreamed of.

Shops & services

Whether you're in need of a tattoo, piercing, some kinky toys or a complete leather outfit, Amsterdam's 'Leather Lane', Warmoesstraat, is where to find it. At the Amsterdam branch of **RoB** (Warmoesstraat 71, 020 422 3000, www.rob.eu), you can pick up a wristband or a full complement of leather/rubber gear. **Drake's Boutique** (Damrak 61, 020 737 0023, www.drakesboutique.com) is a 'sex boutique' and porn cinema. Kinky store **Demask** (Zeedijk 64, 423 3090, www.demask.com) is fun for all. **American Book Center** (Spui 12, Old Centre, 020 625 5537) has a well-stocked gay section.

Gays & Gadgets

Spuistraat 44, Old Centre (020 330 1461, www.gaysandgadgets.com). Tram 1, 7, 19. ***Open*** *noon-7pm Mon-Thur, Sun; 11am -7pm Fri, Sat.* ***Map*** *p70 K7.*

A dazzling and demented array of camp nonsense and household objects, most of it made in China. If a willy or boobs can't be incorporated into the design proper, you can bet your bottom dollar it can be dipped in pink paint or accessorised with a sparkly boa.

Nieuwezijds Sauna

Nieuwezijds Armsteeg 95, Old Centre (020 331 8327, www.saunanieuwezijds.nl). Tram 1, 2, 11, 12, 13, 17. ***Open*** *noon-2am Mon-Wed; noon-6am Thu, Sun; noon-10am Fri, Sat.* ***Admission*** *€21 inc 1st drink; €15 under-27s (€10 Mon & Wed).* ***Map*** *p70 L7.*

Slings, sex cabins, darkrooms and glory holes add some dirt to an otherwise glistening clean and elegant operation , located in a former bingo hall.

Vrolijk

Paleisstraat 135, Old Centre (www.vrolijk.nu). Tram 1, 2, 11, 12, 13, 17. ***Open*** *11am-6pm Mon-Sat, 1-5pm Sun.* ***Map*** *p70 J9.*

The best international selection of rose-tinted reading, whether fiction or fact – plus CDs, DVDs, guides and the best gifts you'll find in town. It also has a second-hand section, and sells a good range of gay T-shirts, condoms and cheeky gifts.

GRACHTENGORDEL

Once unquestionably the gayest stretch of street in Amsterdam, **Reguliersdwarsstraat** had its heyday in the 1990s, when every other bar on the miniature strip between Koningsplein and Vijzelstraat was broadly painted with the pink brush. Following the demise of its most iconic venues, there's much talk of a city-aided renaissance, but it remains to be seen what form that will take. Recent years have seen a move towards more mixed crowds, and there are also enough scene stalwarts and small-scale new initiatives to keep the place ticking over. Not just the main drag for the city's commercial nightlife and tourist hotspots, **Rembrandtplein** is also home to many of Amsterdam's gay and lesbian bars. Although just a few minutes' stroll from Reguliersdwarsstraat, the scene here is much more light-hearted and camp.

Halvemaansteeg is a short lane of brash, loud bars full of male punters of all ages (with the odd lesbian and straight girl to leaven the mix). They're attitude-free and will burst into a Eurovision singalong at the drop of a feather boa. Round the corner on the Amstel are a few more bars that blast out cheesy hits. To the south meanwhile, off busy Leidsestraat, is quiet **Kerkstraat**, home to pioneering cradle of filth **Club Church** and kink shop **Black Body** (*see p221*). It even has a few gay hotels, but it's less posing pink than other areas.

Bars & clubs

Amstel Fifty Four

*Amstel 54 (06 1223 2254 mobile). Tram 4, 14. **Open** 5pm-3am Mon-Wed, Sun; 5pm-4am Thur; 3pm-4am Fri, Sat. **Map** p96 L11.*

Previously known on the scene as Amstel Taveerne, this place has a solid spot in local gay history. It has always maintained a vibe of old-fashioned friendliness and over-the-top gayness. The charming old-school pink interior helps keep the dream alive.

Café Reality

*Reguliersdwarsstraat 129 (020 639 3012). Tram 4, 14, 24. **Open** 8pm-3am Mon-Thur, Sun; 8pm-5am Fri, Sat. **Map** p96 K11.*

Club Church

One of the few bars in town where black and white gay guys regularly meet and mingle, Café Reality is always popular during happy hour (8.30-10pm). Things pump up later on, when ferociously up-tempo Latin and Surinamese music get the crowd moving.

❤ Club Church

*Kerkstraat 52 (www.clubchurch.nl). Tram 1, 2, 11, 12. **Open** 8pm-1am Tue, Wed; 10pm-4am Thur; 10pm-5am Fri, Sat; 4-8pm Sun. **Map** p96 H12.*

This deceptively cavernous venue is more than a little progressive, and sex is unambiguously on the agenda. Erotic theme nights run the full gamut of (mostly male) pervy possibility, from naked parties to fisting to the women-friendly 'Hoerenbal', where those 'dressed for trade' are offered free bubbly. '(Z)onderbroek' (10pm-5am Fri and 1st Sat of mth) is a men-only dance party with an underwear-only dress code: tank tops are tolerated, but only just. Several of the city's fetish parties have also migrated here from smaller venues in the Red Light District. To top it all, Church features a bar with Greek-style columns, a stage perfect for drag-queen acts, a great sound and light system, and various dark, dark chambers.

Club NYX

*Reguliersdwarsstraat 42 (www.clubnyx.nl). Tram 1, 2, 11, 12, 24. **Open** 11pm-4am Thur; 11pm-5am Fri, Sat. **Map** p96 J11.*

Named after the Greek goddess of the night, this mixed club offers three floors of distinct sounds and vibes – making liberal use of graffiti, glitter and concrete – and a toilet DJ keeps the party going while you wash your hands at a giant pink phallus.

Duke Of Tokyo

*Reguliersdwarsstraat 37 (020 777 9322, www.dukeoftokyo.com). Tram 1, 2, 11, 12, 24. **Open** 5pm-1am Mon, Wed, Thur; 5pm-3am Fri; 2pm-3am Sat; 2pm-1am Sun. **Map** p96 J11.*

Housed on the site of former gay bar April, this karaoke bar isn't a specifically gay hotspot, but it is riotously good fun. Decked out like the small alleys of the Japanese capital, it has eight private booths of different sizes for rent, and plenty of Japanese beers, sake, and cocktails, served by your own host. Belting out Cher and Madonna songs never seemed so apt.

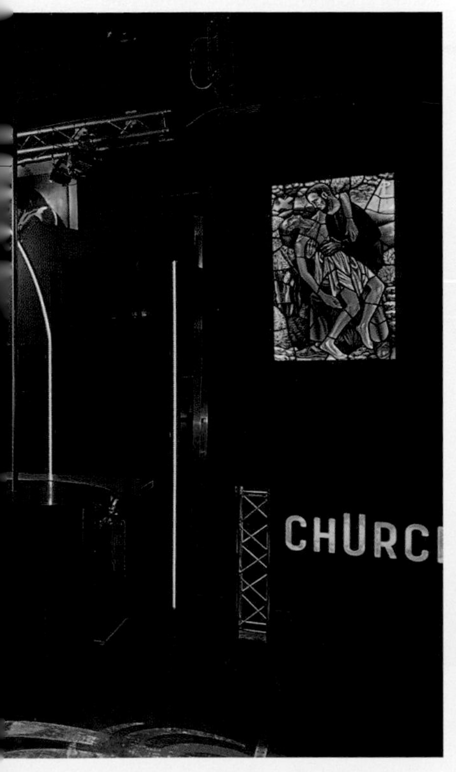

LGBTQ

Big Nights Out

The best gay parties in town

Danserette

www.danserette.nl

This moving gay dance party is for those who aren't afraid to mouth the words to Madonna hits. Also on the decks are disco classics and recent chart tunes.

Femmazing

www.femmazing.nl

Founded to address a lack of social events and parties catering specifically to lesbians and bisexual women, Femmazing organises unique, one-off events and all manner of fancy shindigs around town. The speed-dating nights are great, and there's usually a good few parties thrown to coincide with the city's big, mainstream events such as ADE and Pride. Check the website for what's coming up.

F*cking Pop Queers

www.ultrasexi.com

They may only take place a few times a year, but the ULTRASEXI and F*cking Pop Queers nights are an absolutely riot. Held mainly at Paradiso and Club NYX, they sell out months in advance and are elaborate, themed affairs – one event contemplated what queer culture would look like in 2069...

Rapido

www.clubrapido.com

Very popular – but irregular – club night where shirtless muscle marys dance and flirt to pumping house tunes. Rapido's nights at Paradiso (*see p227*) are legendary, and it also organises 'Funhouse' events at the Westergasfabriek (*see p132*). Check out the website for the latest dates.

Spellbound

www.spellbound-amsterdam.nl

This cheap 'queer underground dance party' is popular with a non-scene crowd. Its success is easily explained by the heavy beats of techno, acid and dub, not to mention the snug bar.

Lellebel

Utrechtsestraat 4 (020 233 6533, www.lellebel.nl). Tram 4, 14. ***Open*** *9pm-3am Mon-Thur; 3pm-5am Fri, Sat; 3pm-3am Sun.* ***Map*** *p96 L11.*

A tiny drag bar where the cross-dressing clientele provides all the entertainment itself. Though most people will be in drag, admirers and friends are welcome, and the atmosphere is friendly.

Lunchroom Downtown

Reguliersdwarsstraat 31 (020 789 0554, www.lunchroomdowntown.nl). Tram 1, 2, 11, 12, 24. ***Open*** *10am-7pm daily.* ***Map*** *p96 J11.*

It's always been about sandwiches, cakes, drinks and international mags here. You might need the latter – service can be slow when the place is busy. At least there's always the hunky, dressed-to-a-T guys to look at in this tiny multi-level hangout. In summer, the popular terrace sometimes attracts straight couples from the nearby Flower Market, who soon realise their mistake.

Mankind

Weteringstraat 60 (020 638 4755, www.mankind.nl). Tram 7, 10, 16. ***Open*** *noon-midnight Mon-Sat.* ***No cards. Map*** *p96 J13.*

A quiet locals' bar tucked down a side street near the Rijksmuseum, and the antiques shops and art galleries of Spiegelstraat. It also provides delicious sandwiches and a cheap dish of the day. Come summer, the canalside patio is perfect to catch some sun, read the international magazines or simply watch the world go by.

Spijker Bar

Kerkstraat 4 (020 233 8665, www.spijkerbar.nl) Tram 1, 2, 11, 12. ***Open*** *4pm-1am Mon-Thur, Sun; 4pm-3am Fri, Sat.* ***Map*** *p96 H11.*

This small boozer was a theatre in its previous life. Punters still liven things up and it can become rather crowded and rowdy. The diverse clientele ranges from cute young guys to older muscle men and a few women, and all mingle happily. On the downside, the pool table always seems to be occupied.

Taboo

Reguliersdwarsstraat 45 (020 775 3963, www.taboobar.nl). Tram 1, 2, 11, 12, 24. ***Open*** *5pm-3am Mon-Thur; 5pm-4am Fri; 4pm-4am Sat; 4pm-3am Sun. Hours may vary during winter.* ***Map*** *p96 J11.*

Taboo was created to breathe some life back into an ailing district. In some ways, it's

just another gay bar – it plays Cher and is festooned in rainbows – but what the place lacks in mould-breaking sparkle, it makes up for in decent prices and a double happy hour (6-7pm, 1-2am). Taboo hosts regular theme nights – check the website or Facebook for updates.

Shops & services

Make your rubber fantasies come true at **Black Body** (Kerkstraat 173, 020 626 2553, www.blackbody.nl). **Mr B** (Prinsengracht 192, 020 788 3060, www.misterb.com) sells anything from a cheap cockring to expensive chaps. It also does tattoos and piercings (there's a female piercer too), plus DVDs and tickets for all the big gay events.

Cuts And Curls

Korte Leidsedwarsstraat 74, Grachtengordel (020 624 6881, www.cutsandcurls.nl). Tram 1, 2, 7, 11, 12, 19. ***Open*** *10am-8pm Tue-Fri; 9am-3pm Sat; appointment only.* ***Map*** *p96 H12.*

This hairdresser's offers butch and basic haircuts with a sensitive side: many of the shampoos and conditioners are vegan-friendly.

OTHER AREAS

Bars & clubs

Bar Buka

Albert Cuypstraat 124, De Pijp (020 341 9460, www.barbuka.nl). Tram 3, 12, 24 or Metro De Pijp. ***Open*** *5pm-midnight Wed, Thur, Sun; 5pm-3am Fri, Sat.* ***Map*** *p181 K15.*

Meaning 'open' in Indonesian, Buka is a new women's bar in De Pijp with a laid-back, unfussy vibe. Alongside decent food, drinks and occasional events, it also organises several LGBTQ walks: Rainbow Strolls around the pink heart of the city.

Saarein

Elandsstraat 119, Jordaan (020 623 4901, www.saarein2.com). Tram 5, 7, 19. ***Open*** *4pm-1am Tue-Thur; 4pm-2am Fri; 1pm-2am Sat; 4pm-1am Sun.* ***Map*** *p117 G10.*

This hardy perennial brown café of the lesbian scene is particularly popular at weekends. The women it attracts tend to be slightly older, but young bucks certainly make an appearance. What's more, the only lesbian pool table in town resides in the basement.

De Trut

Bilderdijkstraat 165, Oud West (www.trutfonds.nl). Tram 3, 7, 17. ***Open*** *10pm-3am Sun.* ***No cards. Map*** *p136 E11.*

If you don't want the weekend to end, head to this alternative dance night in a former squat. With all-inclusive drink offers for €20, it's cheap, crowded and fun, and has been running for nearly 40 years. Arrive early, certainly before 11pm, or you may have to queue for a long time. And note that phones are strictly prohibited; there's no guarded cloakroom or lockers either.

In the know
Film & theatre

The first Wednesday of the month is Gay Classics night at **Pathé de Munt** (*see p208*), where you get a drink – pink champagne – thrown in with your ticket, plus a two-for-one voucher for either **Taboo** (*see p220*) or **Lellebel** (*see p220*) after the show. **De Balie** (*see p210*) regularly presents gay films of a more socially aware nature. The **Queen's English Theatre Company** (www.qetc.nl) gives the queer eye to classic English-language plays a couple of times a year, at the **CREA theatre** (Nieuwe Achtergracht 170, Old Centre, 020 525 1400, www.crea.uva.nl).

Nightlife

The 24-hour city that knows how to party

Once typecast by tales of debauchery and crude excess, Amsterdam's nocturnal scene is now mentioned in the same breath as New York, London and Berlin, despite being a fraction of their size. Whether it's for the stereotypical red light-centred stag do or to dance for three days straight, the city's nightlife is a major draw for the millions who visit each year.

Amsterdam has worked hard to present a more elegant, cosmopolitan face after dark. Hipster bars and cutting-edge cocktail joints have sprung up all across the city, and most of the clubs have a distinctly modern vibe. Amsterdam is still a hedonist's playground, of course, but away from the boozy shenanigans of the Old Centre, partying is more refined. Live music is as plentiful as it is varied and is found in all sorts of venues, from basement bars to opulent former churches. Indeed, on any night of the week, it's not hard to find something to keep you occupied until the wee small hours... or beyond.

Paradiso Noord *p233*

How the Night Mayor Created a Dream Scene

The lasting legacy of Mirik Milan

If you're curious as to how exactly Amsterdam balances a somewhat rambunctious nightlife scene – particularly in the Old Centre – with the needs and concerns of residents, you should examine the work and influence of Mirik Milan. Amsterdam's – and indeed the world's – first Night Mayor, Milan helped rebuild the relationship between nocturnal souls, residents, business owners and politicians, and ensured that the vibrancy of the city's nightlife was properly recognised by those in power as being an essential component of any forward-thinking 21st-century metropolis.

In 2012, when Milan was first formally elected as *nachtburgemeester*, the city's after-dark scene was gradually awakening from a regulation-induced slumber. Locals had complained for years that nightlife was dead, after city by-laws forced clubs and pubs to close early, and underground parties were vigorously monitored and shut. After much lobbying, nine drinking and dining zones were given 24-hour licences; five of these are nightclubs. By 2014, Milan's role was more than just a cool title – it became a paid, fully independent position dedicated to improving the economic and cultural value of the night across all fronts, without alienating residents and public officials. Tough gig, but improve it did.

The *nachtburgemeester*'s approach to nurturing the night as an engine for cultural and economic growth proved so successful that other cities followed suit. Amsterdam hosted the first ever Night Mayor Summit in 2016, and the model has now been adopted by London, Toulouse, Paris and Zurich. One initiative that seems to have enjoyed particular success is a pilot system called Square Hosts, which sees 20 trained 'hosts' patrolling Rembrandtplein between 9pm and 6am every Friday and Saturday, with the aim of making everyone feel safe and welcome. The hosts are paid for by the clubs in return for longer opening hours.

As a result of Milan's efforts, Amsterdam was dubbed the nightlife capital of Europe in 2016. Milan stepped down in 2018 to be replaced by Shamiro van der Geld, but the approach and attitude that Milan instigated remain in place. While the city is best known for its electronic dance scene, its cultural offering is gradually diversifying to cater for a global audience, and the live music scene, while smaller than in some other cities, is going from strength to strength.

CLUBS

Amsterdam's electronic dance music (EDM) scene has long been acknowledged as one of the best in the world, and not just for its homegrown-turned-global talents, including Martin Garrix and DJ Isis among others. The annual **Amsterdam Dance Event** (ADE, *see p204*) attracted a record breaking 400,000 visitors from over 100 countries in 2018, with the Netherlands' EDM industry estimated to be worth well over €200 million. Although infamous dance clubs Trouw Amsterdam and Studio 80 have called it a night for good, pioneers of Amsterdam's ever-evolving club scene were quick to replace them with the likes of **De School** (*see p226*) and **Shelter** (*see p228*), a dance music haven in the basement of Noord's **A'DAM Toren** (*see p174*). Both of these were granted the insatiable club-goer's golden ticket: 24-hour licensing.

Giving venues the option to operate 24 hours a day was one of Mirik Milan's biggest priorities as *nachtburgemeester* (*see above* How the Night Mayor Created A Dream Scene), and is one of the many ways Amsterdam has pioneered a path for club-conscious cities across the globe.

The city's club offering is dance-heavy, but diversification is still apparent. Hip hop and R&B reign supreme at the likes of **Jimmy Woo** (*see p226*), while globally renowned venues **Paradiso** (*see p227*) and **Melkweg** (*see p230*) play host to an eclectic mix of pop, dance and alternative artists in the international spotlight.

There are scuzzy venues for students and rockers, meat markets for stags, and cutting-edge clubs for hipsters. Note that concerts at rock, pop and jazz venues often run into club nights. In recent years, the festival scene has absolutely exploded countrywide (*see p231* Best of the Fests). As after-dark innovators make use of the city's post-industrial warehouse spaces, such as **Pllek** (*see p232*) and **NDSM** (*see p176*), it seems likely that this trend is likely to continue for many moons to come.

Clubbing know-how

Clubbing here requires an element of effortless cool. All venues have bouncers, so show up on time and with a mixed crowd to increase your chances of getting in. Make sure you know who is headlining – because they may well ask you. At most places, trainers are a completely acceptable form of footwear so spare your feet the pain of heels – just ensure your shoes are enclosed. Storing your coat in the cloakroom might incur a fee, as might using the toilets (typically €1-€1.50), but in many clubs outside the city centre these facilities are free. The Dutch aren't great tippers at the bar – ten per cent is considered generous. Almost no one will be inside a club before midnight: people are either at home or in a bar loosening up. It's also worth noting that while many places accept Dutch bank cards, equivalent UK bank cards such as Visa and Mastercard debit are regarded as 'credit cards' here and, as such, are not accepted; having cash is highly recommended.

► *For details of dedicated gay and lesbian clubs, see p216 and p218.*

Old Centre

Bitterzoet

*Spuistraat 2 (020 421 2318, www.bitterzoet.com). Tram 2, 11, 12, 13, 17. **Open** varies. **Admission** varies. No cards. **Map** p70 K7.*

Cool, casual and cosy, 'Bitter sweet' has been around for more than a decade. The key to its success is booking club-night people, bands and DJs who do it more for the passion than the fame. Hip hop, street art, alternative rock, Afrobeat or broken beats may define particular nights – or be all mashed up together in a single night.

❤ Disco Dolly

*Handboogstraat 11 (020 620 1779, www.discodolly.nl). Tram 2, 11, 12 or Metro Rokin. **Open** 11pm-4am Mon-Thur, Sun; 11pm-5am Fri, Sat. **Admission** free-€10. No cards. **Map** p70 J10.*

Formerly the student meat-market dance club, Dansen bij Jansen, Disco Dolly has since found a broader audience, yet doesn't stray too far – expect fairly commercial disco, funk and house. If you feel a bit old among the teen and early twenties clientele, try sister night bar **Bloemenbar**, next door at no.15.

Grachtengordel

► *For details of multidisciplinary club and cultural hub Melkweg, see p230.*

AIR

*Amstelstraat 16 (020 820 0670, www.air.nl). Tram 4, 14. **Open** 11.30pm-4am Thur, Sun; 11pm-5am Fri, Sat. **Admission** €7.50-€20. **Map** p96 M11.*

Like a phoenix from the ashes, AIR Amsterdam rose from the remains of legendary club iT. The musical offerings are varied, and the crowd mixed. Dondairdag on Thursday delivers an urban flavour, with Afrobeat, R&B, dancehall and hip hop; Friday often has a techno feel; on Saturday, it's all a bit more commercial.

Claire

*Rembrandtplein 17 (020 211 1126, www.claire.nl). Tram 4, 14. **Open** 11pm-4am Wed-Thur, Sun; 11pm-7am Fri; 11pm-noon Sat. **Admission** varies. **Map** p96 L11.*

The successor of Amsterdam's iconic Studio 80, which closed in 2015, Claire is the self-described 'best friend, affair and archrival' of the city's nocturnal creatures. The club, which debuted a stellar line-up during Amsterdam Dance Event (ADE) in 2016, is co-owned by Juri Miralles and Marlon Arfman, who also have a hand in popular venues **Bloemenbar** and **Disco Dolly** (*see left*).

❤ Best live music venues

Bimhuis *p233*
Jazz and improv in tailor-made surroundings.

Bourbon Street *p233*
Listen to the blues.

Melkweg *p230*
The cream of musical talent.

Paradiso *p227*
Iconic acts in an iconic setting.

Ziggo Dome *p233*
Vast arena for international stars.

❤ Best clubs

Club Church *p219*
A gay cruising club with a difference.

Disco Dolly *p225*
Pop-lovers eat your heart out.

Jimmy Woo *p226*
A bootylicious sound system.

Pllek *p232*
DJ sets and live bands with a brilliant view of the IJ.

De School *p226*
24-hour hipster house paradise.

Disco Dolly

Club Up/De Kring

Korte Leidsedwarsstraat 26 (020 623 6985, www.clubup.nl). Tram 1, 2, 7, 11, 12, 19. ***Open*** *11pm-4am Thur; 11pm-5am Fri, Sat.* ***Admission*** *€5-€25.* ***Map*** *p96 H12.*

Club Up is an intimate venue with a great sound system, connected via a corridor to artists' members' club De Kring. If you can, visit when both areas are accessible, since De Kring provides the laid-back atmosphere that the often-packed, discotheque-like ballroom of Club Up lacks. DJs spin disco, techno and house.

Escape

Rembrandtplein 11 (020 622 1111, www.escape.nl). Tram 4, 14. ***Open*** *11pm-4am Thur, Sun; 11pm-5am Fri, Sat.* ***Admission*** *€5-€20. No cards.* ***Map*** *p96 L11.*

With a capacity of 2,000, this is as big as clubbing gets in central Amsterdam, and is popular with a younger, more mainstream crowd. It attracts queues on Saturday and Sunday evenings, and the bouncers are wary of groups of tourists, so get in line early. Also note the dress code: no trainers, no sportswear, no 'broken' clothes. Oh, and guests must have a 'groomed appearance', so fix up and look sharp.

In the know
Narcotic no-nos

Despite the perceived relaxed attitude towards drugs in the Netherlands, hard drugs are very much illegal and possession can result in imprisonment and/or a hefty fine. Undercover cops often put in appearances at larger clubs and festivals. Plus, what you think you're buying is not likely to be what you'll get.

❤ Jimmy Woo

Korte Leidsedwarsstraat 18 (020 626 3150, www.jimmywoo.com). Tram 1, 2, 7, 11, 12, 19. ***Open*** *11pm-3am Thur; 11pm-4am Fri, Sat.* ***Admission*** *varies.* ***Map*** *p96 H12.*

Amsterdam has never seen anything quite so luxuriously cosmopolitan as Jimmy Woo. Marvel at the lounge filled with a mix of modern and antique furniture, and confirm for yourself the merits of the bootylicious light design and sound system. If you have problems getting inside, try the equally hip and happening **Chicago Social Club** (Leidseplein 12, 020 760 1171, www.chicagosocialclub.nl), next door.

Jordaan & the West

❤ De School

Dr Jan van Breemenstraat 1 (020 737 3197, www.deschoolamsterdam.nl). Tram 13. ***Open*** *varies.* ***Admission*** *varies.*

Lovers of the night were gutted when legendary Amsterdam club Trouw closed its doors, but they didn't have to wait long for a newcomer to take their mind off the loss. Set in the bike storage building of a

❤ Paradiso

Weteringschans 6-8, Southern Canal Belt (020 626 4521, www.paradiso.nl). Tram 1, 2, 7, 11, 12, 19. ***Open*** *7pm-late daily, depending on event.* ***Admission*** *varies.* ***Map*** *p96 H13.*

Amsterdam's prime music venue, Paradiso is housed in a former church. Fitting, then, that it's now known as the city's 'temple of music'. As is generally the case with iconic music hubs, Paradiso's foundations tell a colourful story.

The building, which has origins in the 19th century, was used by a liberal Dutch religious group as a meeting hall until 1965. A couple of years later, it was squatted by hippies who wanted to take advantage of its position in one of the city's tourism and nightlife hubs and convert the church into a club. The police quickly put a stop to this initiative, and in 1968 the building reopened as 'Cosmic Relaxation Center Paradiso'. The aim? To create an open platform for burgeoning creative talent. This time around it was a success and the name Paradiso soon became synonymous with counterculture and cutting-edge rock music (and, perhaps inevitably, soft drugs).

The years that followed would see countless up-and-coming artists and enthusiastic audiences squeeze through its doors. Almost 50 years later, Paradiso has secured its place as a pop podium and cultural hub for national and international audiences. Its stage has been graced by hundreds of world-famous rock, soul, country and pop music legends. Iconic influencers such as Al Green and Smokey Robinson have brought the house down, and the venue has also helped pave the way for the likes of Franz Ferdinand, Kings of Leon and the White Stripes. With large stained-glass windows and high ceilings, the building still proudly displays its grand origins. In addition to the main hall, which has a capacity of 1,500, the venue showcases independent and break-through talent in a smaller room upstairs.

Paradiso also hosts fashion shows, modern classical ensembles and even the occasional science lecture. The music venue and club nights are most popular among visitors, however, and tickets sell quickly, so check the website well in advance if you want to see one of your favourite acts.

Caravan Palace

school campus from the 1960s, De School is the Trouw team's entry into the thriving electronic dance scene. It's one of a growing number of clubs to hold a 24-hour licence, which means some nights go on until 10am. The 500-capacity club is part of a wider cultural centre at the former campus, which also includes a concert venue, restaurant, café and exhibition space. If you're going to make a night of it, make sure you know who is playing – the exceptionally trendy staff on the door are quick to turn away perceived posers.

Westerunie

Klönneplein 4-6, Westergasfabriek (020 684 8496, www.westerunie.nl). Tram 5. ***Open*** *varies Fri, Sat.* ***Admission*** *varies.* ***Map*** *p117 off map.*

Occupying an old factory building in cultural park Westergasfabriek, Westerunie consists of a large space and the more intimate Westerliefde. For larger events, there's another, even bigger, hall nearby. Fridays usually focus on a particular genre from years past (disco or old-school rave, say). Saturdays tend to have one-offs by the better party organisers around town, such as ExPornStar and the people behind the Loveland festival.

Museum Quarter, Oud West & Zuid

OT301

Overtoom 301, Oud West (www.ot301.nl). Tram 1, 11. ***Open*** *varies.* ***Admission*** *varies.* ***Map*** *p136 C13.*

This multipurpose venue offers cheap bottled beer and a wildly varying programme, including drum'n'bass, funk and hip hop, or a savvy selection of bands and DJs from alternative-minded Subbacultcha. Music varies from underground acts to established names, but tends to be on the less commercial side of things. If you don't like the music, OT301 also has a radio station, vegan restaurant and art-house cinema to keep you entertained.

Jodenbuurt, Plantage & Oost

Canvas

Wibautstraat 150, Oost (020 261 2110, www.volkshotel.nl/canvas). Tram 3 or Metro Wibautstaat. ***Open*** *Club 9pm-2am Fri, Sat.* ***Admission*** *varies.* ***Map*** *p153 P15.*

Canvas's programme ranges from cutting-edge electronica through hip hop to club house and live jazz. Sitting atop a former newspaper-building-turned-hotel, it also sports some of the best views in town – along with the most hilarious toilet attendants. During the day, it operates as a café and cocktail bar.

Waterfront & Noord

Panama

Oostelijke Handelskade 4 (020 311 8686, www.panama.nl). Tram 7, 26. ***Open*** *11pm-4am Thur; 11pm-5am Fri, Sat.* ***Admission*** *€10-€20.* ***Map*** *p166 T8.*

Nightlife anchor Panama opened way back in 2001 on what was a deserted strip, but is now surrounded by high-rise offices, steep rents and the shiny **Muziekgebouw** (*see p236*). Most nights mix up-and-coming Dutch DJs with big international names.

Shelter

Overhoeksplein 3 (www.shelteramsterdam.nl). Bus 38 or Buiksloterweg ferry. ***Open*** *11pm-8am Fri, Sat.* ***Admission*** *varies.* ***Map*** *p166 M5.*

Set in the basement of **A'DAM Toren** (*see p174*) and boasting a coveted 24-hour licence, this is underground clubbing at its finest. The venue opened its doors in October 2016, and has since housed an impressive line-up of big-shot international DJs and local up-and-comers on its decks. If you plan to take advantage of its insomniac-friendly opening hours, you can refuel upstairs at **The Butcher Social Club**, which is open 24 hours on Fridays and Saturdays.

COMEDY

The Dutch have their own cultural history of hilarity, based in large part on their own very singular take on the art and practice of cabaret, so stand-up comedy is a fairly recent import to the Netherlands in general and Amsterdam in particular. However, it's gained in popularity in recent years. Shows usually feature a mix of international and local acts, often performing in English.

Venues

Boom Chicago

Rozentheater, Rozengracht 117, Jordaan (020 217 0400, www.boomchicago.nl). Tram 5, 13, 17, 19. ***Open*** *varies.* ***Admission*** *varies.* ***Map*** *p117 F9.*

This American improv troupe is one of Amsterdam's biggest success stories, with alumni including Seth Meyers (*Saturday Night Live*) and Jason Sudekis (*30 Rock*).

Several different shows, all in English, run seven nights a week (winter is slightly quieter), featuring a mix of audience-prompted improvisation, rehearsed sketches, full-blown themed shows and guest comedians from around the world – coupled with dinner options. 'Shot of Improv' is the showcase Saturday evening show, starting at 8pm. If the improvisers like any of your suggestions and use one or more of them to create a hilarious scene, you might get a bonus beer. Boom Chicago also organises excellent boat tours, gives improv classes and has a fine bar in Bar 117.

Comedy Café Amsterdam

IJdok 89, Waterfront (020 722 0827, www.comedycafe.nl). Bus 48. ***Open*** *Comedy 8.30pm Wed-Sat. Open mic 8.30pm Mon, Tue.* ***Admission*** *€5-€17.50.* ***Map*** *p166 K4.*

Previously located in the Southern Canal Belt, the Comedy Café did a sterling job of bringing comedy to a wider Amsterdam audience by offering shows in a mind-boggling blend of Dutch and English.

Toomler

Breitnerstraat 2, Zuid (020 670 7400, www.toomler.nl). Tram 2, 5, 24. ***Open*** *varies.* ***Admission*** *varies.*

Toomler usually hosts Dutch stand-up, but also organises English-language nights and festivals on occasion.

LIVE MUSIC

On any given night in Amsterdam, you can be sure to find something to suit your aural tastes, from the sultry tones of Portugese songstress Ana Moura to tunes from veteran blues artist Mac Arnold to the all-in sound of the Conservatorium's Jazzband. Alternatively, drink and dance to the DJ-infused mix of The Groove Supplier, or enjoy the eastern European party sounds of the Amsterdam Klezmer Band. The more musical genres you throw into the mix (think heavy metal, art rock, Frisian fado), the longer the list of innovative musical entertainment gets.

The creators are a combination of home-grown talent and international acts. Amsterdam is firmly established as a crucial port of call on the international touring circuit, thanks to such iconic venues as **Paradiso** (*see p227*) and **Melkweg** (*see p230*), ably supported by trendy locations such as **Tolhuistuin** (*see p176*) and **Cinetol** (*see p230*). It's also worth keeping your eyes peeled for what's happening in Haarlem, Utrecht or Rotterdam – you could be a 15- to 60-minute train ride away from your favourite band.

► *For information on classical music in Amsterdam, see p236 Performing Arts.*

Tickets and information

Many of the larger venues sell tickets via their own website. Otherwise, the main ticket retailer is **Ticketmaster** (www.ticketmaster.nl). **The Last Minute Ticket Shop** (www.lastminuteticketshop.nl) shifts tickets at half their face value from 10am, for musical and theatrical events showing that night.

Amsterdam's free monthly cultural magazine *Uitkrant* (pronounced 'out-krant') is available in theatres, bars, bookshops and visitor centres. *A-mag*, an English-language listings magazine published six times a year by the city tourist organisation, is found in many hotels and cafés for free and is also sold at tourist offices and in newsagents.

Rock & pop venues

Bitterzoet (*see p225*) doubles as a venue for jazzy, alternative, world and urban music.

AFAS Live

ArenA Boulevard 590, Zuidoost (0900 687 4242 premium rate, www.afaslive.nl). Metro/rail Bijlmer ArenA. ***Open*** *varies.* ***Admission*** *varies.*

A surprisingly cosy venue in the ArenA complex (*see below*), the AFAS Live (previously the Heineken Music Hall) has a capacity of 5,500 and regularly plays host to pop, rock and dance acts that are too big for the more central venues – from Bob Dylan to The xx. The modern design may lack character, but makes up for it in acoustics.

ArenA

ArenA Boulevard 1, Zuidoost (020 311 1333, www.amsterdamarena.nl). Metro/rail Bijlmer ArenA. ***Open*** *varies.* ***Admission*** *varies.*

When the football season ends, Ajax's stadium is reborn as a musical amphitheatre, hosting tours by the likes of U2 and Beyoncé, and even a few Dutch stars, and staging outdoor raves. Bring your lighter, and don't forget binoculars if you're stuck in the cheap seats.

De Brakke Grond

Nes 45, Old Centre (020 622 9014, www.brakkegrond.nl). Tram 2, 4, 11, 12, 14, 24. ***Open*** *varies.* ***Admission*** *varies.* ***Map*** *p70 K9.*

This Flemish cultural centre and general artists' hangout regularly presents a variety of

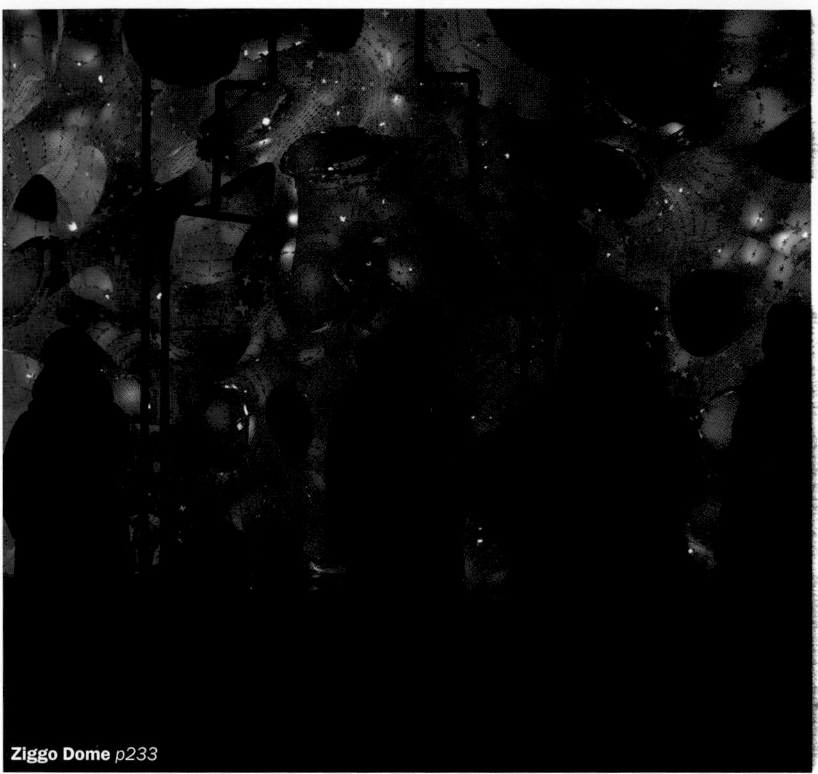
Ziggo Dome *p233*

contemporary music from Belgium – which has an alternative music scene that has long been the envy of the Netherlands.

Cinetol

Tolstraat 182, De Pijp (www.cinetol.nl). Tram 4. ***Open*** *9am-1am Mon-Thur; 9am-3am Fri; 11am-3pm Sat; 11am-midnight Sun.* ***Admission*** *varies.* ***Map*** *p181 N16.*

This small music venue is a self-styled breeding ground for creatives. Musically, it skews towards the fringes of indie and alternative music, but there's much more than just performance here: meeting rooms, studios, rehearsal spaces and the charming Tolbar buzz with cultural energy all day long.

❤ Melkweg

Lijnbaansgracht 234A, Grachtengordel (020 531 8181, www.melkweg.nl). Tram 1, 2, 5, 7, 10. ***Open*** *daily until late.* ***Admission*** *€5-€32. Membership (compulsory) €4/mth; €25/yr.* ***Map*** *p96 G12.*

Located conveniently in the Leidseplein nightlife hub, Melkweg offers a galaxy of stellar programming, from international DJs to theatrical performances, photography exhibitions to dance installations. Melkweg was a milking factory in its past life, hence its name, which translates as 'Milky Way'. The venue is operated by a non-profit group of artists who have run it since they discovered the abandoned factory in 1970. Melkweg acts as a home away from home for music of all styles, and draws a suitably eclectic crowd. Its two decent-sized concert halls – the Max room has a capacity of up to 1,500 – offer a full programme year round. It also has an excellent cinema, gallery and a café. Don't fret about the compulsory membership – you can purchase it at the same time as booking. Opening hours vary depending on what's on, so be sure to check the website and nab tickets in advance if you see something you like.

De Nieuwe Anita

Frederik Hendrikstraat 111, Jordaan (www.denieuweanita.nl). Tram 3, 5. ***Open*** *6pm-1am Mon, Thur; 8pm-1am Tue, Wed; 8pm-2am Fri, Sat.* ***Admission*** *varies. No cards.* ***Map*** *p117 F8.*

Best of the Fests

A round-up of the Netherlands' annual music festivals

Come summer, the Dutch club scene takes a sideways step. Amsterdam's urban beaches begin to host more shows and some crazy parties, and music festivals take place across the country. Even better, some are completely free. Below are the major events (in date order); check www.festivalinfo.nl for a full list and line-ups.

Eurosonic Noorderslag

www.eurosonic-noorderslag.nl. ***Date*** *Jan.*

A rare midwinter shindig, this four-day international industry showcase in Groningen is for those seriously into the rock, pop and indie scenes. The emphasis is on acts expected to make an impact across Europe in the coming year.

Pinkpop

www.pinkpop.nl. ***Date*** *June.*

Attracting a slightly younger and poppier crowd than Lowlands, Pinkpop is somewhat less adventurous than its indie sister. Still, there are plenty of big names in the worlds of pop, rock, dance and metal at the three-day event at Megaland, in Landgraaf.

Parkpop

www.parkpop.nl. ***Date*** *June.*

Loads of European cities claim to hold the largest free festival. The Hague's Parkpop is the Dutch contender: organisers usually expect 300,000 to 500,000 visitors for this family-type affair. Expect some surprisingly big names, Dutch acts and upcoming urban outfits across the event's three side-by-side stages.

Best Kept Secret

www.bestkeptsecret.nl. ***Date*** *June.*

Held in the very south of the country, near Tillburg, this festival doesn't think in terms of genres or styles, it aims simply to programme 'great music'. The wonderful surrounds of the Beekse Bergen Safari Park, with its log cabins, woodlands and a boating lake, add to the sense of uniqueness.

Metropolis

www.metropolisfestival.nl. ***Date*** *July.*

For the last quarter-century, Rotterdam's Zuiderpark has become an alternative-music honeypot for one day every summer. Bands such as Radiohead, the Black Keys and the Strokes played here before they became household names. And, get this – admission is free.

Down The Rabbit Hole

www.downtherabbithole.nl. ***Date*** *July.*

Billed as a trip of 'adventure, confusion, surrealism, and psychedelics', this three-day event in the pastoral, rolling countryside north-west of Nijmegen, showcases some of the biggest names in contemporary indie and alternative music alongside forest walks, wild swimming and a general outoors-y vibe.

North Sea Jazz

www.northseajazz.nl. ***Date*** *July.*

This three-day mega-event, a favourite with Dutch and other jazz fans, stages over 100 acts including some big names. Drawing almost 25,000 visitors per day, it's held in the Ahoy complex in the south of Rotterdam – not the most attractive of locations, but it does allow space for further growth. Running since 1976, it's a veteran event for Dutch jazz fans.

Lowlands

www.lowlands.nl. ***Date*** *Aug.*

Holland's largest alternative-music festival takes place over a long weekend in Biddinghuizen, Flevoland, attracting over 100,000 music fans of all sorts to see assorted bands, theatre acts and street performers. Good weather isn't crucial – all the important stages are inside huge tents.

Crossing Border

www.crossingborder.nl. ***Date*** *Nov.*

Based in The Hague, this gathering puts words before melody. Crossing Border offers a stimulating mix of literature and music, with many well-known international authors and artists arriving in town for spoken-word and musical performances.

Le Guess Who?

www.leguesswho.nl. ***Date*** *Nov.*

Having started out as a celebration of the Canadian independent music scene, this contemporary music festival in Utrecht has bloomed into one of Europe's boldest, most innovative music events. Blending the avant garde, singular talents and those blurring genre boundaries, it's become a celebration of sound in all its forms.

Bimhuis

A big name in Amsterdam's subculture, DNA is a promoter of fresh talent in the world of independent rock and electronica. Programming is sporadic and based on good relations with understanding neighbours, so always check the website before heading there. DNA also operates as a cinema *(see p211)*.

OCCII

Amstelveenseweg 134, Vondelpark (020 671 7778, www.occii.org). Tram 1, 2, 11, 17 or bus 15, 62. ***Open*** *varies.* ***Admission*** *varies. No cards.* ***Map*** *p136 F8.*

Formerly a squat, this friendly volunteer-run bar and concert hall is tucked away at one end of Vondelpark. While its squat-scene days may be over, the legacy remains: the roster offers touring underground rock, experimental and reggae acts, plus adventurous local bands.

❤ Pllek

For listings, see p175.

The shipyard-turned-restaurant-slash-club has added yet another dimension to its offering: a live music stage. Fitted with top-notch sound and lighting, the space can fit up to 300 people. With floor-to-ceiling glass windows set out over the IJ, the view doesn't hurt either.

Q Factory

Atlantisplein 1, Oost (020 760 6780, www.q-factory-amsterdam.nl). Tram 19. ***Open*** *9am-midnight daily.* ***Admission*** *varies.* ***Map*** *pull-out map T14.*

Designed as a one-stop shop for musicians of all stripes, Q Factory claims to be Europe's largest 'music maker center'. The whole building is geared towards those who want to rehearse, perform or record, with three performance spaces, a studio and 50 different rehearsal rooms – one is even big enough to fit a symphony orchestra. There's also a hotel spread over the third and fourth floors.

Tolhuistuin

For listings, see p176.

This arts complex over the IJ has been making waves in the cultural scene since summer 2014. These former Royal Dutch Shell buildings and gardens have been transformed, with the help of a 24-hour licence, to feature an indoor music venue, **Paradiso Noord**, a massive restaurant with views over the IJ, and various gallery spaces and dance studios.

Vondelbunker

Vondelpark 8A, Museum Quarter (www.vondelbunker.nl). Tram 3. ***Open*** *varies.* ***Admission*** *free.* ***Map*** *p136 G13.*

This 1947 bomb shelter, located under a bridge that crosses Vondelpark, is temporary home to Schijnheilig, an activist collective that transforms abandoned places into free arenas for expression. Activities include squatting info nights, film screenings and bands – usually of the more punky variety.

❤ Ziggo Dome

De Passage 100, Zuidoost (0900 235 3663 premium rate, www.ziggodome.nl). Metro/rail Bijlmer ArenA. ***Open*** *varies.* ***Admission*** *varies.*

With a staggering 17,000 seats, this behemoth towers over near neighbour **AFAS Live** (*see p229*), so it's not surprising it pulls in the biggest international names: Lana Del Rey, Drake and Lady Gaga, for example. Bonuses: the acoustics are excellent, and the logistical hiccups that often beset such large venues, non-existent.

Jazz & blues venues

Classical music venues such as **Splendour Amsterdam** (*see p238*) also feature regular jazz gigs.

❤ Bimhuis

Piet Heinkade 3, Waterfront (020 788 2188, www.bimhuis.nl). Tram 26. ***Open*** *varies.* ***Admission*** *from €16.* ***Map*** *p166 P7.*

Jazz and improv musicians from far and wide queue for a chance to grace the stage at the Bimhuis. For decades a smoky jazz joint in the Old Centre, it moved some years ago to the eye-catching new **Muziekgebouw aan 't IJ** complex (*see p236*) – a bit of a shock for some fans. The past few years have seen sporadic pop nights come to play too.

❤ Bourbon Street

Leidsekruisstraat 6-8, Leidseplein, Grachtengordel (020 623 3440, www.bourbonstreet.nl). Tram 1, 2, 7, 11, 12, 19. ***Open*** *10pm-4am Mon-Thur, Sun; 10pm-5am Fri, Sat.* ***Admission*** *€3-€5; free Mon; before 11pm Tue-Thur; before 10.30pm Fri, Sat.* ***Map*** *p96 H12.*

In the heart of the tourist area, this blues club has a spacious bar and a late licence. Musicians are welcome at the regular jam sessions, and international acts drop by at least a couple of times a week. It's by no means a glamorous venue, but if late-night music played live is your thing, you won't be disappointed.

Maloe Melo

Lijnbaansgracht 163, Jordaan (020 420 4592, www.maloemelo.com). Tram 5, 17, 19. ***Open*** *9pm-3am Mon-Thur, Sun; 9pm-4am Fri, Sat. Shows from 10.30pm.* ***Admission*** *free-€10. Some cards accepted.* ***Map*** *p117 F10.*

'Well, I woke up this morning, feeling Maloe Melowed ...' This small, fun juke joint on Lijnbaansgracht is Amsterdam's native house of the blues. Quality rockabilly and roots acts also play here on a regular basis, so shed your gloom and enjoy the boogie.

Paleis van de Weemoed

Oudezijds Voorburgwal 15-17, Old Centre (020 625 6964, www.paleis-van-de-weemoed.nl). Tram 4, 14, 24 or Metro Nieuwmarkt. ***Open*** *varies.* ***Admission*** *varies.* ***Map*** *p70 M8.*

This burlesque theatre and supper club opens its red-velvet curtains to a mixed bag of musicians, who usually veer towards the jazzy side of things. Though there's no official dress code, you may want to consider a zoot suit and fedora as opposed to a pair of tatty jeans and trainers.

Zaal 100

De Wittenstraat 100, Westerpark (020 688 0127, www.zaal100.nl). Tram 3, 5 or bus 18, 21. ***Open*** *varies.* ***Admission*** *from €5. No cards.* ***Map*** *p117 F5.*

Zaal 100 has its roots in the squatting scene, but is tastefully decorated, unlike some of its grungier counterparts. Its stage has been graced by some of Amsterdam's best-known musicians; the venue also books a lot of singer-songwriters. Also a gallery space, it's frequently rented out by local artists. Vegetarian meals are served Wednesday, Thursday and Friday from 6pm.

Performing Arts

The whole city's a stage in the Dutch capital

Amsterdam likes to see itself as a major hub in the cultural universe. Locals give standing ovations to Beethoven symphonies, lap up the latest operas from Pierre Audi or Dmitri Tcherniakov, and keenly support home-grown dance productions.

The city has more than its fair share of world-class venues for every form of cultural endeavour. Add to this an active underground scene, and visitors are spoilt for choice. The breadth and quality of the Amsterdam arts experience was long due to enlightened funding from government and city council alike, resulting in a wealth of arts festivals, plus buildings such as the Muziekgebouw. However, more recent subsidy cutbacks have forced larger companies to merge and smaller initiatives to fight for their very existence.

A Quiet Evening of Dance, International Theatre Amsterdam p242

Tickets

Tickets for most performances can be bought at the venues themselves or via their websites (booking online is usually cheaper). Larger venues often include a free drink and even public transport in the ticket price. If you prefer to play it by ear, jump online to the **Last Minute Ticket Shop** (www.lastminuteticketshop.nl), where tickets for that night are sold at half price from 10am local time. You can also buy tickets from **Ticketmaster** (www.ticketmaster.nl).

CLASSICAL MUSIC & OPERA

One of the most heart-warming aspects of Amsterdam's cultural scene is that the city promotes a classless adoration of beautiful music. Attending a concert is not a grand statement of one's arrival in society; it's simply about love of the music. Many of the greatest international orchestras perform in Amsterdam – typically for little more than the price of the biggest rock or pop concerts, and frequently for considerably less. The city is also home to world-renowned orchestras and soloists, and renditions of the classics are not limited to the grand concert venues, but can be heard alongside canals, in parks, on the streets or in the halls of the Conservatorium van Amsterdam building – whose composers-in-training are being brought to the fore thanks to the likes of the new-music specialist **Asko-Schönberg Ensemble** (www.askoschoenberg.nl). Dutch composer and pianist Louis Andriessen is also on the global radar, having been awarded the prestigious Marie-Josée Kravis Prize for New Music by the New York Philharmonic in 2016.

The renowned **Royal Concertgebouw Orchestra** (www.concertgebouworkest.nl) plays at the acoustically blessed **Concertgebouw** for most of the season (which kicks off in September); try to hear them, if possible, even if just for a lunchtime concert. The German conductor Marc Albrecht, meanwhile, leads the **Dutch National Opera**, the **Netherlands Philharmonic Orchestra** and the **Netherlands Chamber Orchestra** (www.orkest.nl).

Concert venues

Conservatorium van Amsterdam

Oosterdokskade 151, Waterfront (020 527 7550, www.ahk.nl/conservatorium). Tram 1, 2, 4, 5, 9, 13, 16, 17, 26. ***Open*** *times vary.* ***Tickets*** *prices vary.* ***Map*** *p166 O8.*

Concerts and presentations take place almost daily, and often for free, in the Amsterdam Conservatory's gorgeous glass building just east of Centraal Station. You'll find everything here, from classical quartets to jazz big bands.

Engelse Kerk

Begijnhof 48, Old Centre (020 624 9665, www.ercadam.nl). Tram 2, 4, 11, 12, 14, 24 or Metro Rokin. ***Open*** *times vary.* ***Tickets*** *prices vary. No cards.* ***Map*** *p70 J10.*

Nestled tightly within the idyllic courtyard of **Begijnhof** (*see p90*), the English Reformed Church has been hosting weekly concerts of baroque and classical music since the early 1970s. Combined with a particular emphasis on the use of authentic period instruments, the church's acoustics are genuinely haunting. The busy evening schedule also raises funds to help secure the building's future.

❤ Muziekgebouw aan 't IJ

Piet Heinkade 1, Waterfront (020 788 2000, www.muziekgebouw.nl). Tram 26. ***Box office*** *2-6pm Mon-Sat.* ***Tickets*** *prices vary.* ***Map*** *p166 P7.*

Designed by the Danish architectural practice 3xNielsen, the Muziekgebouw is one of the most innovative musical complexes anywhere in Europe, befitting its previous incarnation as the IJsbreker, whose long-lasting ethos was to promote modern variants of classical, jazz and world music. Never afraid to take risks, the centre's schedule bustles with delights, ranging from cutting-

❤ Best for culture

Concertgebouw *see opposite*
World-class concert hall.

DeLaMar Theater *p242*
Show-stopping cabaret.

Muziekgebouw *see above*
Music for everyone.

Nationale Opera & Ballet *p238*
Home of high culture.

Over het IJ Festival *p202*
Ten days of absurdist theatre.

International Theatre Amsterdam *p243*
Ground zero for performing arts.

❤ Concertgebouw

Concertgebouwplein 10, Museum Quarter (0900 671 8345 premium rate, www.concertgebouw.nl). Tram 3, 5, 12. ***Box office*** *1-7pm Mon-Fri; 10am-7pm Sat, Sun (or until 5pm if no evening concert).* ***Tickets*** *prices vary.* ***Map*** *p136 G15.*

With over 900 events and 700,000 visitors each year, it's safe to say the Concertgebouw has made a mark since its opening in 1888. Occupying prime real estate on Museumplein, alongside the Van Gogh, Stedelijk and Rijks museums, the imperious-looking building has been the epicentre of classical music in the Netherlands for decades. Combining beautiful neoclassical architecture with crystal-clear acoustics, it is a favourite venue of many of the world's top musicians and has hosted the likes of Gustav Mahler, Richard Strauss, Yehudi Menuhin and Cecilia Bartoli during its illustrious career. Even if you're not a classical music buff, you will still appreciate the surroundings. Designed by architect Adolf Leonard van Gendt, the Concertgebouw is comprised of three halls – the Main Hall, the Recital Hall and the more recent Choir Hall. The unrivalled acoustic properties of the Main Hall make it one of the most revered classical music venues in the world. Tickets are available online and for purchase at the box office via telephone. If you don't have the time (or funds) to treat yourself to a show, be sure to stop by and soak up the sheer grandeur of the building.

► *The Concertgebouw also holds regular concerts for children; check the schedule on the website for details.*

Aufstieg und Fall der Stadt Mahagonny, Nationale Opera

edge multimedia works to celebrations of composers from the last 150 years. It's also home to the **Klankspeeltuin**, where seven- to 12-year-olds can play with an inspired selection of musical machines, installations and computers. High-quality jazz acts perform regularly at the adjoining **Bimhuis** (*see p233*); see website for details.

❤ Nationale Opera & Ballet

Amstel 3, Jodenbuurt (020 625 8117 information, 020 625 5455 box office, www.operaballet.nl). Tram 14 or Metro Waterlooplein. ***Box office*** *noon-6pm Mon-Fri; noon-3pm Sat, Sun; or until start of performance.* ***Tickets*** *from €15.* ***Map*** *p153 M11.*

Formerly called the Muziektheater, the building – and its primary tenants, the Dutch National Ballet and Dutch National Opera – was reborn as the Nationale Opera & Ballet back in 2014. The stage is used by leading dance companies on tour and to host the latest opera offering. It has a reputation for high-quality performances at good prices. Tickets go on sale three months in advance and often sell out fast, so it's advisable to book early.

NedPhO-Koepel

Batjanstraat 3, Oost (020 521 7500, www.orkest.nl). Tram 3, 14. ***Open*** *times vary.* ***Tickets*** *prices vary.*

The Netherlands Philharmonic and the Netherlands Chamber Orchestra rehearse in this 1925-built church in Oost. The space also acts as a flexible performance space for 200 people to enjoy monthly open rehearsals (free), readings and educational programmes. Both orchestras perform regularly in the Concertgebouw, under conductor Marc Albrecht – a busy man as he's also conductor of the Nationale Opera.

Orgelpark

Gerard Brandtstraat 26, Vondelpark, Oud West (020 515 8111, www.orgelpark.nl). Tram 1, 11. ***Box office*** *by phone 2-5pm Tue-Fri. In person from 75mins before concert.* ***Tickets*** *€10-€22.50.* ***Map*** *p136 D13.*

This church on the edge of Vondelpark provides space for ten organs, which are used for ambitious concerts – from Schubert to improv to electronica – in the hopes of bringing pipe-organ music kicking and wheezing into the 21st century.

Splendour Amsterdam

Nieuwe Uilenburgerstraat 116, Jodenbuurt (020 845 3345, www.splendouramsterdam.com). Tram 14 or Metro Waterloopline. ***Box office*** *45mins before start of performance.* ***Tickets*** *available online or at the door; prices vary.* ***Map*** *p153 M10.*

An inspiring local initiative that has seen a splendid old bathhouse renovated by a collective of musicians, composers and performing artists into rehearsal spaces, along with a bar and a performance hall where they give regular classical, jazz and pop concerts. Children's musical activities also occur frequently.

Westerkerk

Prinsengracht 281, Grachtengordel (020 624 7766, www.westerkerk.nl). Tram 13, 17. ***Open*** *11am-4pm Mon-Fri. Apr-Nov 11am-3pm Sat.* ***Box office*** *45mins before performance.* ***Tickets*** *prices vary. No cards.* ***Map*** *p96 H8.*

This landmark church features a wide range of lunch and evening concerts, many free of charge. Cantatas are performed during services, a chance to hear the music in its proper setting. It's worth visiting to admire the stunning architecture alone.

DANCE

Schizophrenic is probably the best way to describe Dutch dance. On the one hand, it has a boutique, experimental feel, with outlandish domestic creations that are hard on both eye and ear. On the other, its two headline companies, the Dutch National Ballet (based in Amsterdam) and the Nederlands Dans Theater (based in the Hague), are the envy of the international classical and contemporary dance worlds. Foreign choreographers, such as Jirí Kylián, Krzysztof Pastor, William Forsythe, Wayne Eagling and Lightfoot León, have also seen their works flourish with regular premieres at the city's most important venues, the **Stadsschouwburg** (*see p243*) and **Nationale Opera & Ballet** (*see opposite*). Commercial fare passes through the **Amsterdam RAI Theater** (*see p242*), care of the Kirov and Bolshoi Russian ballet companies, while the less classically minded should pay a visit to the city in July, when the Leidseplein theatres host **Julidans** (www.julidans.nl), a festival for the very latest international dance styles.

Dance companies

The **Dutch National Ballet** (*see opposite* Nationale Opera & Ballet) ranks alongside the Royal Ballet and New York City Ballet as one of the largest ensembles on either side of the Atlantic, with the most comprehensive Balanchine repertoire of any European company, and, under artistic director Ted Brandsen, it attracts guest dancers and choreographers from around the world. Its domestic rival is the **Nederlands Dans Theater** (www.ndt.nl), whose progressive success was pioneered by former artistic director and world-renowned choreographer Jirí Kylián. Other

Ballet Imperial, Nationale Ballet

Oerol

An outdoor festival like no other

Terschelling is one of the five Frisian islands that sit off the north coast of Holland, 120km (75 miles) north of Amsterdam. It has a wonderful landscape of dunes, dykes and woodlands, shaped and shifted by the interaction of wind and man. A popular holiday destination for teenagers and twitchers (more than half the island is a bird sanctuary), it becomes a bohemian haven in mid June during the ten-day **Oerol** theatre festival (www.oerol.nl).

Amsterdammers leave the city in droves to attend the festival, which transforms the whole island into a stage for hundreds of acts: there might be international drama groups creating their own environments; world music gigs on the beaches; theatre expeditions through the woods; bicycle tours, or shows in boathouses or barns. And as wacky as this all sounds, Oerol (which began in 1982) reflects a long legacy in Dutch theatre where all things absurd, over-the-top and technologically cutting edge are embraced, and the dividing line between theatre, music, dance and circus is blurred. Think sculpted dreamscape happenings rich in colour, technical wizardry, alien costuming and random exploding bits, all of which have evolved organically in response to the performance's site and context.

You can also witness similar versions of this particular school of performance at festivals in Amsterdam, such as **De Parade** (*see p203*) and **Over het IJ** (*see p202*). But there's something very special about the epic natural setting of Oerol, which makes the performers, spectators and island residents all feel at home.

Installation art, Terschelling

choreographers and companies who have made a name on the world stage include **Krisztina de Châtel** (www.kdechatel.com) and the **Internationaal Danstheater** (www.intdanstheater.net). The **Internationaal Choreografisch Kunstencentrum (ICK) Amsterdam** (020 616 7240, www.ickamsterdam.com) produces high-quality contemporary dance with moody lighting and an unmatched sense of *mise-en-scène*; their performances can be seen locally at the Stadsschouwburg. Another company to look out for is **Don't Hit Mama** (020 463 4449, www.donthitmama.nl), which was formed by theatre-maker Nita Liem and writer/dramaturge Bart Deuss back in 2000. They take inspiration from hip hop and urban dance traditions, involving dancers and choreographers from the US, Africa and Asia.

Performance venues

In addition to the **Nationale Opera & Ballet** and the venues listed below, a number of other places in the city stage occasional dance events. These include **Theater Bellevue** (*see p243*), the **Frascati** (*see p243*), **De Brakke Grond** (*see p242*), **NDSM** (*see p176*) and **OT301** (www.ot301.nl). **Tolhuistuin** (*see p176*) is home to several dance companies who hold regular performances there.

Dansmakers

*Gedempt Hamerkanaal 203-205, Noord (020 689 1789 office, 020 215 9913 box office, www.dansmakers.nl). Bus 38 or IJplein ferry. **Box office** times and ticket prices vary. No cards. **Map** p166 R5.*

As well as staging work, Dansmakers is a production house that allows recent graduates to develop their choreographic talents. Established local names such as Ann van den Broek, Anouk van Dijk, Giulia Mureddu, Muhanad Rasheed and Sassan Saghar all began their careers here. Performances have been staged at least once a month, both here and elsewhere, since 1993. There are also workshops and lessons. Tickets for performances can be bought online or through the box office.

Podium Mozaïek

*Bos en Lommerweg 191, Bos en Lommer (020 580 0380, Box office 020 580 0381, www.podiummozaiek.nl). Tram 19. **Box office** tickets available online and by phone, to be collected after 11am; prices vary.*

In a district west of Westerpark, Bos en Lommer once considered itself up-and-coming enough to call itself BoLo (to the general laughter of residents). But it does have this star venue in a former church, which specialises in presenting a multicultural range of dance, music and drama. In-house café-restaurant Theatercafé Mozaïek is charming as well.

In the know
Language barrier

Don't let the language issue put you off seeing a show. The Dutch have a distinctive, visual approach to theatre-making, and these days many companies employ English surtitles for their shows. All **Dutch National Opera** productions are surtitled in both Dutch and English.

Veem House For Performance

*Van Diemenstraat 408-410, Western Docklands (020 626 0112, www.veem.house). Tram 3 or bus 48. **Box office** times and ticket prices vary.*

A homophone for 'fame', Het Veem Theater occupies the third floor of a renovated warehouse and hosts and co-produces modern dance and multimedia productions from home and abroad. Café/restaurant **Bak** (020 737 2553, www.bakrestaurant.nl), in the same building, is a local foodie haven.

THEATRE

Even the flying visitor to Amsterdam will recognise it as a city of art and artists. Less evident, however, is its active and passionate theatre scene, which tends to thrive in secret back-alley venues. As you might expect from this famously open-minded city, performing artists in Amsterdam are allowed – indeed encouraged – to experiment. Experimentation happens across all forms and genres, and the results are worth investigation, so be sure to hunt out smaller, alternative venues and off-centre cultural hubs. For the bleeding edge of cutting-edge theatre, check out the absurdist multimedia works of **Pips:lab** (www.pipslab.org).

Public subsidy of the arts has come under threat in the Netherlands, as elsewhere. Witness **DeLaMar Theater** (*see p242*), situated near Leidseplein, which programmes mostly Dutch-language theatre, cabaret and musicals. Only a few years old, it was basically a €60 million gift from the VandenEnde Foundation, a cultural fund set up by insanely wealthy international theatre producer Joop van den Ende to support cultural activities in the Netherlands; other beneficiaries include photography museum **Foam** (*see p111*) and the **Stedelijk Museum** (*see p139*).

The language gap is often surprisingly well bridged by surtitles, audience interaction and strong visuals. If language is a barrier, then the multipurpose, multimedia **De Balie** is worth checking out. Alternatively, **NDSM** (*see p176*) mounts regular site-specific pieces that transcend linguistic limitations, and the multi-venue **Westergasfabriek** (*see p132*) combines live performances with other visual and creative arts.

Performance venues

Amsterdam Marionetten Theater

*Nieuwe Jonkerstraat 8, Old Centre (020 620 8027, www.marionettentheater.nl). Metro Nieuwmarkt. **Box office** online until 2hrs before the performance, last minute only by telephone. **Tickets** €7.50-€16. **Map** p70 M8.*

International Theatre Amsterdam

Opera as you've never seen it before. Imagine hand-crafted wooden marionettes wearing silk and velvet costumes, wielded by expert puppeteers in classic works by Mozart and Offenbach, and you'll have an idea of what the AMT is all about. One of the last outposts of an old European tradition, the theatre also offers private lunches, dinners or high teas, to be taken while the puppets perform. Delightful.

Amsterdam RAI Theater

*Europaplein 22, Zuid (020 549 1212, www.raitheater.nl). Tram 4 or Metro Europaplein or RAI rail . **Box office** from 1hr before performance until 30mins after. **Tickets** €20-€90.*

A convention and exhibition centre by day, the RAI is a theatre by night and at weekends. Musicals, operas, comedy nights, ballets and spectacular shows can all be enjoyed in this sizeable hall.

De Balie

*Kleine Gartmanplantsoen 10, Grachtengordel (020 553 5100, www.debalie.nl). Tram 1, 2, 7, 11, 12, 19. **Box office** 4.30-9pm daily. **Tickets** prices vary. **Map** p96 G12.*

This multipurpose venue presents all sorts of performances and events – theatre, films, photographic shows, literature – as well as numerous lectures and debates on topics of current interest, whether social, political or cultural. Add a visit to the café and you've got food for both mind and body. After all, what's culture without a little cake?

De Brakke Grond

*Nes 45, Old Centre (020 622 9014, www.brakkegrond.nl). Tram 4, 14, 24 or Metro Rokin. **Open** times vary. **Tickets** prices vary. **Map** p70 K9.*

At the Flemish Arts Centre, you'll find visual art, literature, dance, theatre, music, performance, film and new media. If you're lucky, you might find an actor or two joining you at the bar of the adjacent café/restaurant. Tickets are also available from the box office at **Frascati**.

❤ DeLaMar Theater

*Marnixstraat 402, Grachtengordel (0900 335 2627 €1 each, www.delamar.nl). Tram 2, 5, 7, 11, 12, 19. **Box office** by phone 10am-10pm Mon-Thu; 10am-8pm Fri; 10am-6pm Sat, Sun. In person 5pm-until start of show, closed if no show. **Tickets** prices vary. **Map** p96 G12.*

The luxurious DeLaMar hosts major musicals, opera and drama. Its two auditoria can accommodate 600 and 900 people respectively, making it a key destination in the Leidseplein theatre district.

Frascati

Nes 63, Old Centre (020 626 6866, www.frascatitheater.nl). Tram 4, 14, 24 or Metro Rokin. ***Box office*** *5-7.30pm Tue-Sat, or online.* ***Tickets*** *prices vary.* ***Map*** *p70 K10.*

Frascati has been a cornerstone of progressive Dutch theatre since the 1960s and gives promising artists the chance to showcase their productions on one of its three stages. Its mission is to challenge the bounds of traditional theatre by teaming up professionally trained artists with those from the street, resulting in a variety of theatre and dance shows featuring MCs and DJs.

❤ International Theatre Amsterdam

Leidseplein 26, Grachtengordel (020 624 2311, www.ita.nl). Tram 2, 5, 7, 11, 12, 19. ***Box office*** *By phone 1-6pm Mon-Sat. In person 1pm-start of performance Mon-Sat; 2hrs before performance Sun.* ***Tickets*** *prices vary.* ***Map*** *p96 G12.*

The former Stadsschouwburg is a striking 19th-century building in the heart of the theatre, club and restaurant district. Situated centrally in Leidseplein, the building is the former home of the Nationale Opera & Ballet. Now, it's the chief subsidised venue for drama, dance and music, featuring work by local companies and touring ensembles. It was the home of Toneelgroep Amsterdam, the biggest and boldest repertory company in the Netherlands, until, in January 2018, the group officially merged with the Stadsschouwburg to form the International Theatre Amsterdam (ITA).

Under the guidance of Flemish director Ivo van Hove, the ensemble has tackled the translated works of Shakespeare, Ibsen, Chekhov and Strindberg, among numerous others, and includes many actors who are nationally recognisable thanks to their appearances on Dutch television. Productions are of a high quality and noted for their sharp aesthetic choices and frequently avant-garde values. Thursday evening performances have English surtitles.

The ITA has two stages: a traditional proscenium with a horseshoe-shaped auditorium (which means compromised sightlines if you sit too far to the left or right), and a gaping but flexible black box with raked seats. There's also a fine café, **Stravinsky**, and a well-stocked theatre and film bookshop.

De Kleine Komedie

Amstel 56-58, Grachtengordel (020 624 0534, www.dekleinekomedie.nl). Tram 4, 14. ***Box office*** *4-6pm or until start of performance Mon-Sat.* ***Tickets*** *€10-€35.* ***Map*** *p96 L11.*

Built in 1786, De Kleine Komedie is Amsterdam's oldest theatre and still one of its most important. Extremely popular with locals, it's one of the city's most colourful venues as well as the nation's pre-eminent cabaret and music stage.

Koninklijk Theater Carré

Amstel 115-125, Jodenbuurt (0900 252 5255 premium rate, www.carre.nl). Tram 1, 7, 9 or Metro Weesperplein. ***Box office*** *By phone 9am-9pm Mon-Fri; 10am-8pm Sat, Sun. In person 4-6pm or until start of performance daily.* ***Tickets*** *prices vary.* ***Map*** *p153 N13.*

Many performers dream of appearing in this glamorous space, originally a 19th-century circus building refurbished in a very grand style. The Carré hosts some of the best Dutch cabaret artists and touring operas, as well as the odd big music name. If mainstream musical theatre is your thing, this is the place to come for Dutch versions of popular blockbusters such as *Grease* and *Cats*. The annual World Christmas Circus brings in the world's classiest acts and clowns.

Theater Bellevue

Leidsekade 90, Grachtengordel (020 530 5301, www.theaterbellevue.nl). Tram 2, 5, 7, 11, 12, 19. ***Box office*** *times and ticket prices vary.* ***Map*** *p96 G12.*

Dating from 1840, this is one of the city's most active venues, premiering lunchtime dramas by emerging Dutch playwrights as well as modern dance and cabaret in the evenings – the programme is extensive and its doors are rarely closed. In spring look out for the Pop Arts Festival held here, offering up the latest and greatest in international puppetry.

Theater het Amsterdamse Bos

De Duizendmeterweg 7, Amstelveen (020 670 0250, www.bostheater.nl). ***Tickets*** *€15. No cards.*

Set in the wooded surrounds of Amsterdamse Bos, this is Amsterdam's answer to the Open-Air Theatre in London's Regent's Park or New York's Delacorte Theater in Central Park. Dreamy midsummer nights can be spent with a picnic hamper and blanket watching an updated performance of, for example, Shakespeare. If, like many spectators, you're there for the champagne rather than the play, you won't mind listening to iambic pentameter in Dutch translation. The season runs from mid July to early September. Its location in the middle of the forest means that you really need to cycle or hop in an Uber/taxi to get there.

Understand

Rokin

History

From boggy marshland to world city

Technically speaking, Amsterdam is a city that shouldn't really have been a city. The bog surrounding a rising river wasn't ever a natural support for urban structures, so the locals built a dam and grouped their houses along the River Amstel. What sprang up as a result over the next eight or so centuries is a triumph of human engineering: a series of picturesque canal rings holding back the rising waters, and hundreds of thousands of buildings standing on pilings driven into sand. Pluck a cobblestone out of the streets today and you'll still find seashells right there.

Amsterdammers are proud that theirs is a city built on the sheer drive and ingenuity of its early inhabitants. In its Golden Age in the 17th century, Amsterdam was the centre of the western world. It was the birthplace of the first multinational corporation – the Dutch East India Company – and quickly became recognised as the cultural capital of northern Europe: Rembrandt, Frans Hals and Jan Steen gave way to Vincent van Gogh, Kees van Dongen and, later, Karel Appel and Piet Mondrian. Not bad for a city built on such shaky foundations.

Inner Amstel, Jodenbuurt, c1656

Boggy beginnings

According to legend, Amsterdam was founded by two lost fishermen who vowed to build a town wherever their boat came ashore. They reached terra firma, and their seasick dog promptly anointed the chosen patch with his vomit.

The reality is much more mundane. Although the Romans occupied the southern parts of Holland, they didn't reach the north. Soggy bog was not the stuff of empires, so the legions moved on. However, recent archaeological findings during the digging of the Noord/Zuidlijn metro line suggest there were some prehistoric settlements dating from 2500 BC. But Amsterdam's site spent most of its history at least partially underwater, and the River Amstel had no fixed course until enterprising farmers from around Utrecht built dykes during the 11th century. Once the peasants had done the work, the nobility took over. During the 13th century, the most important place in the newly reclaimed area was the tiny hamlet of Oudekerk aan de Amstel. In 1204, the Lord of Amstel built a castle nearby on what is now the outskirts of Amsterdam. After the Amstel was dammed in about 1270, a village grew up on the site of what is now Dam Square, acquiring the name Aemstelledamme.

Built on beer

In 1275, the Count of Holland, Floris V, gave Amsterdam a kickstart in becoming a vibrant trade port by exempting the area's traders from tolls. Then in 1323, his successor, Floris VI, made Amsterdam one of only two toll points in the province for the import of brews. This was no trivial matter at a time when most people drank beer – drinking the local water, in fact, was practically suicidal. Hamburg had the largest brewing capacity in northern Europe, and within 50 years a third of that city's production was flowing through Amsterdam. By virtue of its position between the Atlantic and Hanseatic ports, and by pouring its beer profits into other ventures, the city broadened its trading remit to take in various essentials.

Yet Amsterdam still remained small. As late as 1425, the 'city' consisted of a few blocks of houses with kitchen gardens and two churches along the final kilometre stretch of the River Amstel and enclosed by the canals now known as Geldersekade, Singel and Kloveniersburgwal. Virtually all the buildings were wooden (such as the Houten Huis, still standing in the Begijnhof, *see p90*), and so fire was a perpetual threat; in the great fire of May 1452, three-quarters of the town was destroyed. One of the few examples of medieval architecture still standing is the Munttoren (Mint Tower) at Muntplein. Structures built after the fire were instead faced with stone and roofed with tile or slate. These new developments coincided with a rush of urban expansion, as – most notably – new foreign commerce led to improvements in shipbuilding.

During the 16th century, the city started to emerge as one of the world's major trading powers

Radicalism and reaction

During the 16th century, Amsterdam's population increased from 10,000 (low even by medieval standards) to 50,000 by 1600. The city expanded, although people coming to the city found poverty, disease and squalor in the workers' quarters. Local merchants weren't complaining, however, as the city started to emerge as one of the world's major trading powers.

Amsterdam may have been almost entirely autonomous as a chartered city, but on paper it was still under the thumb of absentee rulers. Through the intricate marriage bureau and shallow genetic pool known as the European aristocracy, the Low Countries (the Netherlands and Belgium) had passed into the hands of the Catholic Austro-Spanish House of Habsburg. The Habsburgs were the mightiest monarchs in Europe, and Amsterdam was a comparative backwater among their European possessions; nonetheless, events soon brought the city to prominence among its near neighbours.

Amsterdam's new status as a trade centre attracted all kinds of radical religious ideas that were flourishing across northern Europe, encouraged by Martin Luther's condemnation of Catholicism in 1517. When Anabaptists first arrived from Germany in about 1530, the Catholic city fathers tolerated them. But when they started to run around naked and even seized the City Hall in 1534 during an attempt to establish a 'New Jerusalem' upon the River Amstel, the leaders were arrested, forced to dress, and then executed, signalling an unparalleled period of religious repression: 'heretics' were burned at the stake on the Dam.

After the Anabaptists were culled, Calvinist preachers arrived from Geneva, where the movement had started, and via France. They soon gained followers and, in 1566, the religious discontent erupted into what became known as the Iconoclastic Fury. Churches and monasteries were sacked and stripped of ornamentation, and Philip II of Spain sent an army to suppress the heresy.

The emergence of Orange

The Eighty Years' War (1568-1648) between the Habsburgs and the Dutch is often seen as a struggle for religious freedom, but there was more to it than that. The Dutch were, after all, seeking political autonomy from an absentee king who represented a continual drain on their coffers. By the last quarter of the 16th century, Philip II of Spain was fighting wars against England and France, in the east against the Ottoman Turks, and in the New World for control of his colonies. The last thing he needed was a revolt in the Low Countries.

Amsterdam toed the Catholic line during the revolt, supporting Philip II until it became clear he was losing. Only in 1578 did the city patricians side with the Calvinist rebels, led by the first William of Orange. The city and William then combined to expel the Catholics and dismantle their institutions in what came to be called the Alteration.

A year later, the Protestant states of the Low Countries united in opposition to Philip when the first modern-day European republic was born at the Union of Utrecht. The Republic of Seven United Provinces was made up of Friesland, Gelderland, Groningen, Overijssel, Utrecht, Zeeland and Holland. Though initially lauded as a forerunner of the modern Netherlands, it wasn't the unitary state that William of Orange wanted, but rather a loose federation with an impotent States General assembly.

Each of the seven provinces appointed a *stadhouder* (or viceroy), who commanded the Republic's armed forces and had the right to appoint some of the cities' regents or governors. Each *stadhouder* sent delegates to the assembly, held at the Binnenhof in the Hague. While fitted with clauses set to hinder Catholicism from ever suppressing the Reformed religion again, the Union of Utrecht also enshrined freedom of conscience and religion (at least until the Republic's demise in 1795), thus providing the blueprint that made Amsterdam a safe haven for future political and religious refugees.

The obvious choice for Holland's *stadhouder* after the union was William of Orange. After his popular tenure, it became a tradition to elect an Orange as *stadhouder*. By 1641, the family had become sufficiently powerful for William II to marry a British princess, Mary Stuart. It was their son, William III, who set sail in 1688 to accept the throne of England in the so-called Glorious Revolution.

A social conscience with claws

From its beginnings, Amsterdam had been governed by four burgomasters (mayors) and a council representing citizens' interests. By 1500, though, city government had become an incestuous business: the city council's 36 members were appointed for life, 'electing' the mayors from their own ranks. Selective intermarriage meant that the city was, in effect, governed by a handful of families.

When Amsterdam joined the rebels in 1578, the only change in civic administration was that the Catholic elite were replaced by a Calvinist faction of equally wealthy families. The city, now with a population of 225,000, remained the third city of Europe, after London and Paris. Social welfare, though, was transformed under the Calvinists, and incorporated into government. The Regents, as the Calvinist elite became known, took over the convents and monasteries, starting charitable organisations such as orphanages. But they would not tolerate any kind of excess: drunkenness and immorality, like crime, were punishable offences.

In the two centuries before the Eighty Years' War, Amsterdam had developed its own powerful maritime force. Even so, it remained overshadowed by Antwerp until 1589, when that city fell to the Spaniards. In Belgium, the Habsburg Spanish had adopted siege tactics, leaving Amsterdam unaffected by the hostilities and free to benefit from the blockades suffered by rival ports. Thousands of refugees fled north, among them some of Antwerp's most prosperous merchants, who were mostly Protestant and Jewish (specifically Sephardic Jews who had earlier fled their original homes in Spain and Portugal to escape the Inquisition). The refugees brought the skills, the gold and, most famously, the diamond industry that would soon help make the city one of the greatest trading centres in the world.

The Golden Age

European history seems to be littered with golden ages – but in Amsterdam's case, the first six decades of the 17th century genuinely deserve the label. It is truly remarkable that such a small and isolated

The City of Water

Amsterdam has always gone with the flow

Farmers, beer and water. An unlikely recipe for success, but they made Amsterdam what it is today. Not that the city's rise was universally greeted with delight. In 1652, during one of those periodic downturns in Anglo-Dutch relations, English poet Owen Felltham described the Low Countries as 'the buttock of the world, full of veins and blood but no bones'. But it's that boggy basis that is the foundation of Amsterdam's success and go-with-the-flow reputation.

Originating as a village that subsisted on a bit of fishing and some small-town frolicking, Amsterdam fostered some of the first cheerleaders of democracy: stubborn farmers, who set themselves to build dykes to keep the sea and the mighty Amstel river at bay. The teamwork needed for such a massive task formed the basis for today's famed but seemingly fading 'polder model', where all conflicts are resolved at endless meetings fuelled by coffee and the thirst for consensus. Of course, since flexibility and compromise also made good business sense, the approach turned out to be highly profitable.

Amsterdam was only properly set up as a centre of pragmatic trade and lusty sin in the 14th century, when it was made exempt from the tax on beer. This opened the floodgates to a river of the stuff (flowing from Hamburg) and plenty of beer-drinking new settlers. After beer profits, other profits followed – from sea travels to both the East and the West – and before long Amsterdam was the richest and most powerful port on the planet. The resulting Golden Age saw the construction of the image-defining Grachtengordel 'canal belt', which, together with the more ancient canals of the Old Centre, formed a full circulatory system – and, er, sewage system – in which goods, and people, from all over the world could flow in and out.

As well as demonstrating a flair for building canals, dykes, windmills and ships, the Dutch came up with a whole bevy of other water-worthy inventions during the Golden Age. Inventor Cornelis Drebbel (1572-1634) designed the first prototype submarine (basically, a rowing boat fitted with rawhide and tubes), and local genius Jan van der Heyden (1637-1712) invented the first pump-action fire hose. More curious were the 'tobacco-smoke-enema-applicators', developed in an attempt to reanimate the drowning victims who were regularly pulled from the canals. This ancient technique – also applied with reversed 30-centimetre Gouda pipes – was standard practice and part of the canalside scenery in Amsterdam until the 1850s, when the less dramatic but more effective mouth-to-mouth technique gained prominence. Talk about progress.

Development at the end of the 19th century allowed the building of the Nordzee Kanaal (North Sea Channel), thus giving Amsterdam a more direct route to the open sea and triggering a second Golden Age of sorts. The 1990s can be seen in a similar light, when the Eastern Docklands began transforming into a showcase for modern architecture that sought to blend both private and public spaces with its watery surrounds. The artificial islands of IJburg further east continue this trend, as do ambitious plans to build vast windmill parks in the North Sea, construct new public marinas along the IJ and open up more waterways for recreational purposes.

Water plays a fundamental role in the recreational lives of many folk – and we're not just talking about boys peeing willy-nilly into the canals. Admittedly, 'eel-pulling' – a folk game popular in the Jordaan, which the authorities tried to quash, resulting in the Eel Riot of 1886 and 26 fatalities – is no longer practised as a canal sport. But boating remains very popular (sadly, its winter counterpart, ice-skating, has declined greatly due to climate change).

The opening of the city's first bona fide beach in IJburg (*see p170*) inspired a slew of other urban beaches: Strand West (www.strand-west.nl), Strand Zuid (www.strand-zuid.nl) beside the RAI convention centre, and Pllek (*see p175*).

And while the concept of making Prinsengracht swimmable remains a ploy by fringe political parties to get headline space, a more realistic plan – to redig canals that had been concreted over to cope with increasing motor traffic, such as Elandsgracht and Lindengracht – was all set to go ahead until it was quashed by residents, who decided that since the city is already one-quarter water they didn't need any more of the stuff.

Regardless, Amsterdam remains aware that water is one of its strongest tourist magnets. Compared to the original Venice (aka the 'sewer of the south'), the waters of the 'Venice of the north' are essentially stench-free. In fact, here you can meditate on the wiggly reflections in the canals from up close without fear of succumbing to fumes. Not merely trippy, they act as a constant reminder that Amsterdam is a happily twisted and distorted town – and also remarkably user-friendly; where you can throw your cares overboard and go with the flow.

Oudeschans

Herengracht

The Singel, Amsterdam, looking towards the Mint (Eduard Alexander Hilverdink, 1884-1886)

IJburg

city could come to dominate world trade and set up major colonies, resulting in a local population explosion and a frenzy of urban expansion. Its girdle of canals was one of the great engineering feats of the age. This all happened while the country was at war with Spain and presided over not by kings, but businessmen.

The Dutch East India Company was the world's first transnational corporation

The Dutch East India Company, which was known locally as the VOC (Verenigde Oost Indische Compagnie), was the world's first transnational corporation. Created by the States General charter in 1602 to finance the wildly expensive and fearsomely dangerous voyages to the East, the power of the VOC was far-reaching: it had the capacity to found colonies, establish its own army, declare war and sign treaties. With 1,450 ships, the VOC made over 4,700 highly profitable journeys.

While the VOC concentrated on the spice trade, a new company received its charter from the Dutch Republic in 1621. The Dutch West India Company (West Indische Compagnie), while not as successful as its sister, dominated trade with Spanish and Portuguese territories in Africa and America, and in 1623 began to colonise Manhattan Island. Although the colony flourished at first, New Amsterdam didn't last long. After the Duke of York's invasion in 1664, the peace treaty between England and the Netherlands determined that New Amsterdam would change its name to New York and come under British control. The Dutch got Suriname in return.

Meanwhile, Amsterdam's port had become the major European centre for distribution and trade. Grain from Russia, Poland and Prussia, salt and wine from France, cloth from Leiden and tiles from Delft all passed through the port. Whales were hunted by Amsterdam's fleets, generating a thriving soap trade, and sugar and spices from Dutch colonies were distributed throughout Scandinavia and the north of Europe. All this activity was financed by the Bank of Amsterdam, which became the hub of the single most powerful money vault in all Europe, its notes exchangeable throughout the trading world.

Present and corrected

From 1600 to 1650, the city's population ballooned four-fold, and it was obliged to expand once again. Construction on the most elegant of the major canals circling the city centre, Herengracht (Lords' Canal), began in 1613; this was where many of the ruling assembly had their homes. So that there would be no misunderstanding about status, Herengracht was followed further out by Keizersgracht (Emperors' Canal) and Prinsengracht (Princes' Canal). Immigrants were housed in the Jordaan.

For all its wealth, famine hit Amsterdam regularly in the 17th century. Guilds had benevolent funds for their members in times of need, but social welfare was primarily in the hands of the ruling merchant class. Amsterdam's elite was noted for its philanthropy, but only the 'deserving poor' were eligible for assistance. Those seen as undeserving were sent to houses of correction. The initial philosophy behind these had been idealistic: hard work would produce useful citizens. Soon, however, the institutions became little more than prisons for those condemned to work there.

Religious freedom wasn't what it might have been, either. As a result of the Alteration of 1578, open Catholic worship was banned in the city during the 17th century, and Catholics had to worship in secret. Some started attic churches, which are exactly what their name suggests; of those set up during the 1600s, only Ons' Lieve Heer op Solder (Our Lord in the Attic, *see p79*) survives in its entirety.

The harder they fall

Though Amsterdam remained one of the single wealthiest cities in Europe until the early 19th century, its dominant trading position was lost to England and France after 1660. The United Provinces then spent a couple of centuries bickering about trade and politics with Britain and the other main powers. Wars were frequent: major sea conflicts included battles against the Swedes and no fewer than four Anglo-Dutch wars, in which the Dutch came off worse.

It wasn't that they didn't win any battles; more that they ran out of men and money. The naval officers who led the wars against Britain are Dutch heroes, and the Nieuwe Kerk has monuments to admirals Van Kinsbergen (1735-1819), Bentinck (1745-1831) and, most celebrated of all, Michiel de Ruyter (1607-76).

In the 18th century, the Dutch Republic began to lag behind the major European powers. Amsterdam was nudged out of the shipbuilding market by England, and its lucrative textile industry was lost to other

A Senior Merchant of the Dutch East India Company (Aelbert Cuyp, c1640-1660)

provinces. However, the city managed to exploit its position as the financial centre of the world until the final, devastating Anglo-Dutch War (1780-84). The British hammered the Dutch merchant and naval fleets with unremitting aggression, crippling profitable trade with their Far Eastern colonies.

The Napoleonic Netherlands

During the 1780s, a republican movement known as the Patriots managed to shake off the influence of the *stadhouders* in many smaller towns. In 1787, though, they were foiled in Amsterdam by the intervention of the Prince of Orange and his brother-in-law, Frederick William II, King of Prussia. Hundreds of patriots then fled to exile in France, only to return in 1795, backed by a French army of 'advisers'. With massive support from Amsterdam, they thus celebrated the new Batavian Republic.

It sounded too good to be true, and it was. According to one contemporary, 'the French moved over the land like locusts'. Over 100 million guilders (about €50 million today) was extracted from the Dutch, and the French also sent an army, 25,000 of whom had to be fed, equipped and housed by their Dutch 'hosts'. Republican ideals seemed hollow when Napoleon installed his brother, Louis, as King of the Netherlands in 1806, and the symbol of Amsterdam's mercantile ascendancy and civic pride, the City Hall of the Dam, was requisitioned as the royal palace. However, after Louis had allowed Dutch smugglers to break Napoleon's blockade of Britain, he was forced to abdicate in 1810 and the Low Countries were absorbed into the French Empire.

French rule wasn't an unmitigated disaster for the Dutch. The foundations of the modern state were laid in the Napoleonic period, and a civil code introduced – not to mention a broadening of culinary possibilities. However, trade with Britain ceased, and the cost of Napoleon's wars prompted the Dutch to join the revolt against France. After Napoleon's defeat, Amsterdam became the capital of a constitutional monarchy, including what is now Belgium; William VI of Orange was crowned King William I in 1815. But while the Oranges still reigned across the north, the United Kingdom of the Netherlands, as it then existed, lasted only until 1830.

A return to form

When the French were finally defeated and left Dutch soil in 1813, Amsterdam emerged as the capital of the new kingdom of the Netherlands but very little else. With its coffers depleted and colonies occupied by the British, it faced a hard fight for recovery.

The fight was made tougher by two huge obstacles. For a start, Dutch colonial assets had been reduced to present-day Indonesia, Suriname and the odd Caribbean island. Just as important, though, was the fact that the Dutch were slow to join the Industrial Revolution. The Netherlands had few natural resources to exploit, and clung to sail power while the rest of Europe embraced steam. Add to this the fact that Amsterdam's opening to the sea, the Zuider Zee, was too shallow for new steamships, and it's easy to see why the Dutch struggled.

Still, by the late 19th century Amsterdam had begun to modernise production of the luxury goods for which it would become internationally famous: beer, chocolates, cigars and diamonds. The Noordzee Kanaal (North Sea Canal) was opened in 1876, while the city got a major rail link in 1889. Amsterdam consolidated its position at the forefront of Europe with the building of a number of landmarks, including Cuypers' Rijksmuseum (1885), the Stadsschouwburg (1894), the Stedelijk Museum (1895) and the Tropeninstituut (1926). The city's international standing soared – to the point where, in 1928, it hosted the Olympics.

Misery of the masses

Amsterdam's population had stagnated at 250,000 for two centuries after the Golden Age, but between 1850 and 1900 it more than doubled. Extra labour was needed to fuel the revitalised economy, but the problem was how to house the new workers.

Today, the old inner-city quarters are desirable addresses, but they used to house Amsterdam's poor. The picturesque Jordaan, where regular riots broke out at the turn of the 20th century, was occupied by the lowest-paid workers. Its canals were used as cesspits, and the mortality rate was high. Around the centre, new developments – De Pijp, Dapper and Staatslieden – were built: they weren't luxurious, but they enjoyed simple lavatory facilities, while the Amsterdam School of architecture (*see p266*), inspired by socialist beliefs, designed now-classic housing for the poor. Wealthier citizens, meanwhile, lived in elegant homes near Vondelpark and further south.

The city didn't fare badly during the first two decades of the 20th century, but Dutch neutrality in World War I brought problems to parts of the population. While the elite lined their pockets selling arms, the poor faced crippling food shortages and unemployment, and riots broke out in 1917 and 1934. Many Dutch workers moved to Germany, where National Socialism was creating jobs. The city was just emerging from the Depression when the Nazis invaded in May 1940.

Occupation

On 10 May 1940, German bombers mounted a surprise early-morning attack on Dutch airfields and barracks. The government and people had hoped that the Netherlands could remain neutral, as in World War I, so armed forces were unprepared. Queen Wilhelmina fled to London to form a government in exile, leaving Supreme Commander Winkelman in charge. After Rotterdam was destroyed by bombing and the Germans threatened other cities with the same treatment, Winkelman surrendered on 14 May.

During the war, Hitler appointed Austrian Nazi Arthur Seyss-Inquart as *rijkskommissaris* (state commissioner) of the Netherlands, and asked him to tie the Dutch economy to the German one and help to Nazify Dutch society. Though it gained less than five per cent of the votes in the 1939 elections, the National Socialist Movement (NSB) was the only Dutch party not prohibited during the occupation. Its doctrine resembled German Nazism, but the NSB wanted to maintain Dutch autonomy under the direction of Germany.

During the first years of the war, the Nazis let most people live relatively unmolested. Rationing, though, made the Dutch vulnerable to the black market, while cinemas and theatres eventually closed because of curfews and censorship. Later, the Nazis adopted more aggressive measures: Dutch men were forced to work in German industry, and economic exploitation assumed appalling forms. In April 1943, all Dutch soldiers were ordered to give themselves up as prisoners of war. Within an atmosphere of deep shock and outrage, strikes broke out, but they were violently suppressed.

As Nazi policies became more virulent, people were confronted with the difficult choice of whether to obey German measures or to resist. There were several patterns of collaboration: some people joined the NSB, while others intimidated Jews, got involved in economic collaboration or betrayed people in hiding. The most shocking institutional collaboration involved Dutch police, who dragged Jews out of their houses for deportation, and Dutch Railways, which was paid for transporting Jews to their deaths.

Others resisted. The Resistance was made up chiefly of Communists and, to a lesser extent, Calvinists. Anti-Nazi activities took various forms, including the production and distribution of illegal newspapers, which kept the population informed and urged them to resist the Nazi dictators. Some members of the Resistance spied for the Allies, while some fought an armed struggle against the Germans through assassination and sabotage. There were those who falsified identity cards and food vouchers, while others helped Jews into hiding. By 1945, more than 300,000 people had gone underground in the Netherlands.

The Hunger Winter

In 1944, the Netherlands plunged into the *Hongerwinter* – the Hunger Winter. Supplies of coal vanished after the liberation of the south, and a railway strike, called by the Dutch government in exile in order to hasten German defeat, was disastrous for the supply of food. In retaliation, the Germans damaged Schiphol Airport and the harbours of Rotterdam and Amsterdam, foiling any attempts to bring in supplies, and grabbed everything they could. Walking became the only means of transport, domestic refuse was no longer collected, sewers overflowed and the population fell to disease.

To survive, people stole fuel: more than 20,000 trees were cut down and 4,600 buildings demolished. Floors, staircases, joists and rafters were plundered, causing the collapse of many houses, particularly those left by deported Jews. By the end of the winter, 20,000 people had died of starvation and disease, and much of the city was badly damaged. But hope was around the corner. The Allies liberated the south of the Netherlands on 5 September 1944, Dolle Dinsdag (Mad Tuesday), and complete liberation came on 5 May 1945, when it became apparent that the Netherlands was one of the worst affected countries in western Europe.

Liberation Party, 1945

Amsterdam endured World War II without being flattened by bombs, but nonetheless its buildings, infrastructure, inhabitants and morale were reduced to a terrible state by the occupying Nazi forces. The Holocaust also left an indelible scar on a city whose population in 1940 was ten per cent Jewish. Only 5,000 Jews, out of a pre-war Jewish population of 80,000, remained. When the war was over, 450,000 people were arrested for collaboration, although most were quickly released; mitigating circumstances – NSB members who helped the Resistance, for example – made judgements complicated. Of 14,500 sentenced, only 39 were executed.

The Holocaust

'I see how the world is slowly becoming a desert, I hear more and more clearly the approaching thunder that will kill us,' wrote Anne Frank in her diary on 15 July 1944. Though her words obviously applied to the Jews, they were relevant to all those who were persecuted during the war. Granted, anti-Semitism in Holland had not been as virulent as in Germany, France or Austria. But even so, most – though not all – of the Dutch population ignored the persecution, and there's still a sense of national guilt.

The Holocaust happened in three stages. First came measures to enforce the isolation of the Jews: the ritual slaughter of animals was prohibited, Jewish government employees were dismissed, Jews were banned from public places and, eventually, all Jews were forced to wear a yellow Star of David. (Some non-Jews wore the badge as a mark of solidarity.) Concentration was the second stage. From early 1942, all Dutch Jews were obliged to move to three areas in Amsterdam, isolated by signs, drawbridges and barbed wire. The final stage was deportation. Between July 1942 and September 1943, most of the 140,000 Dutch Jews were deported via the detention and transit camp of Kamp Westerbork. Public outrage at deportations was foreshadowed by the one and only protest, organised by dockworkers, against the anti-Semitic terror: the February Strike of 1941.

The Nazis wanted to eliminate gypsies too: more than 200,000 European gypsies, including many Dutch, were exterminated. Homosexuals were also threatened with extermination, but their persecution was less systematic: public morality acts prohibited homosexual behaviour, and gay pressure groups ceased their activities. Amsterdam has the world's first memorial to persecuted gays, the Homomonument (*see p100*), which incorporates pink triangles, turning the Nazi badge of persecution into a symbol of pride.

The dust settles

Despite deep poverty and drastic shortages of food, fuel and building materials, the Dutch tackled the task of post-war recovery with a sense of optimism. Some Dutch flirted briefly with Communism after the war, but in 1948, a compromise was agreed between the Catholic KVP and newly created Labour party PvdA, and the two proceeded to govern in successive coalitions until 1958. Led by Prime Minister Willem Drees, the government resuscitated social programmes and laid the basis for a welfare state. The Dutch now reverted to the virtues of a conservative society: decency, hard work and thrift.

The country's first priority was economic recovery. The city council concentrated on reviving the two motors of its economy: Schiphol Airport and the Port of Amsterdam, the latter boosted by the opening of the Amsterdam-Rhine Canal in 1952. Joining Belgium and Luxembourg in the Benelux also brought the country trade benefits, and the Netherlands was the first European nation to repay its Marshall Plan loans. The authorities dusted off their pre-war development plans and embarked on rapid urban expansion. But as people moved into the new suburbs, businesses flowed into the centre, making congestion worse on the cramped roads.

After the war, the Dutch colonies of New Guinea and Indonesia were liberated from the Japanese and pushed for independence. Immigrants to the Netherlands included colonial natives, and Turkish and Moroccan 'guest workers'.

The Provos

The 1960s proved to be one of the most colourful decades in Amsterdam's history. Popular movements very similar to those in other west European cities were formed, but because the Dutch have a habit of keeping things in proportion, popular demonstrations took a playful form.

Discontent gained focus in 1964, when a group of political pranksters called the Provos kickstarted a new radical subculture. Founded by anarchist philosophy student Roel van Duyn and 'anti-smoke magician' Robert Jasper Grootveld, the Provos – their name inspired by their game plan: to provoke – numbered only about two dozen, but were enormously influential. Their style influenced the major anti-Vietnam demos in the US and the Situationist antics in 1969 Paris, and set the tone for Amsterdam's love of liberal politics and absurdist theatre. Their finest hour came in March 1966, when protests about Princess Beatrix's

Immigration Matters

The Netherlands is not the haven for minorities it once was

Historically, the Netherlands has been a beacon of tolerance for minorities and refugees fleeing persecution in their own countries, from Spanish and Portuguese Jews in the 16th century and the Huguenots in the 18th century to the Belgians during World War I and Hungarians after the 1956 revolution.

Freedom of religion was accepted at an early stage in Dutch history and laid down in the constitution of 1848, and there was never much tension between the Dutch and the communities of newcomers, which were always relatively small. The situation changed, however, in the second half of the 20th century. After the Netherlands was forced to give up its colonies in the Dutch East Indies, 300,000 Indonesians came to the former motherland, followed, in the 1960s, by tens of thousands of labour migrants from Turkey and Morocco. The next wave of 300,000 foreigners came in the 1970s when another colony, Suriname, in South America, gained independence. Dutch passport-holders from the Netherlands Antilles and refugees from all over the world have also contributed to a serious shake-up of the demographic landscape, which had been pale white for centuries.

Initially, nothing much happened. The predominantly Christian Surinamese and Indonesians spoke Dutch, something the Muslim migrant workers from the Mediterranean countries did not. Not much attention was given to their language skills, because the idea was they would go home after a couple of years. But they didn't. They stayed, brought their families, resulting in an ever-growing number of non-Western immigrants and their offspring, badly educated and with low incomes, often on social welfare, living in dilapidated apartment buildings in areas such as the Bijlmer (recently rebranded as Zuidoost), where crime rates were high and the future looked bleak. Society chose to ignore the problem until Pim Fortuyn – a genuine populist politician, who made no secret of his anti-Islam feelings – made his voice heard. His assassination in 2002 shocked the nation. It wasn't a Muslim extremist who pulled the trigger, though, but a left-wing one.

However, the next bullet did come from an Islamic extremist. In November 2004, Mohammed Bouyeri murdered provocative columnist and filmmaker Theo van Gogh, a big supporter of Fortuyn. For a while, everything seemed to change. Fortuyn's political allies even made it to the coalition government before the movement crumbled, through internal conflicts and empty-headedness. The bleached blond and virulently anti-Islam Geert Wilders and his Freedom Party (PVV) stepped in to fill the void. In 2010, his party shot from nine to 24 seats, which gave him leverage to push through tougher immigration laws. Wilders was accused of encouraging hatred towards Muslims in 2011 but was acquitted of the incitement and continued to gain popularity. At a 2014 rally of his PVV party Wilders infamously encouraged his supporters to chant for fewer Moroccans in the Netherlands. In 2016, Wilders was tried for and convicted of racial discrimination and inciting hatred, although the judge refused to issue a fine or any other form of sanction. Wilders refused to attend proceedings, branding them a 'political trial' and a 'travesty'.

In the 2017 general election, the PVV gained five seats, making them the second biggest party in Parliament. Despite disappointing results in subsequent municipal and European elections, the PVV is likely to remain a significant player on the Dutch political scene for the foreseeable future, as a voice for anti-Muslim, anti-immigrant and anti-EU sentiments. It remains to be seen how more mainstream political parties will respond.

Geert Wilders

Provos demonstration, 17 July 1966

controversial wedding to the German Claus van Amsberg turned nasty after the Provos let off a smoke bomb on the carriage route, and a riot ensued. Some Provos, such as Van Duyn, went on to fight the system from within: five won City seats under the surreal banner of the Kabouter (a mythical race of forest-dwelling dwarves) in 1970.

Squatters

Perhaps the single most significant catalyst for discontent in the 1970s – which exploded into civil conflict by the 1980s – was the issue of housing. Amsterdam's small size and historic centre had always been a nightmare for its urban planners. The city's population increased in the 1960s, reaching its peak (nearly 870,000) by 1964. Swelling the numbers further were immigrants from the Netherlands' last major colony, Suriname, many of whom were dumped in Bijlmermeer. The district degenerated into a ghetto and, when a Boeing 747 crashed there in October 1992, authorities initially found it difficult to ascertain the number of fatalities, many of whom were unregistered. (The official death toll is now set at 39.)

The metro link to Bijlmermeer is in itself a reminder of some of Amsterdam's most violent protests. Passionate opposition erupted against the proposed clearance in February 1975 of the Jewish quarter of Nieuwmarkt. Civil unrest culminated in 'Blue Monday' (24 March 1975) when police sparked clashes with residents and supporters. Police fired tear gas into the homes of those who refused to move out, and battered down doors.

Speculators who left property empty caused acute resentment, which soon turned into direct action: vacant buildings were occupied illegally by squatters. In March 1980, police turned against them for the first time and used tanks to evict squatters from a former office building in Vondelstraat. Riots ensued, but the squatters were victorious. In 1982, as the squatting movement reached its peak, clashes with police escalated: a state of emergency was called after one eviction battle. Soon, though, the city – led by new mayor Ed van Thijn – had gained the upper hand over the movement, and one of the last of the big squats, Wyers, fell amid tear gas in February 1984 to make way for a Holiday Inn. Squatters were no longer a force to be reckoned with, though their ideas of small-scale regeneration have since been absorbed into official planning.

The shape of things to come

Born and bred in Amsterdam, Ed van Thijn embodied a new strand in Dutch politics. Though a socialist, he took tough action against 'unsavoury elements' – petty criminals, squatters, dealers in hard drugs – and upgraded facilities to attract new businesses and tourists. A new national political era also emerged: the welfare system and government subsidies were trimmed to ease the country's large budget deficit, and more business-like policies were introduced to try and revitalise the economy.

The price of Amsterdam's subsequent affluence was a swing towards a polished commercialism as more flashy cafés, galleries and restaurants appeared where the alternative scene once thrived, and a mood of calm settled on the city. But Amsterdam's standing as a pioneer for the creative and liberal still remains. Just ask its resident *nachtburgemeester* – the night mayor – who was appointed in 2014 to nurture the city's thriving nightlife and capitalise on its ever-expanding economy.

Another example of Dutch compromise is the existence of 'artistic breeding places': properties and building spaces handed over to artists and other creative types to do with what they will for a couple of years at a time. It seems the city's reputation as a hotbed for edgy creativity will continue to be nurtured and maintained, at least in the short term, and that Amsterdam is not ready to relinquish its rebel status just yet.

► *For more on contemporary politics and culture, see p28 Amsterdam Today.*

Key Events

All the Dutch dates that matter

Early history

1204 Gijsbrecht van Amstel builds a castle in the area that will eventually become the city of Amsterdam.
1270 Amstel dammed at Dam Square.
1300 Amsterdam is granted city rights by the Bishop of Utrecht.
1306 Work begins on the Oude Kerk.
1313 The Bishop of Utrecht grants Aemstelledamme full municipal rights and leaves it to William III of Holland.
1421 The St Elizabeth's Day Flood; Amsterdam's first great fire.

War and reformation

1534 Anabaptists try to seize City Hall but fail. A sustained and brutal period of anti-Protestant repression begins.
1565 William the Silent organises a Protestant revolt against Spanish rule.
1566 Iconoclastic Fury unleashed. Protestant worship is made legal.
1568 Eighty Years' War with Spain begins.
1577 Prince of Orange annexes city.
1578 Catholic Burgomasters replaced by Protestants in the Alteration.
1579 The Union of Utrecht is signed, allowing freedom of religious belief.

The Golden Age

1602 The Dutch East India Company (VOC) is founded.
1606 Rembrandt van Rijn is born.
1611 The Zuiderkerk is completed.
1613 Work starts on the Grachtengordel.
1623 The Dutch West India Company colonises Manhattan Island.
1625 Peter Stuyvesant founds New Amsterdam.
1642 Rembrandt finishes *The Night Watch*.
1648 The Treaty of Munster is signed, ending the Eighty Years' War with Spain.
1654 England begins a bloody, drawn-out war against the United Provinces.
1667 England and the Netherlands sign the Peace of Breda.

Decline and fall

1672 England and the Netherlands go to war; Louis XIV of France invades.
1675 The Portuguese Synagogue is built.
1685 French Protestants take refuge after revocation of the Edict of Nantes.
1689 William of Orange becomes King William III of England.
1787 Frederick William II, King of Prussia, occupies Amsterdam.
1795 French revolutionaries set up the Batavian Republic.
1813 Unification of the Netherlands.
1815 Amsterdam becomes the capital.

Between the occupations

1848 City's ramparts are pulled down.
1876 Noordzee Kanaal links Amsterdam with the North Sea.
1885 The Rijksmuseum is completed.
1889 Centraal Station opens.
1922 Women are granted the vote.
1928 Olympic Games are held in Amsterdam.

World War II

1940 German troops invade.
1941 The February Strike takes place, in protest against the deportation of Jews.
1944-45 20,000 people die during the Hunger Winter.
1945 Canadian soldiers liberate Amsterdam from the Nazis.
1947 Anne Frank's diary is published.

The post-war era

1966 The wedding of Princess Beatrix and Prince Claus ends in riots.
1968 The IJ Tunnel opens.
1976 Cannabis is decriminalised.
1977 First metro line is opened.
1980 Queen Beatrix's coronation.
1997 The Euro approved as European currency in the Treaty of Amsterdam.
1999 Prostitution is made legal after years of decriminalisation.
2002 Dutch politician Pim Fortuyn is murdered by a left-wing extremist.
2004 Filmmaker Theo van Gogh is murdered by an Islamic fundamentalist.
2007 'Project 1012' clean-up begins.
2009 Bystanders killed in assassination attempt on the Dutch royal family.
2013 Queen Beatrix abdicates, replaced by King Willem-Alexander.
2017 Centre right VVD wins the most seats in the Dutch general election.
2018 New Amsterdam North-South metro line 52 finally opens after years of delays.

Architecture

A 17th-century skyline looks over a post-industrial playground

Amsterdam has been marked by both urban upheaval and prosperous redevelopment during the past decades. There have been improvements in and around Centraal Station, and extensive modernisation has taken place – including a new metro station – along Rokin in the Old Centre. Contemporary and sustainable housing now populates the man-made IJburg but the real structural growth is impossible to miss in the city's waterfront, eastern and northern regions. The former industrial docklands of Amsterdam Noord have been transformed by futuristic structures such as the EYE Film Institute and A'DAM Toren, while Oost's *Oostelijke Eilanden en Kadijken* continues its metamorphosis into a metropolitan residential and work area with Czaar Peterstraat as its beating heart.

Despite the ongoing surge in development, the 17th-century central canal district remains largely unchanged, thanks in part to its designation as a UNESCO World Heritage Site in 2010. General maintenance is required to preserve historical buildings, such as the Zuiderkerk and Oude Kerk, but development is otherwise strictly controlled. Meanwhile, the city on water continues to craft sustainable expansion solutions to cater for a growing population and ever-flowing tide of tourists.

Zuiderkerk *p77*

Damrak, Old Centre

The view from afar

'The colours are strong and sad, the forms symmetric, the façades kept new,' wrote Eugène Fromentin, the noted 19th-century art critic, of Amsterdam. 'We feel that it belongs to a people eager to take possession of the conquered mud.'

The treacherous, blubbery soil on which the merchants' town of Amsterdam is built meant that most attempts at monumental display were destined soon to return to their original element. It's this unforgiving land, combined with the Protestant restraint that characterised the city's early developments and the fact that there were no royals out to project enlarged egos, that have ensured Amsterdam's architectural highlights are often practical places such as warehouses, homes, the stock exchange and former city hall, rather than overblown palaces and castles.

Amsterdam's architectural epochs have followed the pulse of the city's prosperity. The highly decorative exteriors of wealthy 17th- and 18th-century merchant houses still line canals. A splurge of public spending in the affluent 1880s gave the city two of its most notable landmarks – **Centraal Station** and the **Rijksmuseum** (*see p140*). Rather conversely, social housing projects in the early 20th century stimulated the innovative work of the **Amsterdam School**, while Amsterdam's late 1980s resurgence as a financial centre and transport hub led to an economic upturn and thickets of ambitious modern architecture on the outskirts of town and along the Eastern Docklands.

Prime viewing time for Amsterdam's architecture is late on a summer's afternoon, when the sun gently picks out the varying colours and patterns of the brickwork. Then, as twilight falls, the canal houses – most of them more window than wall – light up like strings of lanterns, and you get a glimpse of the beautifully preserved, frequently opulent interiors that lie hidden behind the frontage.

Underneath the paving stones

Amsterdam is built on reclaimed marshland, with a thick, soft layer of clay and peat beneath the topsoil. About 12 metres (39 feet) down is a hard band of sand, deposited 10,000 years ago during the Little Ice Age, and below that, after about five metres (16 feet) of fine sand, is another firm layer, this one left by melting ice after the Great Ice Age. A further 25 metres (82 feet) down, through shell-filled clay and past the bones of mammoths, is a third hard layer, deposited by glaciers more than 180,000 years ago.

The first Amsterdammers built their homes on muddy mounds, making the foundations from tightly packed peat. Later on, they dug trenches, filled them with fascines (thin, upright alder trunks) and built on those. And yet, still the fruits of their labours sank slowly into the swamp. By the 17th century, builders were using longer underground posts and were rewarded with more stable structures, but it wasn't until around 1700 that piles were driven deep enough to hit the first hard sand layer.

The method of constructing foundations that subsequently developed has remained more or less the same ever since, though nowadays most piles reach the second sand level and some make the full 50-metre (164-foot) journey to the third hard layer. To begin, a double row of piles is sunk along the line of a proposed wall (since World War II, concrete has been used instead of wood). Then, a crossbeam is laid across each pair of posts, planks are fastened longitudinally on to the beams, and the wall is built on top. Occasionally, piles break or rot, which is why Amsterdam is full of old buildings that teeter precariously over the street, tilt lopsidedly or prop each other up in higgledy-piggledy rows.

Trials by fire

Early constructions in Amsterdam were timber-framed, built mainly from oak with roofs of rushes or straw. Wooden houses were relatively light and therefore less likely to sink into the mire, but after two devastating fires (in 1421 and 1452), the authorities began stipulating that outer walls be built of brick, though wooden front gables were still permitted. In a bid to blend in, the first brick gables were shaped in imitation of their spout-shaped wooden predecessors.

But regulations were hardly necessary, for Amsterdammers took to bricks with relish. Granted, some grander 17th-century buildings were built of sandstone, while plastered façades were first seen a century later, and reinforced concrete made its inevitable inroads in the 20th century. But Amsterdam is still essentially a city of brick: red brick from Leiden, yellow from Utrecht and grey from Gouda, all laid in curious formations and arranged in complicated patterns. Local architects' attachment to – and flair with – brick reached a zenith in the highly fantastical, billowing designs by the Amsterdam School early in the 20th century.

Force and reinforcement

Only two wooden buildings remain in central Amsterdam: one (built in 1420) in the quiet courtyard of the **Begijnhof** (no.34, known as the Houten Huis; *see p91*), and the other on Zeedijk. The latter, **In't Aepjen** (Zeedijk 1; *see p75*), was built in the 16th century as a lodging house, getting its name from the monkeys that impecunious sailors used to leave behind as payment. Though the ground floor dates from the 19th century, the upper floors provide a clear example of how, in medieval times, each wooden storey protruded a little beyond the one below it, allowing rainwater to drip onto the street rather than run back into the body of the building. Early brick gables had to be built at an angle over the street for the same reason, though it also allowed objects to be winched to the top floors without crashing against the windows of the lower ones.

Amsterdam's oldest building, however, is the **Oude Kerk** (Oude Kerksplein 23; *see p80*). It was begun in 1300, though only the base of the tower dates from then: over the ensuing 300 years, the church, once having the simplest of forms, developed a barnacle crust of additional buildings, mostly in a Renaissance style with a few Gothic additions. The finest Gothic building in town is the **Nieuwe Kerk** (at Dam and Nieuwezijds Voorburgwal; *see p89*), still called the 'New Church' even though work on it began at the end of the 14th century.

When gunpowder first arrived in Europe in the 15th century, Amsterdammers realised that the wooden palisade that surrounded their settlement would offer scant defence, and so set about building a new, stone wall. Watchtowers and gates left over from this wall make up a significant proportion of the city's surviving pre-17th-century architecture, though most have been altered over the years. The **Schreierstoren** (Prins Hendrikkade 94-95; *see p75*) of 1480, however, has kept its original shape, with the addition of doors, windows and a pixie-hat roof. The base of the **Munttoren** (Muntplein; *see p87*) originally formed part of the Regulierspoort, a city gate built in 1490. Another city gate from the previous decade, the St Antoniespoort (Nieuwmarkt 4), was converted into a public weigh-house, **De Waag** (*see p76*), in 1617, then further refashioned to become a guild house and finally a café-restaurant. It remains one of Amsterdam's most menacing monuments.

Call of the classical

A favourite 16th-century amendment to these somewhat stolid defence towers was the later addition of a sprightly steeple. Hendrick de Keyser (1565-1621) delighted in designing such spires, and it is largely his work that gives Amsterdam's present skyline a faintly oriental appearance. He added a lantern-shaped tower with an openwork orb to the Munttoren, and a spire that resembled the Oude Kerk steeple to the **Montelbaanstoren** (Oudeschans 2), a sea-defence tower that had been built outside the city wall. His **Zuiderkerk** (Zuiderkerkhof 72; *see p77*), built in 1603, sports a spire said to have been much admired by Christopher Wren.

De Keyser's appointment as city mason and sculptor in 1595 gave him free rein, and his buildings represent the pinnacle of the Dutch Renaissance style (also known as Dutch Mannerist) – perhaps the greatest being the **Westerkerk** (Prinsengracht

279; *see p104*), completed in 1631 as the single biggest Protestant church in the world. Since the very beginning of the 17th century, Dutch architects had been gleaning inspiration from translations of Italian pattern books, adding lavish ornament to the classical system of proportion they found there. Brick fronts were decorated with stone strapwork (scrolls and curls derived from picture frames and leatherwork). Walls were built with alternating layers of red brick and white sandstone, a style that came to be called 'bacon coursing'. The old spout-shaped gables were also replaced with cascading step-gables, often embellished with vases, escutcheons and masks. There was also a practical use for these adornments: before house numbers were introduced in Amsterdam in the 18th century, ornate gables and wall plaques were a means of identifying addresses.

The façade of the **Vergulde Dolphijn** (Singel 140-142), designed by De Keyser in 1600 for Captain Banning Cocq (the commander of Rembrandt's *The Night Watch*), is a lively mix of red brick and sandstone, while the **Gecroonde Raep** (Oudezijds Voorburgwal 57) has a neat step-gable, with riotous decoration featuring busts, escutcheons, shells, scrolls and volutes. De Keyser's magnificent **Huis Bartolotti** (Herengracht 170-172), a 1617 construction that hugged the canal, is the finest example of the style.

This decorative step-gabled style was to last well into the 17th century. But gradually a stricter use of classical elements came into play; the façade of the Bartolotti house features rows of Ionic pilasters, and it wasn't long before others followed where De Keyser had led. The Italian pattern books that had inspired the Dutch Renaissance were full of the less-ornamented designs of Greek and Roman antiquity. These appealed to those young architects who followed De Keyser, and who were to develop a more restrained, classical style. Many, such as Jacob van Campen (1595-1657), went on study tours of Italy, and returned fired with enthusiasm for the symmetric designs, simple proportions and austerity of Roman architecture. The buildings they constructed during the Golden Age are among the finest Amsterdam has to offer.

The Golden Age

The 1600s were a boom time for builders, as Amsterdam's population more than quadrupled. Grand new canals were constructed, and wealthy merchants lined them with mansions and warehouses. Van Campen, along with fellow architects Philips Vingboons (1607-78) and his younger brother Justus (1620-98), were given the freedom to try out their ideas on a flood of new commissions. Stately buildings constructed of sandstone began to appear around the city, but brick remained the most popular material. Philips Vingboons' **Witte Huis** (Herengracht 168) has a white sandstone façade with virtually no decoration: the regular rhythm of the windows is the governing principle of the design. The house he built in 1648 at **Oude Turfmarkt 145** has a brick front adorned with three tiers of classical pilasters – Tuscan, Ionic and Doric – and festoons that were characteristic of the style. However, the crowning achievement of the period was Amsterdam's boast to the world of its mercantile supremacy and civic might: namely, the Stadhuis (City Hall) on the Dam, designed by Van Campen in 1648 and now known as the **Koninklijk Paleis** (*see p88*).

The 1600s were a boom time for builders as Amsterdam's population more than quadrupled

There was, however, one fundamental point of conflict between classical architecture and the requirements of northern Europe. For more practical reasons, wet northern climes required steep roofs, yet low Roman pediments and flat cornices looked odd with a steep, pointed roof behind them. The architects solved the problem by adapting the Renaissance gable, with its multiple steps, into a tall, central gable with just two steps. Later, neck-gables were built with just a tall central oblong and no steps. The right angles formed at the base of neck-gables were often filled in with decorative sandstone carvings called claw-pieces.

On very wide houses, it was possible to build a roof parallel to the street rather than end-on, making an attractive backdrop for a classical straight cornice. The giant **Trippenhuis** (Kloveniersburgwal 29, De Wallen), built by Justus Vingboons in 1662, has such a design, with a classical pediment, a frieze of cherubs and arabesques, and eight enormous Corinthian pilasters. It wasn't until the 19th century, when zinc cladding became cheaper, that flat and really low-pitched roofs became feasible.

Concertgebouw

Restraint vs refurbishment

Working towards the end of the 17th century, Adriaan Dortsman (1625-82) had been a strong proponent of the straight cornice. His stark designs – such as for the **Van Loon house** at Keizersgracht 672-674 – ushered in a style that came to be known as Restrained Dutch Classicism (or the 'Tight Style', as it would translate directly from the Dutch description: *Strakke Stijl*). It was a timely entrance. Ornament was costly and, by the beginning of the 18th century, the economic boom was over.

The merchant families were prosperous, but little new building went on. Instead, the families gave their old mansions a facelift or revamped the interiors. A number of 17th-century houses got new sandstone façades (or plastered brick ones, which were cheaper), and French taste – said to have been introduced by Daniel Marot, a French architect based in Amsterdam – became hip. As the century wore on, ornamentation regained popularity. Gables were festooned with scrolls and acanthus leaves (Louis XIV), embellished with asymmetrical rococo fripperies (Louis XV) or strung with disciplined lines of garlands (Louis XVI). The baroque grandeur of **Keizersgracht 444-446**, for example, is hardly Dutch at all. Straight cornices appeared even on narrow buildings, and became extraordinarily ornate: a distinct advantage, this, as it hid the steep roof that lay behind, with decorative balustrades adding to the deception. The lavish cornice at **Oudezijds Voorburgwal 215-217** stands as a prime example of such construction.

Remixing masonry

Fortunes slumped after 1800, and during the first part of the 19th century more buildings were demolished than constructed. When things picked up after 1860, architects raided past eras for inspiration. Neoclassical, neo-Gothic and neo-Renaissance features were sometimes lumped together in a mix-and-match style. The **Krijtberg Church** (Singel 446) from 1881 has a soaring neo-Gothic façade and a high, vaulted basilica, while the interior of AL van Gendt's **Hollandsche Manege** (Vondelstraat 140), also from 1881, combines the classicism of the Spanish Riding School in Vienna with a state-of-the-art iron and glass roof.

In stark contrast, the **Concertgebouw** (Van Baerlestraat 98; *see p237*), a Van Gendt construction from 1888, borrows from the late Renaissance, while the **City Archive** (Amsteldijk 67), from 1892, is De Keyser revisited. But the period's most adventurous building is the **Adventskerk** (Keizersgracht 676), which has a classical base, Romanesque arches, Lombardian moulding and fake 17th-century lanterns.

The star architect of the period was PJH Cuypers (1827-1921), who landed commissions for both the **Rijksmuseum** (Stadhouderskade 41; *see p140*) of 1877-85 and what would become its near mirror twin on the other side of town, **Centraal Station** (Stationsplein), built 1882-89. Both are in traditional red brick, adorned with Renaissance-style decoration in sandstone and gold leaf. Responding to those who thought his tastes too Catholic, Cuypers –

Amsterdam School

The brickwork that left its mark on the city

Characterised by its (often rounded) brick constructions and intricate detailing, the Amsterdam School style was used for working-class housing, institutions and schools during the early 20th century. Hendrik Berlage formed the nexus of the movement. Not only did his work reject all the 'neo-'styles that defined most 19th-century Dutch architecture, he also provided the opportunity to experiment with new forms by coming up with the urban development scheme, Plan Zuid.

The Amsterdam School was short-lived; it was forced to simplify within a decade when money ran out, and its greatest proponent, Michel de Klerk, died. Examples of its work, however, are visible in Spaarndammerbuurt, Rivierenbuurt, Concertgebouwbuurt and the area around Mercantorplein.

Located along the waterfront, the epic **Scheepvaarthuis** (now the Grand Hotel Amrâth Amsterdam, Prins Hendrikkade 108-114; *see p284*) is generally considered to be the school's first work. Completed in 1916, it was created by JM van der Mey, Piet Kramer and De Klerk. Among the hallmarks on show are obsessively complex brickwork, allegorical decorations (reflecting its use as shipping companies' offices), sculptures and seamlessly fused wrought-iron railings.

The Spaarndammerbuurt district sports the school's most frolicsome work and remains a huge draw for more dedicated architectural tourists. **Het Schip** (The Ship), as locals call it, takes up the whole block between Zaanstraat, Hembrugstraat and Oostzaanstraat. Completed in 1919, it was commissioned by the Eigen Haard housing association and includes 102 homes and a school. The grand archway at Oostzaan 1-21 leads to The Ship's courtyard and central meeting hall. **Museum Het Schip** (*see p130*), once a post office, is now an exhibition space devoted to the movement; it also runs tours daily visiting other Amsterdam School buildings in the city.

Located at the border of De Pijp and Rivierenbuurt is **Plan Zuid**. It is here that socialist housing association De Dageraad (The Dawn) allowed De Klerk and Kramer (together with their favourite sculptor, Hildo Krop) to do their hallucinatory best. Josef Israelkade, Burg Tellegenstraat and the courtyard of Cooperatiehof are the highlights of what is now known as one of the most successful urban expansions of the early 20th century.

Elsewhere in the city (on Waalstraat and Vrijheidslaan, for example), you'll find later, more restrained examples of the Amsterdam School's work. A window seat at **Café Wildschut** (Roelof Hartplein 1-3, 020 676 8220, www.cafewildschut.nl) offers spectacular views of a whole range of architectural goodies, including **Huize Lydia** (across the street at no.2), which first served as a home to Catholic girls. Finished in 1927, it stands as one of the very last buildings in which wacky window shapes and odd forms were allowed.

while still slipping in some of his excesses later during the construction – decided to organise each building according to a single coherent principle. This became the basis for modern Dutch architecture.

A new age dawns

Brick and wood – good, honest, indigenous materials – appealed to Hendrik Petrus Berlage (1856-1934), as did the possibilities offered by industrial developments in the use of steel and glass. A rationalist, he took Cuypers' ideas a step further in his belief that a building should openly express its basic structure, with a modest amount of ornament in a supportive role. Notable also was the way he collaborated with sculptors, painters and even poets throughout construction. His **Beurs van Berlage** (Beursplein; *see p78*), built 1898-1903 – a mix of clean lines and functional shapes, with the mildest patterning in the brickwork – was startling at the time, and earned him the reputation of being the father of modern Dutch architecture.

Apart from the odd shopfront and some well-designed café interiors, the art nouveau and art deco movements had little direct impact on Amsterdam, though they did draw a few wild flourishes: HL de Jong's **Pathé Tuschinski** Cinema (Reguliersbreestraat 26; *see p208*) of 1918-21, for example, is a delightful and seductive piece of high-camp fantasy. Instead, Amsterdam architects developed a style of their own, a mix of art nouveau and old Dutch using their favourite materials: wood and brick.

A local movement

This movement, known as the **Amsterdam School** (*see above*), reacted against Berlage's sobriety by producing its uniquely whimsical buildings with waving,

almost sculptural brickwork. Built over a reinforced concrete frame, the brick outer walls go through a complex series of pleats, bulges, folds and curls that earned them the nickname *Schortjesarchitectuur* ('Apron architecture'). Windows can be trapezoid or parabolic; doors are carved in strong, angular shapes; brickwork is highly decorative and often polychromatic; and sculptures are abundant.

The driving force behind the Amsterdam School came from two young architects, Michel de Klerk (1884-1923) and Piet Kramer (1881-1961). Two commissions for social housing projects – one for **Dageraad** (constructed around PL Takstraat, 1921-23) and one for **Eigen Haard** (located in the Spaarndammerbuurt, 1913-20) – allowed them to treat entire blocks as single units. Just as importantly, the pair's adventurous clients gave them freedom to express their ideas. The movement also produced more rural variants of their architecture, suggestive of village life, such as the rather charming BT Boeyinga-designed 'garden village' **Tuindorp Nieuwendam** (Purmerplein, Purmerweg).

Architectural rebellion

In the early 1920s, a new movement emerged that was the very antithesis of the Amsterdam School – although certain crossover aspects can be observed in JF Staal's 1930-completed **Wolkenkrabber** (Victorieplein), the first ever residential high-rise in the country, whose name appropriately translates as 'cloudscraper'. Developing rather than reacting wildly against Berlage's ideas, the functionalists believed that new building materials such as concrete and steel should not be concealed, but that the basic structure of a building should be visible. Function was supreme, ornament anathema. Their hard-edged concrete and glass boxes have much in common with the work of Frank Lloyd Wright in the USA, Le Corbusier in France and the Bauhaus in Germany.

Perhaps unsurprisingly, such radical views were not shared by everyone, and the period was a turbulent one in Amsterdam's architectural history. Early functionalist work, such as the 1930s **Openluchtschool** (Cliostraat 40), 1934's striking **Cineac Cinema** (Reguliersbreestraat 31) and **'t Blauwe Theehuis** (in Vondelpark; *see p146*), has a clean-cut elegance, and the functionalist garden suburb of **Betondorp** (literally, 'Concrete Village'), built between 1921 and 1926, is much more attractive than the name might suggest. But after World War II, functionalist ideology became an excuse for more dreary, derivative, prefabricated eyesores. The urgent need for housing, coupled with town-planning theories that favoured residential satellite suburbs, led to the appearance of soulless, high-rise horrors on the edge of town.

A change of heart during the 1970s refocused attention on making the city centre a pleasant jumble of residences, shops and offices. At the same time, a quirkier, more imaginative trend began to show itself in building design. The **ING Bank** (Bijlmerplein 888), inspired by Rudolf Steiner's philosophy of anthroposophy and built in 1987 of brick, has hardly a right angle in sight. A use of bright colour, and a return to a human-sized scale, is splendidly evident in Aldo van Eyck's **Hubertushuis** (Plantage Middenlaan 33-35) from 1979, which seems to personify the architect's famed quotation: 'My favourite colour is the rainbow.' New façades – daringly modern, yet built to scale – began to appear between the old houses along the canals. The 1980s also saw, amid much controversy, the construction of what soon became known as the 'Stopera', a combined City Hall (Stadhuis) and opera house on Waterlooplein; the eye-catching brick and marble of the **Nationale Opera & Ballet** (*see p238*) is more successful than the dull oblongs that make up City Hall.

Housing projects of the 1980s and 1990s have provided Amsterdam with some imaginative modern architecture: examples include the **WoZoCo** apartments in Osdorp by MVRDV and the regenerated Eastern Docklands. You can get a good view of the latter from the roof of Renzo Piano's **NEMO** building (*see p169*). While the area did not achieve the dream of becoming a harbourfront on a par with that of Sydney, Australia, it did help put local architecture on the global map.

Eyes forward

The future for architecture in Amsterdam looks transformative, dynamic and green. The re-energised Noord continues to grow and thrive, as fellow former industrial area in the Oost, Amstelkwartier, is also restored and reinvented. At its centre rises **HAUT**, 21 storeys of energy-generating façades made entirely of wood. The highest wooden residential building in the world, the pioneering project has been awarded with the highest sustainability score.

Those interested in HAUT and other architectural developments should pay

WoZoCo

a visit to NEMO's neighbour, the mighty **ARCAM** – the **Architectuurcentrum Museum Amsterdam** (*see p168*) – or pick up a copy of its excellent publication *25 Buildings You Should Have Seen: Amsterdam*. Bureau Monumenten & Archeologie (BMA), meanwhile, provides an overview of the city's architecture from its origins to 1940 at www.bma.amsterdam.nl (Dutch only).

Architectural travesties of the past have politicised the populace, and referendums are held prior to many developments. Although 130,000 local votes against the construction of **IJburg** – a residential community built on a series of man-made islands in the IJmeer, just east of Amsterdam – was not enough to arrest development around this ecologically sensitive area, they did inspire the promise that 15 million guilders (now around €7 million) would be invested in 'nature development'. Parts of the area have also become a showcase for hyped Dutch concept of *wilde wonen* – 'wild living' – where residents get to design and build their own houses, a radical concept in this space-constrained country.

Similarly, the referendum result against the **Noord/Zuidlijn** on the metro network didn't halt the project – it finally opened in July 2018, after years of problems and delays – but it did establish that the city government needed to be considerably more diligent in its thinking. When planning the line, the powers-that-be apparently overlooked such significant details as financing, loss of revenue for shopkeepers, and the potential for all this digging to bring about the speedier sinking of historical buildings – none of which endeared them to voters.

Superdutch

Modern Dutch architecture – thanks in part to notable exponents such as Rem Koolhaas (his 1991 work, **Byzantium**, is viewable at the north entrance to Vondelpark on Stadhouderskade) – remains very much in vogue. Brad Pitt's own favourite architecture firm, MVRDV, which renovated the futuristic Westerdok, VUmc Cancer Center and **Lloyd Hotel** (*see p286*), shot to prominence at Hanover World Expo 2000 with its 'Dutch Big Mac', featuring such delicious ingredients as watermills and windmills for electricity on the roof, a theatre on the fourth floor, an oak forest on the third floor, flowers on the second floor, and cafés, shops and a few dunes on the first floor. It has remained at the forefront of the industry ever since.

International periodicals continue to see the 'Dutch model' – where boundaries between building, city and landscape planning have blurred beyond recognition – as both pragmatic and futuristic. After all, ecological degradation is now a worldwide phenomenon, and the space-constrained Netherlands has long seen nature as a construct that needs to be nurtured. Expect this principle to define some of the Dutch architecture of the future.

A case in point is seen in the metamorphosis of the **Wibautstraat** in Oost. Nothing but a major traffic route in the 1970s, the wide strip has evolved into an urban lane with universities, hotels, restaurants and, of course, a green centre.

High-budget architectural statements still have a place in the city. The likes of the Zuidoost construction around the **Amsterdam Bijlmer ArenA** train station has pumped much-needed life into what was once essentially an architectural prison. Another hotspot that roped in a veritable who's who of architects is **Zuidas** (www.zuidas.nl) in the south. Zuidas is grouped around the World Trade Center, close to the wacky **ING House** (Amstelveenseweg 500); spot this clog-shaped glass edifice on the ride in from Schiphol Airport. And then there's the compelling **EYE Film Institute** (*see p173*) in Amsterdam Noord, which looks as if it might actually take flight.

Back to basics?

The golden years came to a grinding halt during the global economic meltdown of 2008, which saw 40 per cent of the country's architects out of work. Dwindling budgets meant architects had to look for less pretentious solutions, which led them to find inspiration in such projects as the hundreds of old steel containers turned into living spaces for students at both **Houthavens** in the west and **NDSM** (*see p176*) in the north. Noord's **Kunstadt** ('Art City') has become a versatile skeleton for diverse spaces and the area is now home to the city's first 3D-printed canal house. Others are seeking to rejuvenate disused industrial and mixed community areas, such as Amstelkwartier and Oostelijke Eiland, by turning them into dynamic living and working spaces with a neighbourhood feel.

Sustainability remains a central focus for future plans, both in residential and corporate construction, with aims to build a series of local 'heat networks' to deliver hot water and to have 450,000 houses generating solar power by 2040. Amsterdam has reinvented itself yet again, this time with a carbon-conscious eye on the future.

Art & Design

Art has defined Amsterdam for centuries

Ah, the Golden Age. The living was sweet during those first six decades of the 17th century, starting with the founding of the East India Company (VOC) and ending when the British changed New Amsterdam to New York. Not only did the economic benefits of being the world's leading trading power result in the building of Amsterdam's image-defining ring of canals, but it also led to a flourishing of the arts that continues to this day. That's why it's easy to get lost in the sheer number of viewable works in Amsterdam. Sometimes, it's just better to focus on a few prime works – to stop and smell the tulips, as it were.

Jacob Cornelisz Painting a Portrait of His Wife (Dirck Jacobsz, c1550)

Medieval roots

The groundwork for the blooming of art in Amsterdam's Golden Age was laid by the city's rich medieval artistic tradition under the sponsorship of the Church. Later artists, not content to labour solely *ad majorem dei gloriam*, found more 'individual' masters in the Flemings Bosch and Brueghel. Foremost among these early artists was **Jacob Cornelisz van Oostsanen** (c1470-1533). Also known as Jacob van Amsterdam, he represents the beginning of the city's artistic tradition, and his sharpness of observation became a trademark for all Dutch art that was to follow. The one painting of his that survived the Iconoclastic Fury, *Saul and the Witch of Endor* (on display at the **Rijksmuseum**; *see p140*), tells the whole biblical story in one panoramic, almost comic-book-like, swoop beginning on the left where Saul seeks advice from a witch about his impending battle with the Philistines and ending in the far distance, behind the central witches' sabbath, with his 'poetic justice' of a suicide in the face of defeat.

The Baker of Eeklo is another example that seemingly comes from a very much pre-modern time. It hangs in the **Muiderslot** (*see p193*), a castle outside Amsterdam built for Count Floris V. Painted in the second half of the 16th century by two rather obscure painters, **Cornelis van Dalem** and **Jan van Wechelen**, the depicted tableau – of a busy bakery, where people whose heads have been replaced by cabbages await patiently the rebaking of their actual heads – can probably only make sense to a populace weaned on medieval stories of magic windmills that could grind old people up and then churn them out young again. In this related story, bakers are slicing the heads off clients to rebake them to specification; a cabbage – a symbol for the empty and idle head – was used to keep the spewing of blood to a minimum, although sometimes people's heads came out 'half-baked' or 'misfired'.

The Milkmaid (Johannes Vermeer, c1660)

Painters had no problems with marketing once the Golden Age arrived and the middle classes became hungry for art

Old Masters

Painters had no problems with marketing once the Golden Age proper arrived and the aspirant middle classes became hungry for art. **Rembrandt van Rijn** (1606-69) is, of course, the best known of all those who made art while the money shone. However, *Militia Company of District II under the Command of Captain Frans Banninck Cocq* (1642) didn't prove the snappiest title for a painting. *The Night Watch*, though, is rather more memorable, and it's by this name that the most famous work by Rembrandt is now known (on display at the Rijksmuseum). Amsterdam's Civic Guard commissioned this group portrait to decorate its new building, but rather than conjure up a neat, unexciting portrait, Rembrandt went for spontaneity, capturing a moment of lively chaos: the captain issuing an order as his men jostle to his rear. It's now the city's most popular work in the city's most popular museum.

Rembrandt couldn't decorate Amsterdam on his own, however, and the likes of Jan Vermeer, Frans Hals, Ferdinand Bol, Jan Steen and Jacob van Ruisdael thrived creatively and economically during this time.

Delft-born painter **Jan Vermeer** (1632-75) painted pictures, such as *The Milkmaid* (also on display at the Rijksmuseum), that radiate an extraordinary serenity. In his essential essay, 'Vermeer in Bosnia', Lawrence Weschler suggests that the artist's works are not depictions of actual peace but rather hopeful invocations of a peace yet to come. For Vermeer was painting at a time when exhausted, war-weary Europe was slowly emerging from the ravages of the Thirty Years' War (1618-48); at the time, peace still remained a fervent hope rather than a definite expectation.

Fake or Fortune?

When a Vermeer is not all that it seems

The Dutch are as famed for their business acumen as for their dykes, but this has sometimes led the less scrupulous to a somewhat free and easy attitude towards an artwork's provenance. An estimated 30 per cent of the world art market consists of forgeries, and even the most famous institutions can be caught out.

In 1938, the Rijksmuseum lost a bidding war for a Vermeer to Rotterdam's Museum Boijmans Van Beuningen, which bought the painting for the then-astronomical price of ƒ550,000 (€250,000). Proof, if it were needed, that desire blinds, for how else could Hans van Meegeren's heavy-handed *De Emmaüsgangers* be mistaken for a Vermeer?

It was only in 1945, when the forger was facing a traitor's death penalty for selling the Nazis another 'Vermeer', that Van Meegeren admitted both works were forgeries, painted to avenge himself for a critic's poor reviews. That self-same critic had fallen for the forgeries, although it's unlikely that the sweet taste of revenge was sufficient compensation for Van Meegeren's subsequent imprisonment: he died in jail a couple of years later.

Today, the master forger's legacy remains undeniably (albeit ironically) legitimate. Autumn 2016 saw the release of the film *A Real Vermeer*, about the life and retribution of Van Meegeren by Dutch director Rudolf van den Berg.

Van Meegeren in 1945

Leiden's **Jan Steen** (c1625-79) dealt with the chaos of the times in another way – a way that got him a bad image as being rowdy. While he did run a tavern in his own home, his patchy reputation is more likely based on the drunken folk that inhabit his paintings of everyday life. In fact, if one looks carefully at, for example, *The Merry Family* (at the Rijksmuseum), Steen comes across as highly moralistic. The inscription over the mantelpiece ('As the Old Sing, So Pipe the Young') describes literally what the painting reflects figuratively through a plethora of symbols that represent the emptiness of a life spent smoking, drinking and talking about nothing – a lesson as valid today as when it was painted. Steen himself has a cameo as the puffy-cheeked bagpiper.

After the Golden Age began to tarnish, art continued to develop. The Jordaan-born **Jacob de Wit** (1695-1754), long before the invention of sticky glow-in-the-dark stars, brightened up many a local ceiling with cloud-dappled skies, gods and flocks of cherubs. Initially influenced by Rubens' altar work in Antwerp, De Wit developed a much more delicate and sympathetic touch, which he used to great rococo effect in a number of Amsterdam buildings. Among these are the attic church at **Ons' Lieve Heer op Solder** (*see p79*), the Rijksmuseum, the **Pintohuis** (now a community-run library and reading room; Sint Antoniesbreestraat 69, Jodenbuurt, 020 624 3184) and **Huis Marseille** (*see p100*). However, his mastery of trompe l'oeil, later named *witjes* after him, is probably best seen at the **Bijbels Museum** (*see p102*); one ceiling was painted for local merchant Jacob Cromhout, while the other, entitled *Apollo and the Four Seasons*, was salvaged in the 1950s from a nearby property on Herengracht. Both paintings have since been stylishly restored.

The arrival of Vincent

The 18th century produced Monet's inspiration, **Johan Jongkind**, while the 19th century offered **George Breitner** and **Vincent van Gogh**. The career of everyone's favourite earless genius, Vincent van Gogh (1853-90), is on full display in Amsterdam, most notably at the **Van Gogh Museum** (*see p142*). Here, you can marvel at the fact that the creator of the dark shadows of *Skull with Smoking Cigarette* went on to paint, a mere two years later in 1888, the almost kinetic *Bedroom*. By then, Van Gogh had settled in France's clearer light and abandoned the Vermeer-inspired subdued colouring of his earlier work to embrace the expressionist style that would make him famous. While the self-portrait clearly reflects his restless nature, *Bedroom* depicts the very bed he would, perhaps, have been better off sleeping in. Just two months later, he had the first of the nervous breakdowns that led finally to his suicide.

Like Van Gogh, **Isaac Israëls** (1865-1934) sought to reinvent the relevance of painting in the photographic age. But unlike his buddy George Breitner, who chose to embrace this new technology by using photographs as the basis for his paintings, Israëls chose a more athletic path and achieved the 'snapshot' feel of his paintings by running around like a ninny and painting very fast. *Two Girls by a Canal* (on show at

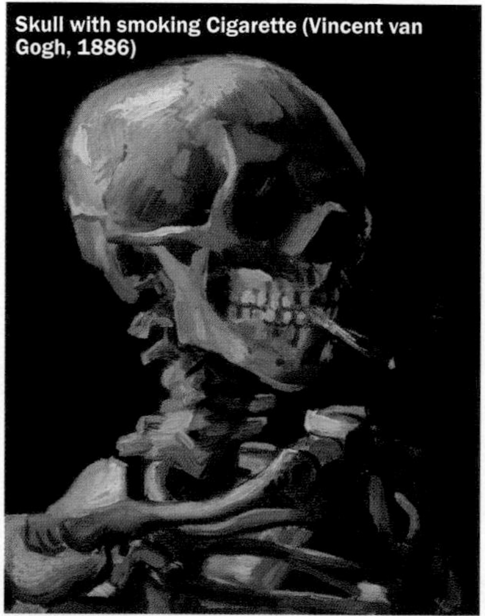
Skull with smoking Cigarette (Vincent van Gogh, 1886)

Bedroom (Vincent van Gogh, 1888)

Where the Art is

Gallery hopping through the city's best art spaces

Galleries, mini museums, ateliers and non-traditional art spaces abound in Amsterdam, in just about every area of the city. The Jordaan is still the congregation point for the more established and internationally minded contemporary art galleries, while the Spiegelkwartier (literally, 'mirror quarter') in the Grachtengordel is where you'll find anything pre-dating 1945, including Old Master paintings, CoBrA art, antiques and genuine Delftware.

In recent years, urban art pioneers have headed to Noord, where the massive shipyard-turned-studio complex NDSM and neighbouring former industrial sites have become a breeding ground of creative production, while others have migrated to De Pijp, West and Oost for cheaper or funkier art digs.

Amsterdam's art spaces can be divided into two categories: commercial art galleries devoted to selling work by more established artists; and non-profit project spaces, where emerging and non-traditional artists have more opportunities to 'play'.

Meanwhile, Amsterdam continues its rich tradition of nourishing a street-art culture (in spite of the police's efforts to curb graffiti), so you'll also find plenty of eye candy around town (*see p129* Street Art). A collection of the best and brightest is showcased at the **Street Art Museum Amsterdam** (Immanuel Kanthof 1, www.streetartmuseumamsterdam.com), a project initiated by an NGO non-profit foundation to enhance the bond between residents, public art and the neighbourhood.

For the most up-to-date list of current shows and spaces, see *Art Alert* (www.artalert.nl – ten issues per year); it's in Dutch, but the galleries are sorted by area and marked on maps. Also check out *Amsterdam Art* (www.amsterdamart.com) for news about upcoming exhibitions and cultural collaborations. English-language city marketing magazine *A-Mag*, available at most newsstands and some cafés, has extensive arts listings too.

the **Amsterdam Museum**; *see p87*) does successfully reflect a quintessentially impressionist view of dynamic Amsterdam.

De Stijl and CoBrA

There's a fair case to be made that the 20th century belonged to **Piet Mondrian** (1872-1944), whose career can also be used as a one-man weathervane of modern art. He moved through realism, impressionism and cubism, before embracing the purely abstract and becoming one of the founders of **De Stijl** ('The Style'). His use of only lines and primary colour blocks inspired accusations of sterility, but actually represented a very personal and subjective quest for essence and harmony. He was also something of a wit, tilting his late and ultra-minimal canvas, *Composition with Two Lines* (on display at the **Stedelijk Museum**; *see p139*) by 45 degrees.

Karel Appel (1920-2001) once said, 'I just mess around' – and many agree when met with his childish forms, bright colours and heavy strokes. But art that chose instinct over intellect was just what people needed after World War II, when **CoBrA** (*see p149*) exploded onto the scene. Appel's rate of production was so huge that Amsterdam ex-forger Geert Jan Jansen claims Appel verified several of Jansen's works as his own. You can admire an Appel mural by the entrance of restaurant **Bridges** (*see p82*), part of the Grand Amsterdam hotel.

Onward to the future

As we move deeper into the 21st century, there is a growing demand for interactivity and a spotlight on sustainability. Take **Annette van Driel** and **Francis Nijenhuis**' UrbanCampsite Amsterdam, a pop-up public art exhibition featuring eclectic works of mobile art made out of renewable products. Visitors can spend the night in the furnished open-air exhibition, which began in 2013 and has been held every two years since. The Stedelijk Museum's celebration of **Jean Tinguely**'s progressive response to avant-garde abstractions is another nod to the interactive trend.

There has also been a significant shift towards design (*see p277* Design for Life). Marcel Wanders' 1997 *Knotted Chair*, part of the Stedelijk's permanent collection, could not be more different from that other iconic Dutch chair of the 20th century: the highly geometric Red-Blue Chair (1918-23) by De Stijl co-founder **Gerrit Rietveld**. But *Knotted Chair* – which reinvents the frumpy hippie art of macramé with the aid of hi-tech epoxy – came to represent the work of a new vanguard of local designers who seek to achieve a fusion of wit, hipness and function. This is also witnessed in **Piet Hein Eek**'s *Waste Table*, made of recycled timber.

It has often been said that Amsterdam, with its soggy climate and bleak winters, was designed to look as good in black and white as it does in colour, making it especially appealing to amateur photographers. And, as home to **Ed van der Elsken** (1925-1990), **Anton Corbijn** and **Rineke Dijkstra**, the city is a strong supporter of the photographic arts, with photography museum **Foam** (*see p111*) and its Unseen photo fair providing solid institutional backing and the perfect playground for up-and-comers. The studio of **Erwin Olaf** functions as a graduate school of sorts for young photographers.

Since the 1980s, there's been a backlash against conceptual art's anti-functional rhetoric

Although painters such as **Marlene Dumas** and existential enthusiast **Peter Bastiaanssen** keep the medium fresh, the local art scene now seems more interested in embracing the blur between street art, design, photography, new media and so on. Since the 1980s, there's been a backlash against conceptual art's anti-functional rhetoric – which would have pleased adherents of De Stijl, who hoped the future would bring a frenzy of cross-disciplinary activity. Photographers, cartoonists and architects are considered to be 'artists', and it's not surprising that the city's creative atmosphere has lured many an expat (one such is UK artist and filmmaker Steve McQueen) to set up canalside studios.

Embracing the new

Amsterdam is home to some of the most instantly recognisable works in history, but art-lovers are lured by far more than Van Goghs and Vermeers. Critics have hailed the city's surge in contemporary art as something of an artistic renaissance. Perhaps it's because Amsterdam has embraced new media like few other cities. The pioneering **Waag Society** (www.waag.org) and the happily subversive **Mediamatic** (*see p169*) both arose from the 'tactical media' scene. From the history of video games to transformation of old Amsterdam warehouses, Mediamatic explores both the possibilities and challenges technology offers art. It also echoes the renewable awareness showcased in UrbanCampsite Amsterdam, with lectures on sustainable food and an on-site aquaponics greenhouse.

Other venues such as **Pakhuis de Zwijger** (*see p170*) and the **Royal Theatre Carré**, formerly a circus theatre, act as hubs for numerous cutting-edge outfits, with a programme of events, conferences and exhibitions.

Artist/entrepreneur/designer **Daan Roosegaarde** (www.studioroosegaarde.net) is a household name and again exemplifies environmental awareness. His studio launched the Smog Free Project to create clean urban skies and an interactive dance floor that generates electricity through dance. His 'social design' lab has also pumped out reality-challenging light shows and dresses that become more transparent based on the wearer's heartbeats.

What makes Amsterdam such a hotbed for creativity in the 21st century? One simple answer might be: money. The cost of living is increasing fast but remains lower here than other urban hubs such as London and New York. Historically, the Dutch government has been incredibly generous with subsidies for artists (for a while, every art-school grad got financial assistance for five years after leaving college). As the home of prestigious art residency the **Rijksakademie** (www.rijksakademie.nl) and acclaimed art/design university **Gerrit Rietveld Academie** (www.gerritrietveldacademie.nl), Amsterdam is teeming with young, up-and-coming artists from all over the world, who are producing work, in all media, like crazy. This international influence helps explain why the city's galleries are more adventurous and welcoming to young artists and curators than elsewhere.

In some respects, the city is one huge gallery. All new construction projects have long had to dedicate a percentage of their costs to public art, so one can hardly walk a metre without bumping into some kind of creative endeavour. This is especially the case in Amsterdam's newly revived **Noord** (*see p172*), where the previously forgotten industrial sites have been taken over and transformed into independent galleries and pop-up venues. Once the largest shipyard in Amsterdam, **NDSM** (*see p176*) has developed into a creative hub hosting anything from music festivals to art exhibits and everything in between. Young artists and entrepreneurs are given free rein at **Kunststad**, a built-in airframe where start-ups can create their own workspace.

Not all exhibits or creative launches are successful, but there's no doubt that the urban landscape is a much richer place thanks to the stained-glass of cartoonist **Joost Swarte** in buildings on the east side of Marnixstraat's northern end; and **Rombout & Droste**'s demented walking bridges on Java-eiland.

To miss out on Amsterdam's art offerings would be a sin comparable with anything you might contemplate in the Red Light District. So open your eyes and start looking.

Design for Life

Functional yet playful aesthetics are at the heart of Dutch creativity

The history of Dutch design has been influenced by the orderliness of Calvinism and the modernist movement De Stijl, founded in Amsterdam in 1917. Drawing upon that part of the Dutch psyche that craves order, abstract artists such as Theo van Doesburg, Piet Mondrian and Gerrit Rietveld sought rules of equilibrium, which can be applied to everyday design as much as art. Just go online or leaf through *Wallpaper** magazine to see the legacy of the style today. And yet a counterpoint has always existed in the Dutch people's strong desire for personal expression (perhaps an echo of the stubbornness required to battle the sea).

Worldwide acclaim has greeted this eclectic mix of functionality and wit – just consider the energy-producing 21-storey HAUT building or the playful, Lego-like residential building Silodam by MVRDV Architects. The **A'DAM Toren** (*see p174*) has retained its original 1970s structure but is not without its futuristic touches, including Europe's tallest swing perched on top.

Furthermore, there's an active sense of city design at work: urban planners carefully quote from the work of American sociologist and urban theorist Richard Florida, who argues that the 'creative class' can play a beneficial role in urban development. Creative types are working in industrial, historically poorer neighbourhoods, ranging from the former shipyard NDSM to the Bos en Lommer district in the west to the new Amstelkwartier in Oost.

To witness how design has infiltrated every level of Dutch life, cross the Damrak from the Red Light District to visit a major outlet of department store **HEMA** (Nieuwendijk 174-176, www.hema.nl). One in eight of the Dutch population dry off using a HEMA bath towel; half of all Dutch babies wear a HEMA bodysuit; and one in four women a HEMA bra. The store sells five fitted sheets every minute and one Dutch smoked sausage, which it is famed for, every three seconds. It may be an economical place to shop for basics, but the store has also made a name for itself as a source of affordable design objects – even its sales flyers are graphics classics. It has featured products by leading designers such as Piet Hein Eek, Gijs Bakker and Hella Jongerius. You might also want to check out supermarket **Marqt** (*see p148*), which has taken branding to the next level.

To put yourself at the heart of local design, head to **The Maker Store** (Hannie dankbaarpassage 39, Oud West, 020 261 7667, www.themakerstore.nl), the **Frozen Fountain** (Prinsengracht 645, Grachtengordel, 020 622 9375, www.frozenfountain.com) or **Droog** (*see p85*), in the Old Centre. You can also visit the higgledy-piggledy Jordaan and get lost in the wacky creativity. A former school here is now the studio of design star Marcel Wanders, another disciple of Richard Florida, and is where you'll find his homeware store **Moooi** (*see p124*). To sit, relax and recharge surrounded by chic design, head to concept-stores-turned-cafés **Friday Next** (020 612 3292, www.fridaynext.com) or **BounceSpace** (020 223 1624, www.bouncespace.eu), both on the Overtoom in Oud West.

Frozen Fountain

Plan

Damrak

Accommodation

With accommodation options in the city running the gamut from B&Bs and privately owned small hotels to enormous, and enormously posh, establishments, Amsterdam does its best to find a bed for everybody. The question of where to put new hotels in this densely packed environment has driven some wonderfully creative and inspired solutions, from updating a youth prison to building designer suites in a crane. Limited space in the city centre means that hotel rooms there tend to be on the small side, and you don't get that much bang for your buck. But many make up for their somewhat modest dimensions with that most prized commodity: a canal view.

Hotel Casa p286

Staying in Amsterdam

Finding a place to sleep in Amsterdam can be a fiercely competitive business. In December 2016, the council declared an official freeze on the construction of new hotels as part of the fight against overcrowding in the city, but the renovation and repurposing of other buildings, not to mention the refurbishment of existing hotels, continues apace, meaning there's no shortage of accommodation options in all price ranges. In 2018, **Soho House** opened an Amsterdam outpost of its all-conquering members' club and hotel chain, and followed **W Amsterdam**'s lead by including a rooftop pool among its list of boutique attractions. They joined the ranks of the **Waldorf Astoria**, which is spread across six grand canal houses; the **Conservatorium**, located in a former 19th-century music conservatory; and **Sir Albert Hotel**, in a former diamond factory – all of which exhibit a local pattern whereby existing buildings are revamped in preference to construction from scratch.

There's also been a drive towards sustainable accommodation, with mid-range ecohotel brand

Hotel Pulitzer p283

Concious Hotels (conscioushotels.com) opening four locations in Amsterdam, each boasting sustainably sourced interior decor, a renewable energy supply and 100% organic food.

The affordable end of the market has been just as creative. In the city's hip Oost district is **Volkshotel**, home to rooftop bar and local hotspot **Canvas**. And **CitizenM** – local folk with global ambitions – came up with their own unique solution: stacking up some shipping containers and renting them out as 'budget luxury' accommodation. Plus, there's been some fierce competition from Airbnb and the like (*see p282* Suite Dreams).

Hotels cluster around particular districts of Amsterdam: the Museum Quarter and the Grachtengordel district have plenty, whereas De Pijp and the Jordaan are prime territory for private apartment rentals. In general, avoid accommodation near Centraal Station or the Red Light District, unless you want to be overcharged for what will probably be an uninspiring – and extremely noisy – place to rest your head.

The best way to experience Dutch hospitality is to stay in a B&B. These are often stylish affairs, with prices to match; www.bedandbreakfast.amsterdam is a good place to start. If you want to rent a houseboat for your stay, check out www.houseboats.nl.

Waldorf Astoria Amsterdam *p283*

Suite Dreams

Fancy an alternative to a conventional hotel?

Tourism is big business in Amsterdam. In 2019, the number of annual visitors flocking to the city stood at nearly 18 million, a 60% increase since 2007. And locals and politicians alike are united in their belief that one company, more than any other, is responsible for much of this increase: **Airbnb** (www.airbnb.com).

The online rental agency currently has over 25,000 Amsterdam properties listed on its site, with nearly 80% of these being entire homes or apartments. Tensions around house price and rent increases, anti-social behaviour and the transformation of entire blocks into de facto unlicensed hotels has led to the introduction of a series of regulations. Since 2017, it's been illegal to rent out a room or space for more than 60 days per calendar year, although that fell to just 30 days in January 2019. With checks, inspections and heavy fines becoming far more prevalent, the city now has some of the toughest laws regarding short-term letting anywhere in Europe.

That being said, Airbnb remains the dominant platform and, given the sometimes hefty cost of hotel accommodation, usually represents good value for money. A private room will set you back anywhere from €50 to €100 a night, while whole apartments go for around €200.

There's also no shortage of unique properties with houseboats, attics, old studios and even windmills pressed into service as a home away from home. Areas outside the Old Centre represent the best value, particularly Jordaan and the West, and also provide a richer experience away from the tourist hordes. And, of course, Airbnb is not the only provider; other agencies include **Homeaway** (www.homeaway.com), **Home To Go** (www.hometogo.com) and **City Mundo** (www.amsterdam.citymundo.com). Longer-term rentals can be found at **Apartment Services** (www.apartmentservices.nl).

Money matters

Hotels in the city are graded according to an official star-rating system designed to sort the deluxe from the dumps – but we haven't followed it in this guide, as the ratings merely reflect room size and amenities such as lifts or bars, rather than other important factors such as decor, staff or atmosphere. Instead, we've listed them in four broad price categories (*see right*).

For the cheapest deals, your best bet will be to look online. Before heading straight to the hotel website, check out www.booking.com, www.tripadvisor.com, and www.hoteltonight.com, which often have seasonal and last-minute deals. The room rate may, or may not, include the city tax of five per cent; it could be added to your final bill. Most hotels have Wi-Fi, but you may be charged extra for it. And finally, note that credit cards aren't always accepted, particularly in smaller places.

In the know
Price categories

Our price categories are based on a hotel's standard prices (not including seasonal offers or discounts) for one night in a double room with en suite shower/bath. Hotel breakfast is usually charged separately and is often ridiculously expensive – you're better off finding a nearby café.

Luxury	€300+
Expensive	€200-€300
Moderate	€100-€200
Budget	up to €100

Luxury

In addition to those listed below, top-notch choices include **Sir Adam** (*see p174*) in Noord and **Soho House Amsterdam** (Spuistraat 210, 020 888 0300, sohohouseamsterdam.com), which brings its members' club aesthetic to a muscular 1930s building on the edge of the Old Centre.

Conservatorium
Van Baerlestraat 27, Museum Quarter, (020 570 0000, www.conservatoriumhotel.com). Tram 2, 3, 5, 12. ***Map*** *p136 G14.*
With a prestigious location on the Museumplein, this grand 19th-century neo-Gothic building, latterly the Sweelinck music conservatory, is a wonderfully stylish place to stay. Italian architect Piero Lissoni embraced the building's rich historical heritage while introducing contemporary clean lines and a muted colour scheme to the 129-room hotel. As well as the ultra-luxe suites and upmarket spa and gym facilities, there's some excellent drinking and dining to be had. The Brasserie & Lounge is a striking space, set in a brick courtyard with soaring windows and a glass ceiling.

Crane Hotel Faralda
NDSM-Plein 78, Noord (020 760 6161, www.faralda.nl). NDSM Wharf ferry. ***Map*** *p171 inset.*
High-end in every sense: three luxury double suites – 'Mystique', 'Free Spirit' and 'Secret' – have been built into the old crane that was once used to position ships in a dry dock at former shipyard NDSM. For an eye-watering €695 a night, you can enjoy all mod cons (including a crane-top hot tub) and amazing views of the city. You may also spot an international DJ or pop star, as it's a favourite with the famous faces that come to town.

Hotel de l'Europe
Nieuwe Doelenstraat 2-14, Old Centre (020 531 1777, www.deleurope.nl). Tram 4, 14, 24 or Metro Rokin. ***Map*** *p70 K11.*
A luxury landmark with fabulous views across the Amstel, this is the place to head for an indulgent splurge or a honeymoon hideaway. As should be expected at these prices, every detail is taken care of. The Provocateur suite has a round bed and an in-room Jacuzzi big enough for two. The hotel is one of the few in Amsterdam to boast a pool, and its Bord'Eau restaurant, with two Michelin stars, is highly rated. Freddy's Bar – named after beer king Heineken – is a woody and evocative place in which to sip a cocktail or suck back a cigar.

Hotel Pulitzer
Prinsengracht 323, Grachtengordel (020 523 5235, www.hotelpulitzeramsterdam.nl). Tram 13, 17. ***Map*** *p96 H9.*
Sprawling across 25 canal houses, the Pulitzer is an ideal destination for indulgent getaways. Guests can arrive by boat, there are antiques galore, rooms are big and stylish, and the facilities are top-notch. A lovely garden nestles at the back. In August, the Grachtenfestival (*see p203*) of classical music takes place in and around the hotel grounds, making it an excellent choice for music fans.

Sofitel Legend The Grand Amsterdam
Oudezijds Voorburgwal 197, Old Centre (020 555 3111, www.sofitel-legend-thegrand.com). Tram 4, 14, 24, or Metro Rokin. ***Map*** *p70 L9.*
Steeped in centuries of history, the Grand is located near the centre of the Red Light District. But the moment guests step into the luxurious courtyard, they feel as if they've been whisked a million miles away from the risqué surroundings. Rooms are spacious and airy, and the art deco-style bathrooms come supplied with Hermès and L'Occitane smellies. There's also a stellar restaurant, **Bridges** (*see p82*).

Waldorf Astoria Amsterdam
Herengracht 542, Grachtengordel (020 718 4600, www.waldorfastoria3.hilton.com). Tram 4, 14. ***Map*** *p96 L12.*
Spanning a collection of six 17th-century canal palaces in one of the city's most iconic districts, the Waldorf Astoria definitely falls into the 'treat yourself' category. In addition to decadently decorated rooms, the hotel has its own courtyard garden and quintessential Amsterdam canal views.

W Amsterdam
Spuistraat 175, Old Centre (020 811 2500, www.marriott.com/hotels/travel/amswh-w-amsterdam). Tram 2, 11, 12, 13, 17. ***Map*** *p70 J9.*
Split across two buildings on the western edge of the Old Centre, this smart hotel delivers all of the luxury one would expect from a W Hotel. Don't be fooled by the W's unassuming brown brick exterior. The inside boasts an intriguing mix of design, which combines influence from the city's heritage with upscale contemporary style. The rooftop spaces – the **W Lounge** (*see p92*) and the steakhouse restaurant **MR PORTER** – offer incredible views of the city's 17th-century skyline and are open to all. The W also boasts one of Amsterdam's rare rooftop pools.

Expensive

Check out **The Hoxton Amsterdam** (Herengracht 255, Grachtengordel, 020 888 5555, thehoxton.com) for pitch-perfect interior design and guest-centred attention to detail.

American Hotel Amsterdam
Leidsekade 97, Grachtengordel (020 556 3000, www.amsterdamamericanhotel.com). Tram 1, 2, 5, 11, 12. ***Map*** *p96 G12.*
The public areas of this dazzling art nouveau monument are all eye-pleasers – especially the magnificently buttressed Café Américain. Now part of the Hard Rock group, the hotel has undergone refurbishment to create stylish guest rooms with contemporary furnishings, quirky wallpaper and artwork that nods to rock'n'roll history. They have good views too, either onto the canal or the bustling square below, and some have their own balcony. Meeting facilities are available.

Doubletree by Hilton
Oosterdoksstraat 4, Waterfront (020 530 0800, www.doubletree3.

hilton.com). Tram 2, 4, 11, 12, 13, 14, 17, 24, 26 or Metro Centraal Station. ***Map*** *p166 N7.*
Just east of Centraal Station near the public library, this is one of the largest hotels in the country. Rooms feature floor-to-ceiling windows, and are equipped with an iMac and free Wi-Fi, while the rooftop SkyLounge bar-restaurant offers a spectacular view across the city and harbour. Corporate clients are particularly well served, thanks to the business centre and convention facilities.

Grand Hotel Amrâth Amsterdam

Prins Hendrikkade 108-114, Waterfront (020 552 0000, www.amrathamsterdam.com). Tram 2, 4, 11, 12, 13, 14, 17, 24, 26 or Metro Centraal Station. ***Map*** *166 N8.*
The Grand Hotel Amrâth nods handsomely to both Dutch sea-faring supremacy and the birth of an architectural movement. Considered the first example of the Amsterdam School (*see p266*), this century-old shipping office, known as the Scheepvaarthuis, bursts with creative brickwork and sculpture. The hotel's feeling of timelessness remains, although you can expect the usual range of deluxe frills, plus (a rarity here) a pool. Some rooms have supplements for specific views. There's also the prestigious three-storey suite in the front tower, complete with 360-degree views from the whirlpool bath.

Mövenpick Hotel Amsterdam City Centre

Piet Heinkade 11, Waterfront (020 519 1200, www.movenpick.com). Tram 26. ***Map*** *p166 P7.*
Large, tall and glamorous, this striped, stone-coloured hotel is a great base for exploring Noord on the bank opposite. Rooms are decorated in soothing greys and woods; pricier ones grant access to an executive lounge and have great views over the city's rooftops, or of the cruise liners ploughing through the waters.

Sir Albert Hotel

Albert Cuypstraat 2-6, De Pijp (020 710 7258, www.siralberthotel.com). Tram 3, 12, 24 or Metro De Pijp. ***Map*** *p181 J16.*
Once a diamond factory, Sir Albert is now a four-star 'luxury boutique' hotel featuring the interior stylings of BK Architects. High-ceilinged rooms are inspired by the great design movements of the past, while old-school service is balanced by the latest mod cons. Its Japanese pub-style restaurant, Izakaya, has already been embraced by local foodies.

Zoku Amsterdam

Weesperstraat 105, Plantage (020 811 2811, www.livezoku.com). Tram 1, 7, 19 or Metro Weesperplein. ***Map*** *p150 N12.*
Described as a 'thriving neighbourhood for global nomads', the award-winning Zoku is designed as a hybrid live-and-work space to accommodate jet-setting entrepreneurs and mobile professionals. In addition to the funky co-working spaces, facilities include a music corner, games room, treatment room and a roof-terrace greenhouse. With commanding views of the city, the bar/restaurant/lounge space on the top floor is open to anyone, though if you're not a guest, working on a laptop requires the purchase of a day pass.

Moderate

Hotel Arena

's Gravesandestraat 55, Oosterpark, Oost (020 850 2400, www.hotelarena.nl). Tram 1, 7, 19. ***Map*** *p153 Q13.*
A holy trinity of hotel, restaurant and nightclub in a former Catholic orphanage, Arena is ideal for lazy young scenesters looking for a one-stop shop. A recent refit has brought all the rooms up a notch – clean, modern lines dominate, although the relative sparse style might not be to everyone's taste – while the extra-large ones and suites, kitted out by leading local designers, look great but come with a matching price tag. The location, while perfect for exploring Oost and Zeeburg, is a bit out of the way, but trams can whizz you into the centre in ten minutes.

CitizenM South

Prinses Irenestraat 30, Zuid (020 811 7090, www.citizenm.com). Tram 5 or Metro Amsterdam Zuid.
Welcome to the future of hotels: the shipping container. Due to the housing shortage in Amsterdam, local students have long been living in these humble units, but CitizenM is now using them as the basis for a 'budget luxury' designer-hotel chain. Created and assembled off-site, the 14sq m (150sq ft) rooms have a wall-to-wall window, a king-size bed with luxury linens, a shower pod, toilet pod and flatscreen TV. Refreshments are available 24/7 from the 'canteen'. **Other locations** Amstel Amsterdam, Sarphatistraat 47, Oost; Schipol Airport, Jan Plezierweg 2, Schiphol (020 811 7080).

Hotel The Exchange

Damrak 50, Old Centre (020 523 0080, www.hoteltheexchange.com). Tram 4, 14, 24. ***Map*** *p70 L8.*
A simple hallway leads back to a red gift-box of a reception, offering just a peek of the statement seating in the mezzanine above. Each of the 61 rooms in this hotel (graded from one to five stars) has been exquisitely dressed by designers from the Amsterdam Fashion Institute – and it shows.

CitizenM

Hotel Vondel
Vondelstraat 26-30, Museum Quarter (612 0120, www.hotelvondel.com). Tram 1, 2, 5, 11, 12. ***Map*** *p136 F13.*
Located near museums and upmarket shopping opportunities, this thoroughly chic place is festooned with art and has a lovely decked garden. Rooms, ranging from small to huge, are designer-driven, with chandeliers and swanky bathrooms. Unusually for such a trendy hotel, families are positively encouraged.
Other hotels in the Vondel group are also recommended, especially the industrial-chic **Hotel De Hallen** (Bellamyplein 47, Oud West, 020 820 8670, hoteldehallen.com), located in a former tram depot. See www.vondelhotels.com for details of other Vondel group options.

Lloyd Hotel
Oostelijke Handelskade 34, Waterfront (020 561 3636, www.lloyd.nl). Tram 7, 26. ***Map*** *p166 U8.*
This one-time youth prison has been reinvented as a stylish hotel offering one- to five-star accommodation – every room is unique in size, shape and style – complete with a new 'cultural embassy'. Lloyd features the work of hotshot Dutch designers Atelier van Lieshout and Marcel Wanders. Expect the unexpected – in the best possible way, of course. The restaurant, with its sunny terrace and modishly simple menu, is a bonus. Its sibling is the fashion-conscious **Hotel The Exchange** *(see p284)*.

Volkshotel
Wibautstraat 150, Oost (020 261 2100, www.volkshotel.nl). Metro Wibautstraat. ***Map*** *p150 P15.*
A 'hotel for the people', Volkshotel is one of the many developments in Amsterdam's Oost district. A newspaper HQ in its former life, the building now comprises 172 hotel rooms that range from cosy and simple to large and more luxurious. Decor features raw materials such as glass, wood and concrete. A great place to stay if you're in town to party: the rooftop bar **Canvas** *(see p161)* offers panoramic views of the city and attracts boozing patrons until the wee hours.

Budget

Cocomama
Westeinde 18, Grachtengordel (020 627 2454, www.cocomamahostel.com). Tram 4, 7, 10. ***Map*** *p96 L14.*
This boutique hostel is located in a former brothel, just across the canal from De Pijp. In the past, it cost €200 for an hour of fun at the 'gentlemen's club' Princess; now it costs from €40 for a whole night. Choose from private doubles, family rooms or dorms for two to six, all decorated in appealing Dutch style. There's a communal garden, living room and kitchen, and the friendly staff cook dinner for guests twice a week. **Other location** Ecomama Hotel, Valkenburgerstraat 124, Jodenbuurt (020 770 9529, ecomamahotel.com).

Flying Pig Downtown
Nieuwendijk 100, Old Centre (020 420 6822, www.flyingpig.nl). Tram 2, 4, 11, 12, 13, 14, 17, 24, 26 or Metro Centraal Station. ***Map*** *p70 L7.*
Not so much a hostel, more a way of life. Young backpackers flock here from around the world, as much for the social life as the accommodation; the hostel organises walking tours and in-line skating for free, and there are regular parties and cheap beer. There's a pool table, chill-out room, DJ nights and 'munchies' for sale: Flying Pig hostels are for visitors who giggle when they say the word 'Amsterdam'. They don't accept guests aged under 16 or over 40 – and our guess is that anyone over 30 will feel like a senior citizen. With locations near Leidseplein and at the beach in Noordwijk (and free shuttle buses between them), you're sure to find multiple ways to get your party on and make plenty of friends.

Hotel Casa
Eerste Ringdijkstraat 4, Oost (020 665 1171, www.hotelcasa.nl). Metro Wibautstraat.
Part-hotel part-student housing, Hotel Casa comprises an eclectic mix of patrons at any given time. Originally dreamt up by four friends who wanted to create affordable living for students, their simple idea grew to become the lively and inspiring hub it is today.

Hotel Prinsenhof
Prinsengracht 810, Grachtengordel (020 623 1772, www.prinsenhof.amsterdam). Tram 1, 4, 7, 19. ***Map*** *p96 M13.*
A good option for budget travellers, this diminutive, ten-room hotel with helpful and friendly staff is right near the city's nightlife, and foodie Utrechtsestraat. The stairs are positively vertiginous – luggage is hauled up on a pulley. Rooms are simple, clean and tidy; some have shared facilities. Best of all, rooms with canal views don't attract a premium.

Stayokay Amsterdam Zeeburg
Timorplein 21, Oost (020 551 3190, www.stayokay.com). Tram 14.
Located in a grand old school building that also houses fab cinema and club **Studio/K** *(see p160)*, this branch of the reliable hostel chain is part of Stayokay's designer concept from Edward van Vliet. It's done out in warm reds, with mosaic floors, sleek but simple furniture and huge photos on the walls. Perfect for families and the more discerning hosteller – HI members get a discount – it offers several special packages; check the website for details. **Other locations** Kloveniersburgwal 97, Old Centre (020 624 6832); Zandpad 5, Vondelpark (020 589 8996).

Winston Hotel
Warmoestraat 129, Old Centre (020 623 1380, www.winston.nl). Tram 4, 14, 24. ***Map*** *p70 L8.*
The legendary Winston, now part of St Christopher's Inns, is renowned for its youthful, party-loving atmosphere and arty rooms decorated in eccentric, eclectic style by local businesses and artists. The dorms (of four, six or eight beds) are much cheaper – but much less appealing. There's also a late-opening bar on site, should you run out of options in the Red Light District.

Getting Around

ARRIVING & LEAVING

By air

Amsterdam's **Schiphol Airport** (020 794 0800, www.schiphol.nl) lies 18km (11 miles) south-west of the city. There's only one terminal building, but within that there are four departure and arrival halls.

Taxis

A fixed fare from the airport to the south and west of the city costs around €40, and to the city centre about €50. Bear in mind that there are always plenty of licensed taxis beside the main exit. You can book taxis on the Schiphol website. Ubers are also common and a lot cheaper (around €30-€35), but be careful to note the pick up point – it's usually far away from the official taxi rank.

Connexxion Airport Hotel Shuttle

Connexxion desk, Schiphol Plaza, near Arrivals Hall 4, Schiphol Airport (088 339 4741, www.schipholhotelshuttle.nl). Departures from Platform A7.
This bus from Schiphol to Amsterdam runs at least every 30mins 6.30am-9pm. Anyone can buy a ticket (€18.50 single, €29.50 return), not just hotel guests. Drop-off points are the 100-odd allied hotels; see the website for schedules.

Trains

Trains leave every 10mins or so 5am-midnight (after which they depart hourly). The journey to Centraal Station takes about 20mins. Buy tickets (€4.50 single) before you board or you're likely to incur a €50 fine. There's a €1 surcharge for buying tickets over the counter or from one of the many machines (with English instructions). This can be saved by buying an e-ticket. Depending on your final destination, it might be quicker to take the train to Amsterdam Zuid and catch a tram/metro from there.

By car

Options for crossing the Channel with a car include: Harwich to Hook of Holland with **Stena Line** (www.stenaline.nl); Newcastle to Amsterdam (IJmuiden) with **DFDS Seaways** (www.dfdsseaways.co.uk); Hull to Rotterdam or Zeebrugge with **P&O Ferries** (www.poferries.com); and Dover to Calais with P&O Ferries. Another option is the **Eurotunnel** to France (www.eurotunnel.com).

By coach

International coach services arrive at Amstel Station, with easy connections to Centraal Station. To book a ticket, visit the **Eurolines** website (www.eurolines.com), which is in English. Fares start from €33 for a single from London Victoria to Amsterdam.

By rail

The fastest route from London is to catch a **Eurostar** train (www.eurostar.com) from St Pancras International to Amsterdam Centraal, with a journey time of around 4hrs. Unfortunately, due to passport checks and the lack of an agreement between the Dutch and UK governments, a direct return journey won't be available until some point in 2020. Until then, you have to get a high-speed Thalys to Brussels, go through security and border controls, and then proceed to London.

The **Dutchflyer** train and ferry service involves a train from Liverpool Street Station to Harwich, Stena Line's superferry crossing to Hook of Holland (*see left*), and then a train to Amsterdam Centraal (with a change in Rotterdam).

If you live in the North of England or Scotland, take the ferry from Hull or Newcastle (*see left*). Transfer buses shuttle from the port to either Rotterdam Centraal or Amsterdam Centraal train stations.

Carbon Offsetting

Direct emissions from aviation account for more than 2% of global greenhouse gas emissions. A return economy flight from London Heathrow to Schiphol airport, calculated as roughly 525 miles (844km), produces 180kg of CO_2. If flying is your only option, then consider offsetting this carbon. Organisations such as www.atmosfair.de, climatecare.org and www.goldstandard.org enable you to calculate the emissions associated with your flight and then pay to offset these by investing in sustainable development and environmental projects around the world. Some airlines also offer the chance to buy carbon offsets directly when booking a flight; always check that these are high-quality certified carbon-offsetting programmes before you commit.

PUBLIC TRANSPORT

Getting around Amsterdam is very easy: there are efficient, cheap and integrated trams, metros and buses, and in the centre most places can be reached on foot. Locals tend to get around by bike, and there are also boats and water taxis. Be warned that public transport provision for those with disabilities is dire.

For information, tickets, maps and an English-language guide to all types of public transport tickets, visit the website of **GVB**, Amsterdam's municipal transport authority (www.gvb.nl).

Trams are the best way to travel around the city by public transport, with a network of routes through the centre (buses and the metro are more useful for outlying suburbs). For a basic map of the transport network, *see pull-out map*.

Fares & tickets

The entire GVB network is now completely cash free, with an **OV-chipkaart** ('chip card', www.ov-chipkaart.nl) system operating across the tram, bus and metro network. The card, which is valid for five years, incurs a one-off €7.50 fee and can be purchased at station ticket machines, tobacconists and many supermarkets, as well as GVB Tickets & Info offices (www.gvb.nl). You load the card in the ticket vending machine, paying with cash or card, and use it immediately. You can also load the card in yellow Add Value Machines at tobacconists and various other shops.

An unlimited 24-hour OV-chipkaart costs €8. You can also buy unlimited 48-, 72-, 96-, 120-, 144- and 168-hr cards (ranging from €13.50 to €36.50). With any type of OV-chipkaart, you have to check in and out when boarding or disembarking a tram, bus or metro, using the card readers in the trams and buses, at the entryway to metro stations or on the metro platform. Hold your card in front of the reader and wait for a beep and green light to flash.

An alternative to the OV-chipkaart is the **Iamsterdam City Card**, which includes unlimited public transport and free entrance to 38 museums and attractions. It can be purchased at shops and newsagents across Amsterdam, or at one of the Iamsterdam tourist offices (*see p296*). The card costs €60 (24hrs), €80 (48hrs), €95 (72hrs), €105 (96hrs) or €115 (120hrs). Don't even think about travelling without a ticket: inspectors make regular checks, and passengers without tickets are hit with €37.50 on-the-spot fines.

Trams & buses

Trams run from 6am (6.30am Sat, 7.30am Sun) until 12:30am. Night buses (nos 348-369) take over at other times. All night buses go to Centraal Station, except 369 (Station Sloterdijk to Schiphol Airport).

Night-bus stops are indicated by a black square with the bus number printed on it. During off-peak hours and at quiet stops, stick out your arm to let the driver know you want to get on. Signs at tram and bus stops show the name of the stop and line number, and boards indicate the full route.

Tram rules

Other road users need to be aware that a tram will only stop if absolutely necessary. Cyclists should listen for tram warning bells and cross tramlines at an angle that avoids the front wheel getting stuck. Motorists should avoid blocking tramlines: cars are allowed to venture on to them only if turning right.

Metro

The metro uses the same OV-chipkaart system as trams and buses and serves suburbs to the south and west. Three separate lines – 51, 53 and 54 – terminate at Centraal Station (sometimes abbreviated to CS), while line 50 connects west with south-east. Line 52 connects Amsterdam Zuid with Noord, stopping at several new stations along the way. Metro trains run from 6am (6.30am Sat, 7.30am Sun) to around 12.15am.

TAXIS

Since taxi services were decentralised, there are more independent taxi companies on the market, which unfortunately means there are some opportunist drivers out there, while others have no idea where they're going. Your best bet is to opt for an official cab from **Taxicentrale Amsterdam**. These can be hired by phone (020 777 7777) or picked up from ranks around the city. These taxis have blue licence plates and red 'TCA' roof lights. Alternatively, get an **Uber** (www.uber.com), which tends to be quicker, cheaper and more convenient.

The best central ranks are outside Centraal Station; alongside the bus station (at Kinkerstraat and Marnixstraat); Rembrandtplein; and Leidseplein. Licensed operators must abide by the official fare structure. Make sure the meter starts at the minimum charge (€3.19); you're then charged €2.35/km. Note that not every taxi will accept cards – some remain resolutely cash only. Ask before you begin your journey. If you feel you've been cheated, ask for a receipt before handing over cash. If the fare seems too high, you can file a complaint (0900 202 1881 premium rate, 9am-5pm, you'll need the taxi number or licence plate) or contact the police. Wheelchairs will only fit in taxis if they're folded. If you're a wheelchair user, you can call Van der Laan BV (020 647 4700, 24hrs daily).

Bicycle cabs (basically rickshaws) operate in the city centre, and bright yellow **water taxis** go up and down the canals.

DRIVING

If you're coming by car to the Netherlands, it's wise to join a national motoring organisation before you leave. To drive in the Netherlands, you'll need a valid national driving licence; **ANWB** (*see below*) and many car-hire firms favour photocard licences. You'll need proof that your vehicle has passed a road safety test in its country of origin, an international identification disc, vehicle registration papers and insurance documents.

The Dutch drive on the right. Motorways are labelled 'A'; major roads 'N'; and European routes 'E'. Seatbelts are compulsory for drivers and all passengers. Speed limits are usually 50km/h (31mph) within cities, 80km/h (50mph) outside, 100km/h (62mph) on expressways, and 130km/h (80mph) on motorways. Speeding and other traffic offences are subject to heavy on-the-spot fines.

If you're driving in Amsterdam, look out for cyclists. Always check carefully before you make a turn and when you open your door. Many streets in Amsterdam are one-way – for cars, that is, not bikes, so don't be surprised to see people cycling against the traffic flow.

Strict drink driving laws only allow 0.5mg of alcohol per ml of blood.

Royal Dutch Automobile Club (ANWB) *Customer services 088 269 2222, 24hr emergency line 088 269 2888, www.anwb.nl.*
An annual membership fee of €15.50 gives all sorts of benefits, but for breakdown assistance you have to subscribe to one of the packages (from €5.25-€11.40 a month). Members of foreign motoring organisations may be entitled to free help. Crews may not accept cards at the scene.

Car hire

Dutch car hire (*autoverhuur*) firms generally expect at least one year's driving experience and will want to see a valid national driving licence (with photo) and passport before they hire a vehicle. All will require a deposit by credit card, and you generally need to be over 21. Prices given below are for one day's hire of the cheapest car available excluding insurance and VAT.

Diks Autoverhuur *Van Ostadestraat 278-280, De Pijp (020 662 3366, www.diks.net). Tram 3, 4.* ***Open*** *8am-7.30pm Mon-Sat; 9am-12.30pm, 8-10.30pm Sun.* ***Map*** *p181 L16.*
Cars from €38 per day. The first 150km are free, then it's €0.16/km.

Hertz *Overtoom 333, Oud West (020 612 2441, www.hertz.nl). Tram 1, 11.* ***Open*** *8am-6pm Mon-Fri; 8am-2pm Sat; 9am-2pm Sun.* ***Map*** *p136 C14.*
Cars from €19 per day. The first 200km are free, then it's €0.18/km.

Parking

All of central Amsterdam is metered from 9am until at least 7pm – and in many places to midnight – and spaces are difficult to find. Most spaces are only for official resident permit-holders – especially within the Grachtengordel. Official parking garages are often the easiest solution but may be costly. For on-street parking, look for the blue boxes marked with a white 'P' to pre-pay with a credit card. You'll have to enter your registration – parking officials from Cition (the local traffic authority) then just scan the plate to see if you've paid. Depending on the area, you'll pay €3-€5/hr.

When leaving your car in the city, be sure to empty it of valuables and leave your glovebox open: cars with foreign plates are vulnerable to break-ins. Apps like Parkopedia can be useful to find cheaper parking places, even in normally pricey multi-storey car parks.

Car parks

Car parks are indicated by a white 'P' on a blue square sign. Also worth considering are the very economical Park and Rides (see www.parkeren-amsterdam.com for locations), which cost between €1 and €8 per day. For more information and a list of locations in English, see www.iamsterdam.com/en/plan-your-trip/getting-around/parking/parking-in-amsterdam.

P1 Parking Amsterdam Centraal *Prins Hendrikkade 20, Old Centre (020 638 5330, www.p1.nl).* ***Open*** *24hrs.* ***Rates*** *€5/50min; €55/24hrs.* ***Map*** *p70 L7.*
Many nearby hotels offer a 10% discount on parking here. You can also save by booking ahead online.

Q-Park Europarking *Marnixstraat 250, Jordaan (0900 446 6880 premium rate, www.q-park.nl).* ***Open*** *24hrs.* ***Rates*** *€1.20-€1.50/15 min; €45/24hrs.* ***Map*** *p117 F10.*

Q-Park De Kolk *Nieuwezijds Kolk 18, Old Centre (0900 446 6880 premium rate, www.q-park.nl).* ***Open*** *24hrs.* ***Rates*** *€1.60-€2/15 min; €55/24hrs.* ***Map*** *p70 K7.*

Parking fines

Fines are €62.70, plus the price of one hour's parking in that section of town, and can only be paid via your bank. For more details, visit www.amsterdam.nl/parkeren-verkeer/parkeerbon and click on 'parking'; include your registration and ticket number when transferring funds. If you suspect your car has been towed, call 14 020 (24hrs). If this is the case, you'll have to pay €373 plus €30/day. Payment is only possible with a card.

Car pound

Daniël Goedkoopstraat 9, Oost (020 351 3322). ***Open*** *24hrs daily.*

Petrol

There are 24hr petrol stations (*tankstations*) at Gooiseweg 10, Sarphatistraat 225, Marnixstraat 250 and Spaarndammerdijk 218.

WATER TRANSPORT

Prior to the opening of the new Metro Noord/Zuid line (Line 52), the most efficient way of crossing the IJ for pedestrians and cyclists was on one of the free ferries that zip back and forth across the water all day long. There are several important routes, most of which leave from directly behind Centraal. **901** goes to Buiksloterweg (take this one for most of Noord's waterfront attractions). **902** goes to IJplein. The **906** heads directly to NDSM. The **915** runs from Azartplein across to Zamenhofstraat and is a very useful link for those in Oost. For details of sightseeing boats and other ways of exploring the canals, *see p99* Canal cruising. When renting a boat, stick to the right-hand side of the canal and keep a look out for larger vessels.

CYCLING

Cycling is often the most convenient means of getting from A to B. There are plenty of good, cheap bike hire companies around, of which we list a selection below. Apart from these, check www.detelefoongids.nl under the section '*Fietsen en Bromfietsen Verhuur*'.

Bike rental

There are many places to rent a bike, for about €10 a day. A passport and/or credit card is required.

Bike City *Bloemgracht 68-70, Jordaan (020 626 3721, www.bikecity.nl). Tram 5, 13, 17.* ***Open*** *9am-5.30pm daily.* ***Rates*** *from €17/day with €50 deposit.* ***Map*** *p117 G8.*

Frederic Rentabike *Binnen Wieringerstraat 23, Jordaan (020 624 5509, www.frederic.nl). Bus 18, 21, 22.* ***Open*** *9am-5.30pm daily.* ***Rates*** *from €15/24hrs.* ***Map*** *p117 K6.*

These bikes are not as aggressively branded as others in the city.

King Bikes *Kerkstraat 143, Museum Quarter (06 4199 9258 mobile, www.kingbikes.nl). Tram 1, 2, 7, 11, 12, 19.* ***Open*** *9am-6pm daily.* ***Rates*** *from €12/24hrs.* ***Map*** *p136 J12.*

Scooter hire and guided tours also available. **Other location** Spuistraat 1.

Mac Bike *Overtoom 45, Oud West (020 683 3369, www.macbike.nl). Tram 1, 3, 11.* ***Open*** *9am-6pm daily.* ***Rates*** *from €8/24hrs.* ***Map*** *p136 F12.*

Bike rental, tours, sales and repairs. Five other outlets around the city.

Mike's Bike Tours *Prins Hendrikkade 176A, Old Centre (020 233 0216, www.mikesbiketoursamsterdam.com). Bus 22, 48.* ***Open*** *Mar-Oct 9am-6pm daily. Nov-Feb 10am-6pm daily.* ***Rates*** *from €8/24hrs.* ***Map*** *p96 J12.*

Guided tours available.

Rent-A-Bike *Damstraat 20-22, Old Centre (020 625 5029, www.rentabike.nl). Tram 2, 4, 11, 12, 13, 14, 17, 24.* ***Open*** *9am-6pm daily.* ***Rates*** *€8.50/24hrs; €25 deposit and passport/ID card or credit card photocopy.* ***Map*** *p70 K9.*

StarBikes Rental *De Ruyterkade 143, Waterfront (www.starbikesrental.com, 620 3215). Tram 2, 4, 11, 12, 13, 14, 17, 24 or Metro Centraal.* ***Open*** *8am-7pm Mon-Fri; 9am-7pm Sat, Sun.* ***Rates*** *from €7/24hrs.* ***Map*** *p166 O7.*

Complete with 'bike gallery' and tour options, StarBikes also has a nice café overlooking the waters of the IJ, and very friendly staff. You may be tempted to just forget the bikes and hang out.

WALKING

Amsterdam is a compact city and everything is easy to reach on foot. The canals, cobbled streets, stunning architecture and sheer number of cafés make a stroll through the city a very pleasant experience. Just be aware that cyclists are ruthless – they stop for nothing and no one, so don't get in their way.

Resources A-Z

Travel advice

For up-to-date information on travel to a specific country – including the latest on safety and security, health issues, local laws and customs – contact your home country government's department of foreign affairs. Most have websites with useful advice for would-be travellers.

Australia
www.smartraveller.gov.au

Canada
www.voyage.gc.ca

New Zealand
www.safetravel.govt.nz

Republic of Ireland
www.dfa.ie/travel

UK
www.gov.uk/browse/abroad

USA
www.state.gov/travelers

ACCIDENT & EMERGENCY

Emergency numbers

In an emergency, call **112** (free from any phone) and specify police, fire service or ambulance. For helplines and hospitals, *see below*; for police stations, *see p295*.

In the event of an accident, go to the **eerste spoedhulp** (A&E) of any hospital (*ziekenhuis*). In the case of a minor accident, call 088 003 0600 (open 24/7) and the service will connect you with an emergency GP in your area. There's also the **Tourist Medical Centre** (020 235 7824, www.touristmedicalcentre.nl), which you can call 24hrs a day for free advice.

You can also just turn up at the outpatient departments of the following city hospitals. All are open 24hrs a day, seven days a week.

Hospitals

Academisch Medisch Centrum *Meibergdreef 9, Zuid (020 566 9111, first aid 020 566 2222). Metro Holendrecht.*

Boven IJ Ziekenhuis *Statenjachtstraat 1, Noord (020 634 6346, first aid 020 634 6200). Bus 34, 36, 245, 293.*

Onze Lieve Vrouwe Gasthuis (OLVG) *Oost Oosterpark 9, Oost (020 599 9111, first aid 599 3016). Tram 1, 3 or bus 37.* ***Map** p153 Q14.*

OLVG West *Jan Tooropstraat 164, West (020 510 8911, first aid 020 510 8911). Tram 13 or bus 282.*

VU Ziekenhuis *De Boelelaan 1117, Zuid (020 444 4444, first aid 020 444 3636). Tram 24 or bus 15, 62, 246 or Metro Amstelveenseweg.*

ADDRESSES

Addresses take the form of street name and then house number, such as Damrak 1.

AGE RESTRICTIONS

In the Netherlands, only those over the age of 18 can purchase alcohol, buy cigarettes, smoke cannabis or drive.

ATTITUDE & ETIQUETTE

Amsterdam's reputation as a relaxed city is well founded, as anyone will find out after a wander around the Red Light District. But not everything goes. Smoking dope is not OK everywhere; smoking it in restaurants is usually frowned upon, and many nightclubs ban sportswear and trainers.

CLIMATE

Amsterdam's climate is influenced by the North Sea. Summers are generally mild, autumns wet and windy, and winters cool – but not bitterly so. There is significant rainfall throughout the year, so remember to pack waterproofs. For further information, *see p292* Local Weather; for information on seasonal Amsterdam, *see p26* When to Visit.

CONSUMER

If you have a complaint about the service you've received from Dutch businesses that you're unable to resolve, contact the **National Consumentenbond** (www.consumentenbond.nl) for advice.

CUSTOMS

The import of meat or meat products, fruit, plants, flowers and protected animals to the Netherlands is illegal.
For more information, refer to www.belastingdienst.nl.

If you're entering the Netherlands from another EU country you may import goods for personal use. The following guidelines are for reference only; UK citizens should also refer to www.gov.uk/visit-europe-brexit:
• 800 cigarettes, 400 small cigars, 200 cigars or 1kg loose tobacco.
• 10l spirits (more than 22% alcohol), 20l of spirits (less than 22% alcohol), 90l of wine (or 60l of sparkling wine) or 110l of beer.

If you enter the country from a non-EU country, the following limits apply:
• 200 cigarettes or 250g of smoking tobacco or 100 cigarillos or 50 cigars (or a proportional assortment of these products).
• 1l of spirits or 2l of sparkling wine or 2l of fortified wine, such as sherry or port (or a proportional

assortment of these products) and 4l of non-sparkling wine and 16l of beer.
• Other goods to the value of €430.

DISABLED

Winding cobbled streets, poorly maintained pavements and steep canal house steps can present real difficulties to the less physically able, but the pragmatic Dutch can generally solve problems quickly. Most large museums, cinemas and theatres have decent disabled facilities. The metro is accessible to wheelchair users with normal arm function, but most trams are inaccessible to wheelchair users due to their high steps. The website www.toegankelijk amsterdam.nl (full site not currently available, although limited viewing is possible) has a list of hotels, restaurants and attractions that cater well for the physically less able. **StarBikes** (*see p290*) also rents a special bicycle for the disabled.

DRUGS

Locals have a relaxed attitude to soft drugs, but smoking isn't acceptable everywhere. Use discretion. Outside Amsterdam, public consumption of cannabis is largely unacceptable. Foreigners found with hard drugs should expect to face prosecution. Organisations offering advice can do little to help foreigners with drug-related problems, although the **Jellinek Drugs Prevention Centre** is happy to provide help in several languages, including English. Its helpline (088 505 1220, 9-11am, 3-5pm Mon-Fri) offers advice and information.

ELECTRICITY

Electricity in the Netherlands runs on 220V. Visitors with British 240V appliances can change the plug or use an adaptor. For US 110V appliances, you'll need to use a transformer.

EMBASSIES & CONSULATES

American Consulate *General Museumplein 19, Museum Quarter (575 5309 8am-4.30pm daily, 070 310 2209 outside business hrs, netherlands/ usembassy.gov). Tram 3, 5, 12, 16, 24.* ***Open*** *US citizens' services 8.30-11.30am Mon-Fri. Immigrant visas by appt.* ***Map*** *p136 G15.*

Australian Embassy
Carnegielaan 4, The Hague (070 310 8200, Australian citizen emergency phone 0800 0224 794, netherlands.embassy.gov. au). ***Open*** *8.30am-5pm Mon-Fri. Passport & notarial services 9am-1pm Mon-Fri.*
This embassy cannot issue visas or accept visa applications. The nearest Department of Immigration and Multicultural Affairs is at the embassy in Berlin. Note that only general visa information is available from the Visa Information Officer.

British Consulate
Koningslaan 44, Vondelpark (070 4270 427, www.gov.uk/ world/netherlands). Tram 2. ***Open*** *9am-12.30pm Mon, Tue, Thur, Fri.* ***Map*** *p136 C15.*

British Embassy *Lange Voorhout 10, The Hague (070 427 0427).* ***Open*** *9am-5pm Mon-Fri, appointments only.*
For visa and tourist information, contact the British consulate.

Canadian Embassy
Sophialaan 7, The Hague (070 311 1600, www.netherlands.gc.ca). ***Open*** *9.30am-1pm, 2-5pm Mon-Fri. Consular & passport section 9.30am-12.30pm Mon-Fri (afternoons by appt only).*

Irish Embassy
Scheveningseweg 112, The Hague (070 363 0993, www. embassyofireland.nl). ***Open*** *10am-12.30pm, 2.30-5pm Mon, Tues, Thurs, Fri. Visa enquiries 10am-12.30pm Mon-Fri.*

New Zealand Embassy
Eisenhowerlaan 77N, The Hague (070 346 9324, www. nzembassy.com/netherlands). ***Open*** *9am-12.30pm, 1.30-5pm Mon-Fri.*

See embassy.goabroad.com for all other embassies and consulates.

HEALTH

It's advisable that all travellers take out insurance before leaving home. EU residents travelling in Europe should obtain a **European Health Insurance Card** (**EHIC**). This allows them to benefit from free or reduced-cost medical care when travelling in a country belonging to the European Economic Area (EEA)

Local Weather

Average temperatures and monthly rainfall in Amsterdam.

	Temp (°C/°F)	Rainfall (mm/in)	Sun (hrs/day)
January	5.8 / 42.4	65/2.5	2
February	6.7/44	52/2	2
March	9.9/49.8	53/2.1	3
April	14.2/57.5	41/1.6	5
May	17.7/63.9	60/2.3	7
June	20.1/68.2	66/2.6	7
July	22.1/71.8	91/3.6	7
August	22.2/72	105/4.1	7
September	19/66.2	81/3.2	5
October	14.6/58.3	85/3.3	3
November	9.7/49.5	84/3.3	2
December	6/42.8	84/3.2	2

or Switzerland. The EHIC is free of charge. For further information, including Brexit-related updates, UK residents should refer to www.nhs.uk/using-the-nhs/healthcare-abroad.

Centraal Doktersdienst *(0900 1515, www.doktersdienst.info).*
A 24hr English-speaking line for advice on all medical services. For health-related emergencies, *see p291* Accident & Emergency.

Dentists

Tandartsenpraktijk AOC
Wilhelmina Gasthuisplein 167, Oud West (616 1234, www.tandartsenpraktijk-aoc.nl). Tram 1, 3, 11. ***Open*** *9am-noon, 1pm-4pm Mon-Fri.* ***Map*** *p136 D12.*
AOC offers comprehensive treatment and dental services, including emergency procedures if required.

TBB *0900 821 2230 premium rate, 020 303 4500, www.tandartsbemiddelingsbureau.nl.*
Operators can put you in touch with your nearest dentist, and telephone lines are open 24hrs for those with dental emergencies.

Pharmacies

Chemists (*drogists*) are usually open 9.30am-5.30pm Mon-Sat. For prescription drugs, go to a pharmacy (*apotheek*), usually open 9.30am-5.30pm Mon-Fri.

The morning-after pill is available over the counter from pharmacies.

Apotheek Leidsestraat
Leidsestraat 74-76, Grachtengordel (020 422 0210, www.leidsestraatapotheek.nl). Tram 2, 11, 12. ***Open*** *8.30am-10pm Mon-Fri; 9am-10pm Sat; 11am-10pm Sun.* ***Map*** *p96 H11.*
The central night chemist for filling prescriptions.

Sint Lucas Andreas Apotheek *Jan Tooropstraat 164, West (020 510 8826, www.olvg.nl/poliklinische-apotheek). Tram 13 or bus 282.* ***Open*** *24hrs daily.*
A 24/7 chemist for prescriptions.

STDs, HIV & AIDS

The subject of prostitution always raises concerns about STDs. Sex workers take their healthcare seriously and will insist on using a condom. There are no laws requiring prostitutes to have medical check-ups but there's an STD clinic in the Old Side's Red Light District where sex workers can go anonymously for free check-ups.

The **AIDS Information Line** (020 689 2577) run by HIV Vereniging offers advice and can put you in contact with every department you need. **SOA AIDS Nederland** has a more general information line (0900 204 2040 premium rate) for questions about safe sex and sexually transmitted diseases.

The city's health department, the **GGD**, runs free STD clinics that are anonymous and open to all. You can also arrange testing through a GP. An AIDS test can also be done at thrift shop chain **Out of the Closet** (www.outofthecloset.org).

There are many active AIDS/HIV-related organisations in Amsterdam, including **Stichting AIDS Fonds** (www.aidsfonds.nl) and **Dance4Life** (www.dance4life.nl).

GGD *Weesperplein 1 Plantage (020 555 5911, www.ggd.amsterdam.nl). Tram 1, 7, 19 or Metro Weesperplein.* ***Open*** *8.30-10am, 1.30-4.30pm Mon-Fri.* ***Map*** *p153 O13.*
Examinations and treatment of STDs, including free and anonymous HIV tests.

HIV Vereniging
1e Helmersstraat 17 B3, Oud West (www.hivnet.org). Tram 1, 3, 11. ***Map*** *p136 F12.*
The Netherlands HIV Association supports those who are HIV positive, including offering legal help. You can get HIV test results in an hour. Call 020 689 2577 (2-10pm Mon, Tue, Thur) to chat, ask questions or make an appointment for a visit or workshop.

SOA AIDS Nederland Info Line *0900 204 2040 premium rate, www.soaaids.nl.* ***Open*** *9.30am-3.30pm Mon-Wed; 1.30-3.30pm Thur, Fri.*
If you need any information or advice on safe sex, AIDS or any other sexually transmitted infections and diseases, call this friendly phone line (€0.10/min).

HELPLINES

Alcoholics Anonymous *020 625 6057 24hrs daily, www.aa-netherlands.org.*
English and Dutch information on the times and dates of meetings, and contact numbers for counsellors. The website has an English section, and you can locate meetings by day or by town.

Narcotics Anonymous *06 2234 1050, www.na-holland.nl.*
Offers a 24hr answerphone service in English and Dutch, with counsellors' phone numbers.

ID

Everyone has to carry some sort of identification all the time. If you're moving to Amsterdam, you have to register with the local council, in the same building as the Aliens' Police (*see p296* Visas & Immigration).

LANGUAGE

Dutch is the official language of the Netherlands, though most Dutch people speak English to a high standard.

LEFT LUGGAGE

There's a staffed left-luggage counter at **Schiphol Airport** (020 795 2843, www.schiphol.nl), where you can store luggage for up to one month, open 24hrs daily, use of intercom 10pm-6am (from €6/24hrs, depending on size). There are also automatic left-luggage lockers, accessible 24hrs a day (from €8/24hrs, for up to 168hrs). There are also plenty of lockers at **Centraal Station**, with 24hr access (from €7/24hrs).

LEGAL HELP

Access *IN Amsterdam, World Trade Center Amsterdam, I-tower, Strawinskylaan 1767, Zuid (0900 222 2377 premium rate, www.access-nl.org). Metro Amsterdam Zuid.* ***Open*** *9am-4pm Mon-Fri.*
This volunteer-run organisation for the international community runs a helpline for all matters and a drop-in centre at the World Trade Center site.

Juridisch Loket *Vijzelgracht 21-25, Grachtengordel (0900 8020 premium rate, www.juridischloket.nl). Tram 24, or Metro Vijzelgracht.* ***Open*** *9am-11pm Mon-Thur.* ***Map*** *p96 K13.*
Qualified lawyers offering free or low-cost legal advice.

LGBTQ

For details of LGBTQ organisations and resources, plus an overview of the scene, *see p212* LGBTQ.

LOST PROPERTY

Report lost property, especially a lost passport or ID card, to the police. Inform your embassy or consulate, too, if you lose your passport. For things lost at the Hoek van Holland ferry terminal or Schiphol airport, contact the company you're travelling with.

Centraal Station *Stationsplein 15, Old Centre (020 751 5155, www.ns.nl). Tram 2, 4, 11, 12, 13, 14, 17, 24.* ***Open*** *24hrs daily.* ***Map*** *p70 H7.*
Items found on trains are kept for five days at the office on the east side of the station (0900 321 2100 €0.80/min), after which they're forwarded to the Centraal Bureau Gevonden Voorwerpen (Central Lost Property Office) in Utrecht. Fill in the 'tracing' form on the website and have items posted (collecting them personally isn't possible) from €15.

GVB Lost Property *Arlandaweg 100 (0900 8011 premium rate, 9am-7pm Mon-Sat; en.gvb.nl/klantenservice/verloren-voorwerpen). Tram 19 or Metro Sloterdijk or bus 22, 61, 69 or Sloterdijk rail.* ***Open*** *9am-5pm Mon-Wed; 9am-7pm Thur.*
Wait at least a day or two before you call and describe what you've lost on the bus, metro or tram. If your property has been found, you can pick it up at GVB head office at Arlandaweg. If you've lost your keys, you don't have to call ahead.

Municipality Lost Property *Korte Leidsedwarsstraat 52, Grachtengordel (020 251 0222). Tram 1, 2, 7, 11, 12, 19.* ***Open*** *In person 9am-4pm Mon-Fri. By phone noon-4pm Mon-Fri.* ***Map*** *p96 H12.*

MEDIA

Freesheet *Metro* is the highest circulation paper in the Netherlands, followed by *De Telegraaf*, *Algemeen Dagblad* and *De Volkskrant*. TV and radio are provided by the Netherlands Public Broadcasting system (with three television and five radio networks) together with a number of commercial channels. Internet channel www.dutchnews.nl has all the latest Dutch news stories in English.

MONEY

Since January 2002 the Dutch currency has been the euro. The Netherlands is well on its way to becoming a cashless society, and many bars, restaurants and services will now only accept payment by debit card (*see right* Credit & debit cards). Contactless payment is extremely common but not everywhere will accept Apple Pay or other phone payment systems; make sure you always have an alternative payment method to hand.

ATMs

Cash machines are found at banks, supermarkets and larger shops such as HEMA. You should be able to withdraw cash from ATMs using any credit or debit card, although it's worth checking with your bank before you go, and also what the charges are.

Banks

Amsterdam has more than its fair share of vast banks. Most are open 9am-5pm Mon-Fri, with Postbank opening on Sat morning as well. There's little difference between exchange rates offered by banks and bureaux de change. Dutch banks buy and sell foreign currency, but few give cash advances against credit cards.

Bureaux de change

GWK Travelex *Centraal Station, Old Centre (020 696 8609, www.gwktravelex.nl). Tram 1, 2, 4, 5, 9, 13, 16, 17, 24, 26.* ***Open*** *9am-8pm Mon-Fri; 10am-5pm Sat, Sun.* ***Map*** *p70 H7.*
Other locations include Leidestraat 103 (9am-9pm Mon-Fri; 10am-8pm Sat, Sun); Schiphol Airport (6am-10pm daily); and Damrak 86 (9am-8pm Mon-Sat, 11am-6pm Sun).

Credit & debit cards

Most restaurants will take at least one type of credit card; they're less popular in bars and shops, and most supermarkets don't accept them at all, so always check first and carry a recognised debit card instead. Also note that the Dutch payment system classifies Visa and Mastercard Debit cards as 'credit' cards, so if an establishment doesn't accept credit cards, it won't accept those either. If you lose your card, call the relevant 24hr number immediately:

American Express *020 504 8000*
MasterCard *0800 022 5821*
Visa *0800 022 3110*

Tax

Sales tax (BTW) – 21 per cent on most items, six per cent on goods such as books and food, more on alcohol, tobacco and petrol – will be included in prices quoted in shops.

OPENING HOURS

As a general rule, shops are open 1-6pm Mon (if they're open at all); 9/10am-6pm Tue-Fri, with some open until 9pm Thur; and 9am-5pm Sat. Smaller shops are more erratic; if in doubt, phone. Many central shops are open on Sun. The city's bars tend to open at various times during the day and close at around 1am throughout the week, except for Fri and Sat, when they stay open until 2am or 3am. Restaurants generally open in the evening 5-11pm (though some close as early as 9pm); many are closed on Sun and Mon.

POLICE

For emergencies, call 112. There's also a 24hr police service line (0900 8844) for the Amsterdam area. To report a crime anonymously, call 0800 7000.

Dutch police (www.politie.nl) are under no obligation to grant a phone call to those they detain – they can hold people for up to 6hrs for questioning for minor crimes, 24hrs for major matters – but they'll phone the relevant consulate on behalf of a foreign detainee.

Hoofdbureau van Politie (Police Headquarters)
Lijnbaansgracht 219, Grachtengordel (0900 8844 premium rate). Tram 5, 7, 19. ***Open*** *24hrs daily.* ***Map*** *p96. G12*

POSTAL SERVICES

Following a reorganisation of the postal services, all but one of the post offices in Amsterdam have closed. Instead, many bookshops, tobacconists and supermarkets offer postal services. Look for the orange illuminated sign with the PostNL logo. The postal information line is available on 0900 0990 (premium rate). The remaining office is at *Singel 250, Grachtengordel (www.postnl.nl).* ***Open*** *8am-6pm Mon-Fri; 9am-5pm Sat.* ***Map*** *p96 J8.*

PUBLIC HOLIDAYS

Known as *Nationale Feestdagen* in Dutch.
Nieuwjaarsdag *New Year's Day* 1 Jan
Goede Vrijdag *Good Friday*
Eerste Paasdag *Easter Sunday*
Tweede Paasdag *Easter Monday*
King's Day 27 Apr
Bevrijdingsdag *Liberation Day* 5 May
Hemelvaartsdag *Ascension Day*
Pinksteren *Whit Sunday/ Pentecost*
Pinkstermaandag *Whit Monday/Pentecost*
Eerste Kerstdag *Christmas* 25 Dec
Tweede Kerstdag *Boxing Day* 26 Dec

RELIGION

The majority of the Dutch population doesn't identify with any religion at all (60% according to Iamsterdam). The largest religion is Christianity, which accounts for 17% of the city's population, just over half of which are Roman Catholics; 14% of the population identify themselves as Muslim. In addition to churches of many denominations, and mosques, the city has synagogues, a Buddhist temple and a Hindu temple. Many of the churches and synagogues offer services in English.

SAFETY & SECURITY

Amsterdam is a relatively safe city, but do take care. The Red Light District is rife with expert pickpockets. Be vigilant, especially on bridges, and don't ever make eye contact with anyone who looks as though they're up to no good.

Be careful to watch out for thieves on the Schiphol train. If you cycle, lock your bike up securely (two locks are advisable). Keep valuables in your hotel safe, don't leave bags unattended, and ensure your cash and cards are well tucked away, preferably zipped up in your bag.

SMOKING

In 2008, the Netherlands imposed a smoking ban in all public indoor spaces. As for cannabis, locals have a relaxed attitude, but smoking it isn't acceptable everywhere in the city: use your discretion, and if in doubt, ask before you spark up. For more on Amsterdam's cannabis laws, *see p34*.

STUDY

The University of Amsterdam is the largest in the country (*www.uva.nl*), with Vrije Universiteit Amsterdam (*www.vu.nl*) and Amsterdam University College (*www.auc.nl*) also in the city.

TELEPHONES

Amsterdam telephone numbers in this guide are listed with the area code, 020, as this is needed for all calls from mobile phones and from landlines outside Amsterdam. Phone numbers in the Netherlands outside Amsterdam are also listed with the relevant area code. There are other types of numbers that appear in this book: 06 numbers are for mobile phones; 0800 numbers are freephone numbers; and 0900 numbers are charged at premium rates. The latter two can't be reached from abroad.

Dialling & codes

From the Netherlands
Dial the following code, then the number you're calling.
Australia *00 61*
Irish Republic *00 353*
UK *00 44 (then drop the first '0' from the area code)*
USA & Canada *00 1*

To the Netherlands
If dialling from outside the Netherlands, use the country code 31, followed by the number. Drop the first '0' of the area code. The first 0 on mobiles is also dropped.
From Australia *00 11 31*
From UK & Irish Republic *00 31*
From USA *011 31*

Operator services

Within the Netherlands
National directory enquiries
1888 (€0.90/min)

Mobile phones

Check with your service provider before leaving your home country about service while you're in the Netherlands. US mobile phone users should make sure they call their phone provider before departure to check their mobile's compatibility with GSM bands. All of the main mobile operators in the Netherlands (Vodafone, KPN, T Mobile, Tele2, Telfort and Simyo) offer pre-paid SIM card bundles of data, calls and texts; prices start from €5. Albert Heijn also sells its own. Avoid purchasing these at Schiphol airport; you'll get cheaper deals in the city. There are also numerous options to rent a cell phone, or purchase a cheap GSM handset.

Public phones

Phonecards are available from stations, the Amsterdam Tourist Board, post offices and tobacconists. You can also use credit cards in many public phones.

TIME

The Netherlands is an hour ahead of Greenwich Mean Time (GMT). The Dutch use the 24-hour clock.

TIPPING

Service charges are included in hotel, taxi, bar, café and restaurant bills. It's polite to round up to the nearest euro for small bills or the nearest five for larger sums, although tipping 10% is becoming more common.

TOILETS

Public toilets are few and far between in the city, though the four-bowls-in-one, grey plastic 'Rocket' urinals and high-tech 'Uri-liften' – which rise out of the ground – have been permanently installed in the city's main nightlife squares. Apart from nipping into a café or department store, there are fewer choices for females. Install the Toilocator app before hitting the town or check out www.hogenood.nu to locate the nearest conveniences.

TOURIST INFORMATION

Iamsterdam Visitor Information Centre *Stationsplein 10, Old Centre (www.Iamsterdam.com). Tram 2, 4, 11, 12, 13, 14, 17, 24 or Metro Centraal.* ***Open*** *9am-5pm daily.* ***Map*** *p70 H7.*
The main tourist office is outside Centraal Station. **Other location** Schiphol Airport, Arrivals Hall 2 (7am-10pm daily).

VISAS & IMMIGRATION

Citizens from the EU, USA, Canada, Australia and New Zealand just need a valid passport for stays of less than three months. Citizens of other countries must have a tourist visa. For stays longer than three months, apply for a resident's permit at the Immigration and Naturalisation Service (Stadhouderskade 85, 088 043 0430, www.ind.nl). For Brexit-related information, UK citizens are advised to consult www.gov.uk/visit-europe-brexit.

WEIGHTS & MEASURES

The Dutch use metric weights, distances and measurements.

WOMEN

Central Amsterdam is fairly safe for women: use your common sense when travelling alone. Call emergency number 112 if you're in danger. The helpline 611 6022 is available for support if you've been a victim of rape, assault, sexual harassment or threats.

WORK

Non-EU nationals must apply for a residence permit (*Machtiging tot Voorlopig Verblijf* – MVV) from the Vreemdelingenpolitie (alien police) if they move to Amsterdam for a period of longer than three months and intend to work. Residence permits are usually valid for one year. Citizens of the EU and EEA do not require a residence permit, although UK citizens are advised to consult www.gov.uk/guidance/living-in-the-eu-prepare-for-brexit. Australians and New Zealand nationals aged 18-30 may not have to apply for a residence permit under the Working Holiday Scheme visa. For further information, contact **IN Amsterdam** (020 254 7999) during business hours.

Further Reference

BOOKS

Fiction

AC Baantjer *De Cock series*
Crime novels by a local ex-cop. Was also a long-running TV series.

Jessie Burton *The Miniaturist*
Mysterious goings-on in 17th-century Amsterdam.

Albert Camus *The Fall*
Writer recalls his Parisian past in Amsterdam's 'circles of hell'.

Tracy Chevalier
Girl with a Pearl Earring
Inspired by Vermeer's painting; set in 17th-century Delft.

John Green
The Fault in Our Stars
The acclaimed novel that inspired the film (*see p298*).

Arnon Grunberg
Blue Mondays
Philip Roth's *Goodbye Columbus* goes Dutch in this 1994 bestseller.

Arthur Japin
In Lucia's Eyes
A coming-of-age tale through a courtesan's eyes.

Herman Koch
The Dinner
Two middle-class families with teenage sons caught up in a murder investigation.

David Liss
The Coffee Trader
Thriller focused on a 17th-century Portuguese Jewish financier, tempted into the emerging coffee trade.

Adrian Mathews
The Apothecary's House
An art historian who processes claims for artwork stolen by Nazis.

Deborah Moggach
Tulip Fever Art, beauty, lust, greed and deception in the 17th century.

Harry Mulisch
The Assault
A boy's perspective on World War II. Also a classic film.

Multatuli Max
Havelaar, or the Coffee Auctions of the Dutch Trading Company
A colonial officer and his clash with the corrupt government.

Janwillem van der Wetering
The Japanese Corpse
An off-the-wall police procedural set in Amsterdam.

Manfred Wolf (ed)
Amsterdam: A Traveller's Literary Companion
The country's best writers on the city.

Non-fiction

Timothy Brook
Vermeer's Hat: The 17th Century and the Dawn of the Global World
An exploration of the Golden Age via various works of art.

Ian Buruma
Murder in Amsterdam: The Death of Theo van Gogh and the Limits of Tolerance
An analysis of tensions over immigration and tolerance in the Netherlands.

Sean Condon
My 'Dam Life
Amsterdam through the adoring eyes of a temporary resident.

Christian Ernsten (ed)
Mokum: A Guide to Amsterdam
A quirky approach to discovering the city.

Fred Feddes
A Millennium of Amsterdam
An illustrated history of Amsterdam's changing landscapes.

Anne Frank
The Diary of Anne Frank
Still-shocking wartime diary.

RH Fuchs
Dutch Painting
A comprehensive guide.

Marielle Hageman and Gerlinde Schuller
Amsterdam in Documents 2010-1275
An illustrated history of the city's most important documents and artworks.

Etty Hillesum
An Interrupted Life: The Diaries and Letters 1941-1943
The moving wartime experiences of a young Amsterdam Jewish woman who died in Auschwitz.

Pete Jordan
In the City of Bikes: The Story of the Amsterdam Cyclist
A personal history of the city's fave mode of transportation.

Geert Mak
Amsterdam: A Brief Life of the City
The city's history told through the stories of its people.

Benjamin B Roberts
Sex and Drugs before Rock 'n' Roll: Youth Culture and Masculinity during Holland's Golden Age
Young, male and horny in the 17th century.

Simon Schama
The Embarrassment of Riches
A lively social and cultural history of the Netherlands.

Russell Shorto
Amsterdam: A History of the World's Most Liberal City

The title nails it. A compelling read.

Russell Shorto
The Island at the Center of the World: The Epic Story of Dutch Manhattan
The Dutch as seen through their influence in the New World.

Wim de Wit
Amsterdam School: Dutch Expressionist Architecture.

MUSIC

Arling & Cameron
Music for Imaginary Films (2000)
Eclectic duo reinvent the history of the soundtrack.

Beach Boys
Holland (1973)
Californians hole up in Holland and start recording.

Chet Baker
Live at Nick's (1978)
In front of his favourite rhythm section, Chet simply soars.

Coldplay
Amsterdam (2002)
Chris Martin wrote the song while in the city.

The Ex + Getatchew Mekuria
Moa Anbessa (2006)
Anarcho squat punks/improv jazzsters team up with Ethiopian sax legend.

Herman Brood & His Wild Romance
Shpritsz (1978)
The classic album from the nation's iconic rocker and 'cuddle junkie'.

De Jeugd van Tegenwoordig
Manon (2015)
Amsterdam hip-hop legends, often incoherent and therefore universal.

Peter Bjorn and John
Amsterdam (2006)
Swedish indie band wrote about the encapsulating power of the city.

Usher
Amsterdam (2016)
The R&B artist sings of a romantic night in the city.

FILMS

Amsterdam Global Village
dir Johan van der Keuken (1996)
A meditative meander through the city's streets (and people).

Of Amsterdam
dir Catarina Neves Ricci (2015)
A documentary about foreign artists living in the Netherlands.

Amsterdamned
dir Dick Maas (1987) Psychotic frogman, lots of canal chase scenes and continuity problems that lead to characters turning an Amsterdam corner and ending up in Utrecht.

Black Book
dir Paul Verhoeven (2006) A Jewish singer goes undercover for the Dutch Resistance.

The Fault In Our Stars
dir Josh Boon (2014)
Two teenage cancer patients embark on a life-affirming journey to Amsterdam.

The Fourth Man
dir Paul Verhoeven (1983)
Melodrama seething with homoerotic desire.

Hufters en Hofdames (Bastards and Bridesmaids)
dir Eddy Terstall (1997)
Amsterdam as a backdrop to twenty-something relationship pains.

Karacter (Character)
dir Mike van Diem (1997)
An impeccable father-son drama.

De Noorderlingen (The Northerners)
dir Alex van Warmerdam (1992)
Absurdity and angst in a lonely Dutch subdivision by the director of Borgman (2013).

Sexwork, Love & Mr Right
dir Clare Struges (2013)
An exploration of the life of a sex worker in the Red Light District.

Yes Nurse! No Nurse!
dir Pieter Kramer (2002)
Musical cult classic for connoisseurs of camp.

APPS & WEBSITES

9292.nl/en Transport information, including route planning and disruption updates. Also available as an app.

FlatTire app An app that allows you to book a mechanic to fix your bike on location. Most repairs take a matter of minutes.

VaarWater app A guide to navigating the city by water.

weCity app Detailed and personalised travel tips, plus reservations for restaurants and more.

www.amsterdam.info
An online travel guide that does what it says on the tin.

www.amsterdamfoodie.nl
Restaurant reviews by a respected food blogger.

en.gvb.nl Official website of the public transport company of Amsterdam, with routes, fares and live information. Also available as an app.

www.holland.com
National tourist board website.

www.Iamsterdam.nl
The official tourist board website is a one-stop shop for visitors.

www.littleblackbook.me
A lifestyle blog packed with food, drink and cultural recommendations. Also available as an app.

www.subbacultcha.nl
All things counter-culturally musical.

Index

INDEX

Photography credits

Inside front cover Xandra R/Shutterstock.com; pages 2 (top) Artur Bogacki/Shutterstock.com; 2 (bottom) Steve Photography/Shutterstock.com; 3, 174 Dennis Bouman/A'DAM Toren; 5 S-F/Shutterstock.com; 6, 115, 120 (left), 173 Harry Beugelink/Shutterstock.com; 11 (top) GiuseppeCrimeni/Shutterstock.com; 11 (bottom), 99 Mo Wu/Shutterstock.com; 12 (top) Erik Smits Fotografie/Rijksmuseum; 12 (bottom) Harry Cooper PhOtography/Shutterstock.com; 13 (top), 141 (bottom) InnaFelker/Shutterstock.com; 13 (bottom) Z. Jacobs/Shutterstock.com; 14 (top), 16 (top), 37, 132, 267 www.hollandfoto.net/Shutterstock.com; 14 (bottom) hurricanehank/Shutterstock.com; 15 (top) Martijn Kort/A'DAM Toren; 15 (middle), 21 (bottom), 209, 217, 227 Melanie Lemahieu/Shutterstock.com; 15 (bottom) Courtesy Carlos Amorales, kurimanzutto and Nils Stærk/Stedelijk Museum; 16 (middle) Martin Hogeboom/fotograaf/Eye Film Institute; 16 (bottom), 23 (middle & bottom), 237 Hans Roggen Fotografie/Concertgebouw; 17 (top) Quince Graphics/Shutterstock.com; 17 (bottom), 184 Albert Cuypmarkt; 18 (top), 111 Brassaï, Foam, 2019 © Christian van der Kooy; 18 (bottom), 79 Arjan Bronkhorst/Ons' Lieve Heer op Solder; 20 ingehogenbijl/Shutterstock.com; 21 (top) kavalenkau/Shutterstock.com; 22 (top Samot/Shutterstock.com; 22 (middle) Mike Bink/Eye Film Institute; 22 (bottom) T.W. van Urk/Shutterstock.com; 23 (top) Monika Rittershaus/Nationale Opera; 24 (top) picturepartners/Shutterstock.com; 24 (bottom), 50 (bottom), 177 fokke baarssen/Shutterstock.com; 25 (top), 60, 91 M. Vinuesa/Shutterstock.com; 25 (bottom) DigiDaan/NEMO Science Museum; 26 (top), 78 Anton_Ivanov/Shutterstock.com; 26 (bottom) Levas/Shutterstock.com; 27 (top) Faustino Gaitan/Shutterstock.com; 27 (bottom) Unique Vision/Shutterstock.com; 29 Aeypix/Shutterstock.com; 30 Frank Cornelissen/Shutterstock.com; 32 Paolo Grassi/Shutterstock.com; 33 DorotaM/Shutterstock.com; 34 Kemedo/Shutterstock.com; 35 (top) De Jongh Photography/Shutterstock.com; 35 (bottom), 280 DutchMen/Shutterstock.com; 36 Kirill Spiridonov/Shutterstock.com; 39, 187 CT Coffee & Coconuts; 40, 128 By Pesca; 41 Casper van Dort/Blauw; 42 &SAMHOUD; 43, 44 Foodhallen; 45 Taste of Amsterdam; 46, 162 Oedipus Brewing; 47 (top) bas@25fps.nl/Twenty Third Bar; 47 (bottom) t Blauwe Theehuis; 48, 183 Ayako Nishibori; 49, 165 Hannekes Boom; 50 (top) Bjoern Wylezich/Shutterstock.com ; 53, 107 Stan Koolen Photography/King Louie; 54 (top), 108 the Otherist; 54 (bottom), 265 Kiev.Victor/Shutterstock.com; 55, 126 (middle & bottom) Moooi; 56 Droog; 57 Wut_Moppie; 58 Edwin Butter/Shutterstock.com; 63 littlenySTOCK/Shutterstock.com; 64 (top), 278 kavalenkava/Shutterstock.com; 64 (bottom), 160, 179 Christophe Cappelli/Shutterstock.com; 65 Daniel jakulovic/Shutterstock.com; 66 BOOCYS/Shutterstock.com; 69, 80 Oude Kerk; 73, 76, 190 (top), 244 Olena Z/Shutterstock.com; 75 (top) Monique Kooijmans/Allard Pierson; 75 (middle & bottom) Lysbeth Holthuis/Allard Pierson; 81 Gert Jan van Rooij ; 84 Anibal Trejo/Shutterstock.com; 87 Richard de Bruijn/Amsterdam Musuem; 88 © Gunther von Hagens, Institute for Plastination, Heidelberg, Germany, www.bodyworlds.nl; 93 Copa Football Store; 95 www.peterkooijman.nl/Museum Van Loon; 98 Mikhail Markovskiy/Shutterstock.com; 101 Julia700702/Shutterstock.com; 103 (top & middle right) Anne Frank Huis; 103 (bottom left) Michelle Grant/Time Out; 103 (bottom right) Cris Toala Olivares; 104 Thijs Wolzak; 105 Gs Holding BV; 110 Museum Willet-Holthuysen/www.amsterdammuseum.nl; 116 T.Withagen-Noordermarkt; 119 Christina Theisen; 120 (right) Marc Venema/Shutterstock.com; 121, 216 Ivo Antonie de Rooij/Shutterstock.com; 122 Michael KN/Shutterstock.com; 123 Angel L/Shutterstock.com; 124, 125 (top) KochxBos Gallery; 125 (bottom) Gunnar Meier Photography/Galerie Fons Welters; 126 (top) Bo van Veen/Lena the Fashion Library; 129 STREET ART MUSEUM AMSTERDAM; 130 Jpstock/Shutterstock.com; 135 M.WILLEMSTEIN/'t Blauwe Theehuis; 138 To follow (Shutterstock); 139 Collection Stedelijk Museum Amsterdam; 140 Marcello Sgarlato/Shutterstock.com; 141 (top) Salvador Maniquiz/Shutterstock.com; 142 Alfio Finocchiaro/Shutterstock.com; 144 Bien Schols @ SeenbyBien/Azzurro Due; 145 Lot Sixty One; 147 maicasaa/Shutterstock.com; 151 www.ruimtesinbeeld.nl/Tropenmuseum; 155 villorejo/Shutterstock.com; 156 (top) Wikimedia Commons; 156 (bottom) Museum Het Rembrandthuis; 159 Merijn Soeters/Verzetsmuseum; 161 Tropenmuseum; 169 Eddo Hartmann/Nederlands Scheepvartmuseum; 170 Elisabeth Aardema/Shutterstock.com; 182 Winds/Shutterstock.com; 185 The Butcher/The Entourage Group; 186 Carly Diaz/Little Collins; 189 HildaWeges Photography/Shutterstock.com; 190 DutchScenery/Shutterstock.com; 191 (bottom) Anton Havelaar/Shutterstock.com; 192 Serghei Starus/Shutterstock.com; 193 Aerovista Luchtfotografie/Shutterstock.com; 194 Okunin/Shutterstock.com; 195 (top) Republiek Bloemendaal; 195 (bottom) dipo58/Shutterstock.com; 196 Angela Sterling/Het Nationale Ballet; 199 http://matthijssimmink.com; 200 Dmitry Kalinovsky/Shutterstock.com; 202 Roel Vincken/SAIL Amsterdam; 205 Jule van Ravenzwaay; 207 Bowie Verschuuren/De FilmHallen; 210 Bowie Verschuuren/The Movies; 213 Wut_Moppie/Shutterstock.com; 214 Nancy Beijersbergen/Shutterstock.com; 218, 219 Remon van den Kommer/Club Church; 221 Ruslans Golenkovs / Shutterstock.com; 223 Ben Houdijk/Shutterstock.com; 226 Fotograafniels.nl/Niels de Vries/Disco Dolly; 230 AngelaLouwe/Shutterstock.com; 232 (top) Bart Grietens/Bimhuis; 232 (middle &bottom) Francoise Bolechowski/Bimhuis; 235 Bill Cooper/International Theatre Amsterdam; 238 Pascal Victormahoganny/Nationale Opera; 239 Hans Gerritsen/Het Nationale Ballet; 240 Robert HM Voors/Shutterstock.com; 242 Jan Versweyveld/International Theatre Amsterdam; 247 By Jacob van Ruisdael via Wikimedia Commons; 251 (top) Altitude Drone/Shutterstock.com; 251 (middle left) Joe Benning/Shutterstock.com; 251 (middle right), 258 Everett - Art/Shutterstock; 251 (bottom) Claire Slingerland/Shutterstock.com; 255 Nationaal Archief/Wikimedia Commons; 257 Alexandros Michailidis/Shutterstock.com; 258 Joost Evers/Anefo/Wikimedia Commons; 261 Dennis van de Water/Shutterstock.com; 262 TravnikovStudio/Shutterstock.com; 268 JJFarq/Shutterstock.com; 271 http://explore.rkd.nl/explore/images/20420; 272 Johannes Vermeer, The Milkmaid, c. 1660. Rijksmuseum, Amsterdam; 273 Koos Raucamp (GaHetNa (Nationaal Archief NL))/Wikimedia Commons; 274 Vincent van Gogh/Wikimedia Commons; 277 Martijn Vonck Fotografie/Frozen Fountain; 281 (top) Per-Boge/Shutterstock.com; 281 (bottom) Sander Baks/Hotel Pulitzer; 24 maxidhoore/Shutterstock.com.

Credits

Crimson credits
Editor Derek Robertson
Proofreader Kate Michell
Cartography Gail Armstrong

Series Editor Sophie Blacksell Jones
Production Manager Kate Michell
Production Designer Emilie Crabb
Print Manager Patrick Dawson
Design Mytton Williams

Chairman David Lester
Managing Director Andy Riddle

Advertising Media Sales House
Marketing Sophie Shepherd
Sales Lyndsey Mayhew

Acknowledgements
This edition of *Time Out Amsterdam* was researched and updated by Derek Robertson. The editor would like to thank Karin Björk, Chloë Björk-Robertson, Lilli Berger and Eva Berger for their invaluable help, plus all contributors to previous editions of *Time Out Amsterdam* whose work forms the basis of this guide.

Photography credits
Front cover Neil Farrin/AWL-images
Back cover Left: Dennis Jarvis/Wikimedia Commons; Centre right: Taste of Amsterdam; Right: DutchMen/Shutterstock.com
Interior photography credits, *see p303.*

Publishing information
Time Out Amsterdam 14th edition

February 2020

ISBN 978 1 780592 80 0
CIP DATA: A catalogue record for this book is available from the British Library

Published by Crimson Publishing
21d Charles Street, Bath, BA1 1HX (01225 584 950, www.crimsonpublishing.co.uk) on behalf of Time Out England.

Distributed by Grantham Book Services
Distributed in the US and Canada by Publishers Group West (1-510-809-3700)

Printed by Replika Press, India